Family Policy
AND THE
American Safety Net

To Bob and Annabelle

with best wishes,

[signature]

August 30, 2012

Contemporary Family Perspectives

Series Editor

Susan J. Ferguson
Grinnell College

Family Policy
AND THE
American Safety Net

JANET ZOLLINGER GIELE

Brandeis University

SUSAN J. FERGUSON, SERIES EDITOR

Los Angeles | London | New Delhi
Singapore | Washington DC

Los Angeles | London | New Delhi
Singapore | Washington DC

FOR INFORMATION:

SAGE Publications, Inc.
2455 Teller Road
Thousand Oaks, California 91320
E-mail: order@sagepub.com

SAGE Publications Ltd.
1 Oliver's Yard
55 City Road
London EC1Y 1SP
United Kingdom

SAGE Publications India Pvt. Ltd.
B 1/I 1 Mohan Cooperative Industrial Area
Mathura Road, New Delhi 110 044
India

SAGE Publications Asia-Pacific Pte. Ltd.
3 Church Street
#10-04 Samsung Hub
Singapore 049483

Printed in the United States of America

Library of Congress Cataloging-in-Publication Data

Giele, Janet Zollinger.

Family policy and the American safety net/ Janet Z. Giele.

p. cm. — (Contemporary family perspectives)
Includes bibliographical references and index.

ISBN 978-1-4129-9894-9 (pbk.)

1. Family policy—United States.
2. Families—United States. I. Title.

HQ536.G52 2013
306.850973—dc23   2012018543

This book is printed on acid-free paper.

Acquisitions Editor: David Repetto
Editorial Assistant: Lauren Johnson
Production Editor: Eric Garner
Copy Editor: Terri Lee Paulsen
Typesetter: C&M Digitals (P) Ltd.
Proofreader: Laura Webb
Indexer: Rick Hurd
Cover Designer: Janet Kiesel
Marketing Manager: Erica DeLuca
Permissions Editor: Karen Ehrmann

MIX
Paper from
responsible sources
FSC® C014174
www.fsc.org

12 13 14 15 16 10 9 8 7 6 5 4 3 2 1

Contents

Series Preface

Contemporary Family Perspectives

Susan J. Ferguson

Grinnell College

The family is one of the most private and pervasive social institutions in U.S. society. At the same time, public discussions and debates about the institution of the family persist. Some scholars and public figures claim that the family is declining or dying, or that the contemporary family is morally deficient. Other scholars argue that the family is caught in the larger culture wars currently taking place in the United States. The recent debates on same sex marriage are one example of this larger public discussion about the institution of the family. Regardless of one's perspective that the family is declining or caught in broader political struggles, scholars agree that the institution has undergone dramatic transformations in recent decades. U.S. demographic data reveal that fewer people are married, divorce rates remain high at almost 50 percent, and more families are living in poverty. In addition, people are creating new kinds of families via Internet dating, cohabitation, single-parent adoption, committed couples living apart, donor insemination, and polyamorous relationships. The demographic data and ethnographic research on new family forms require that family scholars pay attention to a variety of family structures, processes, ideologies, and social norms. In particular, scholars need to address important questions about the family, such as, what is the future of marriage? Is divorce harmful to individuals, to the institution of the family, and/or to society? Why are rates of family violence so high? Are we living in a post-dating culture? How do poverty and welfare policies affect families? How is child rearing changing now that so many parents work outside the home, and children spend time with caretakers other than their parents? Finally, how are families socially constructed in different societies and cultures?

Most sociologists and family scholars agree that the family is a dynamic social institution that is continually changing as other social structures and individuals in society change. The family also is a social construction with complex and shifting age, gender, race, and social class meanings. Many excellent studies are currently investigating the changing structures of the institution of the family and the lived experiences and meanings of families. **Contemporary Family Perspectives** is a series of short texts and research monographs that provides a forum for the best of this burgeoning scholarship. The series aims to recognize the diversity of families that exist in the United States and globally. A second goal is for the series to better inform pedagogy and future family scholarship about this diversity of families. The series also seeks to connect family scholarship to a broader audience beyond the classroom by informing the public and by ensuring that family studies remain central to contemporary policy debates and to social action. Each short text contains the most outstanding current scholarship on the family from a variety of disciplines, including sociology, demography, policy studies, social work, human development, and psychology. Moreover, each short text is authored by a leading family scholar or scholars who bring their unique disciplinary perspective to an understanding of contemporary families.

Contemporary Family Perspectives provides the most advanced scholarship and up-to-date findings on the family. Each volume provides a brief overview of significant scholarship on that family topic, including critical current debates or areas of scholarly disagreement. In addition to providing an assessment of the latest findings related to their family topic, authors also examine the family utilizing an intersectional framework of race-ethnicity, social class, gender, and sexuality. Much of the research is interdisciplinary, with a number of theoretical frameworks and methodological approaches presented. Several of the family scholars use a historical lens as well to ground their contemporary research. A particular strength of the series is that the short texts appeal to undergraduate students as well as to family scholars, but they are written in a way that makes them accessible to a larger public.

About This Volume

Family Policy and the American Safety Net is a comprehensive research volume that examines when and how family policy in America emerged and how it has grown in the last half century. The author, Janet Zollinger Giele (Brandeis University), has studied family policy for more than 40 years, and this volume represents a culmination of much of that scholarship. Giele argues that family policy is more than a historical or political response to societal needs, instead, family policy is an adaptive response to economic and social change. Giele also argues that family policy is all around us and often hidden under other names or programs, such as Social Security, Medicaid, and housing policies. Giele insists on taking this broad approach to family policy in order to understand where resources are allocated in the larger society. Giele begins in the introduction with an analysis of family policy using her personal experience as a form of analysis. This pivotal personal history helps the reader situate Giele's training and experiences in the larger societal discussions about family, work, and gender. After providing this background, Giele examines the emergence of family policy in America and the changing definition of family in the twentieth century. A key variable in any analysis of the family and family policy is gender. Giele reviews the impact changing gender roles have had on the family before beginning her main analysis. Next, Giele divides her analysis of family policy into one of four family functions: caregiving, economic provision, residence, and access to cultural heritage and legal and social citizenship.

To understand the institution of the family in the twenty-first century, we need to understand how family policy affects families across the United States. The last chapter places family policy within the larger contexts of the economy and the government. Giele demonstrates well that, when families can no longer provide the safety net in our modern capitalist state, the government must step in. Giele concludes by arguing that family policy is as critical to the nation's well-being as is foreign policy and national defense. Without strong families, the nation itself is weakened.

A unique feature of this book is Giele's use of a theory of action that posits four main functional requirements of every social system: Adaption, Goal-Attainment, Integration, and Legitimation. Giele adapts this theory to her understanding of the functions of family and structures the main chapters around this analysis.

Family Policy and the American Safety Net is appropriate for use in any class concerned with family structure, family policy, social inequality, gender, and how government affects families in terms of employment, migration, and well being. This book is a valuable resource to teachers and students in beginning and advanced courses in sociology, family studies, women's studies, political science, social work, public policy, and other disciplines. It also finds an audience among any person interested in comparative family studies or among those who work in various human services fields, including human development, social work, education, counseling, health services, and the government. This last statement is particularly true for social service employees who work with welfare or immigrant populations. This volume can help them to better understand how governmental policy can dramatically impact families and improve their lives.

Introduction

This book attempts to answer two questions: What is family policy? Why does it exist, or put another way, why is it important and what function does it serve? The answers given here differ from answers given in the past.

What is family policy? The lay public as well as academic experts think of family policy as fairly specialized public programs that include maternal and child health, child welfare, assistance to poor families, and work and family integration such as found in the Family and Medical Leave Act. The thesis of this book, however, is that family policy is all around us and is hiding in plain sight. Family policy, in fact, includes a very wide range of policies called by other names. Important elements of family policy are embedded in health and disability programs, Social Security, housing subsidies, and immigration policy. I define family policy as any publicly authorized set of supports or restrictions that affects the functioning of family life and the life chances of individual family members.

Why does family policy exist? One familiar explanation is historical: that family policy grew out of a charitable impulse toward widows, orphans, and paupers that eventually was expanded to include more people and was eventually largely taken over by government (Axinn and Levin 1975; Dobelstein 2009). Another important perspective explains the emergence of family-related policies as the result of efforts by reform movements and other interest groups to win mothers' pensions and other forms of social protection (Gordon 1994; Skocpol 1992). While both historical and political explanations are valid, they give relatively little attention to society's need for family policy in order to cope with changing economic and demographic conditions. Economists and sociologists focus instead on the uses of family policy as an adaptive response to economic and social change. Family policy emerged not only in the United States but also in other advanced industrial societies to meet the challenges of economic modernization and the changes in longevity, fertility, and family structure that ensued.

1

It has taken nearly half a century to recognize the need for an American family policy, or what Theda Skocpol (1995) envisioned as a program of "Family Security" to serve not just retirees or poor children, but also everyone "in the middle"—the middle generation of adults, and the middle class in the income distribution. This book represents a stepping-stone on the journey toward that larger vision of social protection for everyone. Almost all social policy is a form of social protection for families, even if the recipient of a particular benefit is an individual, because everyone has a family of some sort that is the first line of defense and a natural safety net in times of sickness, economic need, homelessness, and questions about citizenship. Families must fare well if the society is to prosper. Thus, family policy is a necessary counterpart to economic policy. Economic growth cannot occur without investment in the family infrastructure that reproduces workers with adequate human and social capital to keep the economy competitive. Parents and families must be able to educate and support the children who will make up the future labor force and the civil society. This book is intended to help students as well as the lay public to realize how important and valuable these family-related programs are and how they function both as the foundation for children's education and as social protection for individuals and families.

I have called on my own family history and professional experience for insights into why the various strands of family policy have been developed. From my parents and my childhood I learned the nature of the momentous change from a rural to an urban way of life and the profound impact this has had on the roles of women and men. My first interest in family policy was focused on equal opportunities for women and the need for childcare and more flexible work and family schedules. My professional experience as a faculty member at the Heller School for Social Policy and Management broadened my reach. I was introduced to the many other realms of social policy that affect family life—child welfare; disability policy; employment and training; income maintenance; housing and family wealth; measures to stop racial discrimination; immigrant parents' interaction with the schools; and health, substance abuse, and mental health policies.

Reflecting on my own experience in this way is similar to what Shulalmit Reinharz (2009) terms "experiential analysis" in her book *On Becoming a Social Scientist: From Survey Research and Participant Observation to Experiential Analysis*. While doing research, she found herself as an observer drawing on her own feelings and reactions to understand better the small groups, the survey respondents, and the Israeli kibbutz under attack that were the subjects of her investigations. Because she herself felt puzzlement and fear, she could sympathize with the people she was studying and in the process ask questions and develop hypotheses that would have otherwise been ignored. So too, in telling about my family background and the era through which I have lived, my purpose is to convey an inside view of the momentous changes that have occurred in family life and women's roles over the past 75 years as well as the great range of family programs and policies that I have discovered in doing this research. In hearing my story, I hope that readers of this book will recall their own history and query that of their parents and elders in order to construct a personal inside view of family change and the family-related policies and programs that affect their lives. Such exercises make everyone better able to take responsibility as citizens for shaping the family-related policies and programs of the future.

A Transitional Generation

My personal history spans the mid-1930s to the present. During that time I made the journey from a rural economy to a commuter suburb outside Boston, from a family where the parents had little education to my own where both partners had postgraduate degrees, and from a husband-breadwinner family to a dual-career family. Change in the family structure brought on by the modern economy was something I lived through.

My father grew up in rural Ohio and my mother in the mining country of western Pennsylvania. All four of my grandparents were poor immigrants from Europe who entered the United States in the 1870s and 1880s. Each of my parents came from large families of eight or more children. Neither had a high school education. My father (born in 1894) had to leave his rural one-room school in the sixth grade to help support the family; my mother (born in 1903) grew up in a small mining company town where there was no high school. Her father died when she was 9 and her mother when she was 16. Yet she eventually put herself through business college by doing housework and then living with her sister, brothers, and brother-in-law to work as a secretary and bookkeeper in Akron, Ohio, at a salvage company until she was married. My father had his own business, first in hay baling and threshing for local farmers and later as owner and operator of dragline machines used for digging and cleaning drainage ditches that bordered roads and farms near Wooster, the county seat of Wayne County, an area about 50 miles south of Cleveland. He was very inventive and developed a couple of patents for the design of the booms for his big machines. But he was the ruler of the household because he conceived of the business which he ran as the main support of the family. He therefore believed that he was the family member responsible for making major consumer decisions. At one point he took away my mother's checkbook because she had bought two twin beds from Sears Roebuck that he thought cost too much and were not really needed. But he had no such scruples when it came to buying machine parts and another machine or two that he could take apart for needed repairs. Later, as I taught courses on the family and learned how the patriarchal peasant family had evolved into a more egalitarian modern one, I understood this behavior as consistent with the structure of the pre-industrial family that combined economic production and consumption in one unit. Given this structure, the family must not consume the seed corn or it will forfeit next year's crop. Thus the wife's reproductive labor and consumer decisions are subjected to the husband's authority as head of the production side of family life.

Born in 1934, I was the oldest of four daughters, one of whom died as a young child. In 1942 we moved from Seville, Ohio, to take three rooms in a large farmhouse in Wooster Township while my father built a house on a neighboring property on the road south of Wooster opposite the Ohio Agricultural Experiment Station. Before we moved (when I was 8 years old), I still remember driving by the College of Wooster and my father saying, "Maybe you girls will go there someday." It was especially important to him that we be able to go to the new Township school just across the fields from where we lived. But when it came time for me to go to Earlham College and my parents had to sign the scholarship form, my father balked at signing, I think because he did not realize that getting an education offered the only viable option for the daughter of a self-employed rural entrepreneur. If I had been a son, he probably would have prevailed because there would have been a pathway to carrying on the business. So at last, my mother stood up to my father and signed the scholarship form on her own. Many years later I realized how significant that was in light of her own education and work history.

Something else I learned from my family was what it felt like to be an outsider. My father had many lessons to teach about his own experience growing up, having spoken German at home until he went to school, being made fun of and being jeered at as "Girl's Coat" because of his homemade coat. Many times he also reflected on how important it was to get a "good start in life," by which he meant to have parents who had land and resources, spoke English like natives, and were not poor. My sisters and I to some extent relived this feeling of being out of step with other people. We lived in an unconventional house that Daddy built with cast-off materials during the war. We used the rainwater that flowed from the roof into the cistern for bathing and laundry. Mother cooked on a wood stove that required a steady supply of fuel and taking out of ashes. There was a privy out back to conserve water during dry weather. Although we had electricity, we used the neighbors' phone. Daddy had a machine shop at the back of the house that held lathe, drill press, and a welder with accompanying acetylene and oxygen tanks that he used to construct booms and modify his dragline dippers. His healthy supply of extra machines in the back yard was always a bit of an embarrassment to the rest of the family.

There was a lot of household production that my sisters and I helped our mother to do—canning, making soap, doing laundry with the Maytag gyrator and wringer and rinsing the soap out in two adjoining washtubs, carrying out pails of waste water, and then drying clothes on the line outside. Although my father wasn't a farmer, many friends and neighbors were, and everyone was familiar with the seasonal routines of butchering, canning, preserving, raising one's own chickens for meat and eggs, and growing vegetables in the garden.

Yet we also had a life in the city of Wooster, a vibrant prosperous county seat of about 15,000 that was the headquarters of Rubbermaid, the Bauer Ladder Company, and Gerstenslager Company (which built bodies for mail trucks and other vehicles). We went to town for groceries, church, and shopping and my parents knew many people and their families through Daddy's business and through the church and my sisters' and my schoolmates. I attended Wooster High School and often walked home after some extracurricular activity (about two miles). My teachers were excellent and I excelled in school, which was a source of pride to me and to my parents.

I spent three years at Earlham College and my junior year in France with a special scholarship. After graduating from Earlham in 1956, I entered the PhD program in Sociology at Harvard University. This began a very different life in a sophisticated metropolitan setting that was a great contrast (except for the year in Paris) with my experience up to that point. Besides course work, the immediate challenge was to resolve the conflict I felt between finishing my doctorate to pursue a career as a college teacher (for which I had received a Woodrow Wilson National Fellowship) and getting married and quitting my graduate studies. Fortunately, I had the amazingly good and unusual fortune for that era of finding a life partner who gave up his place in the family printing business in Dayton, Ohio, to come to Boston to seek his fortune in the publishing industry and thereby see to it that I would finish my degree. My husband and I were married in 1957; I received my degree in 1961, and we moved a few months later to Wellesley, a suburb of Boston where our two children were born, and I was able to teach full time at Wellesley College. From that point on, I found myself a member of an urban world in which a new kind of family life had to be invented as we went along.

Like other young women professors who were having children in the 1960s, I was able to continue teaching because I found good help at home and later in the excellent nursery school located at the college. Once the children were in public school, and I had left the college and won a fellowship to the Radcliffe Institute for Independent Study, our family developed a routine of sharing in the work to be done—the children helping with setting the table and doing the dishes, my husband helping with yard work, childcare, and the meals. The challenges of parenting and household management became easier in relation to the work I was doing as a sociologist. But all these experiences and the challenges of going against the typical pattern of the stay-at-home mother had already led me to think about how institutions could be changed to ease the conflicting demands of work and family. By the early 1970s I had begun to focus on questions of family policy. The changing roles of women in general, and my own experience in particular, were such a contrast with that of my mother's generation that it became clear that American society needed new social norms, organizations, and policies to meet these new challenges.

Policies for Women's Equality and Family Well-Being

It was the combination of my training as a sociologist and the challenges of being a young mother with a career that set me on a path to discover new policies to ease the strain between women's two roles. My time as a graduate student in sociology in the Harvard Department of Social Relations was at a golden moment in its history. I had the benefit of distinguished teachers and theorists who taught the four core courses in clinical psychology, social psychology, social anthropology, and sociology.

However, that was also the era prior to the great flowering of Women's Studies and prior to the civil rights and women's movements that would erupt in the following decade. Instead of providing a rationale for social reform, the reigning sociological theories were thought by many to be conservative apologia for the status quo. There was little effort to find connections between sociological knowledge and the solution of social problems. The mood of the 1950s was instead a time of political stability and growing prosperity. In this climate it was a struggle for me to find a thesis topic that would use sociology to understand the connections between the changing roles of women and efforts for social change. In the end I made a comparison of the leadership and ideology of the nineteenth century woman's suffrage movement and the more popular Women's Christian Temperance Union. I discovered that the two movements complemented each other. Suffragists focused on women's rights in the public sphere, whereas temperance advocates emphasized women's rights in the family (Giele 1995). Although

I didn't realize it at the time, this work would eventually launch me into the study of the contemporary connections between change in women's roles and in the family and between the women's movement and changes in laws and social policies to assure women's equality and family welfare.

By the late 1960s, sociologists' interest in social change had begun to expand to include the new social movements of that decade. A few experiments by families in communal living had cropped up around the country (Kanter 1972). Students in my family course at Wellesley College read about the new communes that were being set up among several cooperating families in Cambridge and which showed new possibilities for sharing the many tasks that traditionally fall on women such as cooking, laundry, and childcare. But over time it became clear that communes would never really gain a foothold. Instead of creating new family forms, the general public was more interested in creating new kinds of helping services and support programs *outside* the home—a strategy that produced much of what we consider today to be the subject of family policy.

The concept of family policy moved to the center of my attention in 1972 when I was named a principal consultant to the Ford Foundation's Task Force on the Rights and Responsibilities of Women. My assignment was to meet with the Task Force and prepare papers for its consideration on a variety of topics ranging from the changing role of women in the family to women's education and the economic position of women. Wherever I discovered educational or job discrimination against women, it turned out that more than laws for educational equality or pay equity was needed. The key was to find relief for women's overwhelming responsibility to be the main caretakers of children and other family members. The most frequent suggestion was to create flexibility in working hours and the schedules of working parents. This solution did not fit neatly under employment policy, educational policy, or equal rights policy. Rather, the issue was ultimately one of family policy.

My written report to the Foundation singled out four areas of social policy related to the family that were "now due for critical review in light of changing sex roles and family forms" (Giele 1978:194). The four areas were care of children, economic support to the family, community supports, and changing legal rights. During this period, while still at the Radcliffe Institute, I was also invited by a program officer of the National Science Foundation's RANN program (Research Applied to National Needs) to do a brief overview of family policy development in the United States. Rather than try to name all of the relevant policies, the main effort was to identify academic centers doing relevant research; advocacy groups representing various clients such as children, the elderly, and women; and key reference works (Giele and

Lambert 1975). Partly as a result of the Ford and NSF projects, I was invited by Matilda White Riley, a fellow member of the Social Science Research Council's Committee on Work and Personality in the Middle Years, to cover the topic for the 1979 *Annual Review of Sociology* (Giele 1979). The main categories of family policy (nurturance, economic activity, residence, and legal and cultural identity) that I identified in that article are basically the same as in the present book, which is to me a reassuring correspondence that suggests that my conceptual structure has stood the test of time.

Concurrent with the new scholarly developments in family policy, there was an emerging interest in teaching about existing policies as well as the process of policy making. It was this new interest on the part of policy-oriented professors at the Florence Heller School for Advanced Studies in Social Welfare at Brandeis University that resulted in my being recruited to join its faculty in 1976. In 1977, the National Institutes of Mental Health (NIMH) funded three multiyear academic training programs in family policy: at the University of Minnesota, headed by Reuben Hill; at Duke University, headed by Carol Stack; and at the Heller School of Brandeis University, headed by my colleagues Robert Perlman and Roland Warren, who asked me to teach the basic required courses in the training program.

My experience on the faculty of the Heller School since 1976 has been a boon to my understanding of family policy. Later renamed the Heller School for Social Policy and Management, its faculty taught me how to connect social science to social policy. Its students exposed me to a great variety of programs for women, children, and families that I would otherwise never have known about. Charles Schottland, the founding dean, had been the U.S. Commissioner for Social Security in the Eisenhower Administration. The Center on Economics and Politics of Aging counted three past presidents of the American Gerontological Society—social worker Robert Morris, political scientist Robert Binstock, and economist James H. Schulz. The Institute on Health Policy headed by economists Stuart Altman and Stan Wallack as early as the late 1970s called attention to rising health care costs and eventually took a key role in shaping universal health coverage in Massachusetts. Gunnar and Rosemary Dybwad were leading visionaries and advocates for treating persons with mental retardation in the least restrictive setting. Lorraine Klerman was a distinguished researcher and advocate in the field of maternal and child health and prevention of teenage pregnancy.

My particular mission at Heller throughout the 1980s and 1990s was to bring a sociological perspective to women's changing roles as well as to press for special attention to policies for families, rather than child welfare alone which had always had a place at the school and had been especially championed by David Gil (1970) in his path-breaking study of *Violence against*

Children: Physical Child Abuse in the United States. Beginning with the NIMH Family Policy Training Grant, a course on children, youth, and families was offered annually with special attention to changing family structure and needed policies and programs to compensate for the new realities of parents' work, single-parenting, and ethnic and racial discrimination. In 1990, the School established the Family and Children's Policy Center, of which I was the founding director. The Center served as a meeting ground for affiliated faculty and numerous students in the master's and doctoral programs. In 2005 it became the Institute for Child, Youth, and Family Policy (2011).

In addition to all that I learned from my faculty colleagues about application of social science knowledge to social policy and practical programs, I perhaps learned even more from my doctoral students, many of whose dissertations I have cited in this book. Many came to me because they were doing dissertations on women's work and changing gender roles. But the majority were outside my specialty, and I found myself learning from them about whole new worlds—grandmothers caring for their grandchildren, kinship adoption, formal adoption, open adoption, school choice, childcare programs, women in prison, child sexual abuse, and families in the military— over 50 doctoral committees in all.

Nothing in graduate school or in my sociological training had prepared me for applying social science knowledge to contemporary policymaking. Yet in exposure to the Heller School mission of "Knowledge advancing social justice," I saw how sociological knowledge is necessary to the construction of good social policy. In order for the physician to treat a patient appropriately, she must understand the anatomy, physiology, and many complex systems in the body and how they work in order to recommend an effective treatment. So too, the policy makers who devise social protection systems for families and children must have basic knowledge of how families live and the factors that contribute both to distress and long-term well-being.

Introducing a Theory of Family Policy

This book differs from other books on family policy by including such topics as disability, health care, retirement pensions, housing, and immigration that are usually treated as topics unto themselves. This broad approach is in contrast to the much narrower range that is ordinarily thought of as family policy, namely, child welfare, laws on marriage and divorce, work–family balance, and welfare reform. I have not only extended the boundaries of the way family policy should be defined. I have also grouped family-related policies into four main categories that address universal functions of family life: caregiving, economic provision, residence, and access to cultural heritage and legal and social citizenship. As shown in Chapter 8 of this book, previous works on social policy, family policy, and social protection have generally listed a congeries of relevant programs and government initiatives, but they have provided no rationale for what they enumerate, other than historical or current public attention to the issues at hand. There is universal agreement that caregiving for children and elderly and disabled persons is at the heart of family policy. Consensus on the importance of economic provision is nearly as strong, although opinion is divided over the desirability of universal eligibility versus supports limited to the needy. When it comes to the matter of shelter, which includes housing, neighborhood, and schools, the link to family policy is often unrecognized. Even less common is any awareness that matters of cultural, racial, ethnic, and religious citizenship have implications for the family, especially the current debates over immigration policy. Yet I include all these issues as of serious importance for the nation's family policy, by which I mean social policy, social protection, and the domestic safety net.

In making such claims, I am suggesting that the national focus on economic growth should be balanced by commensurate attention to how the fruits of growth are distributed so that they maximize well-being of the population. In preindustrial societies the household is a system for both production and consumption (and reproduction). These two functions are dependent on each other. People have to have enough to live on in order to produce the food and goods that will sustain them. At the same time they must continue to work in order to have the means to consume and reproduce. The economist Carolyn Shaw Bell (1972) summed up the role of the family in modern society as one of "consumer maintenance." The family maintains the worker's capacity to produce; the family is also the endpoint for consumption.

In our modern society, production has moved out of the home, but it is still necessary for the consumption or reproductive side of the household to be well enough nourished, housed, and integrated into the larger community to work and manage itself effectively. In other words, a feedback loop still exists between production and consumption, but now on a national plane. Economic production and continued growth cannot be sustained without due attention to the well-being of the people who are working in the fields, factories, schools, and offices of the nation.

The theory of social systems and social action has guided this conceptualization of family policy. Social systems are dynamic entities that include small groups (such as the family), social institutions (such as education or the legal system), and whole societies (such as the United States). The members are connected to each other in such a way that events that occur in one part of the system have an eventual effect on other parts. The most common metaphor of a system is the body in which the organs are both interdependent and life sustaining. If key organs such as the heart or the brain experience a trauma, the whole body suffers. In a similar way, the family unit is a system in which its caregiving capacity, economic level, residential location, and cultural status all have an impact on its capacity for sustaining the well-being of its members. If one major function is impaired, the whole family suffers.

Just as the family is a social system, so also is the nation. The strength and capacity of the nation's families to bring up healthy and educated children, and to promote the general health of its population, has long-term effects on productivity in the workplace, the safety and livability of local neighborhoods, and the vitality of participation in civil society. Similarly, the way the nation allocates its resources—whether to national defense, foreign aid, protection of the environment, or to care of its people—affects well-being of children, families, and the population as a whole. When society is thus viewed as a system of interrelated parts, family policy becomes just as important as defense, foreign policy, and economic growth. The safety net and social protection are the society's internal defense against the enemies of sickness, hunger, privation, and despair.

The image of the social system as an entity with visible outlines and visible members is what sociologists refer to when they speak of *social structure*. Within the system are processes or *functions* such as the circulation of money; enforcement of laws; the flow of traffic; or birth, sickness, and death. The *theory of action* treats the connections between the system's structure and its capacity to function as critical to its survival in the face of challenges from within and without.

In his detailed study of the industrial revolution in the English cotton industry, Smelser (1959) demonstrates how structural change in the economy and the family spawned new social institutions such as the public school and the workingmen's cooperatives that helped to fulfill functions that were once performed by the family.

One of the postulates of the theory of action is that to adapt to new challenges in the environment, social systems tend to become more specialized or differentiated in order to meet the challenges effectively. This is what happened in the case of the Industrial Revolution. The family became more specialized in caregiving and spalled off the economic function as it was taken up by the new industrial system. As shown by the great classical theorists of modern social science like Max Weber (1968), Emile Durkheim ([1893] 1964), and Talcott Parsons (1966b), there is along with greater specialization a universalizing trend in which greater capacity is developed to unify and standardize expectations and thereby create broader consensus on basic norms and values.

By using the theory of action to understand current developments in social and family policy, new insights become possible. Changes in family structure can no longer be explained as simply family decline or liberation from patriarchy. What is really going on is a massive process of social differentiation in which the functions of the family are becoming ever more specialized so that family life becomes the main locus for intimacy and satisfaction of the most basic psychological and physical needs. Many, but not all, functions that families used to perform have moved elsewhere: childcare to the daycare center and nursery school, food production to purchases at the grocery store, food preparation to the restaurant, and elder care to assisted living or the nursing home. Yet at the same time that all this splitting off of former family functions is occurring, new social policies and laws are being created to standardize and regulate the many family-related activities that occur outside the family on which many families depend in order to fulfill their purpose.

The social policies and programs that help the family fulfill its purpose are what constitute the corpus of family policy. A key purpose of the family in every society is to bring children into the world and socialize them to become effective adults. In addition, every member of the population who survives infancy has some connection to a family, fictive kin, or a combination of family-substitute groups (such as the homeless shelter, or assisted living) that helps to fulfill basic family functions of caregiving, economic support, shelter, and cultural identity. Grouping policies by major family functions provides some leverage for a critical appraisal of where policies are skewed toward one interest group or another or are missing. For example, data in Chapter 6 on rent subsidies and the mortgage tax credit reveal a huge inequity in the large subsidies being provided to homeowners as compared with renters. Viewed through a family policy lens, a major question is how this disparity affects the many families and children who are involved and whether the policy should be changed.

Still very new to my thinking (and not suggested until the final chapter) is the radical idea that family policy is as important to the nation's well-being as national defense, economic growth, and foreign policy. What is our nation defending, what good is its economic growth, how can it be a leader of nations if in 2006 it ranked 27th among 30 industrialized countries in prevention of infant mortality, has 15 percent of its families living in poverty, and is the highest among advanced industrial nations in the proportion of its population who are in prison? The capacity to reverse these trends is embedded in American values as stated in the founding documents: to enjoy the rights of life, liberty, and the pursuit of happiness and to promote the general welfare. The well-being of families is critical to the realization of these ideals.

Organization of the Book

My purpose in this book is to show that family policy is a well-tested and necessary adaptation by society to the fundamental change that occurred in family structure with economic modernization. The account is both descriptive and theoretical. It provides a map to the field of social policies that helps to organize and highlight the major themes. Rather than focus deeply on one strand such as child welfare and follow it from its origins to its elaboration, application, and evaluation, this book provides an overview of the broader landscape of family policy—why it came into being, where it is well developed, and where it is patchy and weak. The tables at the end of the core chapters summarize the major programs and laws related to caregiving, economic provision, residence, and cultural identity and citizenship.

The organization of the chapters reflects the underlying theory that I use to organize the material and explain its significance. The first three chapters describe the changes in family structure that have driven the search for policies and programs to support family functions. The middle four chapters focus on four major functions of the family that I derive from the theory of action and which also correspond to the major themes of writers and leaders in the family policy field. The theory of action posits four functional requirements that every social system has to meet if it is to survive: Adaptation, Goal-attainment, Integration, and Legitimation. In the case of the family unit as a social system, I identify the four capacities necessary to family viability as caregiving (G), economic security (A), residential location (I), and transmission of citizenship and cultural heritage (L). Each of the four chapters on these major functions describes the major policies and programs that have been devised to support that particular capacity. The final chapter returns to a structural analysis by viewing American family policy as a development that is consistent with modern welfare-capitalism in other countries of the world.

Chapter 1, "The Emergence of Family Policy in America," lays out the central thesis of the book that the new field of family policy has come about in order to support the functions that most families can no longer adequately provide entirely on their own, such as a livelihood, education of the next generation, and caregiving for frail and dependent family members. Family structure changed as a result of modernization. Production moved from farm and small business to the workplace; and the reproductive functions of childbearing and caregiving then took center stage. Thus exposed to new risks, various interest groups have continued to advocate for programs and policies that address these changed conditions.

Chapter 2, "Defining the Family," reviews the main changes that have taken place in the structure of the family during the twentieth century. There has been a dramatic decline in family size and a rise in cohabitation, single-parent families, and divorce. These shifts have produced greater diversity in family structure as well as turmoil and innovation in family law and family policy. The positive and negative effects of these changes have fueled a debate over "family values" in which conservatives emphasize the value of two-parent families, liberals focus on the increased employment opportunities for women that also brought demise of the patriarchal family, and feminists seek ways that women's important caregiving roles can continue without penalty to their incomes or long-term career opportunities.

Chapter 3, "The Gender Factor," connects the changing division of household labor to the resurgent women's movement and rising labor force participation of women. Men's roles have also changed because of the dramatic shift in occupations from agriculture to manufacturing and service industries. Among younger families, husbands' and wives' duties are being reshuffled to bring about a more symmetrical marriage relationship both inside and outside the home. These changes challenge the old family system and spawn new family forms while also creating the conditions that can support greater equality between husbands and wives in their work and family responsibilities.

Chapter 4, "Re-invention of Caregiving," reviews the changes in care for children, older persons, and those who are sick or disabled and the social policies and programs that support them. With more wives and mothers in the paid labor force, care in many cases has been transferred to nursing homes for the elderly, childcare centers, and half-way accommodations for persons with disabilities. The disability rights movement has been a leader in advocating universal access to accommodations and to treatment in the least restrictive setting. De-institutionalization and caregiving in an informal setting promises clients more personalized treatment and more control over their lives. If bureaucratized caregiving can become more family-like, the low-paid caregiving work force may also benefit by being allowed to treat persons more flexibly and humanely in ways that redound to their own benefit.

Chapter 5, "Family Income and Economic Security," describes the income distribution of American families, the extent of poverty, and evidence of increasing inequality. Among the strategies to provide adequate family income, advocates for women's equality have given particular attention to part-time and flexible schedules, employment training, and availability of childcare. Other American policies to protect family income and economic security include assistance for the poor, social insurance, private pensions and benefits, improvement of skills and wages, and work and family integration. Programs such as Social Security are administered by the government, but many job-based benefits such as health insurance and pension contributions are provided by employers subject to government regulations and responsive to government incentives.

Chapter 6, "Housing, Neighborhoods, and Life Chances," begins with a profile of renters and homeowners and then describes the evolution of U.S. housing policy that stimulated the growth of suburbia but never made an equal investment in housing for non-homeowners or those in need of low-cost or subsidized housing. Of particular interest to sociologists of the family are the connections between housing, social class, and neighborhood schools. Poor communities that are characterized by concentrated disadvantage are places of high and chronic stress that interfere with the cognitive, emotional, and physical well-being of the residents whereas prosperous communities are able to insist on high standards, intervene in deviant behavior, and promote school quality and institutional resources that enable their children to succeed.

Chapter 7, "Family Heritage, Identity, and Citizenship," examines the connections between a family's ethnic, racial, cultural, and immigrant status and rights of citizenship. The Immigration Reform Act of 1965 brought a massive influx of immigrants from non-European countries, many of whom have since experienced downward mobility. Language barriers, racial and religious differences, and a lack of technical skills in many cases pushed the new arrivals into menial work and marginal occupations, and their children suffer from discrimination and poorly managed schools. The most successful immigrants maintain parental authority and religious and ethnic ties that enable them to resist the negative aspects of American culture while supporting their children's education. The most immediate policy issue is how to create a path to citizenship for a growing number of undocumented immigrant families and their children.

Chapter 8, "Family, Government, and the Safety Net," places family protection and family policy in the larger context of the modern capitalist welfare state. Family policies are needed to address the structural changes in the economy and family life that accompany modernization. When families can no longer serve as the ultimate safety net, it is government-sponsored programs that must fill the void. In the debate over family values and the purpose of family policy, the goal of supporting family functions prevailed over efforts to influence family structure. Current debate on curbing government deficits points to the need to cut social spending. Some leading economists, however, argue that the best way to fuel economic growth and cut the deficit is to invest in human capital, strengthen families, and improve the health and education of the next generation.

Acknowledgments

I owe personal and intellectual debts to many people, some of whom I have already named in the foregoing account of my own family history and professional experience. Here I especially want to acknowledge the various readers who reviewed my chapters and gave me many helpful suggestions. In the nature of such a broad and synthetic undertaking, I could not possibly know what was most germane in fields such as employment and income security, housing, or immigration. I had to depend on expert colleagues for help, even though I was not always able to follow all of their advice. Special thanks go to Michael Doonan, Margi Erickson Warfield, Susan Ferguson, Hilda Kahne, Jane Roland Martin, Huong Nguyen, James H. Schulz, Connie Williams, and Nicole Witherbee.

In the early stages of the writing, a faculty research stipend from the Brandeis Department of Women's and Gender Studies supported two excellent graduate research assistants, Miranda Waggoner and Ramona Olverez, who helped me in tracking down references and setting up the reference list. When it came time to put the whole manuscript together, Jenna Sirkin brought her extensive bibliographic and editorial experience and impressive knowledge of Endnote to my rescue by filling in many holes and correcting various inconsistencies.

In a more general way I also want to acknowledge the wonderful support I have received from the Heller School faculty, students, and deans who have encouraged my efforts in finding the major intersections between sociology and social policy. I have had the good fortune to know and learn from five outstanding deans of the Heller School, beginning with Dean Charles Schottland. Dean Arnold Gurin let me join the faculty in 1976 and "hang out my shingle." Without the powerful endorsement of Dean Stuart Altman, the Family and Children's Policy Center would never have come into being. Dean Jack Shonkoff was especially invested in questions of family and child well-being, and most recently Dean Lisa Lynch has welcomed my continuing involvement even though I am now in the ranks of the Emeriti.

In particular, I want to express my deep appreciation to Susan Ferguson, the editor of the Contemporary Family Perspectives Series, for her confidence and support throughout the several years it took to complete the book. She early on identified my interest in family policy, then invited me to give a teaching workshop at the 2005 Annual Meetings of the Eastern Sociological Society, and not long after that invited me to write this book. As I gathered up my notes for this introduction, I found that they went back more than twenty years! I would still be writing memos to myself about a possible book some day on the topic of family policy if it hadn't been for Susan who actually made it happen.

Given its position as a leader in publishing titles in the social sciences around the world, it is a pleasure to see this book under the imprint of SAGE. I wish to thank the Sage editorial staff for their excellent handling of the manuscript. Editor David Repetto has been an enthusiastic supporter of the Contemporary Family Perspective Series. From the beginning, he also recognized the need for this book to be somewhat longer than others in the series because of its broad reach and synthetic nature. Editorial Assistant Lydia Balian invited my participation in plans for the cover. As production editor, Eric Garner oversaw the steps leading from manuscript to finished book. Copy editor Terri Lee Paulsen was amazingly efficient and meticulous in correcting errors and noticing omissions under the pressure of a tight schedule. In addition, she communicated her own enthusiasm for the contents of this book, which stemmed from her experience as a journalist, entrepreneur, and (girls') hockey mom.

Finally, as my personal history has already explained, I owe the greatest tribute to my parents, Albert and Ellen Nestor Zollinger, who gave me a good start in life, and to my husband and partner, David Giele, with whom I have enjoyed the fruits of all the care and opportunities that have come to us. Bringing up our two children, Elizabeth and Ben, has given me special insight into both the challenges and pleasures of being a parent. We are all members of families that have come before us and will continue after us.

1

The Emergence of Family Policy in America

The family in the United States has always been seen as a private institution, and it continues to be so. But it is ever clearer that the quality of family life has important effects on public life. A high prison population, a shocking number of high school dropouts, poorer scores in math and science, and a higher rate of poverty than found in other advanced economies—what is to account for these failures? And, on the other hand, economic growth and technological innovation, a healthy and productive workforce—what conditions are necessary for achieving them?

While some of the answers to these questions can be linked to public availability—the quality of police work, the adequacy of schools, or advances in public health—most people would trace the capacity to learn, to be healthy and productive, and to stay out of trouble, to a family upbringing. Certainly there are children from "good" (well-functioning) families who get into trouble, do not do well in school, or cannot get a good job. But more often it turns out that those persons who are not doing well come from families who are poor, live in dangerous places, and have suffered from lack of the kind of support and resources that would maximize their productivity as future citizens and parents of the next generation.

The question of how to reverse the terrible consequences of family poverty and dysfunction and how to strengthen family life to ensure stability and well-being of all is the central question of this book. Its core thesis is that American society must understand that the future of its human capital starts with the quality of family life. Moreover, the qualities that protect physical and mental health, that lead to economic productivity and an active

19

and responsible citizenry are found in the home. Outside public institutions can promote and augment home learning, productivity, and civic engagement, but they will almost certainly fail if the groundwork has not been laid in the family. Teachers understand this, police and social workers understand this. Professors, doctors, and employers all know that the quality of a person's family life is a strong predictor of learning capacity, health and mental health, and productivity.

It is thus in the national interest to promote strong families. Just as states and the federal government support highways and a strong infrastructure in communication to promote trade and a healthy economy, so also the larger society must find ways of supporting the modern family if it is to reap the benefits that carry into the lives of children, students, and the adult workforce. Developing public policies to support the family, however, requires a change in the prevailing American view of the connection between family and the larger society. The American penchant for emphasis on self-reliance, hard work, individualism, and privacy has put any outside support to the family from the government in a bad light. Such help is cast either as a reward for laziness and dependency or as a dangerous move toward socialism and the welfare state such as many associate with "decadent" European countries. Whether seen as an indulgence of dependency or as an imitation of the "nanny state," societal support to the family provided by the government is held to be of questionable legitimacy and hardly appropriate to the American way of life.

This book argues for a change in our fundamental paradigm of the relationship between the family and the larger society. Rather than seeing families as self-contained units that must rely on their own members and avoid dependency of any kind on outside help, the new field of family policy views families in modern society as inevitably *inter*dependent with all of the major institutions of the society—such as the economy, the educational system, or national defense. Moreover, a *policy* toward families is meant to apply across many types of situations in a way that assures social justice to all citizens, whether they are disadvantaged minorities or members of the mainstream middle class.

This interdependence of the family with the larger American society is on the increase because of the complex and ever-tighter integration of regional, rural, and urban economies and populations, as well as globalization and interaction with the rest of the world. No longer can most people live on farms where the family produces its own food, lives within its small community, exchanges needed goods with its neighbors, and expects its children to live nearby and carry on the family enterprise. The reality instead is that children will have to leave home in order to find a paying job; they will need a good education in order to be qualified for that job; and they will need some sort of security for their health care and retirement that can no longer be provided entirely by the assets they inherit. Rather, their security will depend on the assets they are able to build up in the course of a career that involves a number of jobs and a number of employers.

The new field of family policy is emerging precisely to address these functions that most families can no longer adequately provide, such as a livelihood, education of the next generation, and caregiving for frail and dependent family members. In other words, *family policy encompasses all those social policies that support the functions that once were largely accomplished by the nuclear or extended family* and that are now shared with many other institutions outside the family.

Social protection began in the United States in a very piecemeal fashion, first to help the poorest and least fortunate and then to encompass a larger segment of the population. Programs to help the poor and take care of the sick and orphaned were invented in the late colonial period and early 1800s to help a small segment of the population who were most in need. Gradually, however, provisions for economic help, protection of children, or care for the sick were broadened to take in many more categories of people in need of care and support. In the case of an economic support program, such as Social Security, eligibility for coverage has gradually broadened so that almost everyone is covered, and the policy verges on being thought of as an entitlement for all citizens. Concurrently, as coverage has broadened, the focus of social protection has shifted from helping specific categories of needy persons to supporting a range of basic family functions. The four primary family functions that this book will describe are (1) *nurturance*, to meet daily physical needs for food, sleep, and care; (2) *economic provision*, to secure the material necessities of life; (3) *residence*, to provide adequate housing in a specific location; and (4) *legitimation of citizenship* by transmission of a social and cultural heritage and identity. Major social policies have grown up around each of these elemental aspects of family life.

This first chapter of the book lays out a conceptual framework for understanding the types of social policy that are relevant to the family and the conditions for their development. Whether a policy is in the field of childcare, poverty programs, housing, or immigration, the dynamics are roughly similar and involve the following four stages:

1. **Emergence of new social problems and charitable solutions.** The problems that spark a charitable response are the result of the family's inability to perform its traditional functions in the face of changes in the larger society. The most obvious signs of such problems are the appearance of more than the usual number of unfortunate individuals whose families are either absent or unable to care for them or prevent their suffering. Traditional family solutions prove to be inadequate, and public and private benefactors attempt to cope with the problems.

2. **Family change and public response.** Changes in family life begin to be accepted and regularized as a response to general social and economic change. Advocates, professionals, and charitable and political groups begin to propose a variety of solutions such as pensions, free access to education, and subsidies for care that go beyond helping unfortunate individuals. Their effort is to address long-term changes in family structure and functioning in a sustainable way.

3. **Political contests to decide between traditional and innovative solutions.** Protest and reform groups arise which represent the interests of their constituents. Those who decry the proposals for change argue that society should return to time-tested family routines that have worked in the past. Those who propose new programs say that the world has changed and that the family can no longer operate as it used to and still be successful in fulfilling its core functions. Proposals range from appeals for more charity to radical ideas or new ways of organizing family life and public programs.

4. **Institutionalization of new policies and acceptance of family change.** Society at large accepts the fact that families are changing and that social policies are needed for support of key family functions. The family still performs its basic functions of caregiving, sharing income and material necessities, housing, and legitimation of its members as citizens in the larger society. But most people recognize that family functioning is more affected than in the past by the operation of markets, schools, employers, and the state. As a result, the new social policies recognize this interdependence and work on the principle that families need help from the outside.

The story of family policy is a story of social protection against the cruel and unintended consequences of modernization for family life. Modernization is a complex phenomenon that brings many improvements ranging from better roads and communications to the growth of science and technology, a rise in agricultural production, and better education and health. At the same time, however, modernization challenges the adequacy of traditional family structure to support and protect family members. Powerful demographic trends create new groups of dependents who are vulnerable to isolation, poverty, and neglect. The working of the new industrial economy lays bare the inability of individual family units to compensate for the absence or unemployment of a breadwinner and the insufficiency of women's and children's unpaid labor in the home to make up the difference.

We can see the general outlines of this story played out in the development of programs for poor people, children, aged, and infirm persons since the early years of the nineteenth century in America.

Stage 1: Help for Persons and Families at Risk

Family-related charities typically emerge as a result of some condition that reveals the inadequacy of traditional family structure and family life. One major cause of family insecurity is massive structural change in the economy that makes the family more dependent on markets and other forces beyond its control. The American response to the economic dislocations of the early 1800s was prefigured in the Elizabethan poor laws of the 1600s that were a response to the English Enclosure Acts (Polanyi 1944). These new laws converted arable fields to sheep runs and forced the English peasants off the land. Several kinds of public relief measures were tried and gave rise to similar programs in America (Axinn and Levin 1975). In addition, special benevolent associations provided charitable contributions to those in need. In the two decades leading up to the Civil War, a variety of institutions were established to give shelter and sustenance to dependent persons, among them alms-houses, orphanages, and asylums for the mentally ill (D. Rothman 1971).

A second type of major stimulus to social welfare programs is demographic change, because it alters the boundaries and composition of family membership. The rise in the number of lone mothers and poor children that followed the loss of soldiers in the Civil War stimulated the growth of pensions designed for veterans that were gradually adapted to cover widows and their children (Skocpol 1992). At the end of the nineteenth century, when a longer life span raised the proportion of aged persons in the population, social programs were designed to provide an income in retirement and to relieve adult children of the full responsibility for providing care, housing, and sustenance for their aged parents and other relatives.

The earliest forms of social protection were devised to give relief to distinctive groups—the poor, old people, destitute women and children, and those who were thought to be defective or delinquent. All these groups were poor, but their care was organized according to what was seen as the primary reason for their dependency. Care of each of these groups evolved gradually. Some were "put out" by local authorities to townspeople who took them in for a modest fee. Later, others were committed to special refuges and asylums according to their need. Finally, by the end of the nineteenth century more standardized subsidies began to gain acceptance as a better way to relieve families of bearing the entire burden of care.

Poor People

Much of the American way of responding to the poor was influenced by the experience of England, especially the idea that local communities had a public responsibility to look after the dependents in their midst. So long as there were only a small number of very needy persons, neighbors and families could generally take care of them informally. According to Leiby (1978:35–36), the American community in the early 1800s, even after two centuries in the New World, was modeled on the English village. It was assumed that neighbors shared the same language and cultural background, that there was some leading family who could be depended on to look after the poor, and that neighbors would help each other and give particular help to widows, the crippled, or other unfortunate persons.

By the early 1800s, however, the number of poor people had expanded to the point where their needs exceeded the capacity of these traditional arrangements. The factory system spread during the 1820s and 1830s. Rural areas and small towns where people had been able to survive with their gardens and a cow were rapidly being integrated into a larger market system. It became difficult for a family to survive on its own if the breadwinner was unemployed.

Throughout the industrializing world the traditional family and the local community were no longer able to meet the needs through their usual charitable efforts, given the growing number of poor people. In earlier times, these unfortunates would have been taken care of by their families, neighbors, and a local church congregation. By the 1830s, however, the canals were pushing into upstate New York as well as into the hinterlands of Massachusetts, Pennsylvania, Ohio, and Illinois. Manufacturing and trade were changing the social fabric of small-town and rural life. A significant number of workers and families were on the move, and previous patterns of material help were breaking down. As fewer people could depend on farming or crafts such as carpentry or blacksmithing that were located in small towns, more families were put at risk of unemployment and losing their main source of livelihood.

The combination of greater risk of poverty and loss of family capacity to remedy it generated new public efforts to provide help. The two major types were what have been called outdoor and indoor relief. Helping poor and dependent persons by apprenticing or contracting them out to families who could use their help was known as "outdoor relief." What became more common was the establishment of poor farms or almshouses where poor people went to live and perform some sort of labor in return for their keep; this was known as "indoor relief" and was famously experienced in England by Charles Dickens when he was a child. In America this form of aid was seen in poor farms that were established in New England towns. For example, in the town where I live, Wellesley, Massachusetts, the poor farm was established in the 1850s in what was then West Needham. In 1883, when the town of Wellesley broke off from Needham, it located its town hall and town offices on the second floor of the large building that housed the poor farm. Outside of New England, however, the county form of government was the basis for establishing a means of helping poor people. In the community where I grew up, Wooster, Ohio, it was the Wayne County Home (now called the County Care Center) where poor old people lived, and I remember as a child in the 1940s going with my parents to visit some of the people there.

The phenomenon of the poor farm and the county home persisted well into the middle of the twentieth century but was finally made obsolete by the Great Society programs of President Lyndon B. Johnson and the War on Poverty of the 1960s.

Women and Children

Just as people in pre-industrial America were deemed poor when they had no land or livelihood to support them, so women and children were in need of charitable assistance when they had no husband, father, or grandparents who could assure their shelter and care. Of course, the presence of poor women and children was hardly new—it went back to biblical times. But the growing number of poor women and children in the nineteenth century was new and was directly related to the industrialization, migration, and immigration that came with modernization. In 1853, a New York City police report estimated that there were 10,000 orphaned, abandoned, and runaway children in the city (Axinn and Levin 1975). The rural family economy and small craft industries that had relied on help from children were in decline, and the new urban places no longer had a role for them.

The problem of child labor had been growing since the beginning of the century. Between 1800 and the Civil War, 77 special homes or institutions had been established and within another decade the number had grown to 124 (Axinn and Levin 1975). Cities like Boston and Philadelphia established homes of refuge for their children. These houses were considered a great improvement over the previous solution of farming out poor families and children to the highest bidder who would provide food and shelter in return for their labor. Orphanages were better also than the indiscriminate lodging of orphans in poor houses with adults where it was thought they might pick up "bad habits" and "shiftless ways."

Despite the promise of children's homes as places of refuge, where they might learn useful skills and industrious ways, there was disagreement as to their effectiveness. As reformers became interested in child welfare and began to professionalize the field, they began to advocate for foster care as a cheaper and more effective way to bring up abandoned children. Private philanthropic efforts grew through the Protestant Church and Home societies who sent poor children on "orphan trains" from the teeming cities to farms in the West. Catholic organizations, however, concerned that children born into Catholic families would be reared by Protestants, formed church-run schools and homes for children (Leiby 1978).

Eventually these several strands of charitable effort on behalf of children came together in progressive agitation for mothers' pensions. Following the Civil War, the principle of pensions for northern veterans who had served the country was extended to their widows and children. But eventually through the spoils system pensions were granted to many unrelated individuals as a form of patronage. While those interested in clean government perceived pensions to be a byproduct of corruption, the women's movement, which included suffragists, temperance advocates, the General Confederation of Women's Clubs, and a variety of mothers' groups, took up the cause of child protection and argued for the extension of mothers' pensions as a way to assure the welfare of children (Abbott 1938).

With the meeting of the White House Conference on Children in 1909 and the establishment of the Children's Bureau that followed it in 1912, public concern for children was regularized. The further institutionalization of health aid to mothers came with the passage of the Sheppard-Towner Act in 1921 that set up a system of visiting nurses and prenatal clinics in order to lower infant mortality and deliver preventive health care to women and children (Skocpol 1992). Mothers' pensions were institutionalized in the program for Aid to Dependent Children that was a part of the 1935 Social Security Act.

The Aged and Infirm

The story of helping dependent older persons has some of the same features as the story of helping the poor, but consciousness of aging as a social problem came many decades later. Aging as a social problem came to the fore as more people survived into old age as a result of improvements in health care and control of disease. At the same time, the decline of the rural economy and family farms removed the basis of economic security that had sustained elders in the past. In rural society, the traditional pattern had been for the elder to live on the farm with the adult children and grandchildren and help out with small chores, child tending, and the like. But with young people moving west or into town to take a job in the textile mills, the elderly could no longer depend on the younger generation for their care. All over the world, beginning with industrializing countries like Germany, and continuing to this day in the developing world, the question of ways to support the elderly in their old age became a major concern of national governments (Giele 1982b).

In America, the most common pre–Civil War public response to the question of who would look after the aged and infirm was the establishment of the old people's home. Very often it was associated with the poor house, usually being one and the same. The history of social protection for aged persons also bears some resemblance to the evolution of programs for other dependent and vulnerable groups. Prior to the development of almshouses, if there was no heir or family member who could provide shelter and care, old people might be "farmed out" to unrelated families who would fulfill the community's obligation. Following the Civil War, however, the soldiers' and sailors' homes and old people's homes in general became the residence of those who had no family or whose family had no room for them. These institutions lasted up to World War II and the 1950s when they began to be replaced by nursing homes.

For older people who suffered some form of dementia, the state mental hospitals became the residence of last resort. When I was a Harvard graduate student in sociology during the 1950s, I had the opportunity to be an eyewitness to this phenomenon during a summer internship. In order to fulfill my fieldwork requirement, I served as an assistant in the social service department of the Apple Creek State Hospital in Apple Creek, Ohio. There I saw many aged inmates who had been committed to the hospital because of "hardening of the arteries" (atherosclerosis) that made them unable to function normally. Also during that period, I saw many of these elderly, infirm patients with dementia being transferred to nursing homes in rural farmhouses or old Victorian homes in small towns throughout Northeastern Ohio, the idea being that the inmates were harmless and did not require the locked facilities or more specialized treatments available in a mental hospital. Moreover, this "de-institutionalized" care would be provided at much lower cost. But rather than offering more stimulation or improved care, these makeshift nursing facilities merely continued the warehousing of infirm aged persons in their passive state.

The evolution of social programs to help the aged and the infirm had been evolving since the time of the Civil War. The expansion of veterans' pensions, the example of Bismarck's Germany in the 1870s with its public program of old-age support, and the adoption of pensions for railroad workers and other employees around 1900, all contributed to the development of a system of providing resources to elders that would give them greater autonomy and independence (Schottland 1967). Rather than make them rely on the charity of their adult children or the larger community, these innovative programs built later income support on the contributions workers had made earlier. This new type of program that used an insurance principle to share the risks of sickness or income loss would eventually create the foundation for the Social Security Act of 1935, which moved care and income support from a particular location in homes for the aged to a more flexible and universal system that would allow elders to be supported in a variety of settings.

Care for the Sick

Provision of some sort of charitable or public aid for the sick and the insane can be traced back to early Greece and Rome and ancient India. The first hospital was established in the United States in Philadelphia in 1751, the general hospital of Pennsylvania in 1757, the New York Hospital in 1771, and the Massachusetts General Hospital in 1811. Typical of all these efforts was particular concern for the sick, who were poor; those who were well off could be cared for at home. As the number of poor people rose during the nineteenth century, medicine improved, and more medical care was dispensed in hospitals.

Special cases were the asylums for the insane. These institutions were developed after the crusading work of Dorothea Dix in Massachusetts, who exposed the cruel treatment of mentally retarded persons and the mentally ill in jails and almshouses throughout the Commonwealth. She found many kept in barns, cages, closets, cellars, stalls, and pens in ways that might be compared to the condition of domestic animals. In her 1843 report to the Massachusetts legislature she described some beaten with rods, lashed into obedience, and even put up for public auction where care of them was sold to the lowest bidder (Abbott 1941).

Just as saving children and caring for aged persons involved health care and eventually resulted in a patchwork of subsidies and insurance programs to cover their care, so also the general coverage of sickness in the population at large began to be viewed in more universalistic terms. Rather than rely on families or public "homes" to care for persons with chronic illness, new more universal and portable solutions were found. Creation of these deliberate and regularized programs to supplement the functions of the family in more flexible and individualized ways amounted to a new phase in the evolution of family policy.

Stage 2: Public Support of Basic Family Functions

The nineteenth-century solution to crisis in the family was the creation of institutions that would substitute for missing or broken families—public "homes" such as the almshouse and house of refuge for children. In the twentieth century, however, these efforts were gradually replaced by portable and individualized benefits in cash and in-kind that could support individual and family life in a variety of living arrangements and locations. This congeries of measures adopted by public authorities to improve the lives of vulnerable populations is what constitutes *social welfare policy*. It would take the rest of the twentieth century for these measures to be extended from the poorest and most vulnerable to the majority of the population and come under the rubric of what we are now beginning to call *family policy*.

Social welfare policy came about as the result of the changing relation between the family and the economy. Family control of social life declined dramatically with the onset of the Industrial Revolution, as capitalists reorganized work in the factory system and brought adults and children from farms and cottage industries to work in the mills. New social mechanisms were needed to provide the security that families no longer could. As Smelser (1959) demonstrated in his detailed study of the textile industry in Manchester, England, in the 1830s and 1840s, workers and families at first resisted the separation of work and family by bringing children into the factories as child laborers under the supervision of their parents. But this proved to be unworkable as factories speeded up and the production was further rationalized in pursuit of profit. Eventually three new institutions came into being to replace the family and community protective functions that had been disrupted by the factory system. These were the public schools to look after children, the workingmen's savings associations to provide some sort of social protection for those who could not work, and trade unions to win back some control by workers over their hours and wages.

Modernization of Family Functions and the Need for Social Policy

A similar narrowing of family functions took place in America between the Civil War and World War II. The overall process was one of social differentiation in which the internal organization of society became much more complex. The family lost its central role in organizing work and trade as industrialization increased. As work was located outside the home, it became less personal, and community control over adult behavior weakened. Some men went west to seek their fortunes, and women organized to gain equal rights with men to own property, to gain child custody, and to vote.

As the family lost control of economic functions, it intensified its focus on the nurturance and care of its members. Books on cooking, household management, and the best way to care for the health and growth of children began to appear in the middle of the nineteenth century in the works of domestic feminists like Catherine Beecher and Harriet Beecher Stowe

(1869) and in the issues of the *Ladies' Home Journal*. The women's movement demanded the vote to protect home life from the ravages of alcohol and to exert influence on the schools (Giele 1995). In the 1920s, the women's movement achieved major victories with the passage of legislation for maternal and child health and the adoption of mothers' pensions in 42 states by 1927.

It was the Social Security Act of 1935, however, that laid down the first comprehensive framework for a national social welfare policy in the United States. This unprecedented piece of legislation created a federal obligation to underwrite old-age pensions, stipends for widows and lone mothers with children, and other measures to help poor and disabled individuals. In addition, the new Public Works Administration put unemployed people to work to build roads and bridges and plant trees. The Civilian Conservation Corps gave jobs to unemployed young men. Slum clearance and new housing in poor communities were directed to the bottom half of the one-third of the nation, whom President Roosevelt had famously said were "ill-housed, ill-clothed, and ill-fed."

The purpose of these new measures was as much to get the country out of the Depression by stimulating the economy and putting people back to work as it was to help the family. Keynesian economic theory held that government spending would stimulate the economy, and so the expectation was that all these government-funded projects would not only create jobs but also put money into peoples' pockets to buy necessities and increase consumption (Galbraith 2000).

It was not until the massive changes in economy and society following World War II that sociologists in the United States began to consider social welfare policy as especially meaningful for families. In a 1967 issue of the *Journal of Marriage and Family*, its editor Marvin Sussman (1967:5) remarked, "This is, to my knowledge, the first publication effort to review existing governmental programs and their relationships to the structure and functions of the American family." Yet, amazingly, the opening article of the issue quotes a 1934 speech to Congress by President Roosevelt that pinpoints the links between the proposed Social Security Act and the narrower functions of the modern family:

> Security was attained in the earlier days through the interdependence of members of families upon each other and of the families within a small community upon each other. The complexities of great communities and of organized industry make less real these simple means of security. Therefore, we are compelled to employ the active interest of the nation as a whole through government in order to encourage a greater security for each individual. . . . (Cohen and Connery 1967:10)

Since Roosevelt's New Deal, the connections between social welfare policy and family structure and functioning have become more explicit, but the end goal of most public policy has not been family well-being so much as a series of statements focused on national well-being and peace. During the 1940s and 1950s, the goal was to win World War II and return to normalcy. From the 1960s through the 1980s, the focus of domestic policy was on ending poverty by launching and continuing the Great Society programs of President Johnson—Model Cities, the War on Poverty, Head Start, and others. By the 1990s, the bipartisan goal of President Clinton and House Speaker Newt Gingrich was to "end welfare as we know it." Then the terrorist attacks of 9/11 in 2001 changed the national focus to issues of foreign policy and the Iraq and Afghanistan wars.

Not until the closing years of the Bush Administration and the run-up to the 2008 presidential election has attention returned to domestic policy and "nation-building" to strengthen families in the United States (T. Friedman 2008). Conservatives as well as liberals have begun to call for a comprehensive national family policy. They point to the 25 percent high school dropout rate, the challenge to two-earner families of finding time to care for children, and the pressing need for a well-educated younger generation to keep the nation competitive and be able to support the large Baby Boom cohort (born between 1945 and 1964) who are now entering retirement. In a review of Douthat and Salam's (2008) book, *New York Times* journalist David Brooks (2008) notes the potential attractiveness of the authors' conservative agenda for the working class:

> Gaps are opening between the educated and less educated. Working-class divorce rates remain high, while the mostly upper-middle-class parents of Ivy Leaguers have divorce rates of only 10 percent. Working-class kids are unlikely to complete college, affluent kids usually do . . . [Here is] a series of policy ideas to help working-class families cope with economic, health care, neighborhood and family insecurity. . . . it's hard-work conservatism, which uses government to increase the odds that self-discipline and effort will pay off. (Brooks 2008)

What has emerged over the past century of social policy development is a core list of basic family functions that, if they fail, imperil the well-being of the whole society. The most important family function, without which a society cannot survive, is the physical, social, and cultural *reproduction* or *nurturance* of the next generation. Only then will there be a skilled, healthy, and responsible workforce to run the economy and the state, form new families, and care for the older generation. But for families to be able to perform their reproductive function well, they also need adequate *economic security, housing,* and *legal recognition* of their rights and obligations.

Viewed in this way, the major dimensions of family policy turn out to have their roots in prior social policy. This book treats each of these policy domains. In this opening chapter the focus is on showing how each major type of policy is related to a basic function of the *family*, even though it may also have implications for the economy, urban policy, transportation, education, health care, and the nation's place in the world. Furthermore, a probe into any single one of the family policy domains reveals that they are all closely intertwined. How well a family does in rearing its children *(nurturance)* is connected to how well it does economically *(income provision)*, whether it lives in a good neighborhood *(residence)*, and its legal and cultural status *(legitimation)*.

Changes in Family Structure

Along with the modernization of the larger society that has created major changes in family functioning, change has also occurred in family *structure*. A key residual function of the family is the definition of its membership and duties—who can marry, and what obligations parents, partners, and off-spring owe to each other. As families moved from farms to cities to suburbs, several controversial issues emerged because of their potential threat or benefit to families. Rights related to childbearing and control of fertility became a salient issue as did the "proper role" of women and whether they would neglect their families if they took paid work outside the home. All the while, as the structure of the family has been changing, there have been questions about the true definition of family—whether it can include nontraditional forms such as cohabiting partners, single parents and their children, divorced and remarried couples, or same-sex couples. One school of thought is that the family is in a state of decline and that the proper remedy is to restore traditional family forms and values by reducing the number of divorces, nonmarital births, and single-parent families.

For many U.S. citizens the question of how marriage and family is defined is one of the key issues of family policy. An Internet search for references to "family policy" brings up near the top of the list the Family Policy Network, an organization with chapters in a number of states that lists among its main tenets its opposition to abortion, gay marriage, cohabitation, and sexual activity and pregnancy outside of marriage. But on the other side of the controversy is the legal acceptance of gay marriage in a number of states, beginning with Massachusetts in 2004. While large groups of people continue to reject redefinition of the family to include a larger variety of alternatives, the overall trend has been toward greater inclusiveness of different household types in what is considered to be family. Definition of the family is thus a matter of family policy because it defines benefits as well as obligations of family membership. Participants who have previously been denied the benefits of marriage (interracial couples, same-sex couples, or abandoned children) feel that family membership legitimates and normalizes their status; it is a basic human right.

Stage 3: Social Policies to Support Family Life

As the first decade of the twenty-first century comes to a close, there is a new sense of urgency about the need to strengthen and support the American family. Global competition, the energy crisis, the strain in households with two working parents, the mortgage crisis, and growing inequality in the national income distribution all pose a new threat that families will be unable to perform their reproductive function adequately and that the nation as a whole will suffer both economically and politically. The policies being proposed to address this threat touch on all the major family functions: nurturance and caregiving, income provision, housing and residence, and legal and cultural identity.

Reproduction, Nurturance, and Caregiving

Families carry out a reproductive function both in bringing up children and in providing a place of rest and refreshment for the adult members who go to work every day. The economist Carolyn Shaw Bell (1972) referred to the care of able-bodied adults (doing the laundry, waiting for a delivery, caring for a sick child) as the "consumer maintenance" function of the family; it might also be termed "worker maintenance." Having a safe and private place to sleep, eat, enjoy some leisure, and restore one's body and spirit is what most people associate with home. Although many European countries have long had family policies to cover childcare and elder care, the United States has been slow to adopt any comprehensive programs except for the poor. Today, however, one hears Americans in many quarters calling for a better family policy to cover childcare, health care, and long-term care.

Childcare. As mothers' labor force participation rose rapidly during the 1970s, popular demand for preschool childcare also grew. President Nixon had vetoed the Comprehensive Child Care Act of 1973 because he was afraid it would lead to "Soviet style" provision. By the mid-1980s, however, two-thirds of preschool children whose mothers were working were being cared for during some portion of each week by a nonrelative (Hayes, Palmer, and Zaslow 1990), and approximately one-quarter of them received their primary care in an organized childcare facility. By the winter of 2002, 89 percent of preschoolers of employed mothers and 31 percent of preschoolers of nonemployed mothers were in at least one childcare arrangement on a regular basis (Overturf Johnson 2005). Programs for after-school care also were much more common, with a mix of public and private support. The federal government provides subsidies for regulated after-school family childcare for low-income children. In middle-class communities, local school districts provide space and staff, and families pay entrance fees for their children to participate. Child Care Resource and Referral Networks in various states, such as the Sparking Connections initiative in Minnesota, are developing strategies to support family and neighborhood providers of care for school-age children (Afterschool Investments 2007).

Health care. The extensive effort in the 1990s to establish a national system of universal health insurance failed despite vigorous efforts of the first Clinton Administration. Since that time there have been incremental changes that have led in the direction of much broader health care coverage. Beginning in 2007, Massachusetts has required all citizens to have health insurance to be paid for by themselves, an employer, or in the case of those who cannot pay, subsidized by the state. No individual can be denied insurance or renewal due to health, age, or certain other factors. Other states, such as Maine and Vermont, have established comprehensive plans to cover the uninsured. But similar efforts in California failed. The Affordable Care Act of 2010 raised these issues to the federal level and passed the controversial "individual mandate," that similar to the Massachusetts law, imposes a penalty on those who do not use one of the available options to acquire health insurance.

Advocates of universal health insurance believe that penalties to employers for not providing insurance, and to taxpayers, if they are uninsured, will stem the rising numbers of those who are not covered by insurance (close to 47 million nationwide). They also expect to lower costs by centralized bookkeeping, a focus on prevention, and elimination of unneeded tests. Critics decry interference with the free market system and the higher costs to employers that they say will result in layoffs and more jobs moving overseas. Yet Medicare already provides a model of universal coverage for people ages 65 and over, and access and satisfaction have been shown to be greater for patients covered by Medicare compared with private insurers (Davis, Schoen, Doty, and Tenney 2002). Another model is the State Children's Health Insurance Program (SCHIP), instituted by Congress in 1997, which covers uninsured children with Medicaid funds.

Americans are becoming increasingly aware of the high cost and ineffi-ciency of their health care. A series of reports by National Public Radio in 2008 documented the comparative disadvantage of pregnant women and persons with a chronic disability when receiving care in the United States compared with that of France, the Netherlands, or the United Kingdom. One 41-year-old father of four in Philadelphia, diagnosed with multiple sclerosis, reported having to wait 2 years to be covered by Medicare; in the meantime, he lost his job and faced such a high cost of drugs ($3,400 per month) that he lost his family's home to foreclosure and bankruptcy. A woman with the same diagnosis in the United Kingdom had access to regular treatment with only a $30 per month charge for physical therapy and coverage of over £5,000 in drug costs by the National Health Service (Silberner 2008).

Long-term care. Prior to the 1960s, it was still considered the obligation of adult children to provide as much care and support of their aged parents as they could. This was the "filial responsibility" principle of the original Social Security legislation. By the end of the twentieth century, however, the high cost of nursing homes (now over $70,000 a year) had resulted in heavy reliance on Medicaid, not just by the indigent aged for whom it was intended, but also an increasing number of middle-class families seeking to preserve an inheritance for the next generation. The larger family policy issue for most families is how to care for elder family members who are frail and infirm, especially if they live at a distance, and need either nursing home care or assisted living.

Several reform efforts are afoot. Economists and political scientists in the field of aging suggest that some form of mandatory long-term care insurance would be in the best interest not only of the aged but also their loved ones who need help in managing and paying for their care (Schulz and Binstock 2008). Another more service-oriented reform is an effort by the Pioneer Network and the Commonwealth Fund to change the architecture and culture of nursing home care in such a way as to make it more intimate, private, and home like. Providing small living units with a regular staff and giving the residents more autonomy helps to eliminate the warehouse atmosphere of long corridors and hospital-like treatment. Research shows that residents are much happier and more alert under such conditions (Doty, Koren, and Sturla 2008).

Income Provision

Policies to undergird economic support of the family have until recently focused on alleviation of poverty. But the decline of manufacturing and decrease in well-paying blue-collar manufacturing jobs during the 1970s made clear that something more than a good work ethic is needed to have a secure job. Moreover, even among those who are working, there is a growing gap between the top and bottom of the income distribution, making it more difficult for those in the lower income groups to accumulate assets and help their children get a higher education. Three kinds of policy solution with direct implications for family life are being discussed to strengthen equal opportunity. First is a concern that young people be adequately educated for future jobs. Second is the effort to make parents' employment more flexible and compensate for their unpaid labor in the home. Third is the use of tax policy to give incentives for families to invest in their children's education and thereby increase their likelihood of achieving economic independence.

Youth education and training. It stands to reason that a nation, to retain its competitiveness in the global economy, must have a well-trained generation of young workers who are able to perform the jobs that are needed. Currently U.S. high school dropout rates average about 25 percent, about 5 percent higher than in the late 1960s, and proficiency scores of American 10th graders in math and science rank below the average of those in other industrialized countries. To raise the number of college-educated youth requires not only higher graduation rates but also the promise of scholarship aid to students who come from the sizable group of families who cannot pay rising college costs even at public institutions. Although there is as yet no universal publicly funded initiative to pay for college tuition, positive developments include the Massachusetts governor's proposal in 2008 to give full access to community college for anyone who seeks it. A 2008 bill that passed both houses of Congress would provide veterans of the Iraqi and Afghanistan wars with tuition and stipends to publicly funded colleges and universities in their states (Kotok 2008).

Schedules to promote work and family integration. The dramatic and continuous rise in women's labor force participation since World War II has forever changed the male breadwinner/female caregiver model of family life. With the change has come widespread recognition of the "time bind" that usually overburdens the wife by adding a double burden of household work and childcare to her paid work (A. Hochschild 1989). Numerous proposals have been made over the past 30 years to right this imbalance by making more accessible such alternatives as part-time work, flexible hours, job sharing (by two people who work at different times), and parental or family leave. There has been some progress, although the existing programs are more of a patchwork than a comprehensive plan. The Pregnancy Disability Act of 1978 laid down a precedent for the Family and Medical Leave Act of 1993 (FMLA) that now provides for up to six weeks of unpaid family leave for pregnancy, sickness, or care of another family member. In 2004, California began using its state disability insurance fund to pay up to 55 percent of a worker's weekly wage for family leave; however, there is no guarantee that the worker's job will be held open for his or her return. New Jersey and Washington have provisions for paid family leave that took effect in 2009, suggesting that state initiatives may become the main way to fund the federal FMLA mandate.

Tax incentives for families with children. Not so long ago, the world was worried about overpopulation, but recently in the advanced industrial nations, there is new concern that birth rates are so far below replacement levels that there will be too few young workers to support the large baby boom cohort of retirees (Shorto 2008). The problem is most severe in those countries, such as Italy and Spain, which make it difficult for women to have both families and careers; the birth rate remains stable in the Scandinavian countries in part because they have generous provisions for childcare, family leave, and flexible schedules in the workplace, especially for women. To reverse the tide of "illegitimacy and family instability" that breed financial anxiety among working-class families, Douthat and Salam (2008:169, 171) encourage investment in children by offering an income tax credit of $5,000 per child. But to do so, they would be willing "to stigmatize illegitimacy indirectly by tying tax relief to responsible parenting," presumably by denying such relief to unwed mothers. In addition, they advocate more flexible ("family friendly" as compared with "business friendly") working schedules for parents. Subsidies, pension credits, or tuition credits modeled on veterans' benefits could be given to parents who provide childcare, "since both military service and parenthood are crucial to the country's well-being."

Housing and Residence

Surprisingly, recent publications by family sociologists and policy analysts have had very little to say about housing. Although the 1967 issue of *The Journal of Marriage and Family* on "Government Programs and the Family" carried an article on housing policy, the latest decade review of that journal in 2000 did not treat the subject; nor do other leading works on social policy and the family (Bogenschneider 2000; Cherlin 2009; Gornick and Meyers 2003). The omission is unjustified, given the huge investment that most families make in their homes, the large part of their income that goes to housing, and the many amenities or lack thereof that are associated with where they live. The mortgage crisis of 2007–2008 and the concurrent energy crisis have brought to the fore the importance of housing to family well-being. Three topics are of current interest both to sociologists and to the general public: housing and family wealth, the relation of residence to quality of schools, and housing location and urban planning in relation to poverty alleviation and the fuel crisis.

Home owning and family wealth. Just how important a home is to a family's wealth was never very much appreciated by sociologists until an award-winning book *Black Wealth, White Wealth: A New Perspective on Racial Inequality* by Oliver and Shapiro (2006) showed the stark contrast that comes when whites are able to sell their homes for more than they paid while blacks are saddled with housing debt and very little gain because they live in neighborhoods plagued by poverty, poor schools, and declining value. The authors further document how the black middle class were denied access to home lending, favorable mortgage rates, and prosperous neighborhoods because of race prejudice. The policy implication is that redlining of neighborhoods (through which banks refuse to lend to black homebuyers) and predatory and prejudicial lending policies have resulted in unequal opportunity in housing and inability to accumulate wealth just as positive policies have been a boon to those who were covered by them. In the mortgage crisis that started in 2007, predatory lending practices have been even harder on minority neighborhoods, where higher rates of foreclosure and vacancy have threatened the very safety and stability of such communities.

Residence and school quality. Housing is much more than a provision of shelter. It also links a household to the surrounding community, and for families moving into a new neighborhood, the major question is likely to be where their children will go to school. Since American public schools are largely supported by local property taxes, there are vast differences from one city and school district to another (Kozol 1991). Poor neighborhoods tend to have poorer schools, less-involved parents, and teachers who are less well paid and possibly less well trained. One response has been a movement toward charter schools and voucher schemes that would allow "free-market mechanisms" to operate by giving parents a choice of where to send their children. Another strategy is the No Child Left Behind legislation that mandates use of testing to reward good schools and punish bad ones according to how well their pupils do on the tests. Still a third approach is a program like Teach for America, which recruits recent college graduates as teachers and sends them into poor schools to bring enthusiasm and exposure to higher standards.

Is this sort of educational issue really a matter of family policy? Well, yes, in the sense that schooling so heavily depends on where a family lives and how the schools are funded. A number of states have reimbursement formulas that compensate to some extent for differences in quality of local school districts. Nevertheless, the question of how to bring all schools up to a higher standard is the larger issue, and it continues to be intimately connected to family wealth, local property taxes, and where the family lives.

Housing location, poverty, and the fuel crisis. During the fuel crisis of both 1973–1974 and sharply rising gasoline prices since 2008, reliance on individual automobiles to get to work fell, and there was more use of car pools, walking, bicycles, and public transportation. But in both periods there were two fundamental problems that remained despite changes in behavior: first, the public transportation system was in many places quite restricted and underdeveloped; and second, houses were built far apart in suburbs and were far from city centers and bus stops and rail transportation. "Edge City" had replaced the hub-and-spokes configuration of central cities, so that navigation to work, shopping, and leisure activities was very difficult without an automobile (Garreau 1991). Progressives and environmentally oriented reformers look for ways to revise housing policy and zoning laws to achieve greater density and proximity to public transportation. But the two young conservatives Douthat and Salam (2008) praise the suburbs for their richer social networks and greater affordability. Writing before the recent fuel crisis, they thought that "Sam's Club" working-class and family-oriented conservatives were looking for wider and more efficient highways for commuting as well as the potential for more work to be done at home that would be made possible by an improved "world-class" telecommuting infrastructure. As high fuel prices continue, it has became unclear whether the cheers of "Drill, baby, drill," as heard at the 2008 Republican National Convention, will resurface, or whether efforts to improve public transportation and rethink the ecology of working and commuting might gain the advantage.

Transmission of Ethnic Heritage, Identity, and Citizenship

Increasing numbers of citizens of minority race, religion, or national origin bring diversity that is key to another family function—the transmission of a cultural heritage to children and the creation of a responsible citizenry. The majority population may find it difficult to accept other family lifestyles than they deem worthy of opportunity equal to their own. Differences in race, use of "foreign" languages, and religious and cultural practices of immigrant families make it difficult for them to be treated as equals. An immense power that government holds over families is the definition of citizenship. Undocumented immigrants can be exported summarily in raids on plants where they work, forcing them to leave their children behind. (Their children *are* citizens if they were born in this country). Ideological conflict runs deep in the current immigration debate, one major part of the electorate feeling that immigrant workers are badly needed and that they should be given an orderly means of becoming citizens, while another segment resents the competition from foreign workers and extension of services and entitlements to people who come from another country, speak a different language, have a different skin color, and in some cases practice a different religion. This issue is not just "immigration policy," but it is also closely tied to family policy. The acceptance or rejection of immigrants is importantly tied to the reproductive function of families—who will bear the children of the next generation, who will be the workers, and who has the right to receive help and support for the care and protection of family members.

Equal rights are still contested for racial minorities, foreign-born persons, and individuals of Muslim or other non-Western religious traditions. While one can see a general trend toward regularization and unification of services and entitlements for all types of families, many Americans question whether government involvement in family life is going too far or not far enough. Debate on the alternatives is to be expected, and in hammering out the solutions, different segments of the American population register their interest and have their say. It is to the dynamic of these debates that we now turn.

Stage 4: Public Acceptance of Family Policy

Understandably, the changes in the modern American family and the question of how society should respond are fraught with strong emotions. Some worry that families are in a state of decline. Others applaud any change that promotes individual freedom. This book takes a third, sociological perspective, which is to understand family changes and the emergence of family policy as an inevitable consequence of societal modernization.

The way a society adapts to change in family structure is not automatic. Nor is there a single template for developing needed policies. American family policy developed differently and generally later than in other developed countries. Reform movements rather than central planners have been the visionaries behind innovation. New policy is finally accepted when changes in popular life and opinion have caught up with the innovators, and political leaders of both conservative and progressive factions begin to find common ground.

The Exceptional Nature of American Social Policy

American and international observers ever since Alexis de Tocqueville have noted that American history and politics are distinctly different from that of other countries, whether because of their Puritan origins, the American

Revolution, the conquest of the frontier, or the absorption of so many immigrants (Lipset 1996). In its social policy, the United States exhibits a unique combination of public and private means for realizing the ideals of life, liberty, and the pursuit of happiness. With a focus on individual freedom so firmly established, there has always been a worry that government will exert "too much" control. Despite American individualistic values, it is still surprising that the richest country in the world ranked 27th in infant mortality rates in 2006, behind many other industrialized countries.

In matters of social welfare policy, the United States is more similar to Great Britain and Commonwealth countries, like Australia and Canada, than to Scandinavia or countries of continental Europe. The economist Esping-Anderson (1990) has distinguished among three types of welfare state regime. The Anglo-American "liberal" (i.e., so-called "free market") pattern is more compatible with market forces and focuses on individual responsibility as the best vehicle for supporting the general welfare. Government aid tends to be viewed as the safety net of last resort. The Scandinavian "social democratic" systems focus on redistributing the wealth of the nation so that extreme inequality is evened out by a highly progressive tax system and by social programs that are generously funded to cover health and welfare of all citizens. The continental "conservative" regimes of Germany, France, Italy, and Spain see government as the central coordinator of the major institutions of society—business, the voluntary sector, the family—all of which share responsibility for the general welfare of the people.

Americans, with their tradition of free-market capitalism and incentives to stimulate entrepreneurship, hard work, and prosperity, have generally disdained the European welfare states which they view as tolerating inefficient economies and unmotivated workers. But the Great Depression of the 1930s and World War II made clear that markets alone are inadequate for addressing national crises, and then government must intervene. Social Security legislation and other programs of the New Deal created new precedents for undergirding the general welfare through government action. The World War II childcare centers made it possible for mothers to work in war plants, and the G.I. Bill of Rights made education and other benefits available to veterans. These innovations set a precedent for social policies and family services that still serve as models today.

While Americans value an energetic "can-do" spirit of achievement and capacity to solve problems and overcome obstacles, they also believe in equal opportunity. They eschew government handouts to the lazy and the undeserving, but they want everyone to be given an equal chance. Equal opportunity means having access to education and good health care in order to be able to succeed. Now, in the first decade of the twenty-first century, there is a new consciousness born of hard times—high personal debt, a climbing national deficit, a falling dollar, rising unemployment, and homelessness. The nation as a whole is once again looking for more government intervention to solve these problems. These are propitious conditions for establishing a more generous and universal family policy.

Social Movements and Reform Proposals

Along with the national lethargy in bringing government aid to ordinary families, there has long been a spate of serious reform proposals coming from women, labor, civil rights leaders, and preachers of the Social Gospel. As historian Richard Hofstadter (1955) has shown, it was the Progressive calls for wage and hour legislation, collective bargaining, a minimum wage, child protection, pensions, and other benefits that set out the agenda for the reforms adopted during Roosevelt's New Deal.

The question today is who are the foot soldiers of the social movements fighting for a more comprehensive family policy? The labor movement is smaller. The women's movement has been more occupied with women's rights (Title IX, equal pay, abortion) than with family policy (childcare, parental leave, health care). Civil rights leaders lack the attention they received in the 1960s. Religious conservatives want to maintain "family values" by resisting gay marriage and abortion but do not seem particularly oriented to getting more support for existing families. Without a coalition of reformers who are passionate about family policy, progress is unlikely.

There are potentially three likely advocate groups to push for major expansion of family policy: working parents, a new conservatively oriented working class (e.g., Reagan Democrats), and business and congressional leaders. Working parents are interested in getting more flexibility in working time, preschool and after-school care, and health care for themselves and their children. Any help with housing costs and transportation is also in their interest. Douthat and Salam (2008) think working-class conservatives will be another group of supporters interested in family values to welcome flexibility in work schedules for parents and generous tax exemptions for each child. National business and political leaders are the third potential group of advocates to see family policy as a key part of any domestic policy that will stimulate economic growth and productivity.

Just as the nation needs to rebuild and strengthen its physical infrastructure of roads, energy production, and communications, it must see to the maintenance and strengthening of the nation's families who are the foundation of its social and cultural infrastructure. This means attending to the health, education, and productivity of the working population and providing a decent standard of care for dependents—children, old people, and persons with disabilities. Economists are now emphasizing the need for the nation to build its human capital if it is to stay competitive. Goldin and Katz (2008) emphasize the importance of education for national prosperity and show that the relative standing of the United States in the educational levels of its citizens has *fallen* in the last forty years. Nobel economist James Heckman (2006) has documented the critical importance of family environments during the first five years of life for preparing children to learn in school. Disadvantaged families produce children who do poorly in school, but early enrichment, such as that by the Perry Pre-School Project in Ypsilanti, Michigan (and a forerunner of Head Start), can help parents and children reverse these effects. No single national leader has yet put forth a vision that links the economic fate of the whole nation to a more comprehensive family policy, but the elements of that larger vision are beginning to take shape.

Changes in Lifestyle and Popular Opinion

Of course, visionaries and reformers can put forward many different policy proposals, but only those that somehow resonate with the electorate will eventually be adopted. Up to now public programs to help families have focused on the "unluckiest," those most in need. Many poor people's programs, however, are stigmatized and poorly funded. Theda Skocpol (2000) diagnosed the problem as one of "the missing middle," the absence of a broad group of the population who see the need for social policies to benefit *them.*

But American society now appears to be at a turning point where a more generous family policy makes sense for the "missing middle." One of the most visible engines of change is the new more "masculine" role of women as workers in the paid labor force. The welfare functions that families have been able to provide in the past—caring for children, long-term care of elders, protection for the disabled—are all under increasing pressure to be "commodified" and paid for as outside services. The result is a strain on most families. The old breadwinner/homemaker model of family life is increasingly rare, yet most people have to carry on their caregiving responsibilities to children and elders and can only add such duties to the demands of their paid work. They lack easily available and affordable childcare. Some husbands are uneasy with caregiving, especially if the task is very demanding. So women take less employment than they would like and than their families need, with a resulting loss of about 15 percent to the GDP (Esping-Andersen 2009), while others bear a double burden of family work and paid work.

But the implicit gender contract is changing. Women are increasingly expecting to be employed most of their lives, but without giving up marriage and child bearing. And men increasingly are partners to these new role bargains where there is more sharing of productive and reproductive functions between the sexes. Gradually, people are coming to expect a new set of policies and services that will help them integrate their work and family roles. While these changes are still spotty, great strides have been made in the last thirty years related to working times; hiring practices; availability of childcare and family leave; and access to pensions, benefits, and other entitlements (Giele 2006).

The Politics of Finding Common Ground

When social and demographic change brings the majority of the population into synchrony with the ideas of the reformers, policies that had been only experimental and limited become institutionalized for the society as a whole.

A couple of famous examples come from Europe of the 1930s, when countries like Sweden and France were facing demographic decline because of falling birthrates. Alva Myrdal ([1934] 1968) traveled in Sweden and France to discover what families needed in order to be interested in having more children. Subsequently, both France and Sweden instituted housing and income supplements for families with children. These nations supported such family policies because they were in the long-term interests of both family and society. In the early 1970s, I had the opportunity to meet with Alva Myrdal, and she explained to me what she thought to be the key to success in family policy. The whole nation has to think not just in terms of "my" children or "your" children but of "all our children."

The importance of thinking in terms of "all our children," "all our elders," and "all our citizens" is that family policy can only serve the general social welfare if it serves the interests of the country as a whole. The well-being of the whole nation is at risk if a significant number of people are ignorant, hungry, unemployed, sick, or alienated and disaffected. Just as parents are held responsible for the misdemeanors of their children and are congratulated on their successes, so a nation that has many people hungry or in prison must be asked about the cultural and social policies that allow such conditions to prevail just as it is lauded for its can-do spirit and ability to put a person on the moon.

For a sociologist of the family, and for citizens and political leaders alike, the challenge of moving family policy forward is to find the golden mean of political consensus and compromise that somehow allies new programs and benefits for families with the basic values and long-term interests of the society. This unity of interests appeared in France when it passed its flexible working time and childcare policy. The rallying cry was that everyone needs "time to live" (Letablier 2004). Similarly, the conservative government in Great Britain is as much concerned with quality of life as with economics. British conservatives are thinking about strengthening the social infrastructure by increasing the number of health visitors to new parents, rewriting the tax code to be more family friendly, and making childcare more accessible (Brooks 2008).

Developing a Sociology of Family Policy

The sociology of the family combines many strands—anthropological studies of marriage and kinship in other societies, marriage and family counseling, and the many departments of Home Economics and Human Development associated with schools of agriculture such as Cornell University, and the Universities of Minnesota and Wisconsin. The topic of family policy is quite new in this mix. Yet, it is one of the most exciting and relevant aspects of current family studies. In this opening chapter I have drawn together the main strands of family policy in an implicit theory of social change that involves four main elements:

1. *Societal change that reshapes key family functions.* Families have had to adapt to new challenges to provide for the basic human needs of nurturance, material provision, residence, and legitimation of social and cultural identity.

2. *Family modernization.* Family structure has had to change in response to urbanization and industrialization: Families have become smaller and divorce, separation, and single parenting have become more common. Family functions also changed in their execution: Production moved from farm and small business to the workplace; reproductive functions of childbearing and caregiving then took center stage.

3. *Individual and societal adaptation to family change.* Reform movements such as women's and civil rights have reflected changes in individual and family life; they advocate social policies to address the new reality.

4. *Institutionalization:* Successful policies, programs, and life changes are being incorporated into the normal patterns and rules of everyday life.

Sociologists, other social scientists, and the general public all have a role in helping to hammer out the best and most workable family policies. To assess which proposals will work best and be the most likely to be adopted, it is necessary to do research and to collect facts, not just argue from legal precedent or moral principle. This is the method of the famous 1908 "Brandeis Brief" that won for women workers the right to work no more than 10 hours a day and have time to eat lunch and take a rest. Instead of relying solely on arguments about freedom of the workers and employers to make their own labor contract, Louis Brandeis and his sister-in-law Josephine Goldmark documented the actual practices in a laundry in *Mueller v. Oregon* and demonstrated that the workers' commitment to the job was not "free" when the employer had the upper hand in dictating working conditions. The Brandeis method was used again in the famous 1954 Supreme Court decision of *Brown v. Board of Education*. Social scientists provided evidence that separate educational facilities for blacks and whites were *not* equal. The principle of "separate but equal" in *Plessy v. Ferguson* (1896) did not hold up in the face of such evidence.

Today there is a similar challenge to demonstrate how childcare, health policies, working hours, housing and school quality, and immigration are affecting children and families and the well-being of the nation. Arguing from preconceived religious, moral, liberal, conservative, or feminist arguments is not sufficient to win the day or to convince those who hold different views. Social policy for the future will not be designed by simple ideological arguments about too much government intervention, too little family responsibility, or whether the economy is getting better or getting worse. What is needed for intelligent and rational action is a clear-eyed understanding of how families, the economy, and the state are all changing in interdependent ways.

On top of that, we need good research on the actual effects of different types of policy. This is where social science comes in. The sociology of family policy can be a meeting ground for information not only about what social arrangements are most appealing and productive of happiness and quality of life, but also about what families say they want and need. The contributions of political experts and journalists are also valuable for sounding out the potential common ground that can bring together liberals, conservatives, and those in the middle. This book is intended as an invitation to students and teachers in the sociology of the family to begin mapping this new field of family policy in America. Chapters 2 and 3 take up the structural changes in family that have occurred in family composition and the transformation of gender roles. Chapters 4 through 7 focus in turn on the four key functions of nurturance, provision, residence, and legitimation. The final chapter places the growth of family policy in America in a wider historical and international context.

2

Defining the Family

E ver since the rise of the women's movement and the civil rights revolution of the 1960s, there has been a debate over the proper form of family life, some claiming that the traditional family is in a state of decline; others, that greater diversify in family structure is both needed and proper. The majority of Americans think of the family as made up of a husband, wife, and children with an extended kinship network that includes grandparents, cousins, in-laws, and other relatives. That raises a question of whether unrelated persons cohabiting in a household should also be counted as families or should be discouraged because they are harmful to children and adults alike.

This chapter will review the ideological spectrum of opinion about the best and least desirable family forms and how to evaluate them, and then examine how the idealized family matches up with the actual demographics of family life in America. It is important to understand why the main changes in family life have occurred and what their effects have been on family members. With that knowledge it is then possible to evaluate various public policies and programs toward single-parent families and new family forms. The basic argument of this chapter is that citizens support the types of family life that are most in tune with their own experience as well as their own religious and moral outlook. As the society becomes more diverse and the economic basis of family life moves further away from a rural economy and small-town life, support has grown for permitting and legitimating a wider array of intimate living arrangements that perform much the same functions as traditional families: namely, caregiving, income-sharing, providing a place of residence, and holding similar goals and values in common.

Despite what may be a growing consensus, however, the debate between conservatives, liberals, and feminists runs throughout the entire scholarship about current American family life. There is a difference of opinion on how to interpret changing demographics, how to explain the new trends, how to evaluate whether the effects on children are good or bad, and how to construct the policies that are most needed. Before reviewing the various implications of these different views of family life, it is useful to summarize the main tenets of each of the main ideological positions.

The Debate Over Family Values

American family patterns have changed dramatically over the last half century, with a sharp increase in single-person households and single-parent families; a majority of mothers with young children are now active in the labor force. Yet citizens differ on whether these changes are good or bad and whether they are damaging to children as well as to the society at large. At the conservative end of the spectrum are those who are alarmed at the decline of the traditional breadwinner–homemaker family. But liberals note the economic contributions made by the rising number of women in the labor force; and both liberals and feminists emphasize the progress that has occurred in recognizing the rights of women who, in many cases, experienced violence or oppression in traditional families. Liberal and feminist critics also believe that the constitutional rights of persons living in nontraditional families are abridged when they experience discrimination and prohibition of marriage to a partner of the same sex or of a different race. Standing between the traditionalists and feminists are those social scientists and pragmatic liberals who argue that family form follows family function and that the law is likely to lag behind informal mores of behavior. In their view, the new family forms are not so much the result of a decline in family values or a failure of moral choices as efforts to find satisfactory living arrangements under changing economic and social conditions.

During the 1950s, the family debate in America had yet to emerge. The post–World War II population was relieved to be done with the conscription of men for national defense and the mobilization of women to work in war factories. Family life represented to most people a haven of safety and fulfillment that had long been delayed. Veterans returned from the armed forces, and women were demobilized from wartime production and were sent home to make room for men in the labor force. The suburbs mushroomed, and the baby boom lasted from 1947 to 1964 (May, 2008).

By the 1960s, however, it was becoming evident that some family arrangements were less than optimal. Betty Friedan's book on *The Feminine*

Mystique (1963) analyzed women's confinement to the home and their resulting frustration as the "problem that has no name." In 1968, Daniel Patrick Moynihan in his report to President Johnson on *The Negro Family: The Case for National Action* warned that the growing number of single-parent families was imperiling the future success of black children (Rainwater and Yancey 1967). By the 1970s, Christopher Lasch (1977) was viewing traditional families as an endangered species in his *Haven in a Heartless World: The Family Besieged.* Meanwhile, large government-funded research projects such as the Seattle and Denver Income Maintenance Experiments examined the effects of government-provided income supports on family structure. The overall conclusion was that when women have sufficient income either from their own earnings or the state, they are able to leave abusive or dysfunctional marriages (Widerquist, Lewis, and Pressman 2005). The most prominent conservative commentator on all this social change and experimentation was Charles Murray (1984) in his book *Losing Ground: American Social Policy, 1950–1980,* which argued that government-supported welfare projects had encouraged the breakdown of the traditional family by giving women an incentive to have children out of wedlock while being assured they would be taken care of by public support.

How shall we make sense of the wide array of ideological positions on the future and fate of the family? My view is that each perspective has a place because each captures some aspect of the crisis in family life and focuses on that part of the social problem that is a cause for concern. The crescendo of the contemporary debate on family values reached its peak in the mid-1990s, during welfare reform, when conservative arguments prevailed and the program of Aid to Families with Dependent Children (AFDC), established in the 1930s, was shut down. Nevertheless, families have continued to change in much the same directions as before without any major reversal in prevalence of cohabitation, numbers of single-parent families, divorce, or acceptance of alternative family forms. In fact, the permission of single-sex marriage began in Massachusetts in 2004, in Connecticut in 2008, and in Maine, New Hampshire, Vermont, and Iowa in 2009, which suggests that the general public is gradually accepting a wider variety of family forms. The following review summarizes the main claims of the conservatives who want to strengthen two-parent families, the liberal centrists who accept much of family change as pragmatic adaptation, and the feminists who focus on the need to support a wider variety of family forms in order to promote caregiving while safeguarding individual rights. Given the tenets of each perspective, it is now worth considering whether there may be a new synthesis emerging in public opinion and scholarship that combines all three perspectives by giving more emphasis to the basic caregiving and income-sharing functions of family life than to the composition of the family unit (Cherlin 2009; Giele 1996).

The Conservative Focus on Family Values

To "family values" advocates, the most important aspect of family change is the breakdown of the two-parent family and the rise of divorce, cohabitation, illegitimacy, and fatherlessness. Conservatives say these changes have put children at greater risk of school failure, unemployment, and antisocial behavior. The remedy is to restore traditional moral values and family commitment while limiting government support to unwed mothers and mother-headed families (Giele 1996).

The Conservative Model

| Cultural and moral weakening | → | Family breakdown, divorce, father absence, family decline | → | Poverty, disadvantage, school failure, crime, drug use | → | Need to restore family values |

Cultural and moral weakening. To conservatives, it is the secularization of modern religious practice and decline of religious affiliation that have undermined the norms of sexual abstinence before marriage and prohibitions against abortion, adultery, and divorce. In her famous *Atlantic Monthly* article, "Dan Quayle Was Right," Barbara Dafoe Whitehead (1993) defended the 1992 vice presidential candidate's negative comment on the television serial that had glowingly depicted a young mother (Murphy Brown) having a child out of wedlock. Conservatives found great comfort in Whitehead's argument because it put a spotlight on the remarkable recent change in family structure that appears to have been generally accepted without much attention to its defects. Conservatives have three main arguments: First, the family is being weakened; second, family breakdown is destructive for children; and third, the solution is to treat marriage as sacred and thereby to delay sexual intimacy until marriage and discourage divorce.

Family breakdown. The most visible sign of family erosion is the decline of marriage. The proportion of all households headed by married couples fell from 78 percent in 1950 to 60 percent in 1980, 52 percent in 2000, and 48 percent in 2010 (Tavernise 2011). Rising cohabitation, divorce rates, and nonmarital births all contributed to the trend. The rise in persons living alone (single-person households) also was significant: from only 10 percent of all households in 1950 to 23 percent in 1980, and 27 percent in 2010 (Goldscheider and Waite 1991; U.S. Census Bureau 2010c).

Destructive consequences. The growth of single-parent households was especially worrisome because of strong links to child poverty. By 1988, only 35 percent of children in poverty had two parents and 57 percent lived with a mother only. These developments were fed by rising rates of divorce and nonmarital births. Between 1940 and 2010, the divorce rate rose from 8.8 to 21 per thousand married women in 1995, fell slightly lower to about 20 in 2000, and has held steady at that rate through 2009 (Carter 2006; Kreider and Ellis 2011:7). Out-of-wedlock births exploded from 5 percent in 1960 to 26 percent in 1990, and 41 percent in 2009 (Hernandez 1993; Martin, Hamilton, and Ventura 2011:Table 13).

Return to family values. The remedy that conservatives advocate is to revitalize and re-institutionalize marriage. The culture should change to give higher priority to marriage and parenting. Jean Bethke Elshtain (1995), a leading political theorist, views marriage as the basic building block of the civil society. Marriage holds together the fabric of volunteer activity and mutual support that underpins any democratic order (Popenoe, Elshtain, and Blankenhorn 1996). Some conservatives support movements such as the National Fatherhood Initiative to raise awareness of the importance of fathers and their distinctive role in child development (which they believe to be different from women's). Some fatherhood groups advocate taking a pledge to abstain from sex prior to marriage. Other groups offer support to women who want to stay at home with their children through such organizations as Family and Home Network (2011) and Mothers of Color at Home (2011).

Maggie Gallagher (1996), spokeswoman for the conservative perspective, believes that no-fault divorce has led to a "culture of divorce" where breaking up a family has become so responsive to the plaintiff's wishes that there is insufficient consideration of the costs to children and to the partner who is left behind. The Family Research Council (2011), founded in 1983, has been a strong opponent of abortion and embryonic stem cell research. While it supports family tax credits, it endorses the federal Defense of Marriage Act, passed in 1996, which prohibits treatment of same-sex relationships as marriage, even if recognized by a state.

The Liberal Position: Family Structure as Adaptation

Liberals agree that family life is changing, but they attribute this change to economic restructuring more than to a loss of family values. As the family has lost economic functions to the urban workplace and many of its socialization functions to the school, it is left with the intimate relationship between parents and children and between the marital couple as its main reason for being. Marriage, left unshielded by the traditional economic division of labor between men and women, is subject to very high demands for emotional fulfillment and is thus more vulnerable to breakdown and structural change when it falls short of those demands. The liberal solution is to seek more comprehensive family policies that support families by promoting work–family integration, childcare programs, and caregiving for other sick, aged, or disabled family members (Giele 1996).

The Liberal Model			
Changing economic structure	→ Changing family & gender roles	→ Diverse effects: child poverty or well-being	→ Family policies needed for work–family balance, childcare, etc.

Economic restructuring and family adaptation. Liberals find the main source of family change in the marketplace rather than in weaker family values. The male-breadwinner/wife-homemaker family has decreased in numbers because it is less viable in an urban, post-industrial economy. Proof of this connection is found in the remarkable rise in married women's labor force participation rates that grew from one-fifth of all wives in the 1940s to half by 1980 and to two-thirds of those with children under 18 years of age (66.0 percent) by 2010 (U.S. Census Bureau 2011:Table 601). By 1987, over half of all mothers of infants under a year old were in the labor force at least part of the year and this proportion continued to rise, although only slightly to 56.4 percent in 2008 (Bureau of Labor Statistics 2009b). Not only had labor-saving devices in the home and growth of the service professions increased the supply and demand for women workers, but a rising standard of living and the cost of higher education for children also gave families a strong incentive to encourage the wife-mother to work for pay (Oppenheimer 1982). This massive change resulted in three major changes in family structure. First, the husband-earner/wife-homemaker ideal gave way to a dual-earner model of family life. Second, the divorce rate grew after 1950 and by the age of 40 approximately one-third of married men will have experienced a divorce. Third, many fewer men and women are marrying at all, a decline from 90 percent who ever married among those born in the 1940s to roughly 75 percent of those born in the 1960s (Kreider and Ellis 2011:6, 9). All of these transformations threatened the major childcare and protective functions of the family. Mothers' paid employment created a huge time deficit for the care and socialization of young children. Rising divorce raised difficult conflicts over child support and child custody that in many cases threatened poverty and emotional damage to children (Wallerstein and Blakeslee 1989). Finally, the decline in percentage of the population ever marrying portended a continued high rate of nonmarital births.

Positive and negative consequences of family change. But against conservative claims that these changes in the family have brought unquestionable harm to many children, liberals noted positive outcomes along with the negative. Research on the effects of mothers' working is a good example. The early presumption was that it was harmful for children. But further research has shown that much depends on the educational and occupational level of the parents and the availability of outside services (Schneider and Waite 2005). Similarly, Coontz and Franklin (1997) argue that a mother's educational level is more important than her marital status to her child's well-being. While Blankenhorn (1995), Popenoe (1996), and other conservatives insist that divorce and single-parent households are the main factor in child poverty, the economically oriented liberal analysts argue that having sufficient income may be a *precondition* of marriage rather than a consequence. For example, a young black woman's marital choices are limited by the large number of black men who are incarcerated or unemployed; thus, it may be more rational for her to avoid marriage than be saddled with another dependent (Wilson 1987).

Work–family integration policies. Consistent with an economically oriented analysis, liberal policies focus on how the work–family relationship might be restructured to mitigate working parents' time deficits, or how to boost parents' earning power to prevent child poverty. The Family and Medical Leave Act of 1993 is a major example of legislation to further work–family integration. While family leave is federally mandated for firms with at least 50 employees, it is unpaid except in states such as California that are using unemployment insurance funds for that purpose. Another major initiative following the successes of the famous Perry Pre-School program in Michigan and of Head Start is to provide preschool programs and childcare for all children, but especially for those from poor and low-income families. A federally funded program such as the Even Start Family Literacy Program, begun in 1988, aims to improve parents' literacy along with providing childcare. By and large, however, the advocates of parental leave and provision of childcare are more vocal than the advocates of improving parents' earning power. Middle-class individuals can more easily make their own accommodations in their personal schedules or career plans; this may involve one or both parents working part time during the children's early years (Bailyn 1993). This is more difficult for working-class parents.

The Cultural Perspective and Feminist Views

In contrast with liberals who focus on structural change in families, feminists emphasize the importance of changing cultural ideas about the nature of the family. The feminist perspective challenges biological determinism and views men as being capable of caregiving just as women are capable of breadwinning. Feminists are skeptical of conservative solutions because they know of the exploitation of women that so often has been associated with caregiving in the traditional family. They are also to some degree suspicious of liberal solutions because of the "male" bias that accompanies a focus on independent individuals in the marketplace and a lack of recognition that so-called *independence* is possible only when there is hidden *dependence* on the caregiving of others.

By articulating the value of caregiving along with individual autonomy, feminists are in a position to examine modern capitalism critically for its effects on families and to offer alternative policies that place greater value on the quality of life and human relationships. They judge the strength of families not by their *form* (whether they have two parents) but by their *functioning* (whether they promote human satisfaction and development) and whether they provide both adequate income and adequate care. They attribute difficulties of children less to the absence of the two-parent family than to the very low wages of single mothers and poorly educated fathers, inadequate childcare, and inhospitable housing and neighborhoods. They would work for reforms that support equality between the sexes and that build and maintain social capital of the volunteer groups, neighborhoods, and communities that are necessary to the well-being of all families and neighborhoods (Giele 1996).

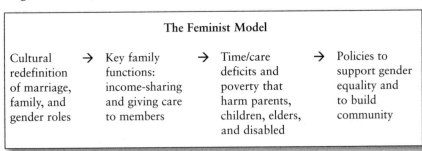

The Feminist Model

Cultural redefinition of marriage, family, and gender roles → Key family functions: income-sharing and giving care to members → Time/care deficits and poverty that harm parents, children, elders, and disabled → Policies to support gender equality and to build community

The family as culturally defined. Perhaps the simplest way to distinguish between the conservative, liberal, and feminist perspectives is to think of each as associated with a particular historical period. Margrit Eichler (1997) sums up these three models of family life as based on *patriarchal, individual,* or *social* responsibility. Conservatives look back to the all-encompassing role of family life in premodern society. Liberals focus mainly on the two-parent "modern" family ideal that has been prominent since 1850. Feminists emphasize a new broader and more differentiated definition of family that coincides with postmodern and postindustrial society (Gillis 1996). In the words of Dill, Zinn, and Patton (1993:14), "Feminist thinkers have demonstrated that family forms are socially and historically constructed, not monolithic universals that exist for all times and all peoples, and that the social and legal arrangements governing family life are not the inevitable result of unambiguous differences between women and men."

Gender, work, and caregiving. Postmodern ideas about gender roles come out of two streams of feminism—the first, *equal rights feminism,* which emphasizes the similar capacities of women and men; the second, *maternal or domestic feminism,* which notes capitalist society's lack of concern for caregiving and concentrates on the emotional and domestic needs of all people, including children and other dependents or vulnerable citizens (Giele 1995). It is not only men who can earn an income, and not only women who can give care. Feminists insist that women should receive sufficient income to help support their families, and men should engage in the emotional work of family life as well as carry their fair share of parental and domestic duties (Coltrane 1996).

Such views lead to complex and not altogether unitary views about the fatherhood movement and about the consequences of divorce. Stacey (1996) is skeptical about the fatherhood movement because she worries that it is a subterfuge for bringing back patriarchy. Gavanas (2004), in her ethnographic study of the fatherhood movement, discovers both a pro-marriage group who believe that two-parent families can significantly lower the child poverty rate and the "fragile family" organizations who focus on the disadvantages that prevent fathers' attachment such as unemployment, racism, and discrimination. With respect to divorce, Wallerstein and Blakeslee (1989; 2004) estimate that four-fifths of divorced women and half of divorced men are happier after divorce whereas children almost universally suffer. These observers contend that relatively more consideration should be given to the needs of children in the event of divorce, especially in the division of marital property to assure the children's economic well-being in case of a second marriage and in plans for custody and visitation to safeguard their emotional development and psychological health.

Policies to support flexibility and interdependence. Feminists are skeptical that any single-family form is better able to promise happiness and well-being. They focus instead on gender equality and the need to develop

institutions that support the integration of work and family life. The
Council on Contemporary Families (2009), for example, promotes understanding of "the latest research and clinical findings about the ways that
boys, girls, men, and women have become more similar in recent years—
and why they continue to be different." Some research shows that couples
in more flexible egalitarian marriages are happier than those with a more
traditional division of labor (A. Hochschild 1989; Turk 2009). On the
other hand, there is also evidence that marriages where the husband is
the main breadwinner are happier than dual-career couples (Wilcox and
Nock 2006). In any case, feminists generally agree that women and men
have similar capacities for productive work and caregiving. Accordingly,
they favor an egalitarian division of labor between women and men in
heterosexual marriages, fair treatment of women and men in the event of
divorce (while also safeguarding the interests of children), and the establishment of gay marriage as a constitutional right of the individual partners
as well as an acknowledgment that families need not be founded on the
traditional heterosexual couple.

The Changing Demographics of Family Life

The moral turmoil over what constitutes the best form of family life is the
direct result of the remarkable changes in family size, marriage, divorce, and
household composition that have occurred since the onset of the Industrial
Revolution. The most powerful explanation of these changes is the dramatic
decline in fertility that began in the mid-1800s and is known as the *demographic transition*. All over the modernizing world, families began to change
their reproductive behavior to have fewer children. The change was driven
by two major factors: first, the decline in infant mortality meant more children survived to adulthood; second, the decline of the rural economy meant
having numerous children was no longer an economic asset (because they
could work on the farm) and instead became an economic liability (as additional mouths to feed in a consumer economy).

Demographer Judith Blake (1982:300) explains the new smaller families
and the new patterns of marriage, cohabitation, and household composition
as transitional forms that have helped American society attain a new permanent state of low fertility. The family is being "updated" as marriage no longer
defines "whether people are 'inside' or 'outside' a family-type situation. . . . We
are seeing a rise in nonmarital domiciliary norms and a decline in stable
marital ones." These general trends were also taking place in other parts of

the world (Mason, Ysuya, and Choe 1998). Blake (1982:302) explained the process as one of adaptation to a new reality:

> The importance of these familial changes is that they are making for non-familial goals in people's lives, at the same time that they are providing various types of intermediate, intimate, flexible solutions along the way. This is vitally important for a developed country that requires a permanent "tilt" toward very low fertility. Such a society has got to define status away from reproductive goals. Such a society has got to involve people, on a long-range basis, in demanding nonreproductive activities that are meaningful to them. . . . Given the fact that we appear to be taking a major leap toward the long-range institutionalization of very low fertility, I would say we are doing so with minimum disruption and with singular flexibility.

This adaptation toward low fertility is reflected in the many new ways that children are now being conceived and adopted. The biggest change is in births outside of marriage, a rate that has quadrupled in the last 50 years. The resulting decline in the number of American children available for adoption has resulted in 15,000 to 22,000 adoptions per year from other countries such as China, Latin America, and Russia. Since the 1990s, new reproductive technology (in vitro fertilization, sperm donation, surrogate pregnancy, etc.) also has expanded the methods for achieving a live birth as well as the types of families who are able to have children. Homosexual couples as well as single persons, both men and women, have become parents, who by aid of the new technology have the possibility of being genetically related to their children.

New attitudes toward sexuality also help to explain the increased acceptance of sexual intercourse as a pleasure in itself that need not lead to reproduction. By 2002, 90 percent of women in the childbearing ages of 15 to 44 had used some form of birth control, with two-thirds of women ages 40 to 44 reporting either their own sterilization (40 percent) or that of a male partner (20 percent). The right to abortion made possible in *Roe v. Wade* was a watershed event consistent with the new choice that Blake refers to between reproduction and other nonreproductive goals that abortion makes possible. Abortion was not only made legal, but also its use could be monitored. In 1970, before the Supreme Court decision, the abortion rate was 51.9 per thousand live births, compared with 136.6 in 1971; it then peaked in 1981 at 431.6 and has since gradually fallen to 285.4, as of 2008 (Johnston 2011).

The adaptation that Blake describes that moves the society toward low fertility has three major aspects: (1) smaller families, (2) changes in family formation and dissolution, and (3) greater variety in family composition.

Changes in Family Size and Reproductive Behavior

A stark worldwide indicator of the effects of modernization on the family has been the dramatic decrease in family size. Over half of all children born in 1800 had *eight or more* siblings. Even children born a century later typically had *five to seven* siblings. It was not until the birth cohort of 1920 that three to four siblings became typical, and not until the 1980 birth cohort that one or two siblings became the norm. The cause of the fall in family size was the drop in the total fertility rate (the total number of children born to the average woman). In 1917, the earliest year for which this figure is available, the rate was 3.3 births per woman, a number that fell to 2.1 in the depths of the depression of the 1930s, rose again during the baby boom to 3.6 in 1960, but fell to 2.0 by 1972 and to 1.8 in 1980, less than the replacement rate of 2.1, but had risen again to 2.1 by 2008 (Hernandez 1993; U.S. Census Bureau 2011:Table 83).

Those reading these statistics will undoubtedly be able to think of examples from their own families where their parents and grandparents came from much larger families than their own. I think of one girl in my rural grade school class in the 1940s who came from an Italian immigrant family of 22 children! My own father, born in 1894 of parents who emigrated from Switzerland and lived on a farm, had eight siblings, one of whom died in infancy. My mother, born in 1903 of Scandinavian immigrants who lived in a mining town in western Pennsylvania, came from a family of nine children, one of whom died as a baby. Yet my parents, who lived outside of a rural county seat in Ohio, but were not farmers, had only four children, one of whom died in early childhood. When my husband (born in 1924) and I (born in 1934) started our family in a Boston suburb, we had only two children, born in 1963 and 1965. Clearly the widespread change in fertility and family size was quite deliberate, aided not only by a change in attitudes but by changes in law and technology. Yet it was not until the 1960s and 1970s that *Griswold v. Connecticut* (1965) struck down a state law prohibiting sale of contraceptives on grounds of the right to marital privacy, and *Roe v. Wade* (1973) protected abortion as a part of a woman's constitutional right of privacy. From the beginning of the twentieth century, reformers like Margaret Sanger had worked to educate the public and change the laws to permit women to control their own fertility. By the 1960s and 1970s, the sexual revolution had dramatically loosened the tie between sexual intercourse, pregnancy, and childbirth. Development of the birth control pill in the 1950s and its introduction in the early 1960s had the most far-reaching effect. It rendered obsolete the Church-approved rhythm method (intercourse during the nonfertile days of the menstrual cycle) and use of barrier devices such as cervical caps or condoms. Taken together, these transformations in law and technology weakened the link between sexual relationships and marriage and between marriage and family formation. While no more than 5 percent of white children were born to single mothers in 1960, two-fifths of all American children today are born to unmarried parents (Martin et al. 2011:Table 13).

Marriage, Sexual Behavior, and Divorce

Both the laws and the demographics of marriage tell a story of the loosening of the connection between sexual intimacy, marriage, and the attainment of status as an adult. Before roughly 1500 in the West, marriage was a mainly private matter between two consenting adults and their families that was consummated by sexual union. In the ensuing 500 years, however, church and state succeeded in establishing a set of requirements—publishing the intentions (banns), betrothal, presence of at least two witnesses, marriage before a religious or governmental official, and registration in the public record (Glendon 1977; Thornton, Axinn, and Xie 2007). Over the last century and a half, however, these rules have rapidly become more flexible or have fallen away, so that the essentials of mutual consent of the couple and their sexual union are the two main elements still left standing.

Correlated with this retreat from formality has been a rapid rise in sexual intercourse and cohabitation before marriage, a rise in the number of children born outside of marriage, and a rapid decline in the taboos against premarital sex and single parenthood. These changes have resulted in two tiers of marriage, both legitimated by society. People with higher education and incomes gravitate to bigger weddings and greater ceremony, whereas the common law pattern is more often found among less educated and poorer people. Thornton et al. (2007) thoroughly document the change in attitudes toward sex and cohabitation before marriage by analyzing the results of a longitudinal survey of mostly white mothers in the Detroit area who had a child born in 1961. The survey revealed general continuity in attitudes between the mothers and their children when interviewed in 1985 and 1993 about timing of marriage and the importance of having children. But the younger generations were markedly more accepting of premarital sex and nonmarital cohabitation than the parental generation. Compared with less than 10 percent of their mothers, roughly half of the younger generation had experienced cohabitation. These trends parallel findings from the National Survey of Family and Households on attitudes of younger and older cohorts in 1987–1988 and 1992–1994. Almost three-quarters of people under the age of 30, compared with slightly less than a quarter of people 70 and over, considered unmarried sex, cohabitation, and unmarried births to be acceptable

(Bumpass 1998). A Pew public opinion survey in 2007 confirmed this general pattern of a generation gap in values and behaviors in which those under age 35 were much more accepting of cohabitation and nonmarital births than people ages 65 and over (Pew Research Center 2007).

The age at first marriage has risen sharply; and fewer people are marrying today, although 80 to 90 percent of people believe they will eventually marry. Men's employment (not women's) still predicts both cohabitation and marriage (perhaps because women are more likely to choose a man who has a job or because only those men who are employed feel that they can undertake marriage). In general, lower rates of marriage are found among those young people who have a positive attitude to gender equality, lower religiosity, a more permissive attitude toward cohabitation, and higher career aspirations. A comprehensive study in *Sex in America* has shown that along with acceptance of cohabitation *before* marriage, there is considerable acceptance of sexual behavior *outside* of marriage. The study delineates three major attitudes toward sex: *traditional*, *transitional*, and *recreational* (Laumann and Michael 2000). It is the recreational orientation that has recently appeared among a considerable number of adolescents and young adults who are fascinated by such TV shows as *Sex and the City* and who speak of "friends with benefits" and "hooking up" as a way of enjoying sex without making a commitment. Studies of college students have found that about 60 percent of college students have been in one of these relationships, but only 10 percent of them (6 percent overall) found any lasting relationship as a result (Carey 2007). Nevertheless, Waite (2001:5313) contends that "the married couple remains the locus of the vast majority of sexual activity."

While the sharp increase in cohabitation and sexual activity outside of marriage is relatively recent, divorce rates have been steadily rising over the past century, from under 2 percent of married women in 1860 to nearly one-quarter in 1980. This is the highest rate of any advanced industrial society (Bumpass 1998; Ruggles 1997). It is currently expected that half of all marriages will be disrupted, and among cohabiting couples, one-fourth will break up after only 3 to 4 years compared with less than 5 percent of marriages (Waite 2001). There are several explanations for this change. The most prominent theory argues that the sexual division of labor has changed such that women's rising labor force participation has enabled them to support themselves independently and to leave a bad marriage (Ruggles, 1997). The alternative view is that the key variable is men's economic opportunity. When it is blocked, marriages go down and separations are more likely (Oppenheimer 1994). This theory helps to explain the much lower rate of marriage and higher rate of separation among blacks compared with whites as being the result of lower employment opportunities for black males

(Ruggles 1997). A third theory attributes higher separation and divorce (and delay of remarriage) to culture and changing attitudes, in which individualism has resulted in an aversion to long-term commitments and at the same time has brought greater equality to women and liberation from confinement to the domestic sphere (Bumpass 1998).

Family Composition

One of the most important consequences of separation and divorce is the type of household where children will grow up—whether or not the family unit is poor and whether or not both parents are present. The overall trend has been toward a greater variety in the structure of families and households. The leading demographers of our time sum up the dramatic changes that have occurred in family structure by pointing to several major trends: (1) the decline of the intergenerational farm family made up of parents, grandparents, and children; (2) smaller family size because of fewer children; (3) change in the roles of men and women; and (4) growth of single-person and nonfamily households and group quarters (Farley 1996; Goldscheider and Waite 1991; Hernandez 1993; Ruggles 2006). The most important underlying factor associated with all these changes was the decline of the rural economy in which family structure was closely intertwined with farming. Women were dependent on men for heavy labor; and men relied on women to do the cooking and necessary household production. Elderly parents who lived past their productive years stayed on and helped with lesser chores. Children were valued workers also. Single people found it difficult to live entirely on their own and stayed with parents until they married or otherwise lived with relatives.

With the decline of the rural economy, the family no longer was bound together as the main unit of productive activity. Adaptation to the new industrial and service jobs in an urban economy affected all family members and brought new living arrangements to children and parents, husbands and wives, young adults, and single men and women.

Figure 2.1 shows the massive change that took place in the predominant family forms over the past century. Two main trends are evident. The two-parent farm family with an occasional member of the older generation was replaced by the husband-breadwinner and wife-homemaker couple and their children. At the same time, the intergenerational rural family that had been dominant gave way to many more types of family and nonfamily households. The patriarchal farm family in which the father had been in charge of the means of production and wives and children held subordinate status gave way to more egalitarian relationships between the children and parents and between the sexes. Children, who were no longer production workers,

Figure 2.1   Household and Family Change, 1920–2010

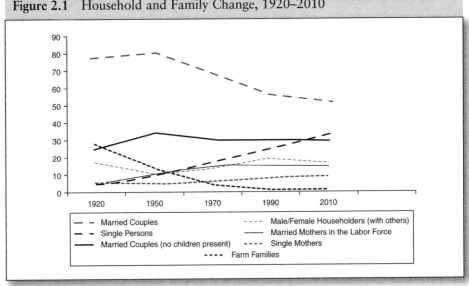

Source: Calculations based on Carter et al. 2006: Table Ae29–37, Table Ae79–81, Table Ae221–244, Table Ba 425–469; U.S. Census Bureau 2011: Table 59, Table 68, Table 601, Table 830; Elliott 2009: Figure 1.

became a new status object of pride and consumption for their parents, while an increasing number of families had no children at all (Zelizer 1985). Wives, having received further education and no longer having to meet so many demands for home production, entered the paid labor force. These changes gave rise to four distinct family forms where only one major type had existed before: namely, husband-wife families with wives either in or out of the labor force, and with or without children under 18.

Four other types also became more common: lone mothers or fathers with children, single-person households, and households of unrelated individuals. Availability of paid work for women enabled them to form households on their own without having to depend on a husband. Similarly, men could survive without a wife to help with cooking and other necessary domestic work. People who wanted to avoid having children whom they were "expected to raise to be independent rather than obedient" no longer had them (Goldscheider and Waite 1991:18). Single-person households also grew steadily after 1950 due to greater affluence and an increase in housing stock that supported the undoubling of families who had shared living quarters during World War II (Downs 1977; Kobrin 1976). This change was supported by an increased feeling that moving out of the parental home was a sign of maturity. Also, as attitudes became more accepting of single persons and people gained more experience with nonfamily living in group quarters such as dormitories or barracks, the number of single-person households became a significant component of the total mix as shown in Figure 2.2.

Whether all of these family forms are benign or not, I see in them a potential for a more inclusive definition of what constitutes a family. Rather than one form predominating as was the case in the nineteenth century with the intergenerational and patriarchal farm family, there is no single pattern that stands out as representing a majority or even a significant plurality. As Simmel (1955) argued in *Conflict and the Web of Group Affiliations,* many cross-cutting axes of differentiation and identification in a group can lead to solidarity. Or, as Durkheim ([1893] 1964) explained in *The Division of Labor in Society,* greater specialization and differentiation in social life can lead to an organic sense of interdependence. Thus, the great variety of family forms in the United States, which is being read by some as a decline in the family, can also be interpreted as assimilation and incorporation of family-like groups and behaviors into the family sphere, with the result that basic needs for intimacy and care can be met in many more ways. This potential for an expansion and generalization of family norms to encompass a wider scope of modern life is a theme that I will return to in the concluding section of this chapter on changing policies related to marriage, divorce, and responsibility for care of children, elders, and dependents.

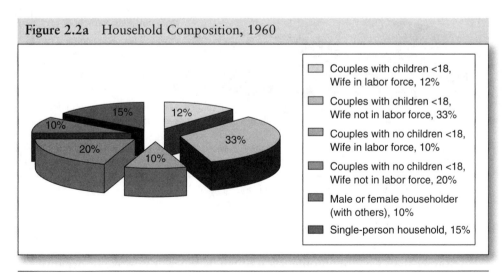

Figure 2.2a Household Composition, 1960

- Couples with children <18, Wife in labor force, 12%
- Couples with children <18, Wife not in labor force, 33%
- Couples with no children <18, Wife in labor force, 10%
- Couples with no children <18, Wife not in labor force, 20%
- Male or female householder (with others), 10%
- Single-person household, 15%

Source: Based on calculations using household composition, presence of children <18, and labor force participation of women with and without children present (U.S. Census Bureau 1961: Table 31; U.S. Census Bureau 1991: Table 643; Carter et al. 2006: 1–674).

Figure 2.2b Household Composition, 1976

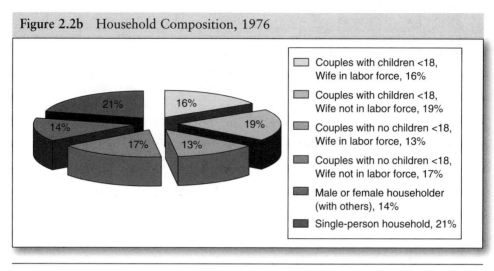

Couples with children <18, Wife in labor force, 16%

Couples with children <18, Wife not in labor force, 19%

Couples with no children <18, Wife in labor force, 13%

Couples with no children <18, Wife not in labor force, 17%

Male or female householder (with others), 14%

Single-person household, 21%

Source: Barrett 1978: Table 2, "Characteristics of Households: 1976."

Figure 2.2c Household Composition, 2010

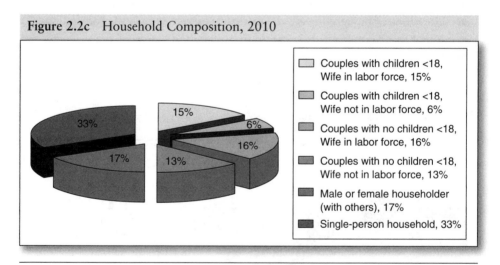

Couples with children <18, Wife in labor force, 15%

Couples with children <18, Wife not in labor force, 6%

Couples with no children <18, Wife in labor force, 16%

Couples with no children <18, Wife not in labor force, 13%

Male or female householder (with others), 17%

Single-person household, 33%

Source: U.S. Census Bureau 2011: Table 59, Table 68, Table 601.

Effects of Family Structure

Rather than view the proliferation of family types as positive or negative, most research has focused on whether the effects of increased divorce, single-parent families, and more mothers in the workforce are harmful or beneficial in the long run. Some researchers have investigated family-related factors in various child and parent outcomes. Main topics include divorce, single parenting, stepfamilies, use of new reproductive technologies, and maternal employment. While the findings are complex and subject to many qualifications, Paul R. Amato (2005:75) probably sums up the general conclusion as well as anyone: "Compared with other children, those who grow up in stable two-parent families have a higher standard of living, more effective parenting, more cooperative parenting, are emotionally close to both parents, and are subject to fewer stressful events and circumstances."

Family-Related Determinants of Well-being

There are a number of ways to conceptualize varieties in family form and family behavior. Most common has been comparison of consequences for children living in an intact two-parent family with those children who have experienced divorce, living in a stepfamily, or single-parent family. The leading researchers in this field have used longitudinal studies to examine effects of family structure on the economic and emotional well-being of both adults and children. McLanahan and Sandefur (1994) were some of the earliest researchers to review research on the consequences of growing up in a single-parent family. Their findings were a surprise to many—that these children experienced higher rates of school dropout, teenage pregnancy, and difficulties in employment, even when differences in family income and social status were factored into the analysis. Amato (2004) reviewed a decade of research on the effects of divorce on adults and children and found that the most positive changes occurred when there had been high conflict in the marriage; but for others the story of divorce was largely a picture of loss. Based on several decades of intensive research with families and children who had gone through a divorce, Wallerstein (2003; Wallerstein and Blakeslee 2004) concluded that a larger percentage of women than men were happier after a divorce. The experience of most of the children, however, was that of considerable suffering and emotional loss.

Other aspects of new family behavior are the focus of Parke's (2004) review of research on family features that affect the development of children. He examines the influence of different ethnic patterns of parenting in African American, Asian, and Hispanic families and reports parenting styles in all these groups that reflect somewhat stricter discipline. Social networks also tend to be more family oriented, with stronger intergenerational ties. When Parke reviews the research literature on effects of growing up in a gay or lesbian family, he discovers that the children are similar to those growing up in two-parent heterosexual families, but the same-sex parents share their caregiving tasks more equally than heterosexual couples. As to the effects of new reproductive technologies such as in vitro fertilization, sperm donation, and surrogate mothering, research is still in a very preliminary stage. Parke suggests that the important questions to investigate are how the technique of reproduction and level of disclosure about circumstances surrounding the child's birth and anonymity of sperm donors or surrogate mothers affect the emotional relationships between parents and child.

Parke also investigates the effects of parental employment and parental incarceration. Unlike earlier research that focused on whether a mother's working was harmful to her children, the newer studies take work of both parents into account as well as the nature and amount of their employment. The child-rearing style of parents with more autonomy in their work is associated with higher school achievement on the part of their children (Kohn 1995). Sadly, parents in prison have more difficult and emotionally distant relationships with their children because their incarceration was in many cases preceded by periods of violence, abuse, or neglect.

Poverty and Inequality

How divorce and single parenthood affect the economic status of adults and children is possibly the most important theme in recent research. Findings are quite consistent that women's economic status declines by about half after a divorce whereas men's status rises by approximately one-quarter (Amato 2004). The reasons are not surprising. Women are usually the ones taking care of the children and thus are more likely to have an interrupted career history, fewer hours of work, and lower pay. Men, who generally have just the opposite employment characteristics and who do not have care of the children, are better off economically (McLanahan and Percheski 2008).

As to the economic consequences for children of divorce or of having a single mother, their economic status is linked to that of their mother. They not only are more likely than children of two-parent families to be poor; their life chances for future upward mobility through education and employment also are worse. Just why this is so has been the subject of various investigations to discover whether it is personal characteristics that predispose parents to divorce or to nonmarital childbearing, or whether it is the process of divorce itself or father absence that disadvantages children of such unions. The answers are mixed. It appears that for a fraction of the families observed, self-selection factors are at work (Amato 2004). But given the very rapid increase in unmarried childbearing and divorce over the last 30 years, it seems more likely that family structure itself may be a major contributor to the rise and perpetuation of income inequality. One pathway for these effects may be detriments associated with father absence. Children who experience death of a father also are less likely to finish school, have more behavioral problems, and lower psychological adjustment than children with two married parents (McLanahan and Percheski 2008).

School Achievement, Emotional Well-being, and Successful Adulthood

Aside from poverty and economic status, divorce and single parenthood have been examined for their effects upon parents and children's emotional well-being. Again, the consequences are most likely to be positive if a breakup follows a marriage or cohabiting relationship that was full of conflict. In cases of low conflict, the divorce process is associated with higher depression in the adults and problems of psychological adjustment for the children.

Children of divorce and single parent families are more likely to have difficulty in school and in making a successful transition to adulthood. They are more likely to engage in early sexual activity and bear children outside of marriage. Although Furstenberg (1987) has shown that teenage mothers 20 years later have successfully overcome welfare dependency, gone back to school, and become self-supporting, their transition to independence takes place on a delayed timetable.

In general, the last 15 years of research showing the long-term negative effects of single-parent families and stepfamilies has raised interest in what policies might be adopted to strengthen and stabilize families and enable their children to avoid suffering and disadvantage and at the same time improve their life chances.

Diversity of Outcomes

Fortunately, the good news is that over an extended period of time the accumulation of negative economic and emotional outcomes is limited to a minority of those who have experienced divorce, remarriage, or a single-parent family. At the end of a 20-year study of unmarried teen mothers, Furstenberg, Brooks-Gunn and Morgan (1987) found that roughly 70 percent of the women and children had recovered from the disruption to their life course that was caused by having a child between the ages of 14 and 19. By their early thirties, a majority had finished high school, found employment, and were off the welfare rolls.

Hetherington and Kelly (2002), in a 30-year longitudinal study of divorce, remarriage, and stepfamilies, likewise found that 75–80 percent of the adults and children were leading normal lives several years after a family breakup or remarriage. They concluded that human beings have an innate ability of "righting themselves" in the face of difficult circumstances. The reasons that a minority continue to have difficulty are several. An important explanatory component may be personality characteristics such as irritability and depression that predispose a couple to conflict and limit their ability to solve problems agreeably. Their children may in turn inherit these characteristics so that they also have difficulty in school, employment, and friendship. But aside from pleasant or difficult personality features, outcomes of divorce, remarriage, and single parenting are due to myriad combinations of various risk factors and protective factors.

Risk factors. As Hetherington and Kelly note, divorce itself is a high-risk life event, but worth taking the risk if a marriage is full of conflict and acrimony and seriously limiting to the growth and happiness of either partner. The risk is compounded when combined with low education, poverty, and the breakup of a second or third marriage. In addition, it is usually somewhat more difficult for parents to establish closeness with their stepchildren than their biological children. Similarly, the relationships between stepsiblings or half siblings may be more challenging than between children of the same mother or father. Another factor is age of the child at the time of the divorce or remarriage: Adolescents find the transition more difficult than either younger or older children.

Protective factors. Not surprisingly, couples with higher income and more education tend to fare better through the disruption of divorce. Hetherington and Kelly also point to the possibilities for new growth and redirection that are opened up when a conflict-ridden marriage is ended and positive new lasting relationships are formed. A loving stepparent who works hard at helping a child to learn and grow is a major protective factor just as a good partner is for the child's parent. In the words of Hetherington and Kelly (2002:280):

> A caring partner who shares responsibilities and joys of raising children, and who is there for advice and support when problems arise, is the most potent protective factor a parent can have. But happy and confident children can and do develop in all types of nurturant, well-functioning families, including divorced, single-parent, and remarried families, through the courageous, self-less, and frequently dedicated caregiving of parents.

Policies to Govern Family Formation and Dissolution

It is remarkable how much family behavior has changed since 1950. The question for citizens and policy makers is which of these changes should be welcomed and which others should be turned back or at least be curtailed. There is a range of proposals for reform in the arena of marriage, reproduction, and divorce that parallels the conservative, liberal, and feminist perspectives that were treated in the chapter opening. Conservative critics note the poverty that accompanies children born outside of marriage and call for a stronger emphasis on marriage. They emphasize the perils of divorce, fatherlessness, and unmarried childbearing. Liberals and equal rights feminists see the advent of no-fault divorce as positive recognition of the new position of women in the workforce and a rejection of the patriarchal family. Maternal or "difference" feminists, however, observe that it is the custodial parent, who is most often the mother, and who with her children is typically consigned to a lower standard of living after a family breakup than the husband or father.

In this concluding section of the chapter my purpose is not just to summarize sociological changes in the family or to report on the ideological spectrum of response to it. Instead, I hope to use sociological understanding of the connections between American values and the evolving sexual mores and family norms to suggest which policy directions are more likely to prove adaptive and productive for addressing the risks of family fragility.

How families are formed, organized, and dissolved falls into several broad categories of concern. They include sexual and mating behavior that results in forming a union, the changing laws of who can marry whom, the evolving rules defining which types of childbearing and termination of pregnancy are legitimate, and the grounds for divorce and disposition of marital property and child custody. The United States already has rules regulating each of these processes. But they have changed rapidly in the past fifty years and the question is which norms and laws should be retained and strengthened, and which should be changed. The broad trend, as we have seen in marriage, cohabitation, and divorce, is toward deregulation and dejuridification. In the realm of private association and intimate feelings there appears to be reluctance to interfere. But family life, to the extent that one of its most important functions is to care for minor children and dependents, also requires a sense of social responsibility for others. When these dependents are put at risk, the public has an interest in defining which sexual, marital, procreative, and custodial aspects of family life are legitimate and which others are to be prohibited or at least discouraged.

Sexual Mores, Courting, and Mating

The precocious sexual activity and mating behavior of some adolescents and young adults is currently a matter of growing concern. Reports of girls in middle school servicing boys with oral sex have raised alarm about the larger effects of such early sexual activity on the subsequent life course of the children involved. Several commentators have speculated that the boys are getting more gratification out of such interaction than the girls (Levin and Kilbourne 2008). Thoughtful critics worry that youthful intrigue and deception that goes with such behavior is likely to interfere with schoolwork and create a climate of lying to parents and teachers that negatively affects the young person's development. In addition, it may be that sexual intimacy that was once reserved for committed relationships is now being changed into indiscriminate liaisons and an entirely recreational attitude toward sex (N. Glenn and Marquardt 2001). Conservatives worry that the loss of courting and dating etiquette gives less time for gradual and thoughtful consideration of marriage (Cere 2000). Some feminists such as Rossi (1984) believe that girls and women, whose sexuality includes the potential for pregnancy and lactation, are being drawn into a male paradigm of sexual gratification that is primarily self-interested. For these and other reasons, sexual activity at very young ages is generally regarded as hazardous both to healthy development and stable marriages.

What is to be done? Modern sexual activity and mating does not require legal sanction even though in prior times there was publishing of the banns (announcing the couple's intention to marry) and clear rules about the level of intimacy permitted the engaged couple. In the late nineteenth century, the women's temperance and suffrage movements supported a state-by-state drive for raising the age of consent through laws that established the minimum age at which minors could marry or legally consent to sexual intercourse (at that time, typically age 14 for males and age 12 for females) (Giele 1995:210). These laws are still enforced in cases involving adults and a minor, but sex between two consenting teenagers occurs under the radar.

Not surprisingly, modern proposals for reform in the realm of sexuality and mating are focused on education and persuasion rather than law enforcement. Better recreational and training opportunities are thought to be an effective antidote for inappropriate teenage sexual activity. The theory is that students pursue sexual pleasure to make up for hopelessness and lack of success in school. To end that vicious cycle, more rewarding and productive training alternatives are being made available through such programs as YouthBuild, under the auspices of the U.S. Department of Labor (YouthBuild USA 2011).

Marriage and Cohabitation

Thornton and his colleagues' (2007) study of the changes in marriage and cohabitation over the last 50 years shows that behavior that was once considered immoral or illegal, such as cohabiting before marriage or having a child out of wedlock, is increasingly acceptable if freely chosen by the partners and in tune with their desires. Restrictions on marriage eligibility that barred interracial marriage or prohibited unions between distant kin have gradually dissolved. One of the most famous Supreme Court decisions is *Loving v. Virginia,* which in 1967 declared the state miscegenation law unconstitutional and struck down the prohibition against interracial marriage.

Now in the twenty-first century, the last bastion of marriage regulation appears about to fall—the prohibition of marriage between persons of the same sex. As of early 2012, seven states (Connecticut, Iowa, Maine, Massachusetts, New Hampshire, Vermont, and Washington), along with the District of Columbia, had either by court ruling or legislative action declared the right of two persons of the same sex to marry. The recent changes have sparked heated opposition especially by religious groups who believe such unions are immoral. But from a sociological perspective also, the changing law requires explanation. How is it that a form of marriage that was once unthinkable has been accepted to the point of winning legal sanction? To answer such questions it is useful to recall the work of Durkheim (1947) and Weber (1963) on the sociology of religion. They found a correspondence between the social structure of a society and its religious beliefs. Similarly, the legitimation of gay and lesbian marriage in the contemporary United States can be understood as a reflection of the changing social reality of marriage and gender roles. If marriage no longer requires a breadwinner-husband who is strong and capable of farming or other manual work, or a homemaker-wife who bears the children and manages home production, then a marriage need no longer require persons of the opposite sex. And if the purposes of marriage are as much companionship and sharing of property and benefits as procreation, the couple need not consist of a man and a woman.

The most urgent topic of policy reform related to marriage is how to forestall or stem the rapid rise in the divorce rate that has soared over the past fifty years. Scholars and preachers alike suggest that marriage education and premarital counseling should be instituted wherever possible to prevent marriages that will likely end in divorce (Gardiner et al. 2002; Russo 1997). Another alternative is covenant marriage, which has been instituted in Louisiana, Arkansas, and Arizona. The marrying couple agrees to obtain premarital counseling and accept more limited grounds for divorce such as abuse and adultery. So far, however, no more than 2 percent of marriages are covenant marriages in those states where it is available (Baker, Sanchez, Nock, and Wright 2009:150).

Finally, there is concern with the high rate of cohabitation that frequently results in nonmarital births, family breakup, and fatherlessness, with all the negative economic and social consequences for children that accompany such unions. Two main solutions have been offered: first, to encourage young women to delay pregnancy until they are in a stable partnership; and second, to raise the employment prospects of poor young men so that they are more attractive candidates for marriage to the young women. The biggest factor in whether a couple marries or not is in the man's economic prospects. If the couple is poor, they are more likely to cohabit but not to marry (Mincy and Pouncy 2007).

Old and New Issues in Procreation

One of the main goals of family planning advocates has been to lower the rate of teen births. In fact, the rate has decreased markedly over the last thirty years due to a combination of factors including abstinence and more effective contraception. However, the rate of *unmarried* teen pregnancies has risen dramatically (Boonstra 2002). Policy makers and the general public have worried that AFDC subsidies in the past either gave an incentive or provided enough of a safety net to fuel the rise. In response, the 1996 welfare law imposed a residency requirement on never-married teen mothers to live with a parent or guardian and to finish high school or a training program or the equivalent (Mass. Legal Reform Institute 2002).

Alongside natural births, new technologies have sprung up to assist couples and individuals who experience infertility. With the decreasing number of children put up for adoption because unmarried mothers want to keep their babies, those with difficulty in having children of their own have turned to other means. One result is the dramatic increase in international adoptions that doubled during the 1990s from just under 10,000 to almost 20,000 by 2001 (Evan B. Donaldson Adoption Institute 2011). Another result is the growth in treatment of infertility through artificial insemination, in vitro fertilization, and surrogate mothering (as seen in the case of the celebrity Michael Jackson's third child). Critics worry that practices such as anonymous sperm donation and closed adoption (where the identity of a biological parent is unknown) can put an unwanted burden on the child who does not know the parent's genetic or social history nor has any chance of interaction with that parent (Hanssen 1997; Marquardt 2006). Not only can infertility treatment be extremely expensive; its demanding schedules also pose a hazard to couple intimacy and later resilience of the parents. Ellender (2005) recommends that infertility clinics be much more aware of these psychological costs and more frank about the often slim prospects that the treatments will result in a live birth.

The most controversial reproductive issue is abortion. At first glance the public appears to be polarized between pro-choice and pro-life forces. Pro-choice advocates focus on a woman's constitutional right of privacy, and the most ardent would permit late-term abortions, whereas extreme pro-life advocates would ban abortion even in cases of rape and endangerment of the mother's health. In actuality, the general public is closer to a middle ground than might be supposed from either extreme position; a majority would permit abortions under at least some circumstances while 22 percent say it should always be legal, and just as many that it should never be legal (D. Sussman 2009). President Clinton voiced this emerging consensus in 1994 when he said that abortion should be "safe, legal, and rare" and should not be used as a substitute for family planning (Alan Guttmacher Institute 1994).

International data show that compared with other developed nations, the United States is at the extreme end of the abortion policy continuum both in its abortion rate and its lack of restrictions in the law (Glendon 1987). Given the deep ideological divisions over abortion in the United States, the most likely outcome seems to be an eventual convergence on a middle ground so that the procedure is safe and affordable in early stages of the pregnancy but much more restricted and rare later on.

Glendon (1987) points out that the relatively permissive American abortion policy is coupled with a stingy approach to child allowances and support for mothers and children. She implies that more generous child support would both lower the abortion rate and at the same time lessen the demand for unrestricted access. She supports this claim with evidence from the Netherlands which has both a permissive policy and very low abortion rate but also generous child allowances. She further notes that a number of Gilligan's (1982) respondents who chose to have an abortion mentioned not only the needs of their other children but also the unwillingness of the father to acknowledge paternity or contribute to child support, thus suggesting that their decision might have been different if more generous provision had been available.

Marital Dissolution and Divorce

The trend toward no-fault divorce in the United States in the 1970s had its counterpart in every other advanced industrial nation. Glendon (1987) suggests that the main function of marriage and family is no longer passing on property through inheritance to the next generation. Rather, companion-ship between the couple and having children on whom to lavish one's atten-tion and material wealth have replaced an earlier land-based patriarchal ideal (Zelizer, 1985). Thus, divorce is no longer a bargaining tool whereby fault of an improvident or philandering spouse is used to influence a prop-erty settlement and the custody of children. Instead, the theory behind no-fault is that the partners should be treated equally as both breadwinners and parents, and the divorce should thus deal with them equally in its distri-bution of property and arrangements for custody of their children.

But no-fault hasn't worked that way in reality. In some cases the standard of living of wives and children decreases whereas the husband's rises substan-tially. Weitzman's (1985) analysis of divorce cases from Los Angeles became famous because she claimed that wives' income fell by 73 percent and hus-bands' rose by 42 percent following a no-fault divorce. A re-analysis of her data by Peterson (1996), however, showed that her findings were in error—that wives' income dropped by 27 percent, while husbands' rose by only 10 percent, a considerable difference even though these findings still reveal loss by the wife and gain by the husband. In some cases the presumption of equal custody can become a potential threat to the mother's claims since the father can in many cases get the mother to accept a lower support settlement for herself and the children if she fears loss of custody (Glendon 1987).

The main suggestion for improving no-fault divorce is to require stan-dardized implementation of both custody agreements and property settle-ments. Judges in the past have been more inclined to protect the husband's standard of living than to safeguard the welfare of the children and the mother who is the custodial parent. More than 20 years ago, Glendon (1987) suggested that a clear set of guidelines for judges, cost-of-living increases, and supplementation of child allowances by the state could result in fairer settlements. Clearer expectations would stem the destructive bar-gaining down of support payments to gain custody. Safeguards also are needed to keep the negotiations from developing into an argument over the fitness of the custodial parent—another potential bargaining chip in domes-tic battles over custody and support.

The understanding of what constitutes marital property has changed along with the emergence of no-fault divorce. No longer is land or real estate so important as pension rights, health insurance, and Social Security benefits that may cover a spouse during marriage but can be terminated with a divorce (Glendon 1979). Some legal scholars and feminists argue that termi-nation of coverage is justified in cases where women have had their own careers. But for a wife or husband who has invested time and effort in sup-porting a spouse through graduate school, entertaining business associates, and taking primary responsibility for care of the children, no-fault divorce can mean a serious loss of security and standard of living. One suggestion in such cases is that the calculation of property division be based on "career assets" whereby a partner's prior investment in the spouse's career is taken into account (Carbone 1994). Despite the general pattern of the wife's being left worse off than the husband financially, it should be remembered that there are many individual variations where, for example, there *is* fault by one partner, say, for infidelity or gambling. In a no-fault state this can mean an equal division of property in which the faithful partner or the nongambler has to divide assets equally with the malefactor or else spend money and emotional investment to fight the no-fault guidelines in court. Or it may be that one partner is unhappy, attributes the problem to the marriage, and simply seeks a divorce without due consideration of the costs imposed on spouse and children. Wilcox (2009) was evidently thinking of such cases when he explained the rapid rise in divorce and adoption of no-fault divorce laws between 1960 and 1980 as follows:

> The nearly universal introduction of no-fault divorce helped to open the floodgates, especially because these laws facilitated unilateral divorce and lent moral legitimacy to the dissolution of marriages . . .
>
> More important, the psychological revolution of the late '60s and '70s, which was itself fueled by a postwar prosperity that allowed people to give greater attention to nonmaterial concerns, played a key role in reconfiguring men and women's use of marriage and family life. Prior to the late 1960s, Americans were more likely to look at marriage and family through the prisms of duty, obligation, and sacrifice. A successful happy home was one in which intimacy was an important good, but by no means the only one in view. A decent job, a well-maintained home, mutual spousal aid, child-rearing, and shared religious faith were seen almost universally as the goods that marriage and family life were intended to advance.

In the meantime, there are a variety of strategies for mitigating the inequities of property settlement and custody arrangements, depending on the roles of husband and wife prior to the divorce. Glendon's (1987) first priority is provision for the children before attention to the property settlement between the spouses. Provision for the children can be assured with clear rules that designate the mother as the preferred custodian for young children and with clear guidelines on support from the noncustodial parent. There seems to be a consensus that disposition of property should take into account the division of labor between husband and wife prior to the divorce. A traditional couple with husband-breadwinner and wife-homemaker will require a different formula from a two-career marriage to assure a just division of assets. Until such standards become clearly worked out in the law, it is, as Glendon says, a risk for a woman to spend her time primarily in child rearing. The homemaker-wife is well advised to get an education and maintain her employability as "insurance" against loss of the husband who supports her.

One further development in child custody is the growing importance of grandparents where neither parent is available or competent to care for the children. At least 1.5 million grandparents are responsible for children under 5 years old and another million for children between 5 and 18 (U.S. Census Bureau 2009c). In cases of mental illness, parental incarceration, drug use, and alcoholism, it is increasingly grandparents rather than adoptive parents or group homes that take in the child, a practice known as *kinship care* (Nichols 2002). These new arrangements are requiring schools, health care providers, and child welfare departments to develop procedures that enable grandmothers and other kin to act in the role of the custodial parent (Addison 2007).

Conclusion

This chapter shows how policies and laws to define family form and function are based on a combination of conflicting ideological perspectives, changing demographics of family life, and positive and negative experiences that result from new types of family-related behavior.

Of these major factors, the ideological debate over family values has captured the most attention. Conservatives and a number of social scientists see much of the change in family life as a process of breakdown in family values that is accompanied by rising divorce, cohabitation, and illegitimacy. These changes along with fatherlessness are putting children at risk for school failure and poor prospects for later employment and stable marriage. The proposed solutions are to restore emphasis on the value of marriage and the two-parent family.

Liberals and advocates of dual-earner families emphasize changing economic reality as the engine that has brought more mothers into the labor force and given them the independence to leave a bad marriage or be able to support a child as a single mother. But for these parents and their children to survive in the new economy, they need more extensive childcare and after-school programs along with provisions for leave time and flexible working schedules.

Feminists generally applaud the demise of the patriarchal family and celebrate a more egalitarian division of breadwinning and caregiving between marriage partners. Their main concern is that caregiving gets short shrift and little reward compared with paid employment. Their reforms would support higher wages for women in low-paid jobs and would ask for more help in childcare from both fathers and the community at large.

The changing demographics of family life are evident in the dramatic decline in family size, changing marriage practices and cohabitation, and the rising divorce rate. The result has been a dramatic shift in family composition toward much greater diversity in family form. In just a century the average number of children per family has dropped from five or more to fewer than two. Population experts see all these changes as an adaptive "tilt" toward low fertility and a refocusing of personal and family life on other goals besides reproduction. Widespread adoption of birth control and the gradual acceptance of abortion are all part of this picture.

In a similar vein, the connection between mating behavior, marriage, and reproduction has been loosened significantly. There is greater acceptance of cohabitation before marriage and of sexual intimacy that does not lead to marriage. At the same time more parents are having children without being married. The result is that no one family form predominates the way the patriarchal farm family once did in the past. There are almost equal proportions of families with wives in and out of the labor force and with or without children present. Single-parent families and single-person households also add to the complexity.

The main topic of research to evaluate different family forms concerns the effects on children. The predominant finding is that children from intact two-parent families tend to do better in later life; they are more likely to finish school, be employed, and form stable marriages of their own. But there are many qualifying statements that must be added to this general conclusion. Whether a family breakup is preceded by high conflict and acrimony is a very important factor in the relative harm done to children. There is general agreement that when the family is riven by severe conflict or violence, children are better off after a divorce than they were before. In addition, having adequate income is an important mitigating factor in the effects of divorce on children. Negative outcomes in school achievement, employment, and future family formation are exacerbated by poverty. There are less severe difficulties if the family is able to gain or maintain middle-class status.

Taken together, the family values debate, demographic changes in family composition, and experience with positive and negative effects of the new family behavior have resulted in both turmoil and innovation in family law and family policy. New and debated policies touch on every aspect of family-related behavior—informal mating and sexual mores, contraception, childbearing, and abortion, and the rules of marriage, divorce, property settlement, and child custody.

The main themes throughout this chapter are the trend toward deregulation of family behavior, the principle of sex equality, and greater reliance on the state as a source of support when dependents are in need. Many legal and policy reforms such as no-fault divorce, contraception, and abortion have been instituted as a result of the decline of the patriarchal family and concern for the equal rights of women. But flaws have become apparent in the implementation of no-fault divorce and joint custody that can disadvantage a mother if she is not employed or that can hurt the partner when one spouse wants to end the marriage and the other does not. Also, the well-being of children is put at risk when a focus on property settlement and custody rights overshadows their needs. Those who would reform abortion law or no-fault divorce emphasize the obligation of the couple and the state to protect children as the highest priority. Then better decisions on marriage, divorce, property settlement, custody rights, and women's reproductive choices can follow.

3

The Gender Factor

Probably the most important single factor in the growth of family policy has been the change in women's roles. I say women's roles, not gender roles, because the change in men's roles has been of a different order and much less dramatic in its impact on the family. Since women's traditional place has been in the family, their movement into the workforce has meant that family life has had to change and that some other way of doing the household chores such as cooking, cleaning, laundry, and child tending has had to be found. The massive recent changes in family life challenge everyone's sense of meaning and expectations of how to be good husbands and wives, what to expect of one's children, and how to take care of aging parents.

Whenever you have such general questions about meaning and proper behavior, you have a problem of *culture*. What is right and legitimate? What is decadent or wrong or otherwise beyond the pale? While social conservatives have generally fought the new patterns as representing a decline in the family, feminists defended the new patterns of women's roles as good and as the means to women's liberation. Thus the redefinition of gender roles was at the heart of changing the culture of family expectations as well as family structure.

Changes in gender roles have fueled the growth of family policy through five main developments: (1) the changing economic division of labor between husbands and wives, (2) the emergence of the modern women's movement, (3) women's new life course patterns, (4) changes in men's roles, and (5) the rise of the two-earner family.

The trigger event for the sea change in gender roles was the sudden growth in married women's labor force participation following World War II. The demand for women workers in the service industries broke down old norms that women should not work outside the home. All of a sudden the traditional husband-breadwinner and wife-homemaker family was turned upside down. The entire economy was being modernized and with it the basic division of labor between work and family life. The questioning of age-old gender expectations helped spawn a new women's movement.

The women's movement that formed in the 1970s built on the women's temperance and suffrage movements of the nineteenth and early twentieth centuries, but its goals were somewhat different. Getting the vote or access to higher education was no longer the issue because these battles had been won. The new challenge was to uncover hidden job and pay discrimination in the workplace and question traditional expectations that women be employed only until they were married and then become stay-at-home mothers.

Even more basic was the change taking place in women's lives. They were having fewer children, living longer, and getting more education. It began to make less sense for them to prepare for a lifetime of homemaking if their children would be leaving home when they still had 20 or 30 years of productive life yet to live. The result was a shift in the normative expectations of the timing of women's lives. Rather than a serial pattern of employment before marriage, homemaking while children were young, and a possible return to the workforce in midlife, more women began to combine work and family life continuously in multiple roles.

Out of this combination of a changing division of household labor, a resurgent women's movement, and the changing life patterns of women came some change and a new more egalitarian ideal of family life. Husbands' and wives' duties were reshuffled to bring about a more symmetrical division of labor inside and outside the home. There is now more agreement than before that a husband should help with some of the cooking, that a father should share in childcare, and that both parents are likely to be employed at least part-time if not full-time during a major period of their adult life.

While the two-earner ideal displaced the patriarchal breadwinner family by what some people now think of as the ideal family form, it is far from being fully realized. An enlarged family policy appears to be the most promising way for modern families to benefit from the support of a larger community of concern.

Changing the Division of Work and Family Labor

Fundamental to the new landscape of gender roles following World War II was the changing economic relation of family to the cash economy and the forces of production. Gainful employment by and large had left the family. In 1900, nearly two-fifths of all employed workers were in agriculture, a figure that dropped to slightly less than one-fifth by 1940 and only 3 percent by 1970. Up until 1940, the rural small-town culture of family life still held sway throughout the country. Household production—canning, curing meat, sewing, raising animals, getting produce from local farms—was still a common way of life. But with World War II and the migration of tenant farmers to the city and wide-scale employment in war industries, the close links between family life and economic life were at last broken. White-collar workers who made up only 21 percent of the civilian labor force in 1900 had grown to almost one-third by 1940 and nearly one-half by 1970 (U.S. Census Bureau 1975). These are the changes that precipitated the postwar demand for women workers and at the same time made women want part-time or full-time paid employment.

From Rural to Urban

As a society, Americans are now technologically and temporally far enough away from the rural small-town family life of the pre– and post–World War II period that it is difficult to reconstruct what a typical day was like for the average woman or man or to see the logic of the traditional division of labor by sex. The prewar era for many women was somewhere between the total do-it-yourself rural barter economy of *Little House on the Prairie* and the modern home. Rural electrification was a major advance during the 1930s. The majority of households in 1940 did not have telephones. Dishwashers were still a rarity. Washing machines were the agitator type that first required rinsing each load in separate tubs before putting them through a wringer and hanging them outside to dry. Monday was washday (Remember the nursery tune: *This is the way we wash our clothes, wash our clothes, wash our clothes . . . so early Monday morning*). Tuesday was ironing day. Wednesday might be for baking or sewing, and the end of the week for other chores like cleaning. It felt good to the housewife to sit down for a rest and have a chance to do the mending. Winter heat came from a furnace that had to be constantly stoked and which produced soot and dust that every spring required cleaning the curtains and other furnishings. People had gardens and raised chickens that they depended on for a good part of their food supply.

As a girl growing up in the 1930s and 1940s, I remember one butchering day at my parents' friends' farm and the sausage, head cheese, blood pudding, and ribs and steaks produced that day, some of which were taken to the local locker for freezing. The prelude to roast chicken was seeing my mother catch the fowl, take an ax to cut off its head, next pour boiling water over it to loosen the feathers, then draw out the innards, and finally stuff it and roast it. My father dressed rabbits he had hunted, and then hung them outside on the clothesline to lose their wild taste. In summer we made jam from strawberries we picked; some came from the Smucker family farm near Orville, Ohio (the forerunner of the multinational corporation with the advertising slogan, *With a name like Smucker, it has to be good!*). We peeled bushels of peaches from local orchards for canning. We even made soap with lye from the ashes of our wood cook stove and from rendered fat of cooked meats. We had no telephone and only one car that my father drove (although my mother had learned to drive in the 1920s before she was married). Our wash water came from the cistern that collected water off the roof. We carried our drinking water from a nearby well. That was the household life of a semi-rural family in the 1940s and 1950s.

And what was my father doing while the women took care of the household? He had an excavating business and dug ditches with his big dragline machine for farmers who needed a pond or a drainage canal, as well as for the county, which needed ditches along the roadsides. He worked long hours at physically demanding labor. Cooking and cleaning, sewing, and food preparation were not his work. Nevertheless, he was the overall manager of the household and its flow of income and expenses. In his view, buying any consumption item such as clothes, furniture, and other non-basic goods was to be kept to a minimum because such expenditure was like "eating up the seed corn." Every bit of surplus was to be plowed back into the business because it was the source of support for the family as a whole. Without it the family could not survive.

Now contrast this picture with the urban and suburban home life that took shape in the 1950s after World War II. The new suburban developments that sprang up in Levittown, New York, and Levittown, Pennsylvania, were far removed from the possibility and necessity of traditional home production. *Crestwood Heights: A Study of the Culture of Suburban Life* (Seeley 1956), described the husband's dedication to his career while his wife managed the household and advanced the family's social standing through her civic and volunteer activities. Laborsaving appliances made far fewer demands than tending a stove, washing clothes the old way, or butchering one's own meat. Not only the father's career but much of what had been the wife's home production had moved outside the family. Yet even as successful careers were associated in the popular mind with more masculine and aggressive qualities, and having a family was thought essential to women's fulfillment, male and female roles were becoming more interchangeable.

Postwar Demand for Women Workers

The new improved household appliances and the preparation and marketing of ready-made food and clothing freed housewives to do other things.

Betty Friedan (1963), in *The Feminine Mystique,* suggested that a lot of unnecessary make-work of cleaning and laundry was taking up the slack. Housewives were avoiding boredom by laundering the sheets twice a week instead of once a week. Ironically, housewives in cities were spending more time in housework than the typical farm family. But if a woman had decided to study or work part time, Friedan observed that she was much more efficient, did the housework in much less time, and was happier overall. Ultimately, however, having fewer children and more free time gave women the opportunity to answer the growing demand for female office work, nursing, and teaching.

Valerie Oppenheimer (1970), in her classic demographic analysis of the growing female labor force in the United States, shows the remarkable confluence of three factors that moved married women into the labor force. The first was growing demand for services due to economic expansion and the baby boom. Second was the traditional labeling of many of the new jobs as women's work. Third was the shortage of young unmarried women to fill these positions because the birth cohorts of the 1930s were unusually small. Given the scarcity of young unmarried women who were the preferred employees for these positions, the ban against employment of married women was eventually dropped. Until the 1950s, women teachers typically had to leave their jobs when they married or became pregnant. During World War II, married women had worked in war factories. But as the film *Rosie the Riveter* shows, they were demobilized after the war to make a place for men returning from military service. By 1960, however, employment of married women had been normalized and was no longer associated with a national emergency.

Supply Factors in Married Women's Employment

Along with responding to the rising demand for women workers and having more time available, women also had an *incentive* to take employment rather than spend their time in leisure. Why did they *want* to work? This is a question that was addressed by several leading economists. Jacob Mincer (1962) introduced the concept of the *reservation wage* as constituting the tipping point where a woman decided that she would make more money by taking employment than she would save by doing the home chores. If there was no net gain, there was no reason to take a job. Glen Cain (1966) refined the analysis by examining census data on women's employment in metropolitan areas with different industries and occupations. Using employment statistics from 1950 to 1960, he found not only that the type of work available, but also a woman's age, how many children she had, her education, and her husband's income determined the proportion of married women in a given metropolitan area who were employed.

Higher education was a particularly critical factor in women's rising employment because it brought higher wages. Since women's levels of education rose with each new generation, their increased labor force participation rate was an important result, as demonstrated by women's employment histories in the National Longitudinal Surveys of Mature Women (Goldin 1997). Gary Becker (1981) showed how these key factors fit together—the reservation wage, background characteristics, and the importance of higher education (human capital). In *A Treatise on the Family,* he presents a gender-neutral theory of labor force participation in which he argues that it is not foreordained whether it will be the husband or the wife who goes to work or stays at home. Rather, the decision is made on the basis of which partner's market wage is higher. If the wife has higher earning power than her husband, the couple will have an incentive to make it possible for her to work at least as much as or more than her partner. There have been many critiques of Becker's application of economic theory to marriage and fertility decisions because of his omission of cultural and normative expectations (Bergmann 1995). Yet my own findings on factors in a woman's choice of staying at home vs. maintaining her career are consistent with Becker's analysis of the relative market wage of husbands and wives as an important if not entirely determining element in the couple's division of labor in the home and in the market (Giele 2008; 2009).

What about Feminism?

These classic economic explanations are certainly plausible about why more married women entered the labor force. But they leave out any mention of the women's movement that coincided with the widespread increase in married women's paid employment. What is the connection?

The Second Wave of Feminism

From 1920 to 1960 many American citizens considered the "woman problem" solved. Women had been given the right to vote. They were no longer denied admission to colleges and universities or such basic rights as custody of their children, owning property, or controlling their own earnings. But rising divorce rates were making clear the need for women's economic independence. With growing awareness that they could earn much more outside than inside the home, they began to see a contradiction between their dependence as homemakers and the need to be autonomous and self-supporting if they were ever widowed or divorced.

It is instructive to examine Betty Friedan's *The Feminine Mystique* (1963) for its charges against the contemporary feminine role. Hers was the voice of a smart woman who graduated from Smith College, was a writer before her marriage, and in her book peeled back the layers of domesticity expected of all women to reveal their dissatisfaction and boredom. She deconstructs the advertising in magazines and television that exploits them to sell laundry soap or electric mixers. She analyzes the hidden assumptions of the reigning anthropological and sociological theories that imply that women's confinement to the home is based on natural differences between the sexes. The result is a stinging critique of the status quo and an impassioned plea for change in the scholarship, economics, and politics of gender.

The women's movement of the 1960s and 1970s took two main forms. One branch was based on informal consciousness-raising groups of local friends and neighbors. Their purpose was to help individual women begin to question the social expectations that oppressed them while at the same time helping them discover their own desires for independence and change (Carden 1974). The other branch consisted of formal organizations such as the National Organization of Women (NOW) that focused on changing laws that permitted discrimination against women in education, pay, and various types of employment (Ferree and Hess 1994). During this period a stunning list of legislative achievements resulted: the Equal Pay Act of 1963, Title VII of the Civil Rights Act of 1964, and Title IX of the Higher Education Act of 1972. The President's Commission on the Status of Women uncovered sex discrimination in access to jury service, and Bernice Sandler of the Project on the Status and Education of Women at the Association of American Colleges brought cases of sex discrimination against more than 250 institutions in the 1970s (Giele 1978; Sandler 2011).

Concurrent with the sex-role revolution was a sexual revolution in which men's greater freedom in romantic attachments and sexual encounters was increasingly seen as an unfair double standard alongside the expected chastity of women. Changing consciousness about women's equal rights eventually extended to the physical realm. The birth control pill introduced in the 1950s went far toward erasing the double standard. However, it was still illegal to buy contraceptives at a drugstore until the Supreme Court in 1965 ruled against such laws in *Griswold v. Connecticut*. Back-alley abortions were also the rule until *Roe v. Wade* in 1973 made abortion legal at least under some circumstances.

Current Influence of Feminism

In the first women's movement there were domestic feminists like the temperance women who wanted to increase women's power as mother and homemaker, while equal rights feminists like the suffragists focused on discrimination in the public sphere and the right to vote (Giele 1995). So also today there is a spectrum of opinion about what is truly feminist. Some feminists believe that differences between males and females are important and should be acknowledged. They observe that women's needs have frequently gone unmet because they were assimilated to a universal male model. For example, cardiologists have found that women's heart attacks do not generally begin with the same classic symptoms characteristic of men. Some psychologists argue that women are more likely to think about the needs of others rather than focus on their own autonomy and independence (Belenky 1986; Gilligan 1982). On the other hand, a large group of feminists see equality of the sexes as the key truth to be emphasized. They focus on the fundamental similarities between women and men. They note the many forms of discrimination against women in education, employment, and the law that stem from assuming that women and men are different (Faludi 1991; Lorber 1994). Both the difference and equality perspective provide insights for understanding variations in self-image that affect the way a given couple will divide their household labor and provide care for their children.

Self-image of women and men. An example of how different forms of feminist ideology play out in practice comes from the research of Kristin Luker (1984). In the life stories behind the opponents and proponents to abortion rights, Luker discovered that the identity of women who opposed abortion was in accord with their roles as wives and mothers in the home. Legalization of abortion represented to them a fundamental assault on their sacred trust to physically carry a child to term in a way that no father can. Proponents of abortion, on the other hand, derived their sense of self from their public responsibilities outside the home. They saw the right to choose whether to carry a pregnancy to term as a fundamental constitutional right to control their own bodies that is equal to the rights of men.

These matters of male and female self-image and gender ideology especially affect every household's division of labor. In her detailed research on the National Survey of Families and Households to distinguish egalitarian from non-egalitarian households, Jema Turk (2009) discovered that a couple's gender role ideology played a major role in just how much they shared household chores. For example, couples were much more likely to share laundry, cooking, and cleaning fairly if they disagreed that "It is better for everyone if the man earns the main living and the woman takes care of the home and family" and thought instead that "It is all right for a woman to work full time when she has children younger than five years old" (Turk 2009:83).

In my own case, even though it was the late 1950s and prior to the feminist revolution, my husband believed I should finish my doctorate before we had children. After our children were born, he supported my commitment to college teaching and sociological research by joining in the responsibility for childcare, cooking, and general household management and being willing to rely on some outside help. A contrasting picture, however, comes from Arlie Hochschild's (1989) *The Second Shift: Working Parents and the Revolution at Home.* In it Joey's mother is having to constantly bear the main burden of childcare and household chores while her husband watches TV or works with his tools in the basement. Clearly Joey's father doesn't see it as his role to help with household work; but this is a source of frustration and anger for Joey's mother, who feels the household division of labor is unfair.

Childcare and education of boys and girls. Two big consequences of the feminist movement are now so accepted that it is difficult to imagine how extraordinary they were as recently as the 1960s. First came the widespread acceptance of preschool childcare. Yet the prevailing sex-role ideology in 1970 as captured in the National Fertility Study showed that over 70 percent of the respondents thought it was better if a man was the achiever outside the family and the wife took care of the home and that "A preschool child is likely to suffer if his mother works" (Mason and Bumpass 1975:1219). Yet by 1984 there had been a huge change: Over half of all married women with children under 6 were in the labor force (U.S. Census Bureau 1985:399, Table 671), and 70 percent of children under 5 of employed mothers were being cared for outside the home in group facilities, family day care, or by a relative (Hayes et al. 1990:29). By 1995, only 20 percent of a national sample disapproved of married women working (Farley 1996:44).

A second significant change was a new effort in primary and secondary education to remove discrimination against girls and encourage them to participate in sports, take mathematics, and go as far as they could in school. Where home economics had once been offered only to girls and shop to boys, the middle school and high school in my town began in the 1970s to change their curricula. Boys, my son included, were encouraged to take home economics and sew their own athletic bags and girls to take shop. Girls' sports were also expanded. The Higher Education Act of 1972 had set a new standard that "No person . . . on the basis of sex . . . shall be denied the benefits of, or be subjected to discrimination under any education program or activity receiving federal financial assistance." By 1992 the numbers of girls in school sports had grown from under 300,000 in the early 1970s to over 2 million (Giele and Stebbins 2003).

The New Complexity of Women's Lives

Along with changes in the economy and the emergence of the new feminist movement, the lives of American women were actually changing whether they liked it or not. Women's survival into adulthood more than doubled between 1880 and 1920 (Uhlenberg 1969). Their life expectancy rose from 58 years in the 1920s to over 70 years in the 1950s. At the same time, fertility declined, and where in earlier years a woman's childbearing might last into her mid-forties, the typical age for the birth of the last child in the 1950s was age 26, giving the average woman at least 30 more "child-free years" between the time of her youngest child's entry into school and her own death (Giele 1978:143). Although in 1948 only 35 percent of women ages 20 to 59 were in the labor force, that proportion had almost doubled to 67 percent by 1983 (Giele 1998:235).

The timing of major life transitions also changed for both men and women. Until the late nineteenth century, the typical sequence had been to finish school, take a job, and only then leave home and get married. But studies by historical demographers showed that a new pattern emerged in the latter half of the nineteenth century in which the events in the transition to adulthood were more often either out of the usual order or happened about the same time (Furstenberg, Lincoln, and Menken 1981; Modell 1989). In a study of Wellesley College alumnae who graduated between 1911 and 1960, I found that this new pattern of concurrent activities in employment, family, and education first appeared among college-educated women in the late 1920s and early 1930s and became the norm among the graduates of the 1960s (Giele 1982a; Perun and Giele 1982).

From the 1950s on, the shape of women's typical life course pattern was in flux. The definition of what was normal went through several distinct phases that resulted in three different patterns that continued over time. The first pattern was *women's two roles* that recognized a tension and contradiction between home and work. A second pattern was expressed as the *three-phase model* in which women's labor force participation was reflected in an M-shaped curve, which was high in young adulthood, low during early marriage and childbearing, and high again from midlife on. By the 1980s a third *multiple role pattern* had emerged in which it was considered relatively normal for women to have a family and at the same time work outside the home.

Women's Two Roles

The earliest and best description of the tension that women in the 1950s were feeling in navigating between home and workplace appears in Alva

Myrdal and Viola Klein's *Women's Two Roles: Home and Work*. In their words, ". . . when most social and economic life was carried on at home these aims [family and work] did not conflict with each other," but "they appear to do so today" (A. Myrdal and Klein 1956:xvi). In other words, "women's two roles" give rise to role conflict in which adult women are being torn between two sets of obligations—as wives and mothers and as gainfully employed workers—in which they experience internal tension between the demands and rewards of "Home and Work." This tension plays out in the truncated ambitions of girls choosing a career, the compromises required of married women professionals in the workplace, and the low prestige and financial dependence of housewives confined to the home.

This two-role definition of the women's situation lasted through the 1950s and 1960s. Beginning with *The Second Sex,* by Simone de Beauvoir ([1949] 1953), a spate of feminist literature decried the subordinate position that women were expected to occupy relative to men. Betty Friedan (1963) unmasked the implicit disparagement of women's intellect and competence in the general cultural priority placed on women's domestic roles. A decade later in *The Future of Marriage,* Jessie Bernard (1973) attacked statistical reports that married women were happier than single women. Arlie Hochschild (1975) analyzed the clockwork of male careers and showed how academic women in their faculty positions were expected to conform to the working hours and timetables for career achievement that had been set by men.

The Three-Phase Model of Women's Employment

The moderate and accommodating response to the two-role ideal was to accept the situation and work to improve women's lot. Continuing education programs sprang up around the country to allow middle-aged and older women to return to school after their principal child-rearing duties were over (Campbell 1973). In 1961, in the shadow of Harvard University, Mary I. Bunting founded the Radcliffe Institute for Independent Study to which hundreds of women sent letters of application to continue their writing, artwork, or independent scientific research. Then in 1964 sociologist Alice S. Rossi published a revolutionary piece entitled "Equality between the Sexes: An Immodest Proposal" that was to become a watershed between the two-role and gradualist models of women's lives and a radical reconceptualization of the family as an equal partnership (Rossi 1964). She "immodestly" suggested that men could be trained to do cooking and childcare just as well as women. By the same logic, women could be expected to reach the highest levels of public responsibility if they were treated equally with men.

The New Ideal for Women: Multiple Roles

Eventually the soul-searching and angst about women's being torn between contradictory expectations of work and family began to die down. The popular ideal of the 1970s and 1980s eventually came to be "having it all," which meant being able to get an education, command a managerial or professional job, and still marry and have a family. A new ideology began to be articulated which was voiced by National Public Radio reporter Cokie Roberts at the Bryn Mawr graduation of 1990. She told the graduates: "All of us learned we have to combine careers and family. You can do it all" (Bronzaft 1991:110).

This change in popular culture was neatly explained by the new cohort comparisons of women's life patterns. Various studies of college alumnae showed that women born after 1930 were much more likely than their predecessors to continue their education beyond college and continue working either part time or full time while their children were still at home (Giele 1993; Giele and Gilfus 1990). Moreover, this pattern also was emerging in other countries (Blossfeld 2009; Giele 1998).

What made the trend in multiple roles even more interesting was its connection to mental health. Psychologists showed that women who had families and were employed were likely to be more satisfied, less often depressed, and healthier over all (Barnett and Rivers 1996; Helson and Picano 1990).

Despite the promising reframing of women's options in these flexible and positive ways, there were still disparities in the workloads and pay levels of women. Some employers were very rigid in permitting fluid movement between home and work. Some husbands didn't cooperate. Outside services like childcare were not always available or affordable. As a result, the consensus on the possibility and value of women's multiple roles began to seem illusory.

A Variety of Options

Longitudinal research comparing full-time homemakers and family women with careers raises the question of how much self-selection goes into type of career and the timing of employment in relation to marriage and childbearing. In *Competing Devotions: Career and Family Among Women Executives,* Mary Blair-Loy (2003) found that in the particular fields of accounting and business that she examined, high-status women executives in whatever their job, believed that their work required their full devotion. So having to compromise on job demands in order to meet family demands pushed them to abandon the job in favor of children and family. In a recent study comparing 50 black and white college-educated career women and homemakers, I gathered retrospective life histories and found that the career women had a distinctive identity as being different, with high achievement motivation, an egalitarian marriage, and an innovative approach that enabled them to persevere in a career despite the odds. I surmise that being a stay-at-home mother is the culturally approved default position and that anyone who departs from that must have a distinctive personal identity and style in order to be able to survive. In addition, the career women whom I interviewed may have been able to persist because they had sought out the type of occupation that is more compatible with being able to combine both family and work (Giele 2008; 2009).

A somewhat different life course perspective comes from Lotte Bailyn (1993), who pictures the possibility of multiple roles for both women and men as being sequential rather than simultaneous. Bailyn observes that the most intense demands of establishing families and careers occur together during early adulthood. She proposes that the couple manage these demands by taking turns—one focusing on family while the other focuses on career. Then in midlife when childcare demands are lighter, the main earner in the couple can pull back a bit from work demands while the stay-at-home partner puts career at center stage.

Change in Men's Roles

Given the immense transformation in women's roles over the past half century, it seems logical that men's roles also would have changed. Indeed they have, but the changes have been less dramatic. In addition, much less research has been devoted to how men's lives have been transformed. Some big trends are well known: longer life expectancy, earlier retirement, more education. But whether men spend much more time with their families to make up for women's employment is not all that clear. Whatever data are available come from statistics on educational attainment and working hours, time diary studies, and individual life histories.

Education, Employment, and Marital Status

Along with women, men shared in the general improvement in health and longevity that raised their life expectancy from 54 years in 1920, to 67 years in 1950, and 75.5 years in 2010. Over the same period their educational attainment improved from 16 percent of 17-year-olds who had completed high school in 1920, and 41 percent who had completed high school or more in 1950, to 86.6 percent with a high school diploma or more by 2010 (U.S. Census Bureau 1975:379; U.S. Census Bureau 2011:Tables 104, 230).

Along with the general urbanization of American society that occurred during the twentieth century, men began to retire earlier. Between 1920 and 1980, the share of 65-year-old men in the workforce declined from 60 percent to 20 percent. Likewise, the proportion of 55- to 64-year-olds who were employed fell from 85 percent in 1940 to 70 percent in 1990 and held steady at 74.4 percent in 2010 (Bureau of Labor Statistics 2009a; Friedberg 2007). The increase in leisure time made possible a more egalitarian division of labor in the home among older couples.

Educational and job segregation between women and men also declined. Formerly all-male Ivy League schools such as Yale, Princeton, Amherst, and Williams began to admit women in the late 1960s. Former all-women's colleges like Vassar and Skidmore began to admit men. As barriers to entrance of women were lifted at elite law and medical schools such as Harvard, the male-labeled professions like law and medicine saw a dramatic fall in the proportion of men students, from over 90 percent in the 1950s to around 50 percent or less by the 1990s (Farley 1996:40).

As already discussed in Chapter 2, changes in family structure reflected the changing marital status of men. The percentage of men who were single more than tripled between 1950 and 2000 while the proportion of female-headed households with children more than doubled. Among married couples, where in 1950 three-quarters of wives were not in the labor force, by 1970 this figure had fallen to 59 percent and by 2010 to 38 percent (U.S. Census Bureau 1975; U.S. Census Bureau 2011:Table 601).

The large-scale changes in men's experience of studying and working alongside women and then being in a household where their wives were employed must have had some effect in decreasing prejudice against women and opening men's minds to more egalitarian attitudes. Faludi (1991) argues, however, that feminism and efforts to bring about equality for women also spawned a cultural backlash that portrayed women as sluts and bitches in film and TV, which was correlated with an unprecedented rise in rape and pornography. The backlash also pictured young women as suffering from loneliness, failing to find eligible marriage partners, and suffering infertility due to delayed marriage and childbearing because of their feminism. Faludi concluded that those men and women who were threatened by the very possibility of equality between the sexes were digging in for a battle of resistance to block any truly significant advances by women.

Time Use

Before comparing time use of men and women in the workforce and the home, it should be noted that the combined number of working hours of both sexes has increased overall in recent times by about 10 hours per week (Bianchi and Mattingly 2004:104). As early as the 1970s, scholars began to examine whether the change in women's work outside the home was having any corresponding effect on men's work inside the home. Their assessment was quite bleak. In the late 1960s, where a wife was a full-time homemaker, she did 72 percent of the household work and he did 14 percent. If a wife was employed, she did 62 percent of the domestic work and her husband 18 percent (Roos 1985:16–17). This proportion had not changed a great deal by the time of Gerson's interviews with 150 men in the late 1980s. But there was one bright spot. It was in childcare, where it appeared that fathers shared about one-third of the responsibility. Gerson (1993:8–9) cites Joseph Pleck's studies of married men that estimated they contributed on average about one-third of the housework, and that one out of six fathers was sharing childcare as the main backup arrangement for a working wife.

More recent data on men's time use comes from time diary studies. Between 1965 and 1998, the proportion of men's time spent in market work fell from 49 percent to 40 percent while their time in housework more than doubled from 5 percent to 12 percent, and childcare increased from 2 percent to 3 percent. But whereas men's free time increased slightly from 38 percent to 41 percent, women's free time decreased slightly from 38 percent to 36 percent. Bianchi and Mattingly (2004) point out that one of parents' evolving strategies for increasing time with their children is to combine childcare with shopping or recreation, a tactic used by both fathers and mothers. Another perspective on changes in time use comes from Jerry A. Jacobs and Kathleen Gerson (2004) who point to a bifurcation in the work force in which more than 35 percent of professionals work 50 or more hours a week whereas less than 10 percent of nonprofessionals do so. They conclude that the culture of overwork is proving a detriment to families, communities, and children. In addition, the time divide between those who are over-worked and underemployed contributes to growing inequality among families and in society at large.

Masculinity and the Life Course

Along with changes in men's objective life circumstances has come an integral subjective transformation in what many consider to be their proper roles. Early signs came from research on men in midlife. Gail Sheehy (1976) and Daniel Levinson (1979) both perceived a "midlife crisis" that was upending the normal workaholic lives of middle-aged men born in the 1920s who had reached their fifties in the 1970s. Signs of the crisis were an inward turning, a search for the meaning of life, and a new sensitivity to inner feelings and one's limited time on earth. Some critics surmised that this "discovery" was confined to a particular age cohort of men born in the 1920s. Nonetheless, the discovery of midlife as a distinct stage had the positive effect of extending theories of development beyond adolescence and raising the possibility that men as well as women had an intimate "feminine" side to their personality. Cross-national studies by Guttman (1977) confirmed that in various cultures around the world older men frequently became less striving and more contemplative and women more assertive and autonomous in employment and public life. Understandably such a rethinking of men's psychological development would be very encouraging to those observers who thought men should be helping more in the home (Giele 1980).

Several scholars have examined how male roles and conceptions of masculinity continue to change. Kathleen Gerson (1993) investigated the life paths of 150 men toward three alternative role patterns: *breadwinner, involved parenthood,* and *autonomy* (which included divorced fathers and single men). She found distinctive factors in each person's life that shaped his turn toward one or another of these alternatives. The men who were involved fathers were distinctive in choosing a career for its intrinsic rewards and satisfaction rather than money or status. They became committed to a nondomestic woman and developed an egalitarian outlook that resulted in considerable willingness to participate in child rearing. They also found it very fulfilling to care for their children and felt reinforced as a nurturant parent as revealed in their reflections: *There was something about holding a little baby and changing diapers that I liked a great deal,* and *I really didn't know how much fun it was being a father* (Gerson 1993:172).

Many of the same themes reappear in the work on men who are egalitarian husbands and involved fathers by Coltrane (1996), Coltrane and Adams (2001), and Connell (1995). Men who are involved family men generally admire women who are competent and independent. Coltrane, a sociologist, also tells of how immensely satisfying it was for him to care for his own child.

Although never the equivalent in strength to the new women's movement, a men's movement related to male rights and responsibilities and revitalization of fatherhood began to take shape in the mid-1990s. One manifestation was the Million Man March of October 1996 that focused on raising the status of African American men. Writers like Levine (1976) and Blankenhorn (1995), and others (Clayton, Mincy, and Blankenhorn 2003; Horn, Blankenhorn, and Pearlstein 1999) represent an ideological spectrum that ranges from a feminist emphasis on equal partnership with mothers and more active involvement with children to claims embraced by many on the religious right that fathers know best and should forcefully assert their rights to equal custody and equal presence in the lives of their children. Whether one views these developments positively or darkly, they represent signs of change in the family roles of men that are inevitably tied to change in women's roles and the structure of the larger family system.

Emergence of the Worker-Carer Ideal

The ultimate effect of the dramatic changes in women's and men's roles and their typical daily lives has been to create a new image of the ideal marital partnership, one in which both husband and wife engage in paid work as well as unpaid caregiving in the home. From the beginning of the modern revolution in women's roles, there have been efforts to re-envision how couples could achieve a fair division of labor, given the weight of tradition and the real-world obstacles presented by working demands and family responsibilities. A few sociologists wrote as early as the 1950s and 1960s about symmetrical and dual-career families as ideals that were beginning to be realized (Holmstrom, 1972; Rapoport and Rapoport 1976; Young and Willmott 1974). Even as sociologist Ann Oakley (1975) documented the dissatisfaction, boredom, and low status felt by housewives in doing their housework, and Arlie Hochschild (1989) famously wrote about women's *Second Shift*, families were nonetheless changing. There are now several studies that document the reality of an emerging worker-"carer" role pattern that exists in a significant segment of American society as well as in other advanced industrial countries.

Change by Age Cohort

Using data from the National Longitudinal Surveys of Women, economist Claudia Goldin (2004) has shown how the dual career pattern of family life evolved over time. She compared the proportion of each age group of white college-educated women who were able by age 40 both to have at least one child and gain an income equal to or greater than the 25th percentile of men's annual income.

Goldin found that it was only the most recent graduates of the 1980s who had a goal of "having it all," and only about one-quarter of them were able to attain their ideal by age 40. The earliest college graduates from the beginning of the twentieth century who graduated between 1900 and 1919 were not only a very small proportion of the total population; they also were likely to follow a pattern of *career or family*. Fully half were not married or had no children; and those who did were unlikely to be employed.

The pattern of the next identifiable group, who graduated in the 1920s and 1930s, was one of *work, then family*—which entailed jobs in teaching and other women's professions, then leaving the labor force after they were married and had children. The graduates of the 1940s and 1950s were likely to follow the pattern of the M-shaped curve of labor force participation— *work, then family, then a return to work*.

It is not until women college graduates are surrounded by the civil rights and women's movements of the 1960s and 1970s that their mindset changes to encompass the possibility of simultaneous involvement in career and family. This is the era that corresponds with the discovery of the dual-career family by Holmstrom (1972) and the Rapoports (1976). But even though this generation of college women envisions the possibility of combining family and career simultaneously rather than sequentially, only 10–13 percent of them are able to succeed in doing so before they reach age 40.

As to the family and career paths of educated women who left college after 1990, they were not included in Goldin's study because they had not yet reached age 40 when she did the research. Schneider and Waite (2005) report that by the 2000 census families in which both parents were working had become the predominant pattern in middle-class families. One important distinction is the difference between *dual-career* and *dual-earner*. The former is more common in the middle class and is associated with higher education of women, a more egalitarian gender ideology, and the implication of choice in whether or not to work. Dual-earner, on the other hand, is likely to mean a woman "has to work" to help make ends meet.

Social Class, Race, and the Two-Earner Family

From the beginning of research on evolution of the modern family there has been a suggestion that educated middle-class couples are more likely to embrace a symmetrical family while the working class holds on to the traditional belief that men are the natural breadwinners and women the natural caregivers of family and the household (Young and Willmott 1974). Even where women are being paid for their work and contribute to family income, working-class families are portrayed as maintaining a fiction that men are the real providers and women's main contribution is in the home (Rubin 1976). Research on middle-class two-earner families, on the other hand, shows them to believe in equality and be ready to hire outside help if neither spouse can do the necessary childcare or household work (Schneider and Waite 2005).

The typical family pattern for black educated women and men has long been quite different. The pattern of *work or family* lasted much longer for black educated women, as shown in the high proportion of single women among the graduates of Spelman College from 1934 to 1962. At the same time among those who did marry, many more had careers than white women of comparable age and education (Giele and Gilfus 1990). Landry (2000) has argued that black educated women have led the way in forging the family–career combination. In 1950, 45 percent of black middle-class wives were in the labor force compared with slightly less than 30 percent of white middle-class wives. The employment rates of both groups rose steadily over the next four decades but with the black rates in 1990 still exceeding white rates for both middle-class wives (83 percent versus 70 percent) and working-class wives (57 percent versus 51 percent). Among married, black, college-educated women with children, stay-at-home mothers are very few and far between. In my research since 2000 on those who had chosen to be at home, I found that most intended their time there to be temporary, and they regarded it as the best way to protect their children and at the same time reinforce their husband's self-esteem against the pervasive negative stereotypes of African American men (Giele 2008; 2009).

Yet even if there seems to be a steady trend toward the dual-career or dual-earner model of family life, there is still debate about whether it will continue. Belkin (2003) and J. Warner (2005) have both documented signs of career women's relinquishment of their jobs in a return to the home so that they can be more available to their children and husbands. The implication in Belkin's article "The Opt-out Revolution" in the *New York Times Magazine* was that these women chose to put family first. But Pamela Stone (2007), in her book *Opting Out?: Why Women Really Quit Careers and Head Home,* documents the unending discouragement and discrimination that mothers face when they request any reduction in hours or relief from the inflexible schedules of their highly paid and demanding careers.

Given these competing accounts, what is the likely direction of change? The evidence suggests several possible adaptive responses, all of which are viable. There are some "greedy occupations" (Coser and Coser 1974) that almost certainly demand career-committed workers with a supportive family-oriented partner. For example, time pressures and very long hours appear to have become the norm among stockbrokers, lawyers, and those in business and accounting where any attempt to moderate the schedule is interpreted as a sign of flagging commitment. When women executives in these fields are pulled between home and family, they are likely to "choose" the home—at least for a time (Blair-Loy 2003; P. Stone 2007).

There are other occupations and industries, however, where some flexibility is possible and where dual-career couples may be better able to thrive. If one member of a couple is in a field such as teaching, nursing, or certain types of consulting, the couple may be able to maintain a dual-career pattern. Thus one explanation of whether a worker stays in or opts out may be due to a hostile or tolerant culture in the workplace. In addition, self-selection into that firm or occupation may reflect the individual's personal beliefs that tip the balance one way or the other toward choosing between family and career or making compromises that allow a continued commitment to both home and work (Giele 2009).

Policy Implications of the Emerging Earner-Carer Ideal

In their book comparing family policy regimes in 12 Nordic, continental, and English-speaking countries, Gornick and Meyers (2003) use the term earner-*carer* families instead of dual-earner or dual-career. Their terminology emphasizes what they believe is the future gender division of labor within the family, namely, that both partners will engage in paid employment outside the home and both partners will be responsible for caregiving inside the home. On this basis they describe and evaluate each country's social programs in terms of the degree to which they support this ideal. In their view, three main types of family policy are needed to realize the worker-carer ideal. First is family leave policy to ensure time to care for young children. Second is regulation of working time to ensure flexibility for meeting family needs. Third is public provision of childcare for preschool-age children as well as public schools and after-school programs for those of school age.

In all their comparisons of national family policy, Gornick and Meyers find the United States the least developed. Because of rigid work schedules and long hours, working parents in the United States have remarkably little time for caregiving during their children's earliest years. Much more could be done to grant employed mothers job security and wage replacement during their leave time. Both parents could be granted paid leave between them to spend at least one full year at home. Other countries entitle mothers and fathers to time off work with pay in order to meet unpredicted needs such as care during a child's illness. If such benefits were made available to fathers, they would provide an incentive to participate more in childcare. If the costs of such entitlements were distributed across the whole society through employee contributions and public subsidies, parents would have some relief in doing the work of childrearing that ultimately benefits the whole society.

In working toward a reduced-hour week, the United States also lags behind other countries. Ironically, as Juliet Schor (1991) has pointed out,

Americans work longer hours than their peers in other advanced industrial nations even though they are richer. American workers do not trade higher income for more leisure, and their children and families suffer as a result. Yet when some highly successful women try to cut back their hours or gain greater flexibility in their work schedules, they end up being punished by being laid off or being sidelined for promotion (P. Stone 2007).

Gornick and Myers recommend that employers limit weekly employment hours by setting the normal workweek at 35 to 39 hours for parents. This change would allow mothers and fathers more time with their children. They also call for making more part-time work available that would not be excluded from equal pay and prorated benefits (as Kahne, 1985, has shown to be the typical pattern). In addition, employees would be allowed to move more easily between part-time and full-time work. Parents would be allowed to refuse nonstandard schedules that require overtime or nighttime work. Finally, Gornick and Myers highlight the abysmally stingy number of vacation days enjoyed by American workers. Where all the other countries they studied set the number of vacation days by statute (20 days, except for Canada with 10 days), American law requires no vacation time. American union workers, who represent only 15 percent of the workforce, typically get 9.6 days after one year of employment and 16.8 days after 10 years.

Gornick and Meyers describe their third category of family policy—public provision of care—as very patchy and highly privatized in the United States. Much depends on a family's personal resources and income. A great deal of concern about public care is focused on early childhood education and childcare, but public provision is also very relevant to care of family members with disabilities and to elders whose capacity for driving, walking, or self-care is impaired. National entitlements can be linked to local services and a mixed system of public and private services to subsidize care through public funds while also charging fees scaled to family income. Such a system for childcare has been very successful in France, where it is coupled with strong oversight, an emphasis on quality care, and service by highly trained and well-compensated childcare professionals (Bergmann 1996; Letablier 2004). Gornick and Myers also suggest that length of the school day and the school year be adjusted to fit better with parents' working schedules.

Conclusion

The revolution in sex roles helps us see the family as a changing *system* of interrelated parts. When the economy changed to draw more women into the paid labor force, families responded by rearranging the daily schedules of women and men, parents and children. These changes in everyday life then came up against long-held beliefs about women's proper place and their obligations as wives and mothers. Women began to live their lives differently, as did many men. The upshot was a more egalitarian vision of family life. For the vision to fully be realized, however, families require help from the larger society in delivering care, in making working hours flexible, and in making schools and communities family-friendly.

The big change that was the initial shock to the traditional family system was urbanization and the modernization of the economy that brought many more married women into the labor force. Rural life relied on the family as an integrated unit of production and reproduction. Goods that the family took to market brought in the cash that would support its out-of-pocket expenses. Many met their subsistence needs by growing their own food, sewing their own clothes, and engaging in one kind of barter or another. The long-term movement of jobs into manufacturing and offices separated the performance of caregiving from earning an income. This separation of family from workplace was further completed and cemented by the demand for women workers in growing professions and office jobs. The scarcity of young *un*married women put married women in a position where they were pulled between gaining tantalizing wages in the paid labor force and fulfilling their unpaid responsibilities in the home. The result was a steady stream of married women into the labor force that tripled between 1940 and 1990.

Such dramatic changes in everyday life had an effect on the consciousness of women, all of which became apparent in the rise of the new feminist movement of the 1960s and 1970s. Women met in informal local groups to discuss the intimate details of their lives, and they critically examined traditional expectations of housewives and mothers to discover new ways of meeting their obligations to their families and themselves. In so doing they resisted oppression and affirmed their own autonomy and self-worth. The formal national groups such as the President's Commission on the Status of Women and the National Organization for Women (NOW) documented the many ways in which women were treated unjustly in home, school, and workplace. They then helped to pass and implement major pieces of legislation that made sex discrimination illegal. Some of the most famous landmarks were the Equal Pay Act of 1963, Title VII of the Civil Rights Act of 1964, and Title IX of the Higher Education Act of 1972. The mere existence of the women's movement in its many guises undoubtedly raised the aspirations of younger women and gave them a new outlook on women's roles in work and family life. This carried over into changes in education of boys and girls so as to remove many barriers to girls in science, mathematics, and sports, and at the same time break down the view that only a mother should be the caregiver for her preschool children.

Not surprisingly, the broad cultural changes in definitions of male and female roles both grew out of and were reflected in the actual life course patterns of younger generations of women. Three main orientations evolved over the years. The two-role pattern tended to be an either-or choice of work or family life. The three-phase model described a sequence where young women worked before marriage, then dropped out of the labor force for marriage and childbearing, then returned in midlife to paid employment. These two earlier orientations were succeeded by a multiple role pattern in which more women combined marriage, motherhood, and continuing education or paid work. It is likely that even though these three models emerged in chronological order, all now coexist and are found in the wider population in different proportions according to the age, occupation, education, and geographical location of any given woman.

Although the change in men's roles may seem less noticeable, it is nonetheless significant. Men have experienced a similar improvement in life expectancy. However, their dramatic shift in occupations from agriculture to manufacturing and service industries is of a different order from women's—having to do with a change in type of job rather than with a switch from unpaid to paid work. In addition, despite increasing longevity, men on average have retired earlier, leading to more years of leisure that are clumped at the end of the life course rather than being spread throughout.

Of particular relevance to family policy is how men spend their time and whether they are in fact more inclined than they once were to take on duties that were traditionally the province of women. Time use studies show that men have indeed increased their time in helping at home and with childcare; but where their leisure time has increased slightly due to fewer working hours, women's leisure time has decreased slightly. The good news is that men appear to find childcare rewarding and on average help with about one-third of the household work. It is also encouraging to see a fatherhood movement that speaks directly to men about their obligations to take an active role in their children's lives. Those men who are most involved in family life value the intrinsic satisfactions of the job and are comfortable being married to a career-oriented or nondomestic woman.

The shift from a rural to an urban economy, the growth of the women's movement, and changes in women's and men's actual life experiences have together challenged the old family system and resulted in a new more symmetrical partnership between husbands and wives and between household partners in general. In place of the breadwinner-homemaker family, the dual-career or dual-earner family now represents the dominant pattern. There are variants—such as full-time and part-time work on the part of one or both of the partners—that are related to ideology, education, occupation, and social class. Some are more egalitarian than others, but in general the patriarchal relationship is on the wane.

Dual-earner families have become more common all over the postindustrial world, but the United States is one of the least progressive countries with respect to family policies that promote the worker-carer solution in which both sexes are employed and both contribute to family caregiving. The most needed policy changes for supporting the continuing trend toward earner-carer families are those that use public subsidies along with private initiatives to provide childcare and elder care. Such policy would also assure that care providers are well trained and well paid and held to standards of high-quality care.

4

The Reinvention of Caregiving

Given the economic changes that have taken place in family structure, one of the main functions of the family—nurturance and caregiving—is under siege. Smaller families with fewer generations present, longer life expectancies, and more mothers in the paid labor force have all resulted in a dearth of caregivers for children, older persons, and anyone with a short-term illness or a long-term disability. American families have adapted to this change in two ways. First, specialization has occurred so that there are different kinds of care for different ages and different needs: nursing homes for the elderly, childcare for preschoolers, and accommodations for persons with one type of disability or another. The second major trend is toward universalization of process and coverage. The earliest supplements to family caregiving were for poor people, old people, and those with handicapping conditions. Gradually over the course of more than a century, the bases for entitlement have become much more inclusive.

It is not as though American society has let these changes come about with no adaptive response. Caregiving has been rationalized so as to serve a greater number of children, elders, or ill people. But this kind of care by professionals such as teachers, doctors, nurses, orderlies, and childcare workers takes place outside the family in institutional settings. For example, the movement from a sick bed at home to a bed in the hospital has saved lives. Yet at the same time, since the 1950s, it has become ever clearer that rationalized and bureaucratized care can result in assembly-line treatment or warehousing of frail elders in nursing homes or of severely disabled persons in the back wards of state-run mental hospitals. Moreover, paid care for dependents in a specialized setting costs more than unpaid caregiving by family members at home.

For more than a generation, since the Kennedy family's crusade in the 1960s and 1970s to de-institutionalize care of persons with cognitive disabilities, advocates have argued that it is more effective, economical, and humane to provide care in the least restrictive setting. In addition, rather than segregating categories of individuals by age or type or severity of disability, the new paradigm of caregiving calls for treating aging and development as a lifelong process in which earlier experiences shape and help to determine capacity later on. This perspective leads to a focus on prevention and individualized care in naturalistic settings rather than treatment that is delayed until a person enters a specialized institution.

These general trends toward treating caregiving as a normal and natural lifelong need and a lifelong process can be found in three major domains of caregiving: elder care, childcare, and family health care, as well as care for persons with mental or physical disabilities. Up to now, these programs have been seen as separate entities oriented to different categories of persons who need a variety of different kinds of services. The central theme of this chapter, however, is that these separate streams of caregiving are all related to each other as a major part of family policy because they all have to do with lifelong development and the family's central caregiving function from birth to death. When the family is unable to give the care that is needed, it is outside help from charitable organizations or government-sponsored services that step in to supplement care from the family. Family policy encompasses both the facilitation of care by the family and the provision of care outside the family.

Elder care became an issue as people lived longer and urbanization and industrialization took away their traditional pattern of living with their children. Charitable organizations and town governments responded to the growing elder population by providing relief or a place to live. In the 1935 Social Security Act, Old Age Assistance was made available to needy elders, and the institution of Medicaid in the 1960s provided financial support for care in nursing homes for those at or near the poverty line.

Services for children and youth also grew out of charitable efforts to help widows and orphans. Child support and mothers' pensions were regularized in Aid to Dependent Children in the 1935 Social Security Act. Other programs for children and youth eventually included childcare, preschool education, child welfare, child protection against abuse and neglect, foster care programs, and the juvenile justice system.

Family-related health and disability services are one of the most active and growing areas of family policy. Beginning with the work of the Children's Bureau, maternal and child health programs grew throughout the 1920s under the provisions of the Sheppard-Towner Act, and then following defeat of its reauthorization emerged again in programs established in the

1930s. More recent additions include the Women, Infants, and Children (WIC) program and the Children's Health Insurance Program (CHIP). The Affordable Care Act of 2010 is a major attempt to advance universal health insurance coverage for families. Also related to health care are extensive programs in mental health and services for persons with disabilities. One of the most vibrant developments in the world of caregiving is the disability rights movement, which has worked for greater autonomy and control by the persons receiving care.

One important by-product of the past rationalization and institutionalization of caregiving outside the family is the development of a *reproductive* labor force (which is "reproductive" in the sense that caregivers are helping to sustain life rather than produce material goods or services). The top tier of this labor force includes a growing cadre of professionals such as medical personnel, childcare workers, teachers, or social workers. The bottom tier, however, is low paid, and of largely minority status—a group who are often insecure in their jobs despite their indispensable work as practical nurses, food workers, or janitorial staff. An important question for improving caregiving both inside and outside the home is how the reproductive workforce is organized, how caregivers perform their work, what rewards they receive for doing a good job, and how they interact with family members. Critics point out that improvement of caregiving will not happen until the organization of care becomes more person centered than rule driven. Rank-and-file workers in caregiving must also be accorded due respect, dignity, adequate pay, job security, and opportunities to improve their qualifications.

This chapter first examines how the modern care system has developed in the specialized domains of elder care, childcare, health care, and disabilities. The chapter concludes with a review of trends in the caregiving labor force.

Trends in Elder Care

Homes for elders got their start during the nineteenth century as poor farms or poorhouses, which were the charitable solution to care for older people when they had no family members to whom they could turn for housing or other forms of assistance. For those veterans who had served in the Civil War or Spanish-American War there were Soldiers' and Sailors' Homes in cities and towns throughout the country that eventually took in veterans of later wars as well. Such institutions were a new development because for most of human history, elders did not live so long. Old people who did survive were generally treated with respect and provided a place to live where they could contribute some help to the family and partake of its benefits. With improvement in health conditions, the demographic pyramid became wider at the top as the population of elders grew larger. At the same time, economic modernization led to the downsizing of the family and its specialization in consumption rather than production. Together, these demographic and economic trends brought about a major change in the living situation of older people.

In her cross-cultural studies of aging based on 1960s data, Shanas (1973) found that in the United States, as in other Western countries, parents preferred to live independently and avoid placing a burden on their children. Yet at the same time, American elders generally lived within a short distance of children or another relative and could call on them if in need of help. This picture contrasted sharply with that in many Asian countries where elders typically expected to live with their children (Giele 1982b). The Western pattern of separate living arrangements had come about as a result of economic modernization and urbanization. No longer in control of a family farm or business, seniors could not command rights to live with or be cared for by their children (Cowgill and Holmes 1972). Yet, as late as the 1940s some states still tried to enforce filial responsibility laws that required adult children to support their parents if they needed public assistance (Schorr 1961).

The increasing population of older people and their new vulnerability helped to stimulate the growth of several new social institutions to provide for their welfare such as pension systems, new types of living arrangements, and provision for medical and long-term care. To understand the evolution of caregiving for older persons, it is necessary to examine three trends that are intertwined: demographic change, invention of retirement and pension systems, and the expansion of social services and home care.

Growth of the Elder Population

Just as infant mortality dropped dramatically with the advent of modern medicine, so also life expectancy improved, and this allowed many more individuals to survive into adulthood and old age. Between 1900 and 1950 the life expectancy of both sexes increased on average by about 20 years, from approximately age 50 in 1900 to age 70 in 1950 (Kinsella 1992). By 2015, life expectancy for males is projected to rise to 76 for men and 81 for women. In 1900, only 4 percent of the population was 65 years old or over, but that proportion had risen to 11 percent by 1985 and is projected to reach over 14 percent by 2015 (U.S. Census Bureau 2009b).

So many more people living longer means that illnesses cured at younger ages result not only in longer life but also more people with chronic disabilities or age-related diseases such as stroke, heart failure, loss of hearing or vision, arthritis, and neurological diseases like Alzheimer's and Parkinson's.

The growing need for care of older people with chronic health problems imposes a significant burden on society and on families to provide care. Yet at the same time that more people are living longer and have a need for more care, families have become smaller and less self-sufficient, and women who have been the traditional family caregivers are less likely to be at home full time. A recent study by the Urban Institute estimates that in the year 2000 slightly fewer disabled older adults (22 percent) were receiving paid help (which averaged 163 hours per month) while slightly more (28 percent) were getting unpaid help from their families. If family size continues to decline and the great majority of adult women continue to be employed, it is likely that the balance in the future will shift to slightly more reliance on *paid* than unpaid help (R. Johnson, Toohey, and Wiener 2007).

These demographic changes have helped to bring about a reorientation in the field of aging research over the last 40 years. An important breakthrough was the realization that the aging process varies greatly by age cohort because each group grows up in a somewhat different set of economic and cultural conditions. Concern has shifted from a focus on post-retirement elder needs and services to consideration for the whole life span and how the aging process can be improved.

Differences among age cohorts. It was once thought that older people declined intellectually as they aged. But when psychologists tested people using longitudinal methods (comparing people of specific age groups over time), it turned out that people born earlier in the century had less education and therefore scored lower on the cognitive tests (Schaie 1977). Economists, sociologists, and demographers made similar discoveries when they compared the life patterns and work histories of different age groups (Ryder 1965). Wives born in the 1880s had only 18 years between the birth of their last child and their own or their spouse's death, whereas a woman born in the 1950s had about 30 such "child free" years (Giele 1978:147).

The cohort perspective is also relevant to demographic projections for the future. For example, Asian, African American, and Hispanic populations predominate in younger cohorts and white non-Hispanics in older cohorts. Due to the higher fertility rates of these ethnic groups, half of all Americans will be from these minority groups by 2050 (J. Angel and Angel 2006). These family-based demographic changes will have major implications for social policy and social provision in the future. Much will depend on the poverty levels, education, and health of these groups and whether the nation will be able to provide economic security and health and social services to its older population. It is in the national interest for families to be able to promote good health over the life span, from birth to death.

Healthy aging. If different birth cohorts have quite different life patterns depending on the economic conditions and cultural climate in which they were born and grew up, the quality of old age also varies with differences in life history. How does one define successful aging and the key factors that contribute to quality of life and subjective well-being?

Baltes and Baltes (1990), in their book on *Successful Aging: Perspectives from the Behavioral Sciences,* used the life course perspective to suggest three characteristics of older people who age most successfully. In contrast with *normal* aging that always involves some loss of capacity and *pathological* aging due to disease, *optimal* aging occurs when individuals maintain a high level of performance by *selecting* a few satisfying activities on which to focus, *optimizing* performance by practice and hard work, and *compensating* for age-related losses by using technical aids or performance strategies that minimize the loss (Baltes and Baltes 1990:26).

More recently, the concept of successful aging has been debated in terms of whether it varies with socioeconomic and cultural context. Based on a ten-year study by the MacArthur Foundation, Rowe and Kahn (1998) conclude that there are three main components of successful aging: avoiding disease and disability, maintaining a high level of physical and cognitive functioning, and engagement with life. Isolation and a lack of social ties is a powerful risk factor for poor health. Conversely, social and emotional supports help to diminish some of the health-related losses of aging. The key source of such social support is, of course, family and friends. When a spouse dies or friends move away, it is thus important to find new forms of social engagement and develop "convoys of social support" that will compensate for these losses while staving off poor health and promoting healthy aging (Rowe and Kahn 1998:161).

One critique of Rowe and Kahn's synthesis is that it puts undue emphasis on individual agency and control while failing to take into account working-class perspectives that may be more accepting of structural limitations and objective conditions that work against an independent lifestyle (Hendricks and Hatch 2006). Likewise, George (2006) suggests that different definitions of "successful aging" can be encompassed within a broader concept of "subjective well-being." Thus, the person with a disability may still feel that she has a high quality of life.

The new interdisciplinary program on Life Span Development and Healthy Aging at Brandeis University (2010) sidesteps the debate on how to define successful aging by listing five pillars of healthy aging that apply to everyone regardless of social class, ethnicity, gender, or health limitations. To age healthily and successfully, a person should attend to these five factors: (1) have a sense of control, (2) receive social support, (3) reduce stress and anxiety, (4) exercise regularly, and (5) undertake cognitively simulating tasks. The family context and family caregivers can facilitate all five of these dimensions, but especially the provision of social support.

Retirement Security

In stark contrast to contemporary concerns about successful aging, the main worry of older people over the past two centuries has been economic insecurity and poverty. Great improvement occurred as poor houses were replaced by a variety of pension schemes that enabled older men and women to live independently and with dignity. The landmark Social Security Act of 1935 laid the groundwork for a universal safety net in the retirement years. The program has grown steadily from its inception in 1935. In 1940, only 220,000 persons were receiving benefits, but the program has been expanded to include Medicare, Medicaid, and social services as shown in Table 4.1. Today more than 50 million Americans currently receive a Social Security benefit, and more than 90 percent of all workers are in jobs covered by Social Security (DeWitt 2009).

Remarkably, the 1935 Social Security Act was passed in a relatively short time (Schulz and Binstock 2008) and has since been expanded to cover groups

Table 4.1   Major Federal Programs To Help Elders Since 1935

Enabling Legislation	Year	Provisions
Social Security Act (SSA)	1935	Persons over 65 receive income from contributions based on earnings in covered occupations
Medicare and Medicaid (Titles XVIII and XIX of SSA)	1965	Medicare available to persons 65 and over on basis of past earnings. Medicaid for those with low income and assets
Older Americans Act	1965	Area Agencies on Aging to provide services for all 65 years old and over, especially poor, rural, and minority elders
Supplemental Security Income (SSI) (Title XVI of SSA)	1972	Consolidation of categorical state programs for Old Age Assistance, blind persons, etc. to provide income to those without sufficient income from past earnings
Social Services Block Grant (Title XX of SSA)	1974	Funding for states to provide Social Services to promote self-sufficiency, prevent abuse or neglect, and prevent or reduce inappropriate institutionalization

that had earlier been excluded such as self-employed persons and household and agricultural workers. In 1965, Medicare and Medicaid were added as Titles XVIII and XIX of the Social Security Act. In 1974, the Supplemental Security Income program and Title XX, the Social Services block grant, brought a congeries of state programs for needy elders, blind persons, and disabled individuals under the federal Social Security umbrella (DeWitt 2009).

Social Services and Long-Term Care

Even if an older person's retirement income is entirely adequate, there is still a question of financial adequacy if one falls and breaks a hip or develops a degenerative neurological disease such as Parkinson's or Alzheimer's. Adequate income has to be somehow transformed into reliable caregiving that is both compassionate and competent. The provision of such services has been a special challenge for the United States because, as explained by Kamerman and Kahn (1976:377), "U.S. health programs are essentially funding devices, not provision for service delivery." Yet as President Nixon said at the 1971 White House Conference on Aging, ". . . the greatest need is to help all older Americans to go on living in their own homes" (Kamerman and Kahn 1976:315), and such a need can only be met by providing services in the home or in a retirement community rather than in a specialized institution that is focused primarily on health care.

Over the past four and a half decades since the passage of Medicare and Medicaid, a series of legislative and private initiatives has produced a wide array of services to older adults that are delivered to the home. The Older Americans Act of 1965 established Area Agencies on Aging and services for care management, home assessment, and nursing help. The Social Security Amendments of 1965 that established Medicare and Medicaid supported health care for those over 65. By 1970, Medicare covered 97 percent of older Americans, which represented a doubling of the population who had formerly been covered by private insurance (Moon 2006). In 1973, the Supplemental Security Income legislation amended the Social Security Act to cover all those previously covered categorical programs for Old Age Assistance and for blind and disabled persons that had been under the control of the states. The 1974 Title XX of the Social Security Act, known as the Social Services block grant, provided for essential social services such as homemakers and meal preparation for needy elderly. Although that legislation provides a commendable array of services (housework, health aides, home management, personal care, consumer education, financial counseling), only 6 percent of the funds were used for elders in 2000, the remainder being used for younger age groups (Gelfand 2006). In 1982 the Medicare program authorized nursing services, medical social services, and counseling and bereavement support to all Medicare and Medicaid clients (Csikai 2009). In addition to the government-funded social services to elders, there has been phenomenal growth in nonprofit and commercial agencies for delivery of home services, estimated in 2003 to be 7,000 agencies that were certified to receive Medicare and Medicaid reimbursements and another 3,000 to 6,000 that were not. Typically these agencies provide health aides who do chores, light housekeeping, food preparation, laundry, and where required, also help with bathing, exercise, and transfer from bed to chair (Adams 2009).

The result of the growth in provision of such services is that there is a strong grassroots feeling that more long-term care should be provided in the community rather than in institutions. There are several advantages of home-based care for the well-being of the older person. Face-to-face interactions in familiar settings are associated with better cognitive functioning as well as protection from the onset of disability (Moren-Cross and Lin 2006). Other benefits of home services include greater comfort and security as a result of being in familiar surroundings. Moreover, from the standpoint of a caregiver or caseworker, seeing the person at home gives a better understanding of the problem and how to provide help (Adams 2009). There are now programs in some states to use Medicaid waivers to divert payments for care in a nursing home to payments for foster care in a family setting. Another important development is end-of-life palliative care provided by hospice organizations, whose services are paid for by Medicare and Medicaid once a patient has waived the option of future curative treatment (Csikai 2009). Finally, senior centers—partially funded under the Older Americans Act—in some cases provide telephone reassurance and friendly visiting that support community volunteers and the general effort of helping persons remain in their homes (Gelfand 2006).

The spectrum of alternatives for long-term care of seniors is now much broader than in 1965 when the Older Americans Act and Medicare were instituted. The range runs from skilled nursing facilities to assisted living; full-service retirement communities for independent living; congregate housing; and local, state, and federally funded low-income housing projects for seniors (Bookman 2008). The newest development is found in the "village" movement which is modeled on the Beacon Hill Village of Boston (2010). There are now roughly 60 villages around the country from Boston and Washington, DC, to suburbs of Chicago, and Palo Alto, California, that recently formed a network for sharing information and ideas (Village to Village Network 2010). Typically, for a membership fee of $500 to $1,000 per household per year, the village provides an array of services including rides to the doctor, assistance with grocery shopping, friendly visits, and access to vetted fee-for-service providers of home maintenance and home health care, and a variety of opportunities for exercise and social activities that range from bridge games to attending lectures and concerts.

Services to Children and Youth

Just as changes in the number of elders helped to bring about new policies toward aging, so also the modern situation of children has been accompanied by a new realization that their health and future productivity affects the well-being of the entire nation. Declining infant death and family size have led to greater relative investment in every single child (Ariès 1962; Zelizer 1985). Early childhood education has become more important, and young people are encouraged to extend their years in school. Child policy has historically focused on basic welfare (food, shelter, protection) and education, health, and nutrition. Increasingly there is concern about the early years of learning, early brain development, and the capacity to learn, all of which are important for future productivity. A great deal of attention is now directed to the long-term destructive effects of child poverty and the need to provide good early childcare in order to promote optimum growth (Shonkoff and Phillips 2000). Nobel Prize winner James Heckman (2006) points out that families are the major contributors to inequality in social and economic life. This disparity can be remedied by an enriched early childcare environment, and the returns in improved outcomes for disadvantaged children are much higher with early than late interventions.

Policies and programs for children and youth first took root with modernization and the decline of agriculture and rural society. Widows without a husband needed some alternate means of support. Young children without older siblings to watch over them needed care while their mothers worked. Older children with no gainful employment during adolescence could get into trouble. Some children had no living parents or relatives to care for them. Gradually during the late 19th and early 20th centuries, a variety of charitable and public institutions began to address child poverty, day care, child protection, and child health. New programs appeared such as mothers' pensions, day nurseries for childcare, orphanages, and health services for mothers and children. Eligibility for these programs was limited to children at risk of poverty, abuse and neglect, poor health, and lags in development. Much of the reform effort over the past 50 years has been to create more universal programs that cover all children regardless of dire need or low income. Together these policies for child welfare constitute what many early leaders in the field have thought of as the core of "family policy" (Kamerman 1995; Steiner 1981).

Child Support and Mothers' Pensions

Between 1890 and 1920 concerns for child welfare tended to fall into two different camps—one that sought mothers' pensions to keep mothers at home and the other that sought childcare for working mothers. Mothers' pensions were supported by the National Congress of Mothers (later the Parents' and Teachers' Association) along with the Children's Bureau who threw their support behind the "naturalist" idea that mothers' place was in the home. They believed that in case of need or the absence of the breadwinner, the state should pay the mother sufficient income to support her family without going on welfare. The 1909 White House Conference on Children led to a full-fledged campaign for mother's pensions (Sklar 1993; Skocpol 1992). This approach prevailed until passage of the Social Security Act in 1935 and eventually resulted in the creation of the program for Aid to Dependent Children (ADC and later AFDC), which at that time went mainly to widows and their children (Koven and Michel 1993).

The ascendance of child support via mothers' pensions displaced and slowed the growth of the fledgling childcare system that had been started in settlements like Hull House. Yet at the same time, the emphasis on mothers' pensions sowed the seeds of welfare reform in the 1980s and 1990s by protecting the traditional homemaker role even in the face of the significant rise in *married* mothers' labor force participation (Mead 1996). The major reforms in childcare legislation since 1970 reveal the continuing strain between the traditional and progressive views of motherhood—that mothers should stay at home to care for their children or that they can help to support the family if they are given sufficient assistance with childcare.

In the early 1970s, Senator Daniel Patrick Moynihan's Family Assistance Plan (FAP) provided income support for families with fathers who were unemployed as well as for lone mothers. Zigler and Gilman (1996) suggest that President Nixon supported FAP instead of comprehensive childcare legislation because it fit better with the conservative view that mothers should be homemakers rather than breadwinners.

But the inexorable rise in married women's labor force participation and in the number of mothers with young children who were working outside the home raised increasing doubts about the sustainability of paying mothers to stay at home to care for their children. During the late 1970s and early 1980s there was growing demand for stronger regulations to enforce child support obligations of absent fathers. By garnishing their wages and pursuing deadbeat parents across state lines, the AFDC program changed expectations about the support obligations of the absent parent and was also able to recoup some of its costs (Garfinkel, McLanahan, and Robins 1994). Even more radical was the change brought about by the Republican majority in the 1994 elections led by Newt Gingrich and the "Contract with America." The steady rise in non-marital births suggested to some, like Charles Murray (1984), that income support for AFDC families was a perverse incentive to have children outside of marriage and thereby rely on childbearing and dependency in order to qualify for welfare payments. The critics succeeded in getting welfare reform that imposed a strict time limit of no more than five years' reliance on financial support along with a requirement of the mother to seek job training and be ready to take employment. With this legislation the old AFDC program was replaced by Transitional Assistance for Needy Families (TANF).

Childcare and Preschool Education

Running parallel to efforts to fight poverty and provide poor mothers and children with income support, the other main strategy for putting a safety net under poor children has been to help their mothers take employment. While mothers work, children can be kept clean, well fed, and well cared for. In the earliest day nurseries, set up by settlement houses and other charitable organizations at the end of the nineteenth century, there was often an assimilation agenda to help immigrants and their children learn American standards and customs (S. Rothman 1978). The National Federation of Day Nurseries, which was founded in 1898, had a membership of 600 participating programs 10 years later (Michel 1993).

However, because child support payments were the dominant means of helping poor mothers to care for their children by staying at home, the childcare movement had little visibility until the 1960s and 1970s when more mothers of young children entered or stayed in the labor force. One brief and remarkable exception to the relative absence of organized childcare outside the home occurred during World War II with the passage of the Lanham Act. Companies like the Kaiser Industries in Seattle that produced warships employed many women workers with young children. To accommodate these mothers, beautiful nurseries and childcare centers were established near the Kaiser plants. At the close of the working day, mothers could pick up their children along with a hot meal to take home for dinner (Michel 1999:256). After the war these centers were dismantled as men came home from the battlefield and women workers were demobilized to return to homemaking. But in the 1970s and 1980s, with the rising presence of educated women in the labor force, new efforts to offer nursery schools and infant daycare began to surface. Women faculty and staff members at universities like Brandeis and Harvard organized cooperatives to care for their children. Nonprofit nursery schools were set up in churches. By 1985, commercial franchises like Kinder-Care had 1,040 centers serving 100,000 children of mostly working parents (Michel 1999:256). Hayes et al. (1990:29) reported the remarkable statistic that during the 1980s only 8 percent of children under 5 were entirely in the care of their employed mother while 22 percent were in family day care, 23 percent were in center-based care, and 37 percent were in some form of home-based care by a father or other relative.

Concurrent with the rise of these practical solutions to the childcare problem were legislative efforts to guarantee public support. The successful Perry Preschool Project in Michigan that helped poor children escape poverty, as well as the creation of Head Start in 1965, suggested the positive gains to be realized from early childhood education. The 1970 White House Conference on Children called for a comprehensive system that would stem the rise of runaways and "latchkey children." Congress responded in 1971 by passing the Comprehensive Child Care Development Act, which would have set up a network of publicly supported preschool centers throughout the country. But President Nixon vetoed the act with a message that America should not adopt a Soviet-style socialist system and that children were best cared for in their own homes. Zigler and Gilman (1996) explain this fateful reversal by the politics of the period in which conservatives argued that such a public system could undermine the traditional American family. In addition, Senator Moynihan's Family Assistance Plan for poor families had greater appeal to those who opposed the public provision of preschool childcare.

Given the defeat of the 1971 legislation, despite the steady growth in mothers' labor force activity as well as use of child care, government has had to respond in some way, even though in piecemeal fashion. In 1990 the Child Care and Development Block Grant provided less than half as much for federal subsidies of childcare as the failed 1971 Comprehensive Child Care Development Act that President Nixon vetoed. Although the Block Grant provided earned income tax credits (EITC) for working parents to deduct costs of childcare from their taxable income, the resources available were in the expert opinion of Zigler and Gilman (1996) far too little.

More recently, roughly 90 percent of preschool-age children with working mothers are in some form of regular childcare, as compared with about one-third of children whose mothers are not employed. The costs of childcare have averaged about 6–7 percent of a family's income for the past 20 years, and only about 10 percent of families received help from any source in covering these costs.

Child Welfare and Child Protection

In addition to child support and childcare, the field known as child welfare also includes protection from abuse, neglect, abandonment, and delinquency. The protective aspects of child welfare have continued to expand
since the nineteenth century charitable organizations and Children's Aid
Societies began by finding homes for orphans. The current emphasis in child
welfare is on family preservation and keeping children at risk of neglect,
abuse, or delinquent behavior in their homes whenever possible. Child
welfare policy today is based on the principle ". . . that the home is the
best place for children to grow, that the state does not make a good parent,
and that family systems can change and grow as learning communities"
(Lewandowski and Briar-Lawson 2009a:135).

Foster care and in-home services. How to realize this principle of protecting
children while preserving the family has changed quite markedly since the
Social Security Act of 1935. From 1935 to the 1970s through Title IV-A and
Title IV-B, children and their families were kept together and provided services and financial assistance under AFDC. In those situations where the
child was at risk of maltreatment, or the family was unable to cope, children
were placed out of the home in institutions or in foster care, or were put up
for adoption.

In the 1970s the family preservation movement began to change professional views on the best methods of child protection. Rather than placing
abused or neglected children in foster care or institutions, the family preservation movement raised the possibility that these children could do better
growing up in the care of their own families with services provided in their
homes. Title IV-E of the Social Security Act established Permanency Planning
in 1980 to help find family-like settings for foster children. Dobelstein
(2009), a social policy analyst of the Social Security Act, however, sharply
criticizes the family preservation idea; he argues that the 1979 White House
Conference on Families displaced the traditional White House Conference
on Children and thereby caused a wrong turn in child welfare policy
because it shifted the focus from children to families. Nevertheless, the prevailing view is that long-term change is only possible through working with
the whole family as a system. Homebuilders of Washington State has developed intensive services for families accused of child abuse and is able within
three to four weeks of intensive work to see enough improvement to prevent
out-of-home placement of the child (Lewandowski and Briar-Lawson 2009a).

The Social Security Act of 1935 has been gradually amended to discharge
child welfare functions somewhat differently now from in the past. Over the

course of recent decades specific laws have been enacted to address child abuse and treatment; others, to support adoption and family preservation; and still others, to change the treatment of juvenile offenders (as shown in Table 4.2).

In 2006, 3.6 million children received investigation or assessment for abuse or neglect, and one-quarter of them were identified as victims of maltreatment. Almost two-thirds of these cases (64 percent) were cases of *neglect,* a category that is known to be clearly tied to poverty. Despite the emphasis

Table 4.2   Major Federal Programs for Children Since 1935

Enabling Legislation	Year	Provisions
Social Security Act (SSA) Title IV-A Aid to Dependent Children (ADC). Became AFDC in 1959	1935 1959	Income support primarily for widows and their children. Later more qualifying families were headed by single parents and divorced mothers
Foster Care (Title IV-B of SSA)	1935	Support for foster care, out-of-home placement
Lanham Act Public Law 76-849	1942	Provided federal funding for states to pay for childcare services for working mothers
Head Start (updated by the Head Start Act of 1981)	1965	Provides comprehensive education, health, nutrition, and parent involvement services to low-income children and their families
Juvenile Delinquency and Protection Act	1974	Reforms in juvenile justice, due process; focus on treatment more than punishment
Child Abuse Prevention and Treatment Act (CAPTA)	1974	Funding to states in support of prevention, assessment, investigation, prosecution, and treatment of abuse and neglect
Child Support Enforcement (Title IV-D of SSA)	1975	Enforcement of child support orders to the absent parent
Earned Income Tax Credit (EITC)	1975	Refundable federal income tax credit for low to moderate income working individuals and families to compensate for child care costs
Permanency Planning (Title IV-E of SSA)	1980	Assistance in finding a family-like setting for persons under age 22 rather than placement in an institution
Child Care and Development Block Grant	1990	Federal subsidies for child care

on family preservation, however, Title IV-E of the Social Security Act allocated $5 billion to help with adoption and foster care compared to only $300 million under Title IV-B for home services and family preservation. Some fear that this disproportionate allocation to out-of-home services may encourage more out-of-home placements than desirable or necessary. The additional fact of several high-profile child fatalities within the welfare system due to overburdening of child welfare workers has recently led to more of a "rescue and place" or "safety first" emphasis than in the 1980s and 1990s, a trend that some authors decry (Lewandowski and Briar-Lawson 2009b). It must, of course, be recognized that not all families are capable of providing adequate care in cases where a parent is incarcerated, violent, or addicted to drugs or alcohol. In those cases, along with foster care there is a new phenomenon of grandparents who are raising their grandchildren, a development also known as kinship care. In Massachusetts roughly 1 in 20 children are in kinship care (Addison 2007; Nichols 2002).

Juvenile justice. Beginning in the mid to late nineteenth century, the risk for older children and adolescents was getting into trouble, leaving home to go to the city, and there falling into poverty or crime. Child labor laws prevented their employment, and many left school or rural areas where there were no schools beyond the eighth grade. The juvenile courts established between the 1890s and 1920s sought to deal with footloose juveniles. Up until the 1920s the usual treatment was to send the adolescent delinquent to a reform school. Methods for treating juvenile delinquents began to change with the general trend toward deinstitutionalization that took hold in the following decades.

The modern phenomenon of runaway adolescents rose to national attention in the 1960s and raised the question of how such children should be treated (Blehar 1979). Research revealed several possible causes: violence and dysfunction in the family and psychological problems and school-related difficulties of the child. The juvenile courts had been concerned with delinquency ever since the early 1900s, and reform schools and other forms of detention had grown up to handle the problem. In the 1970s, however, an important shift occurred with the passage of the Juvenile Delinquency and Prevention Act of 1974. Responsibility for delinquents was removed from the Department of Child Welfare and placed under the jurisdiction of the Department of Justice. The change was accompanied by important reforms such as a narrower range of juvenile offenses, expansion of due process for juveniles, and more emphasis on treating the offenses and avoiding labeling of the offender. In 2002 the Juvenile Justice Prevention Act further sought to reduce use of institutions and increase support from community and home-based services. Here too, by reframing a youth's problem as a family issue requiring family-based interventions, it is possible to shift the focus of treatment to other contributing factors. The effect is to make family the focus where various systems cross—mental health, substance abuse, educational problems, disabilities, economic need, and child welfare. The challenge is to shift the focus from punishing the offender to finding solutions for managing a variety of difficulties in an integrated fashion. Although this shift is usually associated with efforts at family preservation, an important exception is in cases of domestic violence and spousal abuse, where the best solution may be protection of the family from an abuser in a homeless shelter (Lewandowski and Briar-Lawson 2009b).

Family-Related Health and Disability Services

As one reviews the great range of American social programs that assist families in their caregiving functions, one powerful theme runs throughout. Except for Medicare and Medicaid that are directed to the whole population over age 65, virtually every entitlement is limited to circumscribed categories of people with a particular need—poor people, children at risk, or individuals with a given disability or risk factor. This principle is especially true in the field of health care, where the 2010 national debate over health reform was pulled between efforts to expand coverage and efforts to control rising costs (Swartz 2009).

Health care is especially relevant to family policy because poor health is not only a result but also one of the causes of poverty and the inability of children to become productive workers as adults. In order for families to perform their reproductive function of giving birth to and nurturing children, parents, workers, and elders, they need outside help to gain access to preventive health care, medical treatment, home-delivered health care services when needed, and environmental protection that reduces pollution and promotes healthy nutrition and exercise.

Over the past century there have been two milestone developments that significantly expanded health-related insurance coverage of children and elders. The first was the 1935 Social Security Act that within Title IV set up health-related services for poor families who were receiving Aid to Dependent Children (ADC, later AFDC). The second was the amendment of the Social Security Act in 1965 to establish Medicare and Medicaid with virtually universal coverage for seniors. Surrounding and embellishing this stream of legislation were special laws and amendments directed to nutrition for mothers and infants, and assessment and care of persons with mental illness and physical and developmental disabilities. This review focuses only on those aspects of health care policy that are particularly relevant to the family's nurturance and caregiving function. The emphasis is on what kinds of caregiving are available and who qualifies for assistance. The three main types of service are related to family health, mental health, and disabilities and risk factors.

Family Health Care

The origins of a broad-based approach to maternal and child health can be traced to the early 1900s and the work of the Children's Bureau along with several streams of the women's rights movement. Together, their enlightened efforts culminated in the passage of the Sheppard- Towner Act in 1921 that set up clinics for expectant and postpartum mothers and newborns. These services along with programs on health education were available to all women, not just the poor, and were especially welcome in rural areas and small towns where professional medical care was scarce or absent. In just a few years the high rate of infant mortality in needy populations was reduced, and many mothers expressed their deep gratitude for the health and education they had received from the program as well as from the popular publications *Infant Care* and *Prenatal Care* that were put out by the Children's Bureau (Ladd-Taylor 1993). Despite this success critics complained that this "socialist" approach encroached on the rights of doctors so that the law was not extended beyond its expiration in 1928. Not until the Social Security Act of 1935 were elements of this kind of public health approach revived in provisions for health services to children under ADC. But the new provisions were less universal than the Sheppard-Towner provisions and more categorical (in which eligibility is limited by particular characteristics such as age or income). Since 1935, family health coverage has grown through a variety of programs related to nutrition, public health measures (such as inoculations), family planning, expansion of health insurance for children, and most recently, federal legislation to cover the large population of those who are currently uninsured.

Nutrition and food security. In the area of nutrition, one of the first great successes in family policy according to Gilbert Steiner (Steiner and Milius 1976) was the establishment of the National School Lunch Program in 1946. Even though lunches were already delivered in some schools, the important social innovation was involvement of the federal government (with help from the Department of Agriculture) in supplying food that up to then had been considered a basic family responsibility. (I remember in my own rural township school, when I was in seventh grade, the hot lunches that were wheeled into the classroom on a homemade wooden cart and cost only $.10 each, including $.01 for milk). In the 1960s during the War on Poverty, the Food Stamp program made it possible for low-income families to buy food at reduced cost. This program grew dramatically during the 2008 to 2009 recession to supplement the resources of low-wage workers and their families as well as the unemployed (Deparle and Gebeloff 2010). Another recent sign of public interest in nutrition has been First Lady Michelle Obama's campaign to reduce childhood obesity by improving the choices of what children eat at school and at home, a matter that was once considered to be entirely a private family matter. It is well known that obesity has many long-term negative effects on health and health care expenditures and that in the long run good nutrition serves the public interest as well as the individual.

Maternal and child health. Programs for mothers and children that were authorized under Title IV-A of the 1935 Social Security Act were a direct descendent of the defunct Sheppard-Towner Act of the 1920s but were generally limited to families qualifying for ADC. With the rise in teenage pregnancy during the 1960s and 1970s, new legislation authorized special outreach efforts to promote contraception and family planning. In addition, early screening identified infants with special needs who were eligible for early intervention and follow-up. The Women, Infants, and Children (WIC) program was established in 1972 and continues today to provide supplementary nutrition and health screening to low-income mothers and their children (Klerman 1996; Oliveira et al. 2002).

Expansion of health care coverage. Up until the Social Security Act of 1935, except for the brief life of the Sheppard-Towner Act during the 1920s, there were no general public programs to support medical care. With the passage of the Social Security Act, a two-tier system developed in which public hospitals and clinics provided medical care to the poor and uninsured at no cost. In the two decades following World War II, private insurance coverage expanded, and many employers and labor unions developed benefit plans to cover their workers. With the institution of Medicare and Medicaid in 1965, virtually all persons age 65 or over became eligible for public-supported health insurance, a situation that continues to the present. Medicaid expanded to cover many special groups in the population under 65, but these advances were accompanied by troubling developments. First, the national cost of medical care rose from approximately 8 percent of the total national gross domestic product (GDP) in the 1970s to nearly 17 percent in 2010. Second, despite rising expenditures, the numbers of uninsured steadily rose to almost one fifth of the total population or approximately 45 million people in 2009 (Swartz 2009).

These problems have led to several recommendations from health economists, principally that the United States move to a system of national health insurance ("single payer" or "public option") that would pool risk across the whole population, thus lowering costs. This is the idea behind the initiative that the Obama Administration undertook during its first two years and which finally succeeded with passage of the Patient Protection and Affordable Care Act of 2010. The national debate over the desirability of universal coverage revealed considerable skepticism on the part of the general public about the need for such reform. Yet in early 2010 before passage of health reform, Congress reauthorized the Children's Health Insurance Program (CHIP) that expanded coverage from 7 million to 11 million children. The program was originally created in 1997 as Title XXI of the Social Security Act and covers children and pregnant women in families with incomes too high to qualify for most state Medicaid programs but too low to afford private coverage (U.S. Department of Health and Human Services 2011b). Another important precedent and step toward national health reform was the adoption by Massachusetts of universal health coverage in 2006. By 2008, coverage had been extended to 439,000 more people, and visits by the uninsured to emergency rooms had dropped by more than a third. The changes to the law resulted in $68 million in savings in the pool of money set aside by the state to cover the uninsured (Lazar 2008).

Mental Health Services

Difficult as it has been to expand coverage for general health expenses, it has been even more difficult to provide basic services and support for mental illness. Yet it is estimated that roughly 28 percent of the adult population in the United States has a mental disorder or chemical dependency, but only 15 percent of the adult population is receiving treatment. The comparable figure for prevalence and services received by children and youth is 20 percent (Surgeon General of the United States 1999:408–409). The impact on families of a troubled youth or an alcoholic or substance-abusing parent is enormous, with negative effects rippling out to school performance, employment, and the stability of the family itself. There is increasing recognition of the importance of treating illness and substance abuse not by placement in an institution but by rehabilitation of the client within the family and community.

The contemporary emphasis on treating an ill person in familiar surroundings rather than in institutions is a drastic departure from the out-of-home placement paradigm that was typical into the 1960s. Persons with diagnoses of schizophrenia, depression, and senile dementia were routinely placed in locked wards in mental hospitals far from their home communities. During the summer of 1957, I had the remarkable opportunity of serving as a graduate student intern in the social services department of the Apple Creek State School in Apple Creek, Ohio. There I witnessed the bureaucratic and custodial style of a large institution that housed severely retarded individuals along with the mentally ill. Attendants were well meaning, but there was little interaction of the kind that would lead to rehabilitation and release. Everyone recognized even then that conditions were a lot better than they had been. Miracle drugs like chlorpromazine had made the difference. I was shown the padded cells to which very disturbed patients had once been confined. And even at that time further changes were in progress. Elderly patients with dementia were being discharged from the hospital to nursing homes newly set up in large though rundown Victorian houses that were in scattered rural communities throughout northeastern Ohio. I later realized that I was seeing the beginnings of deinstitutionalization, a nation-wide trend that reached its crescendo in the 1960s and 1970s.

Today many state institutions for the mentally ill have been closed. Federal legislation in the 1960s that set up Community Mental Health Centers and established Medicaid (Title XIX) laid the foundation for treatment of psychiatric cases in the community. The discharge of former patients into the community, however, took place before most had gained needed skills for living outside an institution. Nor were needed services made available to help former inmates cope with the new challenge of living independently. The appearance of "bag ladies" and a rise in the number of homeless persons was a direct result. Still, there was a new awareness that mental illness was remediable. The Social Services Block Grant of 1974 (Title XX of the Social Security Act) further provided for an array of social services to needy populations in the community.

Deinstitutionalization shifted the treatment paradigm to the "least restrictive setting," which meant where possible, keeping a patient in the family and the community. Title XX set out five goals with important implications for families. Services should help clients achieve economic self-support; reduce dependency; remedy abuse, neglect, and exploitation of children or adults; prevent or reduce inappropriate institutional care by providing community and home-based care; and use referral to an institution only as a last resort (Kamerman and Kahn 1976:445). Since that time, important demonstration projects in North Carolina and California in the 1980s have shown how individualized treatment plans and case management can provide "wraparound" services in the community for children who are at risk of out-of-home placement. These pioneer efforts demonstrated ways of bringing together mental health, child welfare, juvenile justice, and special education services to help troubled children and youth. This approach was solidified in 1992 in the Comprehensive Community Mental Health Program for Children and Their Families that provided support to communities "to develop a broad array of community-based, family-based services for children with serious emotional, behavioral or mental disorders" (Knitzer 1996:214). For a summary of these services, see Table 4.3.

Table 4.3 Family-Related Programs for Nutrition and Health Care

Enabling Legislation	Year	Provisions for Nutrition
National School Lunch Program	1946	Subsidized lunches and milk for children in school
Food Stamp Program — Pilot Extended nationwide	1961, 1974	Benefits for low-income households to buy food and avoid hunger and malnutrition
Women, Infants, and Children (WIC) Nutrition Program	1972	Nutrition, health education, and healthy food for pregnant and nursing mothers and children under 5 years old
Enabling Legislation	**Year**	**Provisions for Health Care**
Maternal and Child Health (Title V of SSA)	1935	Access to pre- and post-natal care, treatment and rehabilitation for low-income families and at-risk children
Community Health Services and Facilities Act	1961	Expansion and improvement of community facilities and services for the health care of aged and other persons
Family Planning Services and Population Research Act	1970	Access to comprehensive voluntary family planning services
Comprehensive Community Mental Health Services for Children and Their Families	1992	Creation of community and family-based services for children with serious emotional and behavioral disorders
Children's Health Insurance Program (CHIP), (Title XXI of SSA Reauthorized)	1997 2009	State/federal partnerships cover uninsured children, pregnant women in families with incomes above most state Medicaid limits and too low to afford private health insurance
Patient Protection and Affordable Care Act "Health Care Reform"	2010	Expanded insurance coverage to uninsured; expansion of Medicaid eligibility, premium incentives for employers, acceptance of pre-existing conditions

More recently, the establishment of the New Freedom Commission by President George W. Bush in 2002 has led to an agenda for wholesale transformation of the mental health system and *The Federal Action Agenda* of 2005. Key goals are to send a message that children and adults can *recover* from serious emotional disorders and that treatment should be consumer and family driven. In 2006, the Federal National Partnership for Transforming Child and Mental Health and Substance Abuse Prevention and Treatment began the work of translating these goals into practice by working on the issue of suicide prevention along with other top priorities such as integration of primary health and mental health services. Among the first-year accomplishments was a consensus statement that "Adults with serious mental illnesses and substance abuse disorders and children with serious emotional disturbances can and do recover" (U.S. Department of Health and Human Services 2008).

As a follow-up to this agenda, the Substance Abuse and Mental Health Services Administration (SAMHSA) awarded nine grants to nine states as incentives to reduce fragmentation of services across systems. The entire agenda, together with a treatment philosophy that seeks to "empower individuals to be responsible for their own self care," is evidence of the profound revolution that has occurred in the field of mental health in the last 50 years (U.S. Department of Health and Human Services 2008:5). No longer are persons with mental illness or serious addictions locked away out of sight of friends and family, there to languish sometimes for the rest of their lives. The whole treatment philosophy has shifted to treat mental illness as part of a larger spectrum of impairments that can be overcome. Central to the process is respect for the individual, integration of community-based services, and heavy reliance on help from peers and families.

Provision for Disabilities and Coping with Risk Factors

The transformation of the mental health treatment paradigm presented in President Bush's 2001 New Freedom Initiative builds on the 1990 Americans with Disabilities Act (ADA) and the Supreme Court's 2002 decision in *Olmstead v. L. C.* that emphasizes the requirement that services be provided in the community to the maximum extent possible rather than in an institution (Shirk 2008). Especially with respect to those with intellectual disabilities, it took many decades to accomplish this about face. Only through the sustained efforts of enlightened professionals and determined parents did the general public begin to understand that citizens with mental limitation could live independently outside of institutions (Dybwad 1990). Beginning in 1972 with Chapter 766, in Massachusetts the law required that children with learning disabilities and "special needs" be accommodated in public schools. At the federal level in 1973 Congress passed Section 504 of the Rehabilitation Act that required free public education for children with disabilities. The Education for All Handicapped Children Act (EAHCA) also guaranteed all children with any handicap a public education. This legislation has been reauthorized several times since the 1980s as the Individuals with Disabilities Education Act (IDEA) and provides the foundation for inclusive schooling which requires that every child with a disability be offered a free and appropriate public education in the least restrictive environment (Villa and Thousand 2005). The larger disability rights movement has helped bring families and communities back into the center of the service picture by establishing two principles: first, access to free and appropriate public education; and second, provision of help in the least restrictive environment.

Education and early intervention. In 1975, the Education for All Handicapped Children Act (EAHCA) mandated early intervention for children at risk because of poverty or signs of developmental risk such as delayed speech, motor impairment, very low birth weight, or conditions like Down syndrome or cerebral palsy (S. Allen 2009).

Belief that early intervention would lead to much better outcomes for persons with a disability was founded on the research and activism of psychologists like Urie Bronfenbrenner and Edward Zigler and on the precedent established by the Perry Preschool Project in Michigan in the 1950s and the federal Head Start program begun in the 1960s. During the War on Poverty, the idea had developed that helping poor children to get an early start on their education would make them more likely to succeed later on. Early investment would thus pay off in dollars saved on prisons, social services, and costs of unemployment. While such cause-and-effect relationships were never proved for Head Start, they had been shown for the experimental Perry Preschool Project, which provided an enriched program of early childhood education to poor children. Follow-up studies of the Perry students estimated that for every $1 spent on the program $3 were saved in public funds due to reduced criminality, better educational attainment, and greater self-sufficiency. These findings contributed to the public enthusiasm for Head Start and gave a general aura of legitimacy and support to the whole idea of early intervention (Zigler, Marsland, and Lord 2009).

From a family perspective, the development of what is called an Individualized Educational Plan or IEP was an important turning point because the old system of care for children with disabilities had been dominated by medical experts. It was replaced by a new system that gave a greater role to family decision making and community-based services. The creation of each

IEP requires a meeting of a parent with the child's teacher to work out the most productive learning plan for the child (Dembowitz 2007). At the pre-school level, it is social workers or their representatives who work with families to assess the nature of the child's risk factors or delays and to iden-tify compensatory developmental tasks for work with the infant or toddler (S. Allen 2009; J. Gallagher 1996). Home-based services include work with parents on nursing and nutrition, behavior management, and various other parenting skills. Medicaid pays for these services. However, while poor chil-dren make up 70 percent of the target population to be served by Medicaid, the funds are disproportionately allocated to that 15 percent of the eligible recipients who live in institutions for the mentally ill or mentally retarded and to another 15 percent of disabled elderly living in nursing homes (National Council on Disability 2005). Over half of Medicaid funds are going to persons confined to institutional settings. By favoring institutional over home-based placements, this funding pattern weakens the effort to provide treatment in the least restrictive setting.

The disability rights movement. In contrast with many of the social welfare programs directed to persons with mental or physical limitations which rely on a medical model of treatment, the disability rights movement took its cue from civil rights. From the 1970s on, leaders of the movement worked to change people's thinking from wanting to "cure" a handicap or make dis-abled people well again to thinking of persons with disabilities as being healthy but as suffering from discrimination based on "ableism" in which the world is not set up to allow them to function independently and effectively.

Throughout the period that handicapped children's rights to education were being expanded, demographics of disability were changing. More chil-dren were alive who would once have died in infancy. Many more older people were surviving into later years when disabilities become more com-mon. In addition, brain injuries, motorcycle accidents, and other traumas were increasing the numbers of young adults with disabilities. The civil rights movement was spreading to disabled adults and their families. The groundwork had been laid in Sections 501–504 of the Rehabilitation Act of 1973. It was followed by the Education for All Handicapped Children Act (later known as IDEA). These laws, along with several important court deci-sions, culminated in passage of the Americans with Disabilities Act (ADA) in 1990. ADA required accommodations in architecture and construction of new public buildings. Principles of "universal design" were implemented to create curb cuts, accessible public toilets, ramps and elevators, and both lighted and audible signals that could be used not only by those in wheelchairs or those who were blind or deaf, but also by people wheeling strollers, or elders with physical limitations (Hehir 2002). The ADA further protected persons with disabilities against discrimination in employment and provision of state and local services. The ADA protects not only those with *current* physical or mental impairments "that substantially limit a major life activity such as walking, seeing, hearing, learning, breathing, caring for oneself or working" (Fleischer and Zames 2001:93). It also covers those who have a *history* of impairment such as cancer, mental illness, addiction, or HIV. The U.S. Census Bureau (2009a) estimates that there are over 42 million Americans with disabilities who are living outside of institutions—almost 15 percent of the civilian population. For a summary of legislation that has authorized programs for persons with disabilities, see Table 4.4.

Imbedded in the new accommodations is a new kind of thinking by persons with disabilities. Rather than seeing themselves as sick or damaged and therefore in need of medical treatment, some individuals with handicapping

Table 4.4   Provisions for Persons with Disabilities

Enabling Legislation	Year	Provisions
Aid to Blind (Title X of SSA) Aid to Disabled (Title XIV of SSA)	1935–1970 1956–1974	Grants to the states for Aid to the Blind Grants to the states for the permanently and totally disabled
Rehabilitation Act (Section 504)	1973	Right to a free public education for children with disabilities
Education for All Handicapped Children Act (EAHCA)	1973	Right to inclusive schooling
Individuals with Disabilities Education Act (IDEA)	1975	Early intervention with Individualized Educational Plan (IEP)
Social Services Block Grant (Title XX of SSA)	1974	Funding for states to provide social services to promote self-sufficiency, to prevent abuse or neglect, and to prevent or reduce inappropriate institutionalization
Americans with Disabilities Act (ADA)	1990	Requirement of public accommodations for persons with disabilities
Olmstead v. L. C.	2002	Ruling by U.S. Supreme Court that services be provided *in the least restrictive setting*

conditions have claimed their rights as citizens to freedom of choice, and self-determination as to where they can go, how they should live, what to eat, and where to sleep. In their activism they have combined disability rights with civil rights to demand the just treatment of all citizens. This attitude questioned the prevailing medical model of treating the disabled person as a patient in order to make him better (which was futile) or to get him to accept his limitations and lack of choice as inevitable. The first line of battle was to resist confinement to a nursing home, which has historically been the typical disposition of persons with severe impairments such as cerebral palsy or paralysis of the limbs (Shapiro 1993:252). The next big battles were to set up alternative living arrangements in handicap-accessible apartments with technological aids and personal assistants to enable the residents to take employment, freely associate with others, and make basic choices of daily living on their own terms (O'Brien 2004).

The principle that persons with disabilities should have equal rights to public accommodations, employment, and public services was eventually joined with the idea that they also have equal rights to the kind of social services that most people prefer—delivered to them in their homes or local communities where they can exercise greater autonomy than in a regimented institutional setting. This principle was tested in the landmark Supreme Court case of *Olmstead v. L. C.* (2002), which resulted in a majority decision that persons with disabilities have a right to treatment *in the least restrictive setting* that is appropriate to their situation. The court required the state of Georgia to provide services that up to that time had been denied to L. C. even though professionals had recommended her release to the community. The *Olmstead* decision thereby legitimated home- and community-based treatment and services and required the states to provide them. With *Olmstead,* institutional placement was finally relegated to second choice in treatment of those with serious handicapping conditions.

Now, with the requirement to offer services in the least restrictive environment, the prevailing system for providing long-term services is clearly inadequate on several grounds. There is a mismatch between available alternatives and the mandate to provide care primarily outside of institutions. In addition, the actual disbursement of Medicaid funds goes primarily to long-term care institutions. It is also worrisome that as much as 22 percent of total state budgets go to payment of Medicaid costs, a figure that will become increasingly unsustainable as more people experience disability and as older people live longer with more disabilities. The solution proposed by the National Council on Disability (2005) is to universalize the provision of social services to persons with disabilities. This goal would be accomplished in two principal ways: first, by making middle-income people eligible (who presumably can help pay for some part of the services), and not just the poor; and second, by including people in the middle years, and not just children and people age 65 or older. Delivery of services also should become much more family oriented and community based. Such a change would recognize and support family members and neighbors who in their role as informal caregivers currently provide more than $200 billion worth of unpaid services in their local communities.

Not only the civil rights argument for greater choice and social justice for disabled citizens, but also the need to contain health care costs, is helping to drive the shift from institutionalized care to private accommodations in the local community. The cost savings are stunning. Way back in the 1980s, an experiment by Julian Sanchez, a paraplegic in college in Utah, showed that provision of a personal assistant three hours a day cost only *one-fifth* what it had cost to keep him in a nursing home (Shapiro 1993). A recent Massachusetts experiment using Medicaid to divert elders with disabilities from nursing homes and pay for their foster care in private homes has saved the Commonwealth almost $16 million (Seniorlink, Inc. 2009).

The Caregiver Workforce

Across the major types of caregiving from aging and childcare to accommodations for disability, several stages of change can be observed. The starting point, representing most of human history, was informal care given almost entirely by individual family members, neighbors, friends, and relatives. A big change occurred when industrialization and modernization split off paid work from family life. During that time, care for the most severe cases of mental and physical illness was placed in institutions and not kept at home. In the past half century, the trend toward deinstitutionalization and "mainstreaming" has introduced a third major stage of development: Many who would earlier have been consigned to institutions are once again in the care of families and the community. Nevertheless, many functions such as cooking, sewing, and other types of home production that left the home with industrialization will probably never return.

Given the vast amount of service and caregiving outside the family, it is easy to understand why there has been a massive growth in the numbers of caring professionals such as physicians, nurses, teachers, and social workers. In addition, many paid employees work in food preparation, cleaning establishments such as laundries and dry cleaners, and maintenance jobs that were once done within the household. This growth of the helping professions and service work has enabled families to get help with care of children, elders, and those with special needs. Nonetheless, the great bulk of assistance for persons who need help—whether they are seniors, children, or persons with some type of physical or mental impairment—still comes from family members.

With the rise in married women's and mothers' labor force participation, it is clear that this vast assemblage of both unpaid and paid care workers is needed. Yet there are some recurring patterns of gender, race, and social class inequality among both family caregivers and service workers that call for critical attention. In addition, there is a long-running concern that quality of care in long-term care institutions such as nursing homes is badly in need of improvement and will only be accomplished by addressing the organization, training, and incentives of the workforce (R. I. Stone 2006). The following account outlines four themes: (1) the continuing importance of informal caregiving; (2) the heavy representation of women and minorities among professional caregivers and service workers; (3) the conflict between the mandates of efficiency and care; and (4) the current trend toward care in the community.

Informal Caregiving

In the realm of childcare, there are all the mothers and fathers who care for their children as a regular part of family life. Bianchi and Raley (2005) found that mothers' hours of caring for children were somewhat higher in 2000 (13 hours) than in 1965 (10 hours). Fathers' hours more than doubled, from three hours per week in 1965 to seven hours per week in 2000. These changes were made possible by an increase in multitasking (e.g., watching the children while doing grocery shopping) and by a decrease of almost 15 hours per week in the amount of time spent in housework.

The National Council on Disability (2005) reports that 44.4 million American caregivers provide unpaid care to adults who have some impairment or disability, and 60 percent of these caregivers also have other jobs that are paid. Bookman and Harrington (2007:1005) make clear the important role of family members and other informal caregivers in safeguarding the well-being of an older person in an appointment with the doctor and in everyday life in a nursing home. Their fieldwork with family caregivers revealed that "family caregivers—untrained, unsupported, and unseen— constitute a 'shadow-workforce,' acting as geriatric care managers, medical record keepers, paramedics and patient advocates to fill dangerous gaps in a system that is uncoordinated, fragmented, bureaucratic, and often depersonalized." They conclude that the health care system lacks coordinated care and information and therefore spouses, adult children, or other relatives perform important integrative functions and in so doing raise not only the quality of care, but also help to reduce the costs.

Women and Minorities as Paid Caregivers

The caregiver workforce has a persistent profile. Women and minorities predominate, and they typically receive lower pay and fewer benefits than employees in other occupations who have comparable education and responsibilities. Throughout the world, even in the Scandinavian countries with their very generous subsidies for childcare and elder care, there is very strong sex segregation in the service professions and occupations. Not only do women predominate, their pay scale is low relative to other service jobs performed by men. In the heyday of calls for "comparable worth," an often-quoted statistic was that tree trimmers in Denver, Colorado, earned more than nurses; and that child care workers received pay that was comparable to that of a parking lot attendant. In an analysis of over a thousand occupations from the 1980 census, England (1992) found that in occupations with a high proportion of women, men earn less than men in other occupations with comparable skill and effort. But the biggest single factor in lowering pay of a given occupation was whether it required nurturance (i.e., caring behavior). Findings from the National Longitudinal Survey of Youth for 1982 through 1993 support a similar conclusion and show that "working in a caring occupation leads to a significant net wage penalty of 5–6 percent for both men and women" (England, Budig, and Folbre 2002:464). Chafetz (1991) explains the wage penalty for female occupations as the result of the socialization process that allocates greater power and resources to males. Males learn to break away from identification with their mothers and thus adopt impersonal and business-like styles of behavior whereas females are encouraged to imitate their mothers in concern for others' well-being. Public life implicitly favors the male work style as more professional and rational. The emotional aspect of caring for others is relatively devalued as something that is natural, that anyone can do, and that is therefore worth less pay than work in a male-typed occupation.

Duffy (2005) has tested some of these theories to see whether they are borne out by U.S. Census data over the past century. She examined whether paid care was connected to inequality of gender, race, ethnicity, and immigration status and whether the relationship had changed over time. She found that care workers are indeed part of a stratified labor market with a primary sector of professional jobs that are relatively secure, and a secondary sector that is more part-time and insecure and subject to temporary employment and layoffs. The primary sector comprises nurturant professions such as physicians, clergy, teachers, nurses, and therapists, whereas the secondary sector is made up of non-nurturant service jobs in food preparation, janitorial work, health care, and private households. The primary sector is dominated by white women, whereas the secondary sector is dominated by people of color, ethnic minorities, and recent immigrants. A remarkable collection of the personal stories of women domestics and their aspirations for their daughters can be found in the work of Evelyn Nakano Glenn (1992), a professor of sociology at the University of California at Berkeley, whose own mother was sent to a Japanese internment camp during World War II and who worked as a domestic so that her children could gain an education and have a better life. Parallel stories from black domestics in the South and Mexican American women in the Southwest show that a similar pattern still persists today among the newest immigrants. However, there is the question of whether they will have the same opportunity for upward mobility as earlier generations. Today there is a new global market that brings mothers from the Third World to America. They have left their own children behind in the care of other family members so that they can send cash back home. But the long absences from their own children, coupled with low pay and often-oppressive working conditions, make upward mobility a distant if not impossible goal (A. R. Hochschild 2001).

Glenn contends that several radical changes are necessary to raise the status of caregivers. Similar to the spirit of the Disability Act, every citizen should have the right to receive care when it is needed, and society should treat caregiving as an obligation not only of families but of the nation as a whole. Employers should make it more possible for people to integrate caregiving with work. To make these changes, a fundamental reorientation is necessary in which "the liberal concept of 'society' as made up of discrete, independent, and freely choosing individuals will have to be discarded in favor of notions of interdependence among not wholly autonomous members of a society" (E. Glenn 2001:93).

Bureaucratic Efficiency versus Personalized Care

During the past two decades, a number of feminist scholars have subjected caregiving to a critical perspective. They have been primarily concerned with how paying for caregiving affects the quality of care. Nancy Foner (1994), an anthropologist, conducted fieldwork during 1988 and 1989 in a New York nursing home and documented the inherent conflict between the profit motive and the caregiving ethic in a business enterprise that provides long-term care. The demand for efficiency conflicts with the need to give care and personal attention and show concern for the well-being of each person. Foner compares the situation to Max Weber's "iron cage of bureaucracy" and uses Weber's theory as her basic analytic framework for understanding the behavior that she observed (Weber 1968). Some nurses took time with patients to give them a hug and a smile, but they were criticized for not getting the work done fast enough. Others who were stern and demanding were allowed to be almost abusive in language and demeanor because they finished their work on time. Efficiency trumped caring. Similar observations are made by D. Stone (2000:110) who summarizes the basic principle of bureaucratized care: "Love is taboo; detachment is correct."

Community Care Built on Relationships

Against a general backdrop of the creeping takeover of informal and personalized care by bureaucratic and profit-oriented institutions and care workers, a key question is how to preserve humane and high-quality care in the face of heartless routine. Fortunately, a revolution is afoot in the demands of those who seek care as well as in the managerial science of caregiving. The movement for innovation that would give more control to the client started in the disability rights movement. During the 1990s, protests by disabled people put a spotlight on the right to independent living and to hire their own care providers rather than be subjected to rigid bureaucratic requirements. This action led to a big shift from payments based on eligibility criteria to payments based on type of care needed and to the individual's control over contractual arrangements. Caregiver allowances were paid through Social Security and the tax system to the care user who could then pay the wages of caregivers (Ungerson 2000). Changes during the 1980s and 1990s in the way services were being delivered to children with disabilities also had the effect of wresting power to provide care from the agencies and making it more individualized and family centered. Services for children under IDEA became more interdisciplinary and integrated across therapies. Transitions were better coordinated between infant–toddler and preschool programs (Harbin, McWilliam, and Gallagher 2000). In short, the evolution of family–professional partnerships had been transformed from a focus on counseling and psychotherapy in the 1950s and 1960s to parent training and involvement in the family-centered model from the 1960s to the 1980s, and finally a focus on collaborative empowerment in the 1990s (Turnbull, Turbiville, and Turnbull 2000).

Along with these changes on the ground has come a transformation in the managerial science that guides the health care and services industries. Gittell (2009) uses a relational model to understand the phenomenal success of Southwest Airlines by identifying those features of organizational behavior that are needed for the best and most efficient delivery of caregiving. Gittell shows that Southwest Airlines was able to lead the industry in on-time departures, customer satisfaction, and profitability because flight attendants, mechanics, pilots, and reservation agents were able to work across job boundaries. They had similar goals, shared knowledge, and mutual respect. In research on the orthopedic surgery units of nine hospitals in Boston and New York, Gittell shows that the hospital with the best relational coordination also had the shortest hospital stays, highest potential patient satisfaction, and best surgical outcomes as measured by lower postoperative pain, lower readmission rates, and lower mortality. She identifies the creation of "care paths" that enable specialists to integrate the goals and knowledge across job boundaries as the key ingredient to such success. These care paths, or care protocols, outline a necessary and standard set of procedures that are critical to patient well-being. Having a shared protocol assures that all the specialists will work together to see that each critical step is followed. Signs that such a system might be emerging in family caregiving come from a GAO report that describes state agencies that use a similar integrative strategy to coordinate health care and meet the needs of children in the foster care system (U.S. Government Accountability Office 2009). Application of relational methods is a very promising development that hopefully will be replicated in many other types of caregiving, from long-term care for the elderly to services for younger persons with a variety of special needs.

Nevertheless, there are inevitable dilemmas in how to reach the right balance between informal family-based caregiving and caregiving that must be done inside formal institutions. How can sensitivity to the patient's particular desires and characteristics be encouraged and maintained? Is it possible to compensate family members for giving care, even though such a practice raises issues of accountability, documentation, and quality assurance? Most people know someone confined to a nursing home or assisted-living facility who does not want to be there but for whom living at home is not an available option. How to manage these cases is still an unsolved problem. One of the most promising initiatives is the Green House Project, which strives to create small, homelike living units within a larger institution. The setting, even though it is part of a larger institution, encourages the intimacy and sensitivity to individual personalities and preferences that comes the closest to living in a family and a homelike setting (Green House Project, 2011).

The Robert Wood Johnson Foundation (2010) sees in it a major culture change in the way long-term elder care is delivered and describes it as,

> A model that breaks the mold of institutional care by creating small homes for six to 10 "elders" who require skilled nursing or assisted living care. The homes, which are designed for the purpose of offering "privacy, autonomy, support, enjoyment, and a place to call home," are a radical departure from traditional skilled nursing facilities and are considered to be the peak of culture change.

Conclusion

Most Americans view their national family policy as almost nonexistent in comparison with the robust programs of European countries. But the actual array of U.S. programs for helping seniors, children, and persons with mental or physical impairments is really quite extensive. Historically, the helping services were small, often privately supported, and limited to the neediest cases. Today, however, caregiving services are both more extensive and more specialized to meet the needs of different populations, and they account for a large portion of state and federal budgets. Even as public policies to support caregiving have expanded, there has been a turn away from bureaucratic and profit-oriented institutions as the preferred place of treatment. Experts and users recommend returning more of caregiving to the oversight of individuals, families, and the local community. These themes are visible in all three types of care that are covered in this chapter: care for older people, children, and persons with disabilities.

Programs for care of the aged grew up as a response to a long-term increase in the elderly population as well as modernization of the family and the economy that pushed many seniors into dependency and women, the traditional caretakers, into the paid labor force. Civil War and railroad pensions of the nineteenth century provided a template for the Social Security program established in 1935 that now provides income support and health care to almost everyone over age 65. Current challenges are to sustain these programs even as costs continue to grow. The main strategies are to encourage private savings, healthy aging, and prevention of disability, as well as cooperation of informal family caregivers with experts in the community.

Expansion of programs for children also took place alongside a demographic revolution that lowered infant mortality, led to smaller families, and resulted in greater relative attention to the well-being of each child. Decline of the rural economy and loss of the family's productive function to outside firms also made it clear that child labor was no longer a viable source of family income. What was needed instead were learning and education that would prepare future workers for productive roles in modern society. In the absence of a breadwinner, the family needed income which in the early twentieth century was provided by mothers' pensions, then after 1935 was supported by ADC, then AFDC, with aid to dependent children, and finally after welfare reform in 1996 by TANF (Transitional Assistance to Needy Families). Childcare that began with the settlement houses of the nineteenth century grew into the public programs for Head Start and private cooperatives that emerged in the 1960s and 1970s. Although public funds for care of preschool children are still targeted primarily to low-income families, childcare outside the family for preschool children has become a widespread phenomenon. Yet many experts agree that for long-term productivity of the nation, the years between birth and age 3 are especially critical for optimum development and better life chances.

In addition to helping families with such basic functions as childcare or income support, the child welfare field also has historically been concerned with how to provide assistance when a family is not able to function in the normal way. Programs for protection of children from neglect and abuse, arrangements for foster care, and provisions for treatment of juvenile offenders are all examples of other aspects of caregiving in the field of child welfare. The trend toward deinstitutionalization and working with families and the local community to stabilize and treat these difficult cases has become the new goal among experts in the field.

Health care reform and the disability rights movement have built on the accomplishments and progress that have occurred in elder care and child welfare. Two main themes are the trend toward universal access and the trend toward de-institutionalization. Several nutritional programs illustrate the theme of broader access. The establishment in 1946 of the National School Lunch Program and of the Women, Infants, and Children (WIC) program in 1972 guaranteed nutritional support to children that came from outside the family. The Food Stamp program, established in the 1960s, has helped families faced with low wages and unemployment during the 2008 to 2009 recession. Mental health professionals also advocate broader access to treatment for mental illness, alcoholism, and substance abuse. However, it is especially the disability rights movement that has made the clearest and most insistent claims for equal access and individual control. By using the model of the civil rights movement to identify and resist discrimination against persons with disabilities, advocates built on a series of laws to provide public education to handicapped children and social services to the elderly that culminated in the Americans with Disabilities Act of 1990. Two desired results have occurred. There is agreement that treatment should be given in the *least restrictive setting* (i.e., outside an institution). It should also be possible, in those situations where the person with a disability is otherwise healthy, to hire one's own caregiver and live independently in one's own home with needed services being delivered there rather than being available only in an institution.

Along with these changes in access and standards of care, the caregiving workforce must also be taken into account. Not only are care workers underpaid relative to others with comparable education and skill, but they also are disproportionately of minority status—women, persons of color, or immigrants—who in general suffer the insecurity of existing on the lower rungs of the occupational ladder.

Fortunately, the new paradigm of working with families and communities to provide care rather than relying primarily on bureaucratic institutions may come to the aid of care workers by releasing them from some of the rigid demands of profitability and efficiency and revitalizing the expectation of humane and personalized care. Similarly, the new managerial science of building on relationships across caregiving specialties can raise the level of mutual respect among clients, professionals, aides, and service workers. If this happens, caregiving that has been given by the family to outsiders will become family-like, with benefits for those who are receiving care as well as those who are giving it.

5

Family Income and Economic Security

To provide food, shelter, and a place to live for all its members, every family must have some means of economic support. Throughout the millennia, in hunting and gathering, horticultural, and agricultural societies, family units have been the locus for producing and sharing food and caring for children and old people. With urbanization and a money-based economy, where families are far removed from food production, almost every family is dependent on employment to bring in the income that will pay for the basic necessities of life. The loss of a job, absence of a breadwinner, or low-wage employment are all conditions that may require families to get help from outside. However, since the Reagan years of the 1980s, free market advocates have argued that economic growth and incentives to invest in new ventures and create new jobs are the single most powerful remedy for poverty (Levy 1998; Rich 2010). Yet in the current U.S. economy, which gives higher rewards to more skilled occupations, high unemployment and poverty among the unskilled signal the need for additional mechanisms besides the market to assure the general welfare. These other remedies come in the form of charity, welfare, pensions and social insurance, employment subsidies, and more flexible arrangements between work and family life, most of which are now provided in some form by government policies and programs. In the words of Charles Schottland (1967:71), a former United States Commissioner of Social Security in the 1950s, and a social worker,

Economic programs of government have a significant impact on the American family because the family is a basic economic institution and a distributor of goods and services. In advanced societies such as the United States, the family is dependent upon money with which to purchase the necessities of life. To maintain money income, the United States has established a variety of social insurance, public assistance, and service programs.

This chapter begins by asking what level of income in contemporary America is sufficient to provide for a family's needs. The provision of family security is so complex that many policy solutions are needed to address different aspects of the question and the needs of different families. The current American income distribution varies by family type, geographic location, race, educational level, and age of the householders. Given these multiple influences and how they have changed over time in relation to prices, a central issue is what constitutes an adequate family income. Not only money is involved, but also benefits in kind such as health insurance, pension contributions, or access to amenities such as childcare. Experts differ on what income and resources should be considered adequate for a family.

Policies to assure a family economic security are similar to the policies to support family caregiving described in Chapter 4, in the sense that the earliest examples were designed to help the poorest and the neediest. Nineteenth-century debtors' prisons, poor houses, and charitable societies were primarily concerned with helping only the most desperate. Gradually, however, government-sponsored pension schemes for veterans and workers were developed. Child labor laws beginning around 1900 made it illegal to depend on young children to add to the family income. Protective labor laws against long working hours for women and the concept of the "family wage" strengthened the ideal of the male-breadwinner and female-homemaker family. With the expansion of the Social Security law in 1935, the foundation was laid for a two-tier social welfare and employment system that addressed both poverty alleviation and workers' economic security. That landmark accomplishment laid the foundation for the War on Poverty in the 1960s as well as expansion of job-based benefits. However, President Clinton's call for "the end of welfare as we know it" heralded a sharp turn in antipoverty efforts in 1996 that put new emphasis on "workfare"—time limits on welfare payments and emphasis on work readiness and getting a job. In the aftermath of welfare reform and diminished emphasis on poverty reduction, greater attention is now being given to three other means to improve family income security: expansion of work-based benefits, making work pay, and better accommodation of family time demands.

The purpose of this chapter is threefold. The first priority is to provide a descriptive summary of the actual income situation of American families, how it has changed over time, and the extent of poverty and income inequality. The second goal is to give an overview of the many different strategies and public policies that have been developed to provide adequate family income. My third aim is to show that there is an internal logic to American income-related policies and programs that explains how they have developed. They began with a charitable impulse to help the neediest, but they have evolved in the direction of universal coverage. Understanding their development helps one discern what elements should be kept and what changes are still needed to achieve adequacy and fairness in the income distribution.

This chapter surveys two main types of policies and programs to enhance economic security. These measures are commonly thought of as aimed at individuals rather than families. But this is a fallacy; these programs make a major contribution to economic security of the family. The earliest, and in some ways the most familiar type of assistance, goes to those who are poor. The Social Security Act of 1935 established assistance for the aged, blind persons, and dependent children. These programs have evolved over the years. Aid to the poor disabled was added in 1939. Aid to Dependent Children became Aid to Families with Dependent Children (AFDC) in 1960, and in 1996 was transformed into Transitional Assistance to Needy Families (TANF), with time limits and work requirements to receive aid. A variety of in-kind benefits such as food supplements, subsidized housing, childcare, and health services are also available to those who are at or near the poverty level.

The second main category of support for economic security is based on work-related benefits and programs of which there are three main types— social insurance, wage improvement, and work–family integration. The *insurance programs* include Workers' Compensation, Old Age Insurance, (Social Security), and Unemployment Insurance that are publicly mandated and private pensions that are provided through employers. Programs for *wage improvement* ("making work pay") include measures to raise the minimum wage as well as to allow unionization and collective bargaining. Since the 1960s there have also been a variety of efforts to train employees so that they can command better-paying jobs. For those who are out of the workforce and in need of a job, new programs in community colleges are training workers for positions where there is strong local demand. *Work–family integration* refers to efforts to transform the workplace into a more family-friendly and flexible environment that makes allowances for workers' caregiving responsibilities. Change involves a transformation of the culture of the workplace, which is typically blind to family needs. Examples of progress are legislative measures that support flexible hours, part-time work, and family leave as well as employer-sponsored provision for dependent care.

Ultimately, the families who will enjoy greatest security are those who can assemble a combination of resources from employment, Social Security, private pensions, employer-related benefits, and savings. Data on the current income distribution shows, however, that many families have only one or two of these sources of income, thus making them quite vulnerable to unemployment or an economic downturn.

The American Income Distribution and Family Needs

Implicit in almost any discussion of family income are two underlying questions. First, how much do most people make? Second, how much income is enough? A descriptive answer reports how family income varies across different types of households. A normative answer addresses the issue of what should be an adequate or fair distribution, given the family's characteristics, including the number of children, and the total productivity of the nation. This chapter opens with a general description of current family income and how it has become increasingly unequal among different segments of the population over the past several decades.

Variation in Household Income

In 2009 the median income of all households in the United States was almost $50,000 (when rounded to the nearest thousand). This median amount varies by household characteristics. For example, the 2009 estimate for a married couple family is roughly $72,000 compared with $48,000 for a male householder without a wife present and about $32,500 for a female householder without a husband present. Households in the West and Northeast report incomes almost $8,000 more than those in the Midwest and the South. Households inside metropolitan areas collect roughly $11,000 more than rural households. Householders under age 65 report median incomes of $57,000, compared with $31,000 among those ages 65 and over. Race differences are also striking: Asian families have the highest median income ($65,000), whites are in second place ($54,000), and Hispanic and black families place third and fourth (with $38,000 and $33,000, respectively) (DeNavas-Walt, Proctor, and Smith 2010:5).

Compared with 10 years earlier, median family income was slightly lower in constant dollars in 2009 than 2000. This decline was due in part to unemployment which rose from 4.4 percent in March 2007 to over 9 percent in

2010 because of a "jobless recovery" and loss of benefits. The result was greater difficulty for low-wage workers in finding any job or one with adequate benefits. Those with only a high school diploma in 2007 had 18 percent less income than their counterparts in 1979.

Since the 1970s, the proportion of union members among all workers has dropped by more than half, from 43 percent in 1978 to 19 percent in 2005, which resulted in weakened bargaining power by workers to claim their share of national gains in productivity. As a result, corporate shareholders gained greater power relative to employees. Coverage of employee benefits such as pensions and health insurance dropped from 69 percent of workers in 1979 to 55 percent in 2006 and 51 percent in 2008 (Mishel, Bernstein, and Shierholz 2009). Because these additional forms of compensation imply payment in kind rather than payment in cash, such retrenchment represents a net loss of available income to the employee. Between 2008 and 2009, the proportion of people covered by employment-based health insurance fell from 58.5 percent to 55.8 percent, a percentage that is the lowest since 1987 when the first comparable health insurance data were collected (DeNavas-Walt et al. 2010:22–24).

Mishel and colleagues (2009:15) sum up the policy theme of the decade as "YOYO" economics, meaning "You're On Your Own." Many able workers are not able to find jobs; many bright kids cannot afford college. Increasingly, production, and hence jobs, are shipped offshore to take advantage of cheaper labor costs, and domestic workers must find new work.

Poverty, Wealth, and Inequality

The poverty threshold provides a measure of the adequacy of family income for meeting basic needs. The most common measure was created in 1963 to measure poverty based on the least expensive adequate food budget for a family of two adults and two children. Cost of food at that time was estimated to be about 30 percent of the family's total expenses for basic necessities that also included shelter, clothing, and transportation. Variations were then calculated for families of different sizes, and in different regions of the country. The *poverty threshold* represents the level of income below which a person or family is officially defined as poor. *Poverty guidelines* are simplified criteria based on the threshold that are used to determine eligibility for means-tested programs such as food stamps or subsidized childcare.

Over the past 50 years there have been many suggestions of how the poverty measure should be revised. An interagency task force has developed a Supplementary Poverty Measure that began being used for research and testing in 2011. The food basket will still be a central element but its percentage of the total will be smaller. In-kind income will be taken into account as well as assets in homeownership that lower the costs of shelter. Health care and childcare costs also will be included in the calculation of basic income requirements (Roberts 2010).

Prevalence of poverty. In 2009, using the traditional measure, the poverty threshold for a household unit of one person stood at approximately $11,000, for a household of two at $14,000, for a three-person household at $17,000, and up to $22,000 for a four-person household (U.S. Census Bureau 2010b:Table 694). The number of people in poverty was 43.6 million or 14.3 percent of the total population (DeNavas-Walt et al. 2010:14). This figure was higher than the 11.6 percent in poverty before the recession in 2008–2009. The proportions vary by demographic characteristics: 5.8 percent of married-couple families were poor versus 29.9 percent of female-headed households and 22 percent of unrelated individuals. Poverty stood at 12.3 percent among whites compared with 25.8 percent among blacks and Hispanics. Among native-born persons, 13.7 percent were poor versus 19 percent among the foreign-born.

Improvement in poverty rates since 1960 is nowhere more evident than among the elderly, a change directly attributable to social programs that were specifically designed to improve the situation of older people. The creation of Medicare and Medicaid in the 1960s also replaced a significant portion of income that was earlier needed for health care. The remarkable turnaround is represented by the proportion in poverty of people 65 years and older. Today that figure has dropped to 8.9 percent, which is considerably lower than the 12.9 percent of younger people ages 18 to 64 who are poor today. In 1960, roughly a fifth of the elderly population was in poverty as was reported by Michael Harrington (1962) in *The Other America: Poverty in the United States.*

Some observers believe that the actual poverty rate is much higher than current figures suggest. In fact, there is some worry that when the new Supplementary Poverty Measure is used in the future, there may be "too many" poor people for the funds available from entitlement programs to provide the aid that is required (Short 2011).

Against the backdrop of measurement issues, it is useful to keep in mind a broader definition of poverty as "hardship and social exclusion," meaning lack of access to the material resources that are needed for food, housing, transportation, medical care, education and training, and employment (Haveman 2009). Akin to this approach is the concept of a "living wage," which has been the object of grassroots organizing campaigns among unionized workers at hospitals and universities such as Harvard and Yale (Harvard Living Wage Campaign 2003).

Several components determine the adequacy of a family's economic resources. For most people, the dominant factor is income from wages, which may be supplemented by in-kind benefits such as subsidized health insurance or childcare. Other very important resources are savings, capital investments, or equity in a home or land that may provide interest and appreciation in value over time. Such assets can be used as a resource for buying property, meeting an emergency such as a health crisis or unemployment, or for discretionary consumption of such goods and services as travel or a second home. Accumulated assets can also be used for education and training that lead to upward mobility. Also, these assets, or "wealth," can be used for charitable giving and investment in the wider community (Mishel et al. 2009:10–11).

Oliver and Shapiro (2006) have shown that racial differences in *income* are not really so great as differences in *wealth* that are largely due to a long history of racial discrimination in housing. The result is that home ownership for blacks never led to the high rates of appreciation that were experienced over several decades by whites. The inability to accumulate wealth thus limited the ability of African Americans to pay for higher education and attain the American dream of owning a home that appreciates in value over time. The mortgage crisis that began in 2008 hit minorities particularly hard because they were more often offered subprime loans and were charged higher rates of interest that resulted in a disproportionate number of foreclosures (Merle 2010).

Growing inequality in income and wealth. By 2011 it was apparent that income inequality among American families was on the rise. This increase is a change from the first half of the twentieth century through World War II, when government programs lessened the enormous gaps between rich and poor that dominated the Gilded Age. Since the mid-1970s, however, the oil crisis and lower growth in the GDP allowed inequality to rise again so that the United States now has the highest level of income inequality among industrialized nations (Wolff 2009:86). In 2009 the top 1 percent of wage earners earned 24 percent of total income, up from 9 percent in 1976 and the highest level on record since 1928 (Mishel 2009:12), a condition that Kristof (2010) compares to "banana republics" like Nicaragua, Venezuela, and Guyana.

Economists cite several reasons for the rise in inequality: (1) changing household structure, whereby there are more single-parent families who have lower income than married-couple families; (2) slower growth in the economy; (3) the increasing "skill bias" of the job market which requires more education and training and leaves less well-educated people more likely to be unemployed and therefore relatively worse off than in the past (Levy 1998); and finally (4) a decrease in the tax rate for the wealthy relative to these in the working-class and middle-income groups. Mishel and colleagues (2009) attribute growing inequality to a drop in the real value of the minimum wage, globalization and loss of manufacturing in those industries where U.S. wage rates are higher, and macro economic factors such as high unemployment in the 1980s as well as a slack labor market after 2000. Yet strong demand led to an 11 percent growth in productivity even though ordinary workers failed to participate in these gains, and 26 percent of workers earned poverty-level wages in 2007.

The wealthiest 1 percent of all households controls a larger share of the national wealth than the entire bottom 90 percent. Average wealth of the top 1 percent was approximately $15 million compared with $81,000 for the middle quintile. In 1962, the bottom 80 percent held 19.1 percent of the wealth, whereas in 2004 they held only 15.3 percent, and approximately 10 percent of households had net worth less than $10,000. Mishel and colleagues (2009) sum up the reasons for the trend: the diminished bargaining power of the American worker, cheap imports that displace American-made goods, decline of unions, the low minimum wage, and the high cost of higher education which impedes upward mobility in the lower middle class. Joblessness, even for willing workers, and digitization of college-level jobs that are sent offshore (e.g., use of call centers in India to provide technical help on software problems) together result in a laissez-faire attitude not only toward markets but also toward workers. As a result, workers are no better off than in 1947, and the poverty rate was higher in 2009 than in 2000 (Mishel et al. 2009:15–16).

In the context of growing inequality, what has happened to intergenerational mobility? Surprisingly, given their minority status, black families have not experienced as much of an increase in inequality as white families. The difference by race is due to a combination of factors: urbanization of blacks who came from the low-wage South, a rise in high school graduation rates to 85 percent by 2005, improvement in schools as a result of school desegregation, and federal programs to combat discrimination such as Title VII of the Civil Rights Act of 1964 (Wolff 2009:478). The degree of mobility is, however, gradually decreasing for the majority of the American population, where despite the Horatio Alger myth, the United States now has greater inequality of opportunity in education than Europe and the Scandinavian countries, where children's economic level is less correlated with that of their parents than in the United States (Mishel et al. 2009).

The National Interest in Family Income

Many observers are alarmed at the high rate of child poverty in the United States—22 percent compared with an average of 10 percent in other OECD countries (Mishel et al. 2009). Why should the child poverty rate be a matter of such serious national concern? The answer is that poverty of children and families ultimately exacts heavy costs to the nation in health care, productivity, and social cohesion (Kristof 2011b). To remedy inequality and lower the poverty rate requires behavioral changes related to family size and composition as well as education and training for competing successfully in the labor market. Lowering the poverty rate also requires income transfers from the rich to the poor. The United States is the second richest country in the world after Norway in per capita GDP, yet it has one of the highest poverty rates of the industrial world and one of the lowest tax rates among the industrialized countries. The national proportion of GDP paid in U.S. taxes (including federal, state, local, property, payroll, excise, and income taxes) is approximately 29 percent compared with an average tax proportion of 36 percent among other OECD countries (Wolff 2009). The high poverty rate will not change until the American public understands that lowering poverty and its hidden costs is vital to maintaining American leadership in the world.

Poverty and costs to health and mental health. Recent studies show a strong relationship between low social status and physical and mental illness. Low status causes stress in human beings. In Great Britain, for example, social scientists found that low status among civil service workers was associated with higher rates of heart disease, suicide, some cancers, and poor mental health. When workers become unemployed or lose income they tend to gain weight, and obesity is a much greater problem among the poor than among those who are well off (Kristof 2011b). The mortality rate for blacks is 2.3 times that of whites (Mishel et al. 2009). Moreover, a cross-national comparison by Wilkinson and Pickett (2010) reveals that the countries with the greatest inequality have more mental illness, infant mortality, obesity, high school dropouts, teenage pregnancy, drug use, and homicides. They find the same pattern is evident among the American states, where Mississippi and Louisiana do poorly in this regard in comparison with New Hampshire and Minnesota. Although the United States is the highest among nations in the percentage of its GDP that is used for health care, it has lower life expectancy and higher infant mortality than its peers (Mishel et al. 2009).

Poverty and threats to productivity. The long-term effects of family and child poverty are also worrisome when it comes to the nation's long-term competitiveness in the global economy. Approximately one-third of U.S. children experience poverty at some point in their childhood by living in a poor household. If such poverty is deep and persistent there is risk of intergenerational transmission of economic disadvantage. Harsh child-rearing methods, a home atmosphere of hostility and conflict together with poor housing, high crime, boarded-up neighborhoods, poor schools, and pollution are likely to have negative effects on brain development because they stimulate the stress response and stress hormones and thus interfere with cognitive ability and achievement motivation. The outcomes are well known: poor health, lower educational attainment, and more problematic behavior such as crime, nonmarital childbearing, and poverty as adults (Magnuson and Votruba-Drzal 2009). Given the increasing skill bias in employment, those workers who do not complete high school, and those who do not have some post-secondary education, are at particular risk of long-term unemployment or consignment to precarious low-income jobs. Prevention requires investment in early childhood education and compensatory programs such as Even Start for low-income families, which bolster poor mothers' training and at the same time provide early childcare and education for the children (Carson 2009). As has been shown with the Perry Preschool Program and Head Start, such institutions pay off in preventing dropping out later on and in laying a foundation for success in school (Heckman 2006; Zigler and Gilman 1996).

Poverty and loss of a sense of community. As the sixteenth-century poet John Donne wrote, *"No man is an Island, entire of itself; every man is a piece of the Continent, a part of the main."* Everyone is dependent on social support and the resources of a larger community of family and nation. But great social distance or inequality among income groups is a threat to the cohesion of society. The most graphic illustration of this principle comes from Wilkinson and Pickett (2010), who document the high levels of violence, substance abuse, and suicide in those societies with the greatest income inequality. The most unequal societies need more prisons and police. Wilkinson and Pickett explain that great inequality in society is harmful because it undermines social trust and a sense of community. Human beings feel stress when they are at the bottom of a hierarchy. Their distress eventually affects not only their physical and mental health but also the stability and safety of society as a whole.

Aid to the Poor

As was described in Chapter 4, many of the earliest charitable activities of the nineteenth century were the forerunners of today's safety net. Help was primarily directed to poor women, children, and old people. Over the course of a century, charitable efforts by churches and friendly aid societies were gradually transformed into government-funded assistance or entitlements that are characteristic of welfare states in the modern world. Even though the United States was always more individualistically oriented than the social democracies of Scandinavia and Continental Europe, it too developed a government-supported safety net to help the indigent. Beginning in the nineteenth century, poor houses gave shelter to the elderly; Civil War veterans' pensions were extended to widows, children, and other survivors. Between 1915 and 1934 a number of states provided relief to poor old people, widows, and children, but with very severe restrictions such as liens on property if one accepted assistance (ElderWeb 2011). With the Social Security Act of 1935 these various state programs were brought under the umbrella of federal law, and minimal standards were set for aid to the elderly, the blind, and dependent children. The 1960s War on Poverty further extended government support to those in need. Following the defeat of President Nixon's Family Assistance Program to eradicate poverty through basic income maintenance (a "negative income tax"[1]), the federal program for Supplemental Security Income (SSI) was established in 1972 as a way to shift state control of assistance to the elderly, blind, and disabled to more general oversight by the federal government (Dobelstein 2009).

These policy developments have been subject to criticism from different ideological perspectives. Scholars on the left like Piven and Cloward (1971) understood welfare programs and their eligibility requirements to be mechanisms for "regulating the poor" by quelling social protest such as the welfare rights movement of the 1960s. Assistant Secretary of Labor Daniel Patrick Moynihan, on the other hand, worried that too generous welfare policies were creating a dependent class whose children would grow up to rely on government handouts rather than their own initiative (Rainwater and Yancey 1967).

Garfinkel, Rainwater, and Smeeding (2010), however, interpret American welfare policy in light of American exceptionalism, that is that the United States is fundamentally different in its cultural values and political system

---

[1]The negative income tax, which had been suggested by economists Milton Friedman and Robert Lampman as a way of avoiding the bureaucratic and stigmatizing procedures of awarding welfare payments, never was adopted. The basic concept was that "unlike other filers who would make payments to the IRS, based on the amount by which their incomes exceeded the threshold for tax liability, NIT beneficiaries would receive payments ('negative taxes') from the IRS, based on how far their incomes fell below the tax threshold" (J. T. Allen 2007).

from other advanced industrial societies. The United States spends less on poor relief than any other advanced country because of a strong belief in individual initiative and equal opportunity. Yet at the same time it has historically spent more on education and access to training than the United Kingdom, Denmark, or Germany. However, these trends have been shifting over the past 30 years, and the United States now has less social mobility, greater inequality, and a lag in scholastic test scores and educational attainment that puts it behind its peers. The high unemployment and trauma of the Great Depression shifted politics toward the left and toward helping the working class and poor people. But since then, the social upheavals of the 1960s and the presidencies of Nixon and Reagan have brought a long swing toward the right, which has permitted an increase in inequality and poverty.

Through all these changes, four constant themes reappear. First, Americans believe that government should take some responsibility for aiding the poor. Second, their compassionate impulse is always accompanied by a nagging concern not to encourage dependency. Third, they are less interested in helping those who can work than in aiding those who cannot be expected to work. Finally, they give more generous help to those who conform to their values of self-reliance and hard work. But at the same time, race prejudice or narrow views on the proper role of women or family life can make them reluctant to provide support to those who are different from themselves (Garfinkel and McLanahan 1986).

The following account provides a brief chronology of policies to alleviate poverty of specific vulnerable groups—the elderly, children, and persons with disabilities. In addition, some policies provide in-kind help to poor families and individuals regardless of age or family status. These include programs that subsidize food security, housing, and health care. While there has been much progress in expanding antipoverty programs beyond their early beginnings, it is clear from the much tighter rules of eligibility resulting from welfare reform that poverty relief is still offered somewhat grudgingly.

Americans prefer income programs that offer an entitlement such as work-based *insurance* rather than means-based *assistance*. Those who receive direct aid experience a degree of stigma, as do the programs that offer such aid—a condition which is captured by a saying among some social workers that "means-tested" benefits often seem to come from "mean" programs. As a result, policy makers over the years have sought to move poverty relief toward a guaranteed entitlement that assures a decent standard of living. The history of the Social Security Act according to Dobelstein (2009) shows that this effort partially succeeded in 1972 when assistance for needy elders and for blind and disabled persons was moved from control by the states to the responsibility of the federal government with the passage of the Supplemental Security Income (SSI) Act. Aid to Families with Dependent Children (AFDC), however, was left under the supervision of the states and thus continued without the legitimacy that would have come from its being made an entitlement administered by the federal government.

Transformation of Old Age and Disability Assistance to SSI

Between the 1930s and the 1970s, assistance to the elderly and disabled gradually took on the attributes of an entitlement program. For both age and disability, the 1935 Social Security Act contained two types of help. In the case of age, Title I provided Old Age Assistance, which was directed to the poor who had no other protection, whereas Title II Old Age Security was directed to those persons over 65 whose contributions from current wages were to ensure their retirement income. Similarly, Aid to the Blind was a grant-in-aid for one type of disability whereas Workers' Compensation (which pre-dated Social Security and still continues as an insurance system run by the states) applied to persons who were covered by employer-backed insurance for work-related injuries.

In his masterful history of the Social Security Act, Dobelstein (2009) shows how, between the 1930s and the 1960s, poverty relief gradually shifted from direct aid to programs that tried to use objective standards of eligibility similar to those applied to social insurance. The transformation began in the 1950s with Title XIV of the Social Security Act, which established a federal standard of eligibility for Aid to the Permanently and Totally Disabled. The program was amended further in 1956 as Aid to the Disabled.

By means of the Economic Opportunity Act of 1964, President Johnson's War on Poverty introduced the idea of helping poor people find jobs through services that promoted self-help, vocational education, and job placement. Then, following the espousal of the Negative Income Tax by conservative and liberal economists alike, the idea took hold of converting all public transfers into a single program to include both social insurance and welfare programs. The benefits would be based simply on income level and family size and would thereby remove the stigma of welfare for those unable to work while at the same time helping the working poor (Garfinkel and McLanahan 1986). The Negative Income Tax idea was eventually incorporated into President Nixon's Family Assistance Plan to guarantee a minimum annual income to poor families. After several failures to pass Congress and many amendments that eventually gutted the income guarantee and left out transfers from social insurance, the measure was finally adopted as the Supplemental Security Income Act of 1972 (see Table 5.1).

Table 5.1   Major Programs for Poverty Assistance Since 1935

Enabling Legislation	Year	Provisions
Old Age Assistance Title I of SSA	1935–1972	Aid to persons in need over age 65
Aid to the Blind Title X of SSA	1935–1972	Aid to blind persons
Aid to the Permanently and Totally Disabled (APTD) Title XIV	1950–1956	Aid to persons unable to work because of mental or physical impairment and not covered by Titles I or X.
Aid to the Disabled Amendment of Title XIV	1956–1972	APTD available to persons whose disabilities were neither permanent nor total.
Supplemental Security Income (SSI) Title XVI	1972 Effective 1974- 1990–1996	Provides income benefits to aged, blind, and disabled persons who meet the eligibility criteria of the poverty guidelines. Children on AFDC eligible if they meet SSI eligibility criteria

Supplemental Security Income (SSI) provisions. Since 1974, when it was implemented, SSI has been the poverty program of last resort to supplement the incomes of needy elders, and blind and disabled persons as well as income of some dependent children. The program is seriously flawed for the elderly, however, because it counts Social Security payments as unearned income, which is subtracted from the SSI benefit, and thereby deprives them of the value of their contributions during their working years. The upshot is that SSI favors poor people in some categories (the blind and disabled) more than others (the aged). Moreover, variations among state programs still prevail, which along with complex rules of calculating the monthly benefit, make the program exceedingly difficult to administer. Dobelstein (2009:158) concludes that, "SSI has failed miserably to provide an income maintenance flow for eligible low income individuals that comes anywhere near mitigating poverty among this group of economically needy Americans."

Recipients of SSI. The overall percentage of the American population who receive it has remained steady at around 2.4 percent. Of that number, almost three-fifths were over 65 in 1974 (57 percent), two-fifths were disabled (41 percent), and only 2 percent were blind. By 2005, the disabled portion had doubled to 82 percent (in large part due to de-institutionalization of the mentally ill); the aged had fallen to 17 percent; and the blind were a tiny 1 percent. At least some of the decline in elderly recipients must be attributed to the relatively more favorable calculation of benefits for people under 65 than for those 65 years and older; but another component is the improved Social Security benefits over time for those aged 65 and over. Using SIPP data (Survey of Income Program and Participation), Scholz, Moffitt, and Cowan (2009:220–221) found the percentage of those who are poor even after receiving SSI to be around 29.8 percent. Dobelstein (2009:166) reports that of those who did receive SSI, their incomes reached 91.4 percent of the poverty level in 1975 but only 85.3 percent in 2002. In 2011 the minimum federal monthly payment was $674 ($8,088 per year) for eligible individuals and $1,011 ($12,132 per year) for an eligible individual with an eligible spouse. This can be compared with the U.S. poverty guidelines for 2010 and 2011 that are used in setting eligibility criteria: an annual income threshold of $10,830 for one person and $14,570 for a household of two persons (the average poverty line for the 48 states and District of Columbia). Thus the maximum annual federal SSI benefit reached about 75 percent of the poverty level for an individual and 83 percent for a couple (Institute for Research on Poverty 2011; Social Security Online 2011b).

Although SSI to help needy elders, the blind, and disabled was created after the Nixon income reforms failed, Dobelstein attributes its passage to "policy drift" that moved from a theory of social welfare based on discretionary assistance toward one based on an objective standard of a minimum guaranteed income. In his view the creation of SSI both stifled further development of an income guarantee and at the same time reinforced the American aversion to giving outright aid.

> Instead of a program that provides a basic income guarantee to America's aged, blind, and the disabled . . . SSI has become a program of income support as a last resort. . . . by cobbling together three assistance programs into a single assistance program. (Dobelstein 2009:158)

Aid to Dependent Children

Poor relief for children and their mothers has also been a charity with ancient roots that includes both the assistance and insurance principles of providing necessary income. In the nineteenth century, churches and women's charitable groups established societies to aid widows and their families. The Civil War pensions for veterans extended the insurance principle to the children and families of the veterans. Together with the mothers' pension movement described in Chapter 4, these precedents provided a foundation for Aid to Dependent Children, Title IV-A of the Social Security Act. However, despite a number of changes in the ADC program between the 1930s and the 1990s, it never achieved the legitimacy of an entitlement. Unlike the 1939 amendments to Old Age Security (Title II) that extended insurance-based Social Security benefits to survivors of covered workers, ADC and its successor AFDC perpetuated the concept of aid and relief to poor families in which the children and their mothers were not expected to work. Whereas aid to the old, blind, and disabled was gradually transformed into an entitlement under federal control, assistance to dependent children retained the aura of charity and remained under the control of the states. As a result, regional differences in racial politics and economic prosperity created wide variation in eligibility criteria and size of benefits. In keeping with historical patterns of racial discrimination, many eligible black mothers and their children were denied benefits (Gordon 1994).

Between the 1960s and the 1990s, before AFDC was challenged by welfare reform, several policy initiatives opened up new possibilities for the way that aid to poor families might be structured. In 1964 the War on Poverty through the Economic Opportunity Act began providing services instead of cash for self-help, vocational training, and job placement. In 1975 the new Earned Income Tax Credit (EITC) began providing a subsidy to low-wage workers. Also in 1975 the Child Support Enforcement Amendments (Title IV-D) of the Social Security Act authorized the Internal Revenue Service to locate absent fathers and establish paternity in order to help the states enforce parental obligations for child support.

During this 30-year period between the 1960s and the 1990s, two important waves of social change further undermined acceptance of the AFDC program. One was the rapid rise in female-headed households that resulted from nonmarital births rather than widowhood, a trend that was reflected in the jump from 60 percent of all AFDC recipients who were in female-headed households in 1967 to 90 percent in 1972 (Garfinkel and McLanahan 1986). The rapid increase in *married* mothers' labor force participation dealt a second blow to AFDC. The proportion of mothers in the labor force with preschoolers doubled between 1960 and 1980, from approximately 20 percent to 40 percent (Moen 1992). Together these developments caused Americans to question the need to provide income support to mothers in order that they might stay at home to care for their children. After several decades in which successive administrations had struggled and failed to lower the welfare rolls, the Republican Congress of 1996 passed the Personal Responsibility and Work Opportunity Reconciliation Act (PRWORA), which created a

Table 5.2   Poverty Assistance to Dependent Children and Families

Enabling Legislation	Year	Provisions
Aid to Dependent Children (ADC) Title IV-A	1935–1959	Assistance to children in households without an able-bodied male breadwinner
Aid to Families with Dependent Children (AFDC) Title IV-A	1959–1996	Assistance to custodial parent as well as eligible children
Economic Opportunity Act "War on Poverty"	1964	Provision of services (instead of cash) for self-help, vocational training, and job placement to enhance opportunity for the poor
Earned Income Tax Credit (EITC)	1975	Provides a subsidy to low-income workers
Title IV-D Child Support Enforcement Amendments	1975 1984	Authorized use of IRS data to locate absent parent and establish paternity in order to pursue enforcement of child support by the states
Transitional Assistance to Needy Families (TANF) PRWORA	1996	Instituted work requirement after maximum of 2 years of assistance and 5-year time limit for assistance

new program with a five-year time limit and a requirement that poor mothers make an effort to obtain gainful work. AFDC was replaced by TANF, Temporary Assistance for Needy Families. (See Table 5.2.)

Implementation of TANF. The best-known requirements of TANF are the work requirements and the five-year time limit. While the rules differ somewhat by state, recipients must work as soon as they are ready for a job and no later than two years after being enrolled. Single parents have to work at least 30 hours per week unless they have children under 6 and are unable to find childcare. Two-parent families must work between 35 and 55 hours per week depending on the circumstances. After five years of federally funded assistance a family is not eligible to receive cash payments under TANF but may receive social services and state-only funds.

With the passage of TANF, social workers and service providers were very worried about what would happen to families who had formerly depended on AFDC for basic necessities. Research results were mixed. Interviews with welfare mothers amply demonstrated how difficult it was for them to make ends meet and to get from one month's welfare check to the next. Among the hardships they faced were difficulties finding transportation, being able to pay for childcare, and getting health care to replace Medicaid, if they found a job at a minimum wage (Edin and Lein 1997; Seccombe 2011). Yet the welfare rolls declined dramatically, from over 12 million families on AFDC in 1996 to just over 6 million on TANF in 2001 (Schram and Soss 2001). While it would be reassuring to believe that the change was due to more mothers working, the interview data suggest that many eligible mothers were strongly discouraged by welfare workers from applying to the program. Those who did receive benefits reported that they were encouraged to take any available job regardless of whether it represented an improvement or meant a loss of benefits or neglect of their children. As support for welfare cash payments has fallen, other forms of support have been used more, particularly the Food Stamp Program. Surprisingly perhaps, the use of Food Stamps is now being encouraged for working parents with low income. Unlike "welfare" that in some cases had become associated with fraud and dependency, food aid is seen as a justifiable in-kind program that can lead to better nutrition and relief of basic hunger (Deparle and Gebeloff 2010).

In-Kind Subsidies

The importance of an in-kind transfer such as the Food Stamp Program brings up a larger discussion of the relative importance of cash transfers compared with in-kind goods and services.

Alva Myrdal, in her famous book on Swedish family policy *Nation and Family: The Swedish Experiment in Democratic Family and Population Policy,* addresses this question in a chapter entitled "In Cash or In-Kind" (Myrdal [1934] 1968). Myrdal noted the popular preference for income-based payment in cash, but she argued strongly that in-kind transfers were preferable. They are cheaper, they do not get lost in the family budget, and they tilt the focus of aid toward quality rather than quantity. Most important of all, they circumvent the social class distinction that separates what goes to the poor from the nonpoor. In-kind services and commodities instead express the solidarity of the nation and its dedication to supporting all children and families as a fundamental requisite for national well-being. She sums up this principle as follows:

> Cooperation, finally, may be the key word for this social policy in a deeper sense because it rests fundamentally on social solidarity, on pooling of resources for common aims, wider in their loyalty than just insurance of individual

interest. If children shall continue to be born and if they shall be reared according to standards that our democratic culture can be proud of, the competitive and destructive society of yesterday must yield to a society of solidarity. A new era in social policy will then dawn, a century of childcare and family security. (Myrdal [1934] 1968:151)

Given Myrdal's rationale and strong recommendation of in-kind benefits, it is encouraging to see how many forms of in-kind support are available in the United States, not just for poverty relief but for support of children and families in general, as shown in Table 5.3. The list includes health services and family planning, food aid, housing and heating assistance, and childcare. These

Table 5.3 In-Kind Programs for Children and Families

Enabling Legislation	Year	Provisions
Health Related		
Maternal and Child Health Title V of SSA	1935	Replaced Sheppard-Towner Act. Allocated funds to states to provide health services to mothers and young children
Medicaid, Title XIX of SSA	1965	Medical assistance to the poor, regardless of age administered by the states
State Children's Health Insurance Program (SCHIP) Title XXI of SSA Reauthorized	1997 2009	Health care coverage for low-income children (between 133% and 200% of poverty level)
Food Security		
School Lunch Program	1946	Subsidized milk and lunches for school children
Food Stamps (SNAP)	1974	Benefits for low-income households to purchase food
Women, Infants, and Children (WIC)	1972	Nutrition, education for pregnant and nursing mothers and children under 5
Housing Assistance		
U.S. Housing Act	1937, 1949	Low-Rent Housing Program
Housing and Urban Development Act	1965, 1968	Rent subsidies to low-income families
Heating Assistance (some states)	1981	Aid to low-income families or those with high heating costs

in-kind subsidies are key to the economic security of the family even though they give direct support rather than a cash benefit to family functions of providing care and shelter. My main purpose here is simply to list the major types of in-kind support in order to show the variety of programs that exist and to outline the major developments that have occurred since the 1930s.

Health-related programs. Health care coverage for mothers and children was established in 1935 with Title V of the Social Security Act, which continued the coverage that had begun with the Sheppard-Towner Act, which was repealed in 1929. Federal funds to the states provided health care to mothers and young children. The Maternal and Child Health programs were consolidated under the Health Services Block Grant of 1981 and since then have generally been associated with county health departments (Dobelstein 2009). Following the Maternal and Child Health programs, two other major health programs for poor families and children were added—Medicaid in 1965 and the State Children's Health Insurance Program (SCHIP) in 1997. Medicaid covers medical assistance to people with income at or below the poverty level who have limited assets ($2,000 or less) or who have extraordinarily high medical costs that lower their disposable income. Along with usual medical services that include access to a doctor, lab tests, and X-rays, Medicaid also covers family planning, home health care, and Early and Periodic Screening and Diagnostic Treatment (EPSDT) for persons under age 21. In 2008 Medicaid payments went to 14 percent of the total U.S. population. Minorities were more heavily represented among the young, with black and Hispanic populations around 30 percent of those under 18 years or less (U.S. Census Bureau 2011:Table 144). SCHIP provides coverage for children from families whose family income is slightly higher—an average for the country as a whole of up to 241 percent of the Federal Poverty Line (Medicaid.gov 2011).

Food security. As already mentioned in Chapter 4, the National School Lunch Program established in 1946 makes lunches and meals available to all children in public and nonprofit schools. With the Child Nutrition Act of 1966, the program was expanded to include free and reduced-cost lunches and breakfasts for low-income children. The Healthy, Hunger-Free Kids Act of 2010 added goals of reducing childhood obesity and improving the diets of children (Food and Nutrition Service 2011). The WIC (Women, Infants, and Children) program established in 1972 offers health education and nutritional assistance to pregnant and nursing mothers and children.

The Food Stamp Program is by far the largest government effort to provide subsidies to ensure food security. First established in 1939 to address the double goals of using agricultural surplus and feeding the large unemployed population, the program was closed in 1943 because it had met its goals. It was then reopened by President Kennedy on a pilot basis in 1961. The Food Stamp Act of 1964 established the present program to provide food subsidies to low-income families. The program is now called SNAP (Supplemental Nutritional Assistance Program) and uses an electronic benefit transfer (EBT) system, which is a debit card that can be used in the grocery store. There are currently 40 million Americans receiving these benefits (Food and Nutrition Service 2011). In 2011, the weekly food budget for a family of four was approximately $85, which requires careful purchasing to stretch that amount. This budget compares with at least twice that amount ($154 to $180 per week for a low-cost meal plan, depending on age of children) for a comparable family not on food stamps (U.S. Department of Agriculture 2011). In my hometown of Wellesley, Massachusetts, a middle-class family decided to try living within the limits of the food stamp budget. The homemaker-mother of the family kept a blog and described how she managed. She doubled the quantity of milk by thinning it with water and made flavorful soup with bones and cheap but nutritious staples like beans (Applebaum 2011).

Housing assistance. In their book *Black Wealth, White Wealth: A New Perspective on Racial Inequality,* Oliver and Shapiro (2006) remind us how government assistance to Americans goes back a long way. Pioneers could establish homesteads and become landowners by settling the prairies. Modern housing assistance to low-income families began in the 1930s with the Housing Act of 1937 and establishment of the Federal Housing Authority to help families obtain mortgages and to assist communities to build tracts of affordable housing. In recent years the government has taken less of a role in construction than private developers. There are now three main forms of assistance: public housing, Section 8 vouchers for subsidized rentals, and low-income units that are included within the private subsidized housing plan. Recipients range from elders and persons with disabilities to poor single adults and low-income families with young children (McCarty et al. 2008). Another form of assistance with shelter is the Low-Income Home Energy Assistance Program (LIHEAP) that took effect in 1982 and is run by the Administration on Children and Families of the Department of Health and Human Services (HHS). In 2010, $5.1 billion was spent for heating assistance and reached 74 percent of the eligible households with either an elderly member or a young child. Families eligible for assistance must have income no greater than 150 percent of the poverty level or 75 percent of the state median income or incur very high heating costs in relation to income (Administration for Children and Families 2011b).

Childcare. Head Start, established in 1965, provides childcare to low-income families. In 2009 almost 1 million preschool children were enrolled, half of whom were 4 years old and almost all of the rest under age 4. Roughly two-thirds were black or Hispanic and the remaining third were white (U.S. Census Bureau 2011:Table 572).

The Child Care and Development Fund within the Office of Child Care also helps low-income families and those receiving TANF benefits to pay for child care so that they can participate in educational or job training programs. As of 2009 CCDF had increased the number of accredited childcare centers from almost 10,000 at the beginning of the decade to 15,000 in 2009. The Fund also succeeded in maintaining the proportion of 32 percent of children served, which is at a level commensurate with the number of children in families whose income is less than 150 percent of the federal poverty line (Administration for Children and Families 2011a). The number of children participating ranges between 1.6 and 1.8 million, and come from approximately 1 million families (McKenna 2010).

The Child Care Tax Credit instituted in 1976 is another form of in-kind transfer that benefits a family's overall financial situation. It is not a government benefit but a nonrefundable tax credit that can be applied against the household's overall tax bill. It gives credit for child or dependent care costs so that a single parent, or if married, both parents, can work or look for work. It is available to families at all income levels who can deduct up to $3,000 for one dependent and up to $6,000 for more than one. Between 2004 and 2007 about 4.4 million taxpayers participated in this program (McKenna 2010). (See Table 5.8.)

Impact of Poverty Relief on Poverty Levels

The ultimate question is how the various income transfers and in-kind benefits affect the financial situation of a low-income family. Do they raise them out of poverty? This complicated question requires careful research to answer it. The best data available come from the analysis of the 2004 Survey of Income and Program Participation (SIPP) collected by the Census Bureau. Scholz et al. (2009) show that if no transfers at all were available 30.3 percent of all families and single-person households (not the same as the total population) would be poor. When all transfers including social insurance, means-tested transfers, and in-kind benefits are taken into account, only 12 percent are poor. However, if one considers only the effects of means-tested cash transfers, the result is much less dramatic: 23.5 percent remain poor after cash transfers, and 22.5 percent after in-kind transfers (Scholz et al. 2009:Table 8.2). These results suggest how important social insurance is to the protection of economic security because it has the greatest relative impact on the poverty rate of families and households.

Work-Based Social Insurance and Benefits

Not only is social insurance the single most effective form of benefit for raising the aged and disabled out of poverty, but it is also the most popular single element in the American safety net (Newport and Saad 2011). Anyone, with a few exceptions, who has worked more than 50 hours in a quarter is required to pay 7.65 percent of his or her income in Social Security taxes, an amount that is withheld and matched by the employer. An individual's Social Security number is a major identifier and signifier of eligibility for a pension at retirement. It is also required for benefits to a disabled person or the minor child of parents who receive Social Security. The official name of this social insurance is Old Age Survivors and Disability Insurance (OASDI). As of 2010 some 54 million people were receiving OASDI, roughly 17 percent of the total U.S. population of 308 million.

In addition to Social Security there are two other major types of social insurance that contribute to family income and are based on an individual's or family member's work history: Workers' Compensation, which first appeared in 1908, and Unemployment Insurance, which was established in 1935 as Title III of the Social Security Act. In addition to these major forms of social insurance that were instituted by the Social Security Act, veterans' benefits and private pensions are also important forms of work-related insurance.

Together these insurance programs constitute a different segment of the safety net to individuals and families, one that undergirds those who have jobs with benefits as well as the dependents of those workers. Given the American belief that everyone should be as self-reliant as possible, it is not surprising that these insurance programs enjoy great legitimacy. The recipients feel they are entitled to benefits that they believe they have earned, even though as a result of inflation and the structure of the Social Security Trust Fund, most people, on average, will have received benefits that are about three times what they paid in contributions. Today, as the baby boom generation approaches retirement, there is widespread concern that the workforce, whose contributions pay for the retirees' benefits, will no longer be large enough to pay the bill for Social Security, Medicare, and Medicaid. Proposals for reform include raising the retirement age so that workers make their contributions over a longer period before receiving benefits.

This brief review describes the purpose of each program and how it has evolved, as well as details of eligibility, size of benefit, and characteristics of the participants. A major concern is the amount being spent for Social Security benefits. In 2008 one-fifth of the entire federal budget went to Social Security (the same amount as spent on national defense) (Facing Up to the Nation's Finances 2011). Various proposals have been brought forward to keep social expenditures from swallowing up resources that are needed for other purposes such as education, national defense, environmental protection, or maintaining transportation and communications. These are important questions of social policy that will be addressed in Chapter 8.

Workers' Compensation

The earliest employment-based social insurance was workmen's compensation which, after its introduction in Europe was first established in the United States in 1908. Although employers originally argued that they were not liable

Table 5.4   Work-Related Social Insurance

Enabling Legislation	Year	Provisions
Workers' Compensation (Federal oversight, state control)	1908	Insurance coverage for injured workers from premiums paid by employers to the states
Social Security (Title II) Old Age Insurance	1935	Employer-employee contributions to retirement pension
Disability Insurance	1935, 1956	Coverage for disability. Trust Fund established and eligibility expanded in 1956
Survivors' Security	1939	Pensions extended to survivors of covered employees
Unemployment Insurance Title III of SSA	1935	Compensation for persons who lose their jobs
Employment Retirement Income Security Act (ERISA)	1974	Authorized Pension Benefit Guarantee Corporation to protect pensions from private employer-based plans
		Safeguards for spouse in disposition of partner's benefits

for a worker's illness or injury because it was the worker's free choice to take a job even though it was dangerous, workers' compensation laws spread rapidly, and by the 1920s they had been adopted in 46 states to insure against loss of income by injured workers. Premiums are paid by employers to the states. Guyton (1999) describes workers' compensation as a major success in American social policy even though it is much narrower in scope than the Americans with Disabilities Act (ADA) of 1990 that was described in Chapter 4. Workers' Compensation protects only against loss of income from work-related injury and not against workplace inaccessibility or discrimination. It has succeeded because the employer is protected from being sued, there is a clear compensation schedule, and the potential costs to the employer of paying for a long-term disability provide a strong incentive to pay costs of the worker's rehabilitation.

Nationwide statistics on eligibility rules, compensation schedules, and rates of usage are hard to describe in general terms since each state is different. Statistics from the state of New Jersey give an idea of the program's scope. In 2011, the maximum compensation per week was $792 for temporary, permanent, or total disability. In 2009, roughly one-fifth of the accidents reported resulted in new claims being filed (New Jersey Department of Labor and Workforce Development 2011).

Old Age Security and Disability Insurance (Title II)

The Social Security Act of 1935 had native roots in the veterans' and mothers' pensions that developed in the late nineteenth century and at the same time built on the idea of social insurance that was introduced by Bismarck in Germany in 1881 as a way to fend off social revolution by industrial workers (Schulz and Binstock 2008). Through the late nineteenth century in the United States, several kinds of pension schemes evolved. Pensions for Civil War veterans and for their dependents were government supported (Skocpol 1992). Others like the railroad pensions and trade union retirement programs laid the groundwork for extending social insurance to all older workers (Schottland 1967).

Congress was galvanized for action in the 1930s by high unemployment, the desperate financial situations of older workers, and grassroots social protests such as the Townsend movement that called for government stipends for persons age 65 and over. President Roosevelt, however, resisted a program based on handouts alone and insisted that workers also contribute to the government-run fund financed by employers that would pay monthly benefits after a required period of work.

Social Security Title II, the Old Age Insurance program, which began in 1935, includes three major insurance-based programs—Old Age Insurance,

Disability and Survivors' Insurance. The first two programs were expanded in 1939 to include survivors of retired workers, and in 1957 to benefit persons with disabilities whether or not they had ever been employed. (Another major program within Social Security is Title III, Unemployment Compensation, which, in addition to providing benefits to the unemployed worker, also serves the general social welfare during periods of economic downturn and high unemployment, as indicated in Table 5.4.)

Even by the 1940s, the number of workers covered by Social Security was still very limited. In 1950, however, Old Age Insurance was expanded to include self-employed, agricultural, and domestic workers. (My father, a self-employed small businessman, enrolled himself at that time and was very glad that he had when he needed Medicare coverage later on.) The Disability Insurance Trust Fund was created in 1956 to cover workers who became disabled prior to retirement. Between 1970 and 2010 the number of persons receiving Old Age and Survivors Insurance almost doubled, to 44 million, and constituted 14 percent of the population. The number of disabled workers and their dependents receiving Disability Insurance nearly quadrupled to just over 10 million, or roughly 3 percent of the whole population (Social Security Online 2011a). In January 2012 the average monthly Social Security Benefit in the United States for all retired workers was $1,229 and the maximum monthly benefit for a worker retiring at age 65 was $2,513 (U.S. Social Security Administration 2011).

Unemployment Insurance

Title III of the Social Security Act of 1935 addresses the problems of income loss when a person is unemployed. Unemployment Insurance is not a true social insurance programs since the funds to pay benefits do not come from the worker's previous earnings but from employer contributions. A worker who loses a job in a covered occupation through no fault of his own receives income for only a limited length of time and is required to be looking for a job and be ready to accept suitable work. Given these limitations, unemployment insurance is more like an income maintenance or assistance program than an entitlement like Social Security.

Of the unemployed, only about one-third receive unemployment benefits because of the gap between the official definition of eligibility for unemployment insurance and the worker's actual circumstance of not having worked during the past week or for the number of weeks required. Those among the unemployed who do not receive benefits have either voluntarily left their jobs, are no longer looking for work, or have exhausted their benefits.

During the recession of 2008–2010, the Census Bureau observed in its Current Population Surveys that the numbers of workers experiencing long periods of unemployment were at unprecedented levels so that in 2011 the CPS began recording length of unemployment that lasted beyond two years and up to five years. Also in the fall of 2010, the U.S. Congress extended until January 2012 the program of Emergency Unemployment Compensation to provide a full additional year of benefits in states with unemployment rates of 8.5 percent or higher (Isaacs and Whittaker 2011). These benefits were again extended in February 2012 along with a temporary cut in payroll taxes. The new legislation has been hailed as a historic modernization of the unemployment insurance (UI) system because it allows states to use UI money for programs that help to move the jobless back into the workforce by such means as offering employers wage subsidies for taking on and retraining jobless workers (Lowrey 2012).

Although authorized by the Social Security Act, Title III is administered by the Department of Labor. As a sign of the overall state of the economy, unemployment is measured by the number of claims filed. The number varies seasonally and with occupational sector and geographic location. The highest rates of unemployment are typically found in construction (8.9 percent), professions and business (6.5 percent), and the leisure industry (7.6 percent); the lowest rates in information, education and health, and self-employment (all under 3 percent) (Dobelstein 2009:111–112). Although many once believed that unemployment could never go much lower than 5 percent, by 2002 the rate had dropped to 3.5 percent. On the other hand, in the recession of 2008–2010, it reached as high as 10 percent.

Unemployment benefits coverage and amounts. Although benefit coverage and amounts vary by state, federal rules require earnings of at least $1,500 during any calendar quarter or paid work for at least one day a week for 20 weeks in the previous year in order for the worker to be insured. The rules are somewhat different for agriculture and domestic workers. In general unemployment insurance replaces between 50 percent and 70 percent of the individual's average weekly pretax wages up to a predetermined maximum that varies by state. The basic benefit lasts 26 weeks. That can be extended another 13 weeks when the unemployment rate has risen to 6 percent. Further temporary extensions are authorized by Congress when unemployment is unusually high and persistent, as in the recent past. The U.S. average weekly benefit in 2011 was $297 but ranged from $395 in New Jersey to $127 in West Virginia (Employment and Training Administration 2011). Dobelstein (2009) points out that many of the benefits are at poverty level so that a person working at $10 an hour for a 30-hour week is able to earn more than the UI benefit provides.

Employer-Sponsored Pensions (ERISA)

The major development of pension coverage outside of Social Security was the growth of employer-sponsored pensions, which were either wholly paid for by employers or jointly by employer and employee. In addition to private employers, government workers and the military are also covered by pensions other than Social Security. In 1974 the Employment Retirement Income Security Act (ERISA) was passed to safeguard large "defined benefit" pension funds as well as protect the rights of a spouse in the disposition of a partner's benefits.

Alongside Social Security, a variety of pension programs were developed by employers. Initially, many of these were defined benefit plans, where employers contributed to workers' retirement without requiring an employee match. Now most are defined contribution plans. Although employers had set up these plans partly out of concern for their workers' future, they also used them to make it easier to lay off workers knowing they had been promised a pension (Schulz and Binstock 2008). Yet, until recently, workers have actually been retiring at earlier ages if they have the means to do so (the pension programs have made this possible), and employers' incentives to retire workers early make it difficult to delay retirement until a worker is older (Schulz and Binstock 2008).

Adequacy of Income in Retirement

To maintain a middle-class status in old age, it is desirable to have a pension *and* personal assets *in addition* to Social Security. Yet a significant portion of the elderly population has no private pension and only meager personal savings. Although almost half of non-Hispanics (46 percent) have retirement accounts, only one-third of the Hispanic households do. A large proportion of minority elders have to rely on a "single pillar" of retirement income (R. Angel and Angel 2006). Their economic situation is the result of many earlier life experiences such as poor education, low-income jobs, early marriage, and many children (Crown 2001). The economic situation of older people in any cohort is shaped by the conditions in which they grew up, worked, and entered their retirement years. Between 1951 and 2001, the overall income, on average, of those 65 years and older increased (Holden and Hatcher 2006). A current question concerns whether such improvement will continue, given the lower savings rate of younger cohorts and the likely negative impact of the recession of 2008–2010 on the retirement incomes of the baby boom generation.

Making Work Pay

The earliest features of the American safety net were designed to protect poor families and children, retirees, the disabled, and the unemployed. Just as important to family security and the main working population, however, are the state of the overall economy and the structure of the labor market. Rebecca Blank (2009:86), a leading labor economist, has stated that ". . . the best policy we can pursue for the poor is to keep unemployment low and the economy strong." That is also true for those who are not poor. Policies that keep the economy strong such as introducing a government stimulus, maintaining a lower interest rate, or investment in research and innovation fall outside the scope of family policy. But labor-related policies such as protection of collective bargaining, raising the minimum wage, and investment in job readiness have very clear connections to workers' capacity to earn an adequate income for their families.

This section reviews three main types of labor-related policy that affect family income security. In the 1930s the right of workers to organize and bargain collectively was vigorously contested, and Congress passed legislation to protect that right. The adoption of wage and hours legislation also strengthened workers' power. Since the 1960s, a different kind of program has come to the fore that is aimed at raising the skill levels and job readiness of unemployed or low-wage workers. Significantly, the labor-rights policies of the 1930s were particularly relevant to male workers. But as the gender revolution took hold with two-earner families and female-headed families becoming more common, women increasingly became the objects of "manpower" development.

More recently, other strategies for improving economic security have come to the fore with attempts to improve the remuneration of occupations in the service sector and efforts to create more "good" jobs. But with the recession of 2008–2010, there has been stiff opposition to raising wages and providing adequate benefits for service positions. Nor does the idea of creating more good jobs hold much promise for low-wage workers whose skills and education fall woefully short of the qualifications that such jobs require.

In fact, every one of the major labor-related policies that affect family economic security is being contested in light of the changing economy and the changing demographics of the American population. Big government deficits and the aging of the baby boomers have called into question the right to collective bargaining of public unions of employees of cities, states, and the federal government. The growth in less well-educated immigrant and minority populations and their heavy concentration in low-paying service occupations have raised the question of whether employee training will ever be strong and continuous enough to improve the security of low-income families. Thus the settled policies of the past need to be reexamined for what new policies may be more effective in securing the safety net of the future.

Labor Relations, Collective Bargaining, and Wage Improvement

Following the revolution in labor relations that came with the New Deal, American workers in mining, auto, and other industries experienced long-sought improvements in their wages, working conditions, and job security. As a girl during the 1940s I remember visiting my Aunt Lillie in Akron, Ohio, when we had Sunday dinners with several of my uncles, one of whom was a member of the United Rubber Workers Union at Goodyear Tire and Rubber. All three of these uncles had grown up in a mining town in western Pennsylvania. Unlike my father, a small businessman who was unsympathetic to labor unions, my uncles were all pro-union and sang the praises of John L. Lewis of the United Mine Workers who had fought for better wages and safer working conditions in the coal mines.

Beginning in 1935, The National Relations Labor Act established rights of workers to organize and bargain collectively with employers over wages and benefits, including the right to strike if their demands were not met. With this legislation American manufacturing workers gained tremendous new power to improve their economic situation. At the end of World War II, roughly one-fifth of all workers in the private sector were unionized. From 1960, when union membership stood at about a third of all workers in the civilian labor force and manufacturing jobs were beginning to be lost to technological improvement and foreign competition, there began a slow decline in union membership so that in 2008 only 7.6 percent of private sector employees were unionized. This contrasted with the steady rise in unionization of public sector employees to 36.8 percent in 2008 (Reynolds 2009). Even in their weakened state, unions still have a very strong and positive effect on wages. One estimate is that between 2004 and 2007, comparing unionized and nonunionized workers in each occupation across the United States, union workers were making 11.3 percent more than nonunion workers (Madland and Walter 2009).

Adoption in 1938 of the Fair Labor Standards Act established $.25 as the minimum hourly wage and 40 hours as the standard workweek. Although 40 hours is still the standard workweek for many occupations with overtime pay available for extra hours, the minimum wage has been raised a number of times, most recently in 2009 to $7.25 per hour.

There is increasing concern that the minimum wage is nowhere near adequate to provide the necessities of living for a single person or a family. One estimate is that a single-earner family with one preschool and one school-aged child needs at least $40,000 a year or the equivalent of $19.28 an hour (Kahne and Mabel 2010). A recent calculation by Wider Opportunities for Women estimates that a single worker with two young children needs $57,756 a year or just over $27 an hour to pay for housing, utilities, food, transportation, personal and household expenses, health care, childcare, savings, and taxes. To close the gap between what they actually earn and what is needed for economic security, families go to food pantries and do without savings and other necessities in order to make ends meet (Rich 2011). Yet opponents of raising the minimum wage continue to argue that higher costs will hurt business. The advocates, on the other hand, show that when wages increase, higher productivity also results which can provide the income for consumer expenditures that make up at least 70 percent of the GDP (Madland and Walter 2009). This is a principle that automaker Henry Ford understood very well: Workers needed to be paid high enough wages so that they could afford to *buy* the cars they made.

Employee Development and Training

As the nation became aware in the early 1960s that one-fifth of the American population were poor, the Manpower and Development Training Act was passed in 1962 to address the loss of higher-paying manufacturing jobs and the rise in relative importance of the lower-wage service economy. Efforts to improve the economic situation of workers moved from a focus on job creation to one on training. The Economic Opportunity Act of 1964 and the War on Poverty emphasized federal spending for education and training and at the same time also worked to lessen racial and gender discrimination. By offering education, training, and job placement the Office of Economic Opportunity (OEO) aimed to help people find higher-paying jobs rather than to seek cash assistance. In the next two decades the basic idea of employee training went through many revisions. The Work Incentive (WIN) program of 1967 provided a work program for welfare mothers. The Comprehensive Employment and Training Act (CETA) of 1973 gave assistance to unemployed and underemployed persons through employment counseling, classes, and on-the-job training as well as by authorizing public service employment in areas of high unemployment. The Job Training Partnership Act (JTPA) of 1982 continued the Job Corps and summer youth employment programs that had begun earlier. The Family Support Act (FSA) of 1988 created a JOBS program (Job Opportunities and Basic Skills) to revise the AFDC program to emphasize

Table 5.5 Policies for Making Work Pay

Enabling Legislation	Year	Provisions
Labor Unions and Collective Bargaining		
National Labor Relations Act	1935	Protected workers' right to organize and bargain collectively
Wage and Hour Legislation		
Fair Labor Standards Act	1938	Set standard workweek at 40 hours and minimum wage at $.25 per hour
Minimum-wage law amendments	2007	Set minimum wage at $7.25 per hour after July 2009
Manpower Development		
Manpower Development and Training Act	1962	Federal funding for employee development and training
Economic Opportunity Act (War on Poverty)	1964	Services for help to find jobs: vocational education, job placement
WIN (Work Incentive) program)	1967	Work for welfare mothers
Comprehensive Employment and Training (CETA)	1973	Assistance for unemployed, or underemployed through training and job placement
Job Training Partnership Act (JTPA)	1982	Continuation of Job Corps, Summer Youth Employment, etc.
Family Support Act (FSA) JOBS Program, Title IV-F of SSA	1988	Employment and training for people on public assistance
Workplace Investment Act (WIA)	1998	Replaced JTPA. One-Stop Career Centers for access to training programs and job openings

work, child support, and family benefits and thereby assist needy children by helping their parents to obtain education, training, and the employment needed to avoid long-term welfare dependence. Many of these ideas were incorporated in the welfare reform of 1996 and its rules requiring work effort by needy families receiving transitional assistance (TANF). Most recently the Workplace Investment Act (WIA) of 1998 replaced JTPA with the creation of One-Stop Centers for access to training programs and job openings.

In my state of Massachusetts, the One-Stop Career Centers established under the Workplace Investment Act are enjoying some success. In 2010, the

Massachusetts Workforce Agency reported that in the second quarter of fiscal year 2011 the Career Centers had served about 8,000 employers and more than 136,000 job seekers. Average earnings of job seekers and veterans either held steady or improved after they exited the programs. The only disappointing result was the six-month earnings of older youth after exit that reached just 71 percent of the state goal (Massachusetts Workforce Development System 2011). (See Table 5.5.)

Other reports on employer training are less encouraging. One key problem is that the jobs available may not give access to needed benefits such as assistance with health insurance or childcare costs. An important barrier to higher pay is the low level of basic skills in reading and math that has been reported among single mothers who are trying to leave the welfare rolls. According to Seccombe (2011), fully one-third of test-takers are unable to pass the standard test that measures basic reading and quantitative skills. Many have not finished high school and are therefore unable to succeed in the specialized courses of community colleges that are geared to training in fields where the job openings exist. Partly as a result of reports of superficial training such as learning how to write a resume or respond to a job interview, there is a general perception that workforce development programs are not effective. Holzer (2009) attributes the problem to a combination of concerns. One question is whether labor demand is sufficient to place all the newly trained workers in jobs. Another issue concerns the influence of global competition and the hiring of immigrants for the job openings that do occur. Finally, it is argued that employment and training for these jobs needs to begin in earlier school years, not as adults. Holzer, however, believes that some of the problem is related to the decline in public funding for workforce development over the past 35 years. But in fact, the evidence from a five-year evaluation of funds spent for on-the-job training showed that for every dollar spent on training, earnings were doubled. So Holzer concludes that higher spending under the Workplace Investment Act is clearly warranted.

New Strategies: One-Stops, Community Colleges, and Workplace Supports

The newest strategies for making work pay continue to build on the basic idea of improving human capital through training and on-the-job experience. But several new factors have been added. Kahne and Mabel (2010) outline three major program improvements that are already being tried, although their adoption is still limited. The first idea is to use workplace intermediaries to make a better match between local employers' needs and the local labor supply of job seekers. The second strategy is to create specific training programs in community colleges that prepare workers for the jobs where they are needed. The third important addition is to provide help to workers in the form of health insurance, childcare, or transportation that in effect subsidize the worker's income.

One-Stops: Workplace intermediaries. Under the Workplace Investment Act of 1998 there are already networks of local One-Stop Career Centers at the state level. These centers bring together information about the needs of local employers and local job seekers. The most effective centers typically provide four types of service: (1) listing of job opportunities with local employers in high-level wage sectors, (2) training in basic job readiness and specific skills, (3) counseling on how to manage competing job and family responsibilities, and (4) advice on available work supports such as the Earned Income Tax Credit (EITC), affordable health insurance, and childcare subsidies (Kahne and Mabel 2010).

Holzer (2009:316) provides several examples that tell us what these One-Stop Centers look like. Here is his description of the Wisconsin Regional Training Partnership (WRTP):

> WRTP is a nonprofit association of businesses and unions that has served employers, employees, job seekers, and unions in the Milwaukee area since 1996.
>
> WRTP works in several industries including manufacturing, healthcare, construction, and hospitality. Firms that join WRTP agree to develop education and training programs on-site or at community colleges and provide a payroll contribution. In return, they receive technical assistance to strengthen technology and workplace practices, improve the skills of incumbent workers, and recruit and train new workers. Nearly 100 employers with about 60,000 workers participate.

Community college programs. Training, counseling, and advice on assistance are very often located in a community college. Shoreline Community College in Shoreline, Washington, for example, has a workforce program that lists three areas of assistance: Job Skills Training, High Wage/High Demand Job Training, and Basic Education. The Job Skills Training provides access to over 52 career training programs that "focus on building, strengthening, and maintaining a solid set of skills marketable to industry-specific jobs" (Shoreline Community College 2011). The High Wage/High Demand Job Skills Training offers certificates requiring 11 to 33 weeks for completion, ranging from Nursing Assistant Certificate (NAC) and Bilingual Office Assistant to Business Software Applications, Automotive, and Manufacturing. The third program is Basic Education, which helps students improve their fundamental skills in literacy and in identifying their interests and abilities while also giving them the opportunity to earn a GED. To be eligible one must be a parent of a child age 18 or younger and be receiving Transitional Assistance for Needy Families (TANF).

Work supports for job seekers. Kahne and Mabel (2010) report that along with matching up training of workers with the job openings that exist, an essential factor in promoting job retention and wage improvement is provision of supportive services and benefits including higher wage work that keeps individuals engaged and motivated to complete their training and stay connected to the labor market. These work supports include the Earned Income Tax Credit, food stamps, affordable health care, and childcare subsidies. Yet less than half the workers who are eligible for these benefits are using them, probably because of the difficult application process or stigmatization of applying for help through the local welfare office. Others may be unaware of what is available and still others may be undocumented immigrants. Yet one estimate is that in many locations families would double their household income if they took advantage of the full range of the supports.

Income Packaging

What the new policies for low-wage and unemployed workers tell us is that self-sufficiency of income is often based on what Lee Rainwater, Martin Rein, and Joseph Schwartz (1986) long ago termed "income packaging." The modern family that derives adequate income from only one source is a rarity today. Instead, for the middle class, the "income package" may include the earnings of husband and wife, tax breaks for a house mortgage, subsidies for home energy improvements, employee benefits from a steady job, mileage costs for travel, and the like. For retirees, the ideal combination is Social Security, a private pension, interest on savings and capital appreciation, and possibly some earnings from part-time work. For the low-wage worker, the subsidies are likely to be for childcare, affordable housing, and the Earned Income Tax Credit. No matter which group, the basic principle is the same: not to depend for all one's income on only one source. Not only is the total more likely to be greater when combining several income sources, but hardship is less likely if one earner loses a job or the economy takes a downturn.

Policies for a Family-Friendly Workplace

Work–family flexibility is the most recent addition to the policy arsenal for family security. The ultimate goal is to integrate breadwinning and caregiving more smoothly so that both are optimized and neither function has to be sacrificed to the other. Various schemes have been proposed: cafeteria benefit plans, flexible working hours and places of work, family leave, job sharing and job rotation, childcare for working parents, and flexible scheduling over the life course.

Unlike most antipoverty and wage and benefit programs, work–family policies are not so much directed to making family income adequate as to making work possible while also caring for a family. Work–family policies are intended to respond to a new situation under the sun. Long gone are the small cottage industries and local farming operations that accomplished food production, manufacture, and family care under the same roof. Household production and small farms have been replaced by thousands of consumption-oriented suburban homes and city apartments located far from the fields of food supply and far from the offices and factories that provide a living.

In a post-industrial society modern families and employers and governments have to invent new institutional arrangements that will simultaneously promote economic production, family caregiving, and national goals of prosperity and well-being. Over the last four decades (since the appearance of the women's movement in the 1970s) the visionaries who have imagined how to accomplish work, caring, economic growth, and population renewal have proposed a series of "work–family" policies to facilitate the new institutional arrangements. The policies and programs are of four main types:

1. Equal employment opportunity legislation

2. Employer-provided benefit plans

3. Programs for dependent care

4. Cultural change in work-and-family gender roles

These innovations have been fueled in all advanced industrial societies by what I term "the changing gender contract," namely, the growing belief that women and men have equal rights and are capable of similar work and family responsibilities (Giele 2006). In the following section, I group work–family policies by major type and suggest likely future directions. The basic narrative is one of first establishing the general principle of work–family integration or balance (Kanter 1977) and then implementing it to encompass more people and a larger segment of economic and family life.

Much has been made of the fact that U.S. work–family policies are far less generous and cover a much smaller range of benefits and opportunities for flexibility than are available in other advanced industrial societies. For example, publicly funded childcare for working parents is the norm in Canada, England, France, and Sweden (Waldfogel 2009). The usual reason given for the outlier position of the United States is the strong American belief in independent solutions rather than provision by a welfare state. However, Stebbins (2001) notes another factor, which is the historical evolution of the American housewife's role. In the 1840s, middle-class women felt it a privilege to focus on care of their homes and families while their husbands did the breadwinning. This division of labor gave them an autonomous sphere of activity and expressed greater equality between the sexes than was known in the patriarchal family of an earlier era. Stebbins suggests that this association of women's domestic role with middle-class women's autonomy and privilege left a legacy that later worked against acceptance of organized childcare. Middle-class mothers thought such arrangements inferior to their own care because they associated day care with provisions for poor working-class children whose employed mothers were unable to give them attentive supervision. Yet despite this history, a growing tide of married women entered the labor force during the 1950s and 1960s and changed the rationale for childcare to one that extended the potential for combining work and family responsibilities to all women. A new feminist consciousness helped to fuel a movement to change the circumstances and daily schedules of workers and parents.

Equal Opportunity Legislation

Along with the massive post-war entry of married women into the paid labor force, broad cultural changes were taking place in attitudes toward women and minorities. Even as economists were explaining the lower pay of women and blacks on the basis of differences in skills and human capital, overcrowding into segregated occupations, or employers' "tastes" (Wolff 2009), legal remedies were being promulgated to prevent discrimination and differential treatment of women and men. The Equal Pay Act of 1963 prohibited unequal pay for similar or equal work. Title VII of the Civil Rights Act of 1964 outlawed wage discrimination between men and women in firms of 15 or more employees. The Equal Employment Opportunities Commission (EEOC) was established to investigate and punish violators.

Equal rights legislation extended protection to women in areas beyond the reach of Title VII. Executive Order 11246 of 1968 prohibited discrimination in employment (hiring, salaries, promotion, and benefits) in any institution with federal contracts exceeding $10,000. Title IX of the Higher Education Act of 1972 and the Women's Educational Equity Act of 1974 banned discrimination on the basis of sex in admissions, recruitment, curriculum, and sports. The Pregnancy Discrimination Act (PDA) of 1978 required that pregnant women receive work-related disability coverage equal to that received by men. This act became an important precedent for activists'

Table 5.6 Equal Rights Legislation in Employment[1]

Enactment	Year	Provisions
Equal Pay Act	1963	Equal pay for equal work
Civil Rights Act, Title VII	1964	Outlawed wage discrimination by sex and race
Executive Order 11246	1968	Equal protection for employment (hiring, salaries, promotion, and benefits in institutions with federal contracts)
Higher Education Act, Title IX	1972	Banned sex discrimination in admissions, recruitment, curriculum, and sports
Women's Educational Equity Act	1974	
Pregnancy Disability Act (PDA)	1978	Provided nonwork-related disability coverage to pregnant women
Family and Medical Leave Act (FMLA)	1993	Up to 12 weeks unpaid leave to care for self, newborn or adopted child, or family member

[1]For a more detailed account of the legislation affecting gender equality, see Giele (1978: Table 1, Table 12); and Stebbins (2001: 154-159).

efforts that later resulted in the Family and Medical Leave Act (FMLA) of 1993 (Wexler 1997). The FMLA provides for up to 12 weeks unpaid leave for a worker's own illness or for care of a family member. Workers are eligible if they have worked at least one year in a firm with 50 or more employees (Stebbins 2001:158). Although the law guarantees the right to return to the same or a comparable job following the leave, few low-paid employees are able to afford time off that is unpaid.

These legal landmarks (listed in Table 5.6) are an obvious sign of changes in attitudes toward the work and caregiving capacity of women and men. But from a family policy standpoint they also signify something more. Taken together, the equal opportunity laws represent a fundamental rationale underpinning government policies on work and family. They express society's interest in supporting those who bear and rear children and care for the sick or disabled. As economists Blau, Ferber, and Winkler (2010:330) observe, "[T]he nation also benefits when children grow up to be healthier, better educated, and better trained adults." Those children will be more productive, will contribute more as taxpayers, and will be less likely to become a public burden.

Employee Benefit Plans

Implicit in any leave policy is the idea that a worker has a personal or family life that exists outside of work. The purpose of a leave is to achieve some sort of boundary regulation or reconciliation between the work and family spheres. For over a century leading up to the enactment of the Pregnancy Disability Act in 1978 and the Family and Medical Leave Act in 1993 and other antidiscrimination rules, the connection between work and family was based on the idea that a worker supports not only himself but also members of his family. The same was true for the women factory workers who came off the New England farms in the 1840s and 1850s to work in the Lowell textile mills and sent home much-needed cash to their families. Gradually, from the late nineteenth century up to the present, employers added fringe benefits which in many cases covered family members as well as the worker. Schottland (1967), in his comprehensive review of early employment benefit programs for the family, cites the railroad retirement plans as early examples of income maintenance as distinct from federal or state assistance or private insurance. I remember my father's elderly cousin Katie, born in Switzerland, and the widow of a retired railroad employee, who in the late 1940s was able to ride the trains between Ohio and Pennsylvania with a nominal fare because her husband had been a railroad employee.

Today, employee benefit plans, while having expanded considerably over the last 50 years, still constitute only a partial segment of the economic safety net and have a large voluntary component that is sensitive to general economic conditions of growth or recession. Generous benefits enable greater flexibility between work and family demands, but Blau and colleagues (2010) point out that there are both positive and negative consequences for the employer. On one hand, the employer who provides fringe benefits may ensure high morale and low turnover and rehiring costs. But on the other hand, generous benefits may attract those employees who self-select because of their greater need and thereby drive up costs. Cancian and Danziger (2009) further note that low-wage workers are less likely to be covered by fringe benefits such as health insurance, sick leave, and vacation days. Temporary or part-time employees frequently have no eligibility at all.

Employee benefit coverage. There is a gap between the ideal benefit packages that work–family advocates call for and what employers actually provide. Cancian and Danziger (2009) point out that single parents need more help such as flexible schedules and child care and ideally would get 8 to 12 weeks of paid parental leave to cope with the added challenges of long commutes, unsafe neighborhoods, and the lack of wages to cover market substitutes for childcare and prepared meals. They argue that at a minimum a subsidized payroll tax operated like social insurance would provide for two weeks annual paid care for family illnesses and other family responsibilities as well as the right of parents to request part-time work or flexible hours.

In fact, the 100 best companies regularly listed in *Working Mother* magazine or *Businessweek* make available part-time work and job sharing along with recognition that a job carries intrinsic as well as extrinsic rewards. Telecommuting is also another attractive alternative in that it permits greater flexibility of working hours (Stebbins 2001). But as shown in Table 5.7, fewer than 6 percent of all employers offered a flexible workplace in 2009 (Employee Benefit Research Institute 2010a).

Along with access to flexible scheduling, the most attractive packages offer a choice of benefits in what is known as "cafeteria plans." For example, in a two-earner couple where one member already has health insurance covering the family, the other might choose childcare benefits or contributions to a pension fund (Blau et al. 2010). Information and referral is another popular benefit provided by many employers to help workers find childcare or other needed services. But how the costs of such benefits as health insurance, dependent care, vacations, or pensions are paid for does not have an obvious answer. Employers understandably want to keep costs and benefits low enough to make their business profitable. For example, in the case of the automakers in 2009, it was clear that high "legacy" costs of employees' health and retirement insurance and overtime pay could make American cars unprofitable in comparison with foreign cars with their lower labor costs. In order to avoid a potential backlash of the childless against parents who receive a childcare benefit, another question may be how to provide benefits for childless couples that ensure equivalency of benefits offered to couples with children. The potential for resentment may decrease as society learns to view family obligations as necessary to national well-being and not solely a women's or a parents' issue (Stebbins 2001:57–58). Also, as society ages and single people take care of aging relatives, dependent care benefits can serve their interests as well.

Ruhm (2005) gives some idea of how many employees are actually covered by various types of employee benefits. He estimates that approximately one-half of all workers are covered by the FMLA. Of leaves granted, almost half are for the worker's own health problems, less than one-fifth for maternity or paternity leave, and the rest for care of sick children (Wertheimer et al. 2005). Other countries are much more generous; most provide two to three months paid maternity leave. In the United States, roughly 90 percent of firms with more than 100 employees provide paid holidays and vacation; and two-thirds provide paid sick leave. Less than one-quarter provide paid parental leave. Among firms with fewer than 100 employees, the proportion providing paid holidays and vacations is slightly lower (approximately 85 percent) and roughly one-half give paid sick leave (Ruhm 2005). Wertheimer and colleagues (2005), however, point out that only 12 percent of all establishments are covered by the FMLA statute (presumably because so many have fewer than 50 employees or fewer workers with 1,250 hours of work in the previous year). Nonetheless, one-third of these smaller firms offer full FMLA benefits, and most provide at least partial benefits. The latest data for 2009 show about 85 percent of large establishments have paid holidays and vacations; 72 percent, paid sick leave; 63 percent, health insurance for full-time and part-time employees; 48 percent, wellness plans; 15 percent, childcare benefits; and 6 percent, a flexible workplace. The corresponding percentages for small private establishments are smaller, while state and local governments are similar to small firms with respect to paid holidays and vacations. But they are more generous in provision of paid sick leave, wellness programs, and childcare (as shown in Table 5.7).

Five states (California, Hawaii, New Jersey, New York, and Rhode Island) pay maternity leaves with temporary disability insurance (TDI). Some states have enacted paid parental leave; however, coverage is lower at lower income levels (one-fourth of those with incomes under $10,000 have paid parental leave compared with four-fifths of those with incomes over $75,000). From

Table 5.7 Employee Benefits in Private Establishments and State and Local Governments (in percentages), 2009[2]

Employee Benefit Program	Medium and Large Private Firms	Small Private Firms	State and Local Governments
Paid holidays	86	69	75
Paid vacation	86	71	67
Paid sick leave	72	52	98
Health insurance	63	42	83
Employee assistance	68	24	54
Wellness programs	48	12	54
Childcare	15	3	14
Flexible workplace	6	3	5

[2]*Source:* Employee Benefit Research Institute (2010a), Tables 4.1b, 4.1c, and 4.1d.

a policy standpoint, parental leave has important social benefits that improve maternal and child health by lowering infant mortality and increasing the likelihood of well-baby visits and immunizations (Waldfogel 2009).

Future trends. While considerable progress has occurred over the past half century in expanding employee benefits, both progressive and regressive trends have been at work. A sign of expansion has been the 2010 Affordable Care Act for health care reform, which relies heavily on health insurance provided through an employer (as does the Massachusetts plan for universal health coverage that was created in 2006). Yet at the same time, rising benefit costs put pressure on employers to find ways that will reduce their labor costs. The result may be greater reliance on part-time and temporary positions that do not carry the same level of benefits. The Employee Benefits Research Institute (2010b) finds that access to employer-provided health insurance for Medicare-eligible retirees decreased from over 40 percent in 1993 to around 25 percent in 2009.

Childcare

Although benefits for care of another dependent family member other than a child are available in a few benefit packages, by far the greatest interest and attention has gone to coverage of childcare costs. The Nordic and European continental countries generally cover costs of preschool childcare through their social welfare systems. Canada, the United Kingdom, and the United States typically provide care through private day care centers and family day care (Gornick and Meyers 2003).

Few people realize that publicly supported childcare in war industries was authorized for a brief period during World War II by the Lanham Act; but the new centers were quietly dismantled after the war (Michel 1999). Further development of the American childcare system did not take off again until the 1960s and 1970s when more mothers of young children went into the labor force. Beginning in the 1960s, sporadic grassroots efforts in universities, hospitals, and industry brought forth pilot programs that eventually became permanent. Nursery schools sprouted in church basements, and for-profit franchises such as Kinder Care grew alongside family day care in private homes (Francis 1992; Hayes et al. 1990). By 2006 almost half of all children under 15 were in the care of a parent or a relative, nearly a quarter were in an organized care facility, and the rest were almost evenly divided between care by nonrelatives such as family day care and other arrangements including self-care (U.S. Department of Health and Human Services 2007).

Enabling legislation. Alongside growth of this patchwork system, a number of legislative efforts have been made to establish a comprehensive public system (as shown in Table 5.8). A famous failure was that of the Comprehensive Child Care Act of 1973, which was passed by Congress but vetoed by President Nixon as threatening to bring about a Soviet style of collectivized childrearing to the United States. Since that time the main progress in development of childcare programs has been the elaboration of payment mechanisms that help working families cover the cost of childcare. A small percentage of employee benefits programs now give coverage for childcare,

Table 5.8   Major Federal Legislation on Child and Dependent Care[3]

Legislation	Year	Provisions
Title V, Social Security Act	1935	Grants-in-aid to public welfare agencies for childcare
Lanham Act	1941	Federal funds for childcare for working mothers in war-time industries
Economic Opportunity Amendments	1966	Authorized Head Start
Tax Refund Act	1976	Dependent Care Tax Credit (treated childcare as a work-related rather than personal expense)
Social Services Block Grant (SSBG) of Title XX of SSA	1981	Authorized subsidies for child care for low income families
Title V, Child Care Omnibus Budget Reconciliation Act	1990	Grants to the states for funding child care assistance
Child Care Development Block Grant Act (CCDBG) (Section 418 of Social Security Act)	1990	Access to subsidies for employed parents with children age 13 and younger
Personal Responsibility and Work Opportunity Reconciliation Act (PRWORA)	1996	Childcare assistance for employed parents receiving Transitional Assistance for Needy Families (TANF)
American Recovery and Reinvestment Act	2009	Grants to states for childcare assistance for low-income families and to parents trying to achieve independence from public assistance

[3]See Gornick and Meyers (2003); NCCIC (2010); Stebbins (2001); and Waldfogel (2009).

but the most important innovation was the Tax Refund Act of 1976 which extended the Dependent Care Tax Credit to work-related costs of childcare. In 1981, dependent care became a nontaxable benefit that can be used for childcare or dependent care (Stebbins 2001). Also in 1981, the Social Services Block Grant authorized means-tested subsidies for low-income parents (Gornick and Meyers 2003:Figure 7.1). In 1990 Title V of the federal budget reconciliation provided grants for funding childcare assistance. In addition, the Comprehensive Child and Development Block Grant provides a means-tested subsidy to parents for care of children under 18; TANF does the same for employed parents.

Who uses childcare? The answer depends on the demographics of mothers' employment, whether the care is paid or unpaid, and the amount of subsidy or income available to pay for the care. As of 2007, two-thirds of all mothers with children under age 18 were employed, and over half of mothers with children under age 3. But many fewer were employed full time—just over half of all mothers with children under 18 and two-fifths of those with children under 3 (Blau et al. 2010). Ruhm (2005) reports that 60 percent of childcare for preschool-age children is provided by nonimmediate family and 39 percent of that care is free, a good portion of it provided by a relative or a grandparent. The cost burden, however, varies by income and is at its heaviest at the lowest income levels, which is roughly 20 percent of family income for the lowest decile compared with less than 1 percent for the top decile.

Suggestions for reform. Given the uneven coverage and quality of the American childcare system, there are many worthy ideas for reform that are related to access, affordability, and quality. Ideas for broadening access range from making prekindergarten for 3- and 4-year-olds universal to lengthening the school day and the school year for the benefit of working parents. Closely related to access is affordability, and suggestions for reform include broadening eligibility for childcare subsidies and making the tax credit refundable in cash. In fact, it appears that access and affordability improved dramatically between 1997 and 2006 when spending on subsidized childcare rose from $5.3 to $12.0 billion. Still, only about one-third of all eligible parents receive childcare subsidies (Blank 2009). Waldfogel (2009) suggests guaranteeing assistance to families who are up to 200 percent of the poverty line (roughly $43,000 for a family of four in 2007) (U.S. Census Bureau 2010b). To improve quality, better pay for teachers is needed to reward better preparation and prevent high turnover. Gornick and Meyers (2003) suggest that one avenue to quality assurance is direct public oversight and consistent standards. Not only does a good childcare system help working parents, but it also lays a foundation for success in school and a productive workforce in the next generation.

Culture Change in Work-and-Family Gender Roles

Although the official statistics on employee benefits as shown in Table 5.7 reveal that 6 percent or fewer employers offer some sort of flexible scheduling, over 70 percent typically offer paid vacations, holidays, and sick days. Certainly there appears to be much more talk about the value of flexible schedules than one would expect if only a tiny minority of workers were involved. In fact, the picture is quite complicated. Blau et al. (2010) report that 30 percent of workers have flexible schedules and that the latest statistics available show that only 60 percent of employees work a standard Monday through Friday, 9-to-5 schedule. In 2007, 25 percent of employed women and 11 percent of employed men worked less than 35 hours. In 2004 an estimated 15 percent of all workers did work for their primary job from their own home (Blau et al. 2010). Waldfogel (2009) reports that between 1992 and 2002 workers with access to flextime rose from 29 percent to 43 percent, although low-income workers still had less access than middle and higher income workers. To assess where American family policy currently stands with respect to flexible schedules, it is necessary to review: (1) the evidence on the prevalence of work–family conflict versus work–family balance, (2) the arguments for and against flexibility, and (3) ideas for policy reform.

Work–family conflict versus work–family balance. It is perhaps not surprising that at the same time more mothers of young children are in the labor force, thereby suggesting that work–family integration is moving forward, one also hears more about the problems and conflicting demands of employment and caregiving. What is the actual situation? The simplest answer seems to be that behavior is changing in the direction of more flexible gender roles with shared parenting and breadwinning. But the social institutions of school and work are not changing as quickly. The result is considerable work-related stress that adversely affects health and happiness.

There is ample evidence of a trend toward more integration of work and family responsibilities. As Waldfogel (2009) notes, two-thirds of American children had a stay-at-home parent in 1975 compared with only one-quarter today. Half of all children live in families where both parents are employed, another quarter with a single parent who works, and one-quarter in a family where one parent is not employed. Cause for strain is especially clear in the single-parent families where the sole parent is also employed; many are poor or have low income and this may lead to extra hours at low-level jobs that offer very little flexibility.

Although working parents clearly need greater flexibility to meet family obligations, they risk important costs if they look for part-time jobs or ask for extended family leave. They may be punished with lower pay, less opportunity for advancement, and devaluation by a corporate culture that requires long hours and limits their autonomy (Blau et al. 2010). In fact one main reason women so often receive lower pay than their male peers is the perception that they are less committed to work when they respond to a family emergency or a child's or elder's needs. Stone (2007) recounts the numerous instances of high-level career women in law, finance, and business who were sidelined when they asked for even the most minor variations on the long and demanding hours of their workplace.

Yet despite these known perils of looking for a flexible work schedule, Gerson (2010) in her study of 120 young adults from diverse backgrounds in New York discovered a clear trend toward a *desire and expectation* that women and men should share domestic and breadwinning duties. She observes (p. 218) that "The gender gap in aspirations has closed to a remarkable degree, with most women wishing to be earners, most men wishing to be involved parents, and most people seeking a balance between the two." What Gerson concludes is that gender ideologies have become more flexible while social institutions have remained largely the same. "The social organization of work and caretaking, which still largely presumes a caregiver at home and a breadwinner supporting the household, can meet neither the wishes nor the needs of most 21st-century families" (Gerson 2010:219). Her solution is to create new social policies.

The arguments for flexibility. A variety of research has shown that there are many benefits of flexible work arrangements for the employer as well as workers and their families. Rapaport and Bailyn (1996) have shown that flexibility of the workplace reduces absenteeism and encourages more autonomy and higher productivity (Stebbins 2001). Relaxation and time away from the job are necessary to generate growth of innovation and productivity (Christensen 2005). Family leave is associated with work satisfaction and relief from work–family conflict (Blau et al. 2010). One reason may be that the operative unit according to Barnett (1999) is the work–life system, not the individual worker. Bailyn, Bookman, Harrington, and Kochan (2006) use a collaborative interaction research technique to help workers become aware of the "dual agenda," which is that they need to serve their own personal needs as well as the organizational needs. Only in this way will both the employer and the employee achieve satisfaction. Still and Williams

(2006) take a very pragmatic approach which is to examine Americans' relative interest in childcare and part-time work compared with flexibility. They conclude that there is more promise in limiting working hours than meeting the popular demand for childcare and generous parental leave. The potential effectiveness of regulating working hours is also revealed in a cross-national comparison by Gornick and Heron (2006).

As to individual and family benefits, parents with low stress are more likely to have flexible work arrangements. Long working hours lead to high stress, which is hard on families (Christensen 2005). Gerson (2010) found in her study of 120 young adults that those who came from families with inflexible gender ideologies and little role sharing of work and family responsibilities were less able to handle uncertainties and crises—whether a loss of job or a sudden health problem of a family member. "The inability to develop more flexible strategies for breadwinning and caregiving left these families unable to sustain an emotionally or economically secure home" (Gerson 2010:217).

Wertheimer et al. (2005) note that the level of work–family integration that is possible varies both with the nature of the job (high vs. low pressure) and the worker's stage of life (young parent vs. empty nester). Thus the need for flexibility may vary with the job, the industry, and the life stage of the worker.

The negative effects of high stress and long hours also deserve mention. Twenty years ago in *The Overworked American: The Unexpected Decline of Leisure,* Juliet Schor (1991) was one of the first to point out that Americans have longer working hours than any other advanced industrial nation. After recounting the watershed decision by management and labor in the early 1950s not to use productivity gains to shorten the workweek, Schor shows the endless "squirrel cage" effect of working more to gain more income. Longer working hours and overtime pay result in overwork, less leisure, and the use of money to buy material possessions in order to enjoy the fruits of one's labor. J. Jacobs, Gerson, and Gornick (2004) review cross-national data from the Luxembourg Income Study to show that the average dual-career couple in America works a total of 81.2 hours per week compared with 74 to 79 hours per week by their counterparts in other countries. The distribution is also different. Over 80 percent of American dual-career couples work *more than* 80 hours per week compared with fewer than 50 percent in all the other countries.

Ideas for policy reform. Given the continuing gap between the rigid demands of school and workplace and what is thought to be a healthy balance between work and family life, the remedies proposed all call for innovative social policies that will introduce greater flexibility into existing institutions.

The main recommendations concern (1) more compatible schedules for children, (2) limits on working hours, (3) convenience of work location, (4) options for full- and part-time work, and (5) changing the overall culture of work expectations and the workplace.

Conclusion

Since breadwinners in almost all families today gain a living outside the family, the idea that the family is a basic economic institution may come as a surprise. Yet the Greek root of "economics" is in fact *oikos* or household, and production to gain income and consumption to reproduce and care for the family are economic functions. The challenge for modern families is to gain adequate income when old or disabled, out of a job, earning too little, or swamped by an economic downturn. In order to create an economic safety net in the face of hardship, social policies such as cash assistance, social insurance, and subsidized benefit programs have been instituted.

In the wake of the women's movement, those interested in family policy have given particular attention to part-time and flexible schedules and availability of childcare. Compared with other advanced societies, U.S. family policy is much less comprehensive and more of a patchwork. Nevertheless, a very extensive range of American policies has been developed to protect family income and economic security. The two main types are assistance to the poor and work-based programs that include insurance and pension plans, wage improvement through employee training, and work–family integration.

Each type of family policy operates against the backdrop of the American income distribution. Recent trends are worrisome. Over the past 40 years there has been a steep rise in income and wealth inequality so that the top 1 percent in wealth holds as much in assets as the bottom 90 percent. Upward mobility in the United States today is not as great as in the Scandinavian countries, France, or Germany. Ironically, as the second richest country in the world (after Norway), the United States has one of the highest poverty rates among its peers.

The main programs of assistance to the poor have their origin in the Social Security Act of 1935. Old Age Assistance, Aid to the Blind and Disabled, and Aid to Dependent Children all provided help to people who had little or no other income. Over time these state-run programs evolved so that assistance to poor old people, blind, disabled, and mentally ill persons was gathered under federal oversight in the Supplemental Security Income program. In-kind assistance was also added—health care, housing, food aid, and childcare. In 1996 the movement for welfare reform transformed Aid to Families with Dependent Children into TANF, a welfare-to-work program, with time limits on transitional assistance.

The other main arm of the Social Security Act—Old Age Security—is a social insurance program funded by employer and employee contributions. This retirement program has enjoyed much greater legitimacy than the comparable assistance programs because it is understood to be supported by worker contributions and therefore has none of the stigma that goes with aid to the poor. Other programs that carry similar legitimacy are Workers Compensation, Disability Insurance, and private pensions and employee benefits. Unemployment Insurance is also a part of the safety net. With its many restrictions on eligibility, it combines features of both aid and entitlement.

Another work-based program to strengthen economic security is wage improvement and making work pay. Historically, the growth of unions and the wage and hours legislation of the 1930s had a major role in increasing workers' bargaining power and raising their wages. Since the 1960s, however, with the decline of manufacturing and loss of union power, employee training and development has been the primary strategy for getting people into better-paying jobs. Most of these programs target people on assistance and help them find a job or a better-paying job. The main challenges are to match up employers with the job seekers, and then provide training that achieves the desired results.

Development of a family-friendly workplace has been the primary interest of many family sociologists. But the policies that promote this development are hard to summarize. Most are located in the private sector and except for antidiscrimination and family leave are difficult to document. The main effect of antidiscrimination legislation such as the Equal Pay Act or Title VII of the Civil Rights Act was to establish that women could be workers and breadwinners with rights equal to those of men. The Pregnancy Disability Act and Family and Medical Leave Act wrote into law the legitimacy of family claims on a worker's time. Although employee benefits are much talked about as a way to construct a family-friendly workplace, their actual availability is surprisingly low. Dependent care, especially the need for childcare, is a long-standing interest of working women. Except for tax credits, however, subsidies and public provision of childcare are limited to low-income families. The main hopes for creation of a family-friendly workplace appear to rest with a younger generation of workers who believe that women and men should share work and family responsibility. Indeed, the transformation of gender roles is the direction of the future. Needed changes in the workplace are being reinforced by changes in family structure and gender roles as well as by the actual experience of women and men who are combining work and caregiving.

In constructing its economic safety net, a nation has to understand the interdependence of everyone in the society—rich and poor, maintenance workers and managers, children and parents. No matter how rich a country, if one-quarter of its youngest children are growing up in poverty, the nation cannot continue to prosper. The safety net must therefore provide a way to raise low incomes and also counteract the damaging effects of poverty on family life, neighborhoods, and schools. The United States is just beginning to understand the importance of protecting children and families by strengthening their surrounding communities, which is the topic of Chapter 6.

6

Housing, Neighborhoods, and Life Chances

S ociologists of the family typically do not spend very much time on the topic of housing. My guess is that they consider it a largely material matter that deals with bricks and mortar and pricing but does not cover the interesting connections between people that are of greatest interest to sociologists. In recent years, however, social scientists are beginning to realize that inattention to residential location and housing is a huge omission of a very important dimension of family life. Housing affects not only degree of crowding, presence of indoor plumbing, and availability of electricity, phones, and access to the Internet. The location of a household also brings with it a whole environmental context that includes safety of the neighborhood, quality of the schools, and access to transportation, parks, shops, and services. Thus housing is an important entry point to excellent or limited economic and educational opportunities and to a decent or marginal quality of life.

In the expression "Location, Location, Location!" real estate agents state the basic principle of pricing: The same house in a different location can cost more or less depending on its surroundings—the schools, transportation, social class of the neighbors, type of children and adolescents who live there, and crime or safety of the district. Anthropologists and sociologists have long known that having a residence in a particular location, whether it be a house, a tent, or a cave, is one of the distinguishing features of any household or family. In fact, even homelessness is not only a statement about lack of housing; it also stigmatizes the individuals and families who experience it.

As with nomadic peoples, homeless families occupy a delimited space at one time or another even though their location changes according to the availability of work, access to helpful kin, or a seasonal food supply.

Just as caregiving and securing an income are basic functions of the family, so also is securing a habitable shelter. The quality of individual family housing varies with family size, income, minority status, region of the country, and rural or urban location. Just as families vary in income and wealth or poverty status, they also vary in size and quality of their dwelling, the amount of income they have to pay for rent or a mortgage, the quality of the neighborhood, and access to public services, community connections, and safe surroundings.

The price and quality of a family's housing has consequences for its integration into the larger neighborhood and community. Adult family members' job opportunities and commuting time are influenced by the distance of their homes from their jobs. Children's success in school and their ability to stay out of trouble, delay marriage, continue their education, and find good jobs is shaped by the quality of the neighborhood schools and the safety of its streets. Sociologists, economists, and educators now understand the importance of neighborhood to family life as a matter of *social capital*. Neighborhoods that are unsafe, where there is a lot of moving in and out, and where people do not know each other are poor in social capital. Social capital is that reservoir of trust and mutual obligation that enables innovation and risk taking and further investment in the community to the benefit of all.

The newest thinking about housing policy and the family asks how the nation can make housing more affordable and also improve neighborhood quality for everyone, especially those at the bottom of the income scale. Finding the answers is of utmost importance for promoting the healthy development of children, adult well-being, and productivity of the nation—what the United States Declaration of Independence terms "the pursuit of happiness." The connections between housing policy and quality of family life are fairly direct but largely implicit. The two main streams of housing policy—assistance for the poor and support for self-help among the non-poor—are similar to the two main components of the Social Security Act that were treated in Chapters 4 and 5. Poor support takes the form of slum clearance, public housing projects, and rent subsidies. Assistance for the middle class, which began with settlement of the frontier and continued in tax deductions for interest on a home mortgage, encourages home ownership. Government support for home ownership has far outstripped the amount of investment in affordable housing subsidies for poor and low-income families. A key question is how housing policy can be strengthened in ways that will benefit families at all income levels rather than reinforce existing patterns of inequality and residential segregation.

This chapter is divided into four parts: (1) the current housing profile of the American population, (2) the evolution of federal housing policy, (3) the connection of housing to social class and neighborhood, and (4) the impact of residential location on school achievement and life chances.

A Current Profile of Housing in America

The single most important change in Americans' living situation over the past century has been the shift from living in the country to living in cities and suburbs. Industrialization and urbanization brought change in the nature and quality of housing as well as the type of neighbors and communities that surround the typical household. The farmstead that supported both food production and family life was replaced by a residence that served primarily as shelter and stage for a particular lifestyle. For those who can afford to own their homes, their houses represent attainment of "the American Dream" as well as an investment that can increase their wealth. Thus expecting the average family to own its own home has become a fundamental tenet of American social policy. To appreciate the current housing situation of American families, it is necessary to see how it has changed over the past century. The population has shifted from rural to urban areas. Twice as many families own their homes as those who rent. Housing quality has improved dramatically, but the mortgage crisis of 2007–2010 seriously challenged the idea that almost everybody can attain the American Dream through owning their own home. Many families new to the ranks of homeowners were encouraged by disreputable lenders to invest in properties that cost far more than they could afford. These families ended up in bankruptcy, having lost the resources that would have permitted them to become homeowners.

From Rural to Urban

Even though urbanization and industrialization have been going on since the mid-nineteenth century, it is useful to think of the year 1940 as a major watershed. Change had already begun right after the Civil War, when so many New England country towns had lost residents that they became unincorporated again. Along with this movement of Eastern farmers to the West and Southern blacks to the North, the biggest shift was from country to city. As late as 1939, one-quarter of Americans lived on farms compared with fewer than 10 percent in 1960 and less than 1 percent in 1992. Nevertheless, one-fifth of the total U.S. population was still defined as rural in 2000, a proportion that varied widely by state, from as high as 40 percent in Alabama, Arkansas, Kentucky, Maine, and Mississippi to under 10 percent in California, Massachusetts, New Jersey, and Rhode Island. In 2009, almost half of the U.S. population lived in cities of 500,000 or more, and slightly over half lived in medium-sized cities of 25,000 to 100,000 (27.9 percent) and small towns and cities of under 25,000 (27.5 percent). Farm population was at its peak at 32 million in 1935, up from just under 25 million in 1890 and double what it fell to after 1960 (Carter 2006:Table Da1–13; U.S. Census Bureau 2011:Tables 28–29).

The rural-to-urban shift had a profound impact on family life. The decline in the farm population led to enormous changes in household production and was made possible by growth in manufacturing and white-collar occupations and improvements in utilities and transportation. The effect was particularly evident in women's work. A huge part of their time had gone to cooking (from milking the cow or making butter to tending the garden), cleaning (including laundry), making clothing, and childcare. In 1929, the proportion of household income spent for food that was prepared or eaten outside the home was only 15 percent compared with two or three times that proportion today. Time spent in childcare from birth through nursing, during a child's first year, fell with the fertility rate from an average of 14 years of the average mother's life in 1800 to only four years in our era. As a consequence, more married women joined the paid labor force, and their participation rate grew from 2.4 percent in 1880 to 32.4 percent in 1950 and 57.6 percent in 1990. By 1970, with the decline of agricultural occupations, the proportion of workers in white-collar jobs rose to over half the labor force, and the proportion in manufacturing jobs fell to less than half (Craig 2006). With fewer goods produced at home, trade was necessary to move the food supply to the towns and transportation to move people to their work. Innovations in the railways, highway system, and manufacture of automobiles between 1880 and 1910 made all such commerce much more possible (L. Cain 2006). In the opinion of Sobek (2006:2–39, 40), ". . . all major identifiable occupational subgroups have shared in the improved opportunities offered by the changing occupational structure . . . the entire structure has been shifted upward in terms of occupational desirability toward higher-skilled white-collar work."

At the same time, the rise of corporate agricultural and factory farms for raising livestock such as chickens and hogs have had a huge negative impact on small family farms, making it difficult for them to compete against the mass production and lower prices made possible by monoculture (FamilyFarmer.org 2011).

Homeownership versus Renting

Perhaps because of their rural and democratic origins and their distaste for the inherited status of nobles and princes, Americans have long favored ownership of individual property as a sign of enterprise, independence, and full citizenship. Even men's voting rights before the Jacksonian era were limited to those who owned property. Social historian Oscar Handlin (1963) has observed that the ideal home from the colonial period to the present has been a freestanding dwelling with land around it that, in its modest way, recalls the English manor of the country squire. By 2009, two-thirds of all American households owned their own home compared with less than half (44 percent) who did so prior to World War II. (U.S. Census Bureau 2004; U.S. Census Bureau 2011:Table 987).

The median price of a house in the United States in 2011 ranged from around $175,000 for the United States as a whole to as high as $600,000 in San Jose, California, and as low as $67,000 in Youngstown, Ohio (National Association of Realtors 2012). The median monthly housing cost in 2009 was $1,000 for owner-occupied units and $808 for renter-occupied units (U.S. Census Bureau 2011:Table 989). For those households below the poverty line, the median monthly cost was $502 for homeowner-occupied units and $629 for renters, figures that of course vary by region.

Of a total of 33.6 million renter households in 2003, about half (16.6 million) were eligible for housing assistance. But of those eligible, only about one-quarter (4.3 million) received any housing assistance, whether as public housing tenants (1.1 million), voucher households (1.8 million), or households in privately owned projects (1.4 million). In FY 2010, approximately one-third of the households receiving rental assistance were elderly, 24 percent were disabled, and 40 percent were families and others. Ironically, low-income people who are eligible for housing assistance pay almost half of their income for housing (45 percent) while the nonpoor use only one-quarter (24 percent) (U.S. Department of Housing and Urban Development 2008).

Homelessness. A relatively recent development is the rise of homelessness, which became a matter of national concern in the 1970s. Before that time, tramps and "bums" were mostly vagrant men who rode the rails and asked for a free meal from generous housewives and townspeople. As a little girl in a small Ohio town in the 1940s, I remember my mother giving a hot lunch to the occasional tramp who knocked on the door. (There was a widespread belief that tramps left some sort of sign on a gatepost or tree that indicated the best places to ask for a meal, so the tramp's request may have been something like a compliment to a housewife for her cooking.)

Homelessness since the 1970s is a very different phenomenon from that of the tramps during the 1930s. It was caused partly by the deinstitutionalization of the mental hospitals without adequate preparation of the inmates for life outside. An even bigger source has been the increase in whole families of mothers and children who, having missed a rent payment or escaped from a violent partner, first tried living in a car or with relatives but eventually ended in a homeless shelter because of overcrowding or loss of a job (Burt 2010). Transitional housing programs were first institutionalized by the U.S. Department of Housing and Urban Development in 1986. By 2007 there were a total of almost 7,300 transitional housing programs and about 211,000 beds in the nation as a whole. Just over half are designated for families and serve about 40,000 mostly single-parent families at a time. Yet the estimated number of homeless individuals is several times larger: 250,000 people in families who are homeless, 75,000 homeless veterans, and 50,000 youth (National Alliance to End Homelessness 2011).

Improvements in Housing Quality

In contrast with the worsened housing situation of homeless families, the quality of housing for the general population has clearly improved. Houses are larger, with more running water, electricity, bathrooms, telephones, and TV. The next frontier is penetration of broadband Internet to rural and sparsely populated regions. These technological changes are in marked contrast to the housing censuses of the mid-1930s, when rural electrification was one of the bold new ventures of the Roosevelt Administration and when nearly half of all housing units had incomplete plumbing. The contrast between housing now and 50 years ago was brought home to me by a college development consultant who reported that a great many contemporary college students never shared a bedroom until they moved to a college dormitory. The proportion of new houses built with air-conditioning rose from 45 percent in 1975 to 90 percent in 2007, and the proportion constructed with two full bathrooms increased from 60 percent to 95 percent (Schwartz 2010).

One of the most dramatic changes in housing since 1950 has been what Downs (1977) called the "un-doubling" of American households. Many a family or war bride doubled up with relatives during the housing shortages of World War II. With the post-war housing boom, city families were able to move from small apartments into single-family houses in the new suburbs. Students and young married people moved out of their parents' homes into their own apartments. Between 1950 and 1976 the number of single-person and nonfamily households grew from 15 percent to 22 percent of all households (Goldscheider and Waite 1991). Even though families were smaller, the median size of the single-family dwelling increased from approximately 1,500 to 2,300 square feet (Schwartz 2010).

The Mortgage Crisis of 2007–2010

Unfortunately, the American devotion to the homeownership ideal was part of what led to the housing bubble of the 1990s and early 2000s. At least four other forces also were responsible: (1) use of rising house prices and equity as a "credit card" (Case 2010); (2) improper and discriminatory lending practices; (3) the general downturn in the economy that raised unemployment, making house payments difficult and thereby putting many houses "under water" so that the owner's equity was less than when the house was bought; and (4) questionable financial practices by lenders that obscured the tie between loan amount and underlying property values so that buyers were offered larger loans than they could afford. By the spring of 2011 the backlog of houses that had been foreclosed by the banks was just over 4 million. The estimated time to clear the backlog had risen to over three years, with the supply bringing down prices even further (Dash 2011). Many observers have called it the worst housing market in 75 years.

Such drastic consequences point to a need for better financial decisions by families, tighter lending practices by the banks, and an overhaul of federal housing and lending policy to help families make prudent decisions on how much debt they can undertake. Discriminatory lending practices targeted minority families and sold them property with adjustable-rate mortgages, where interest rates rose over time and their debt obligations were unrealistic, given their limited income and assets. The elderly were also exploited because they had a lot of equity in their homes but little cash for medical expenses and maintenance, and loans promised to ease their cash flow, but they too were hurt by the crisis (Boyer 2008). The debacle was particularly ironic in the case of minority homeowners. They have historically been confined to redlined districts,[1] where housing prices are slow to appreciate, if at all, and where neighborhood deterioration is more likely (Oliver and Shapiro 2006). Yet during the housing bubble these disadvantages appeared to have vanished, only to return with a vengeance. New subdivisions in Cleveland, Ohio, or Southern California were quickly abandoned as families failed to

---

[1]Redlining is a discriminatory practice by which lending institutions and insurance brokers define investment in the "redlined" districts as so risky that they will not underwrite loans to buyers or insurance of properties in those areas.

meet their mortgage payments and their houses were foreclosed, leaving them bereft of their dream yet still burdened by unpaid debt. Between 2004 and the first quarter of 2010 the homeownership rate dropped from 69.2 percent to 66.4 percent, with an expectation that it would eventually fall to 63 percent (Streitfeld 2011).

The only good news at this point is that some states have taken matters into their own hands with new programs that accept a low down payment but carefully counsel families on what is realistic and monitor their performance to forestall further problems. These new programs report success in helping families to meet their obligations by using the income that would have gone to rent to pay down the mortgage instead (Leland 2010). In the process, struggling families have a chance to attain the home ownership they dreamed of.

Evolution of Federal Housing Policy

The earliest schemes for public provision of housing go back to colonial times when workhouses, almshouses, and asylums sheltered those without a home. Although New Deal legislation rationalized and modernized housing for the poor, such housing is still frequently stigmatized because of its location in a poor or dangerous neighborhood. Access to land and homeownership also was established very early for those who were thought to be deserving by dint of their efforts as farmers or soldiers. The 1855 Old Soldiers Act awarded public land to veterans. The 1862 Homestead Act awarded land to pioneers who settled the Midwestern prairies. Whereas public housing assistance to unemployed or dependent persons was usually given grudgingly, land grants to settlers and veterans were seen as rewards to hard-working and ambitious citizens (Vale 2000).

Most relevant for contemporary times are the housing policies that were instituted in the 1930s and have been revised since then. Over the ensuing decades, public housing assistance has evolved from slum clearance and construction of inner-city housing to efforts to disperse and mix low- and middle-income residents and house them in attractive townhouses scattered around the cities. Policies to support homeownership also evolved. While the main focus of the 1930s was to stabilize the mortgage market and the banks, the huge pent-up demand created by World War II brought unprecedented growth in construction of new single-family houses in the suburbs. During the 1970s and 1980s housing prices rose sharply and became a source of investment growth. Fast appreciation, however, ultimately fed a housing bubble that burst with the recession of 2008–2010.

This account focuses on the importance of housing for families and links these developments to the key milestones in housing policy.

Overview: Homeownership versus Housing Assistance

By comparison with a time in the 1930s when President Roosevelt famously referred to one-third of the nation as "ill clothed, ill housed, and ill fed," great progress has occurred in the housing of almost all Americans. However, this progress has taken place in very uneven increments, with the lion's share of public subsidy going to the highest income group who live in the nicest houses. The mortgage interest tax deduction, which was established to encourage homeownership, has become a protection of wealth by subsidizing ownership of very expensive houses and covering also a second home. The top income quartile in 2002 received 62.5 percent of all federal housing benefits (Brassil 2010). Although many millions of dollars have gone into public housing projects, subsidized private units, and rental vouchers, the total amount is dwarfed by the tax deductions given to homeowners for interest payments on their mortgages and local property taxes. The result is that programs to build affordable housing and assist low-income renters have been chronically underfunded. Moreover, the purpose of assisting poor people has at different periods been subordinated to other purposes such as raising the inner-city tax base through urban renewal or creating a more diverse socioeconomic group of renters through selection of middle-income tenants to inhabit affordable housing units.

The current statistics on rental assistance and homeownership, as shown in Table 6.1, are the product of these policy priorities that have evolved over the past 80 years. The figures raise several issues related to equity of funding for various income groups. If the funding for renters were proportional to the $171 billion of tax benefits spent on homeowners (who already have incomes twice as high as renters), the amount would be approximately $57 billion instead of $40 billion. If the number of renters benefiting from assistance were proportional to the number of homeowners, the figure would be closer to 51 million (rather than 7 million). The tax write-offs going to homeowners have helped them increase their net assets substantially, from $174,700 in 1998 to $243,200 in 2008, whereas renters' assets (in constant 2008 dollars) actually decreased during that period, from $5,600 to $5,300 (Schwartz 2010).

One further problem is that rents have continued to increase so that many low-income workers have to spend well over 30 percent of their

Table 6.1 Characteristics of Renters and Homeowners

Characteristics	Renters	Homeowners
Number of Households (percentage)	32.7	63.7
Race or Ethnicity (percentage) White Hispanic Black	 25 51 53	 75 49 47
Married Couples (percentage)	16	84
Median Household Income (in thousands of 2008 dollars) 1988 1998 2008	 $34.1 $33.5 $32.7	 $60.8 $63.3 $63.7
Median Wealth in Assets (in thousands of 2008 dollars) 1988 1998 2008	 $3.4 $5.6 $5.3	 $169.2 $174.7 $243.2
Subsidies to Renters (Rental Housing Assistance) and Homeowners (in tax deductions) (in billions of 2008 dollars)	$40.2	$171
Number of Households Receiving Benefits in 2007	7 million	155 million

Source: Schwartz (2010:7–8, 21).

income for rent. The National Low Income Housing Coalition estimates that it took an average hourly income of $17.32 in 2008 to rent a two-bedroom apartment, and the federal minimum wage at that time was only $5.85 an hour. Matters are made even worse by the low access of eligible renters to housing vouchers and public housing. In 2007, of 15 million low-income families with unaffordable housing costs, only 5 million received assistance through HUD programs (Brassil 2010).

Some understanding of how these patterns came about can be gained from a review of four major eras in modern housing policy: the Depression through World War II; the suburban housing boom of the 1950s and 1960s; community development programs from the 1970s to the present; and the lessons learned from the housing boom and bust since 2000.

Housing through the Depression and World War II

Up until the 1930s, housing conditions were largely treated as the inevitable result of differences between poor people and everyone else. Urban crowding, low-quality construction, and deteriorating buildings were limited somewhat by minimum standards in building codes, but amelioration was primarily up to local authorities and charitable groups (Erickson 2009). The Great Depression, however, precipitated a national response that became the basis of federal housing policy as it has evolved over the last 75 years. First came the National Industrial Recovery Act of 1933, which established the Public Works Administration and provided a legal basis for the federal government to become involved in public housing. It was followed by the Housing Act of 1934, which put in place the financial mechanisms to support homeownership. The Housing Act of 1937 established a national system of public housing coordinated by local housing authorities. The passage of this legislation served the interests of three major constituencies: (1) the construction industry to revive the building trades through new private and public housing; (2) the financial services and banking sector, which benefitted from loan guarantees; and (3) the people living in substandard housing who needed better accommodations. These acts of Congress, as shown in Table 6.2, also set in motion the long-running competition for public resources between renters and homeowners that persists to this day (Mitchell 1985).

In less than a decade, the advent of World War II placed tremendous new pressures on the existing housing stock. Construction of military bases around the country and the massive conscription of 15 million soldiers brought many people to new locations like Southern California, Detroit, or Norfolk, Virginia, where war plants and military bases were located and where existing housing was quite scarce. Building materials were in short supply, as were builders and tradesmen who had gone off to war. My father, a do-it-yourselfer, built a house during this period by using cement blocks instead of wood and old factory windows with metal frames. People doubled up with friends and relatives. Wives of servicemen moved home to live with their parents for the duration of the war. Others took rooms near military bases to be near their husbands.

After the war there was competition for every vacancy. Veterans were given preference, and others made do with what was available. In Dayton, Ohio, the parents of my husband took in the family of a German scientist who after the war was brought to work on a defense project at Wright-Patterson Air Force Base. Crowded conditions thus persisted until they were relieved by the spurt of new housing after the war, which was greatly

Table 6.2   Major Federal Housing Legislation Since 1930

Legislation	Year	Basic Provisions for Public Housing and Homeownership
National Industrial Recovery Act	1933	Established the Public Works Administration and provided the legal basis for federal involvement in public housing
Housing Act of 1934	1934	Established Federal Savings and Loan Insurance Corporation to ensure deposits and mortgages against default
Housing Act of 1937	1937	Established a national system of public housing coordinated by local housing authorities
Housing Act of 1949	1949	Urban Renewal connected to public housing. Authorized 810,000 units to be built between 1949 and 1955
Housing Act of 1954	1954	Urban renewal established as the nation's urban revitalization strategy
Authorization of HUD	1965	Department of Housing and Urban Development established to coordinate all federal housing programs
Fair Housing Act of 1968	1968	Banned discrimination. Established 2.6-million unit 10-year goal for low-cost and affordable housing (Section 235). By 1972, 1.1 million units had been built (McCarty, Perl, Fotte, Jones, and Peterson 2008).
Fair Housing Amendments Act	1988	Expanded scope and strengthened enforcement of Fair Housing Act of 1968

aided by government support of veterans' housing, subsidized loans, and low down payments.

The Postwar Housing Boom, 1949 to 1973

Pent-up demand for housing after the war led to the huge growth in housing construction that created vast suburbs like Levittown, New York. Public housing also expanded, but in unfortunate ways that were shaped by a focus on slum clearance and urban renewal more than provision of decent affordable housing for people who happened to have low incomes. Although the Housing Act of 1949 had as its purpose, "the realization as soon as possible of the goal of a decent home in a suitable living environment for every American family," and authorized construction of over 800,000 units by 1955, this number never materialized (Erickson 2009:4). Public housing advocates had to resist Cold War theories that government projects were the tool of a communist front for socialist purposes. Assistance for the poor, as authorized by the Housing Act of 1954, was converted into a call for urban renewal to improve the inner-city tax base while at the same time clearing the slums. Dark unsafe alleys and dilapidated structures were to be replaced by bright new buildings and clean wide streets, and the projects were to serve as a stabilizing force in the neighborhood (especially when they were seen to serve the worthy poor such as the elderly, the handicapped, and those temporarily out of work). Mitchell (2009:10) concludes, however, that urban renewal ultimately "cheated public housing of its birthright." Land values in Boston's West End did not decline until *after* 1953 when plans for demolition were announced. Moreover, the new public housing built to replace the old crowded (but friendly) West End neighborhood could accommodate only one-third of the families who lived there before urban renewal (Vale 2000). Others were displaced to communities where they were among strangers and far from many of the social and economic supports that were available in their old neighborhood.

Between 1950 and 1973, when the fuel crisis and President Nixon's hostile stance toward public housing brought an end to the housing boom, the homeownership rate rose dramatically from under 44 percent in 1940 to 55 percent in 1950 and 62 percent in 1960. This change was made possible by almost 2 million housing starts in 1950 and well over a million each year through the 1950s. By contrast, construction of public housing lagged, with only 250,000 new units having been built by 1960 and a total of only 470,000 units built during the 18-year period from 1949 to 1968. Partly in response to the urban activism of the 1960s, and under the coordination of the Department of Housing and Urban Development (HUD) that was established in 1965, an additional 375,000 public housing units were built between 1968 and 1973 (Erickson 2009). At the end of this period, a large unmet need for affordable housing still existed. Unfortunately, along with what growth did occur, a pattern of residential segregation developed in which the "projects" became overwhelmingly associated with poverty and people of color even though there was a positive bias toward housing whites wherever possible.

The Fair Housing Act of 1968 had banned discrimination in housing, but spatial segregation persisted in the physical separation of white and colored communities. A disproportionate number of whites were able to gain access to public housing, while at the same time the public housing units that had started out in nonpoor largely white sections of cities such as Boston by 50 years later were found in what had become the poorest census tracts (Vale 2000). The postwar housing boom and urban renewal era came to an end in the early 1970s with the realization that suburbs had their limitations during a fuel crisis, and urban renewal did not necessarily revitalize the cities in ways that had been hoped for.

Community Development Programs, 1974 to 2000

Passage of the Housing and Community Development Act in 1974 set in motion a whole new era in housing policy. Disappointment with the desirability of high-rise public housing projects and a slowdown in housing starts produced a readiness to consider new strategies to create affordable housing and promote homeownership.

The 1974 legislation had greatest effect on public and affordable housing. Its three main goals were: (1) consolidation of housing programs by using block grants to states and local authorities, (2) creation of three forms of rent subsidy (public housing, subsidized mixed-income housing, and rental vouchers), and (3) dispersion of poor and low-income tenants into nonpoor areas in order to avoid the stigma of concentration. These policies set the stage for greater local involvement in planning and construction of public housing and affordable units. Brassil (2010) and Erickson (2009) see these steps in devolution as the beginning of a whole new orientation toward local networking rather than reliance on top-down federal decisions about what should be built and who should be the tenants.

With respect to policies on homeownership, the new era marked a shift toward innovative financial mechanisms to underwrite mortgages and provide tax credits for interest payments and property taxes. Strict federal regulations governing the banking institutions were eased to give more power to the institutions. Although the results at first seemed quite positive, they led in the long run to the mortgage and foreclosure crisis that came after 2007.

Forms of public and affordable housing. The public housing projects built in the 1950s are now almost all gone, having been demolished and replaced by low-rise row houses with porches and gables and bay windows. Most of the original projects that remain have been refurbished and improved. Some had appliances such as dishwashers and air-conditioning that are now standard in new construction.

Housing assistance comes in three forms. Public housing units are reserved for low-income tenants whose rent exceeds 30 percent of their income. Subsidized mixed-income housing is built with public subsidies and includes both moderate and low-income tenants. Vouchers provide rent subsidies for eligible tenants who are able to find a suitable unit in a qualified building. Voucher holders have the same eligibility requirements as public housing tenants but they may have to spend more of their budget in rent. The Public Housing Reform Act of 1998 set tighter eligibility rules for tenants in public housing. The "one-strike" rule excludes anyone with a prison record or history of drug dealing. In some cases the result is that whole families are excluded because of the unfortunate history of one family member.

Housing conditions have greatly improved for those families who have been lucky enough to be accepted as tenants in public housing or to find a unit for which they qualified for subsidized housing or a rental voucher. However, three major limitations remain. First, the overall supply of public and subsidized housing has steadily declined since the 1970s as the old projects are replaced by low-density units. Second, large families, persons with special needs, and those with a record of a criminal or drug offense have particular difficulty in being accepted as tenants. Finally, there is little sign that the supply will increase anytime soon. It is true that the National Affordable Housing Act of 1990 established the HOME program to expand the supply of affordable housing for very low-income families. Yet HUD already spends over 40 percent of its budget on rent subsidies and housing vouchers—and that to house only a fraction of the eligible population. Congress finds it much easier to support homeownership with tax write-offs than to authorize direct housing subsidies which get counted in the budget as expenditures (Schwartz 2010).

In addition to direct subsidies, public support also has been given in the form of financing mechanisms that were developed through the Community Development Block Grants (CDBGs) authorized by the 1974 housing legislation and the Low Income Housing Tax Credit of 1986, which helped various local organizations to cooperate in funding public housing. This financing usually accommodates people with between 40 percent and 80 percent of the Area Median Income, whereas an income of 30 percent or less of the median is required to be eligible for public housing or Section 8 housing. Also, the Housing and Community Development Act of 1992 regulated government-sponsored enterprises (GSEs) to prevent fraud and money laundering of funds used to support subsidized housing construction.

Policies to support homeownership. Beginning in the 1970s and continuing through the 1980s, the established system of home finance changed substantially. Instead of relying on local banks with passbook accounts and savings and loans as the main source of funds, mortgages were securitized and became subject to all the risks of gain and loss that accompany the rise and fall of any market. The Home Mortgage Disclosure Act of 1975 and the Community Reinvestment Act of 1977 were aimed at creating banking regulations that would make home financing more transparent and less prone to discriminatory lending. As inflation rose during the 1970s and 1980s, the value of houses appreciated at an even faster rate. For example, a three-bedroom, two-bathroom house of 1,700 square feet in Wellesley, Massachusetts, that sold for $28,500 in 1961, sold again for $32,000 in 1967, $135,000 in 1982, and in 2011 was listed on Zillow.com with an estimated value of $787,700 and an asking price of $939,000! (In constant 2011 dollars, the price in 1962 would have been $215,384; in 1967, $219,875; and in 1982, $316,116.)

Any homeowner could see that investment in real estate would pay off handsomely, especially given the tax deductions available for interest payments and property taxes. Many began using their home equity to take out a second or third mortgage to pay for a car, college tuition, or other expenses. These positive experiences reinforced a bias toward public investments in homeownership rather than public housing. Ownership was associated with thrift, self-reliance, and middle-class status whereas publicly subsidized housing was associated with dependency. The Housing and Community Development Act of 1992 eased regulatory burdens on financial institutions along with funding several housing initiatives to make home ownership more affordable. HOPE VI (Housing for People Everywhere) in 1992 allowed lower down payments and adjustable interest rates to enable low-income families to buy a home. Many advocates were ambivalent toward HOPE VI because they saw a huge net loss of units that resulted from the program. The American Homeownership and Opportunity Act of 2000 updated rules concerning continuation and termination of residential mortgages. One piece of legislation melded the purpose of helping "worthy" low-income tenants with the purpose of also helping them to become homeowners. The Choice Neighborhoods Initiative is the new version of HOPE VI, which addresses the loss of housing by requiring a one-to-one replacement of the former units and at the same time invests in the whole neighborhood (National Housing Law Project 2011).The summary of policies related to public and subsidized housing and homeownership appears in Tables 6.3 and 6.4.

Lessons on Public Housing and Homeownership since 2000

During recent decades, the disparity in allocation of public resources to subsidized housing and homeownership has become increasingly clear. Public housing is starved for funds. The home mortgage industry has

Table 6.3   Public Policies for Rental and Mixed-Income Housing

Legislation	Year	Provisions
Housing Amendments (Brooke)	1969	Linked payments for public housing to tenants' ability to pay rather than to operating costs
Housing and Community Development Act	1974	Three features: (1) categorical programs combined into a block grant for capital improvement and home services; (2) rent supplement program for rentals, rehabilitation, and construction (Section 8); and (3) dispersion of low-income housing
Low Income Housing Tax Credit	1986	Part of Tax Reform Act of 1986. Incentive for developers to construct low- and moderate-income housing
National Affordable Housing Act	1990	(Cranston-Gonzales) Established HOME program to expand supply of affordable housing for very low income families
HOPE VI (Housing for People Everywhere)	1992	Replaced distressed public housing projects with mixed-income housing. Provided housing vouchers to enable some of the original residents to rent apartments in the private market
Housing and Community Development Act	1992	Title I on Housing Assistance, public and Indian housing, Section 8 vouchers. Title III on preservation of low-income housing
Public Housing Reform Act (QHWRA)	1998	Quality Housing and Work Responsibility Act. Limited funding for low-income households to discourage new generation of poor from ever getting into public housing (Vale 2000:384).
Choice Neighborhood Initiative	2009 2010 2011	Authorized funding from federal budget to replace deteriorated dwellings in high-poverty areas. CNI to create mixed-income neighborhoods with counseling for work opportunities and educational and social services

grown so much that its recent failure imperiled the general economic health of the nation. The big question going forward is the appropriate balance between these two major components of the housing market. There is continuing evidence that a substantial level of public housing will always be needed, but there is a lack of broad public support for it. At the same time there are suggestions that homeownership is not the panacea that it has been assumed to be.

Table 6.4   Policies to Support Homeownership

Legislation	Year	Provisions
Home Mortgage Disclosure Act	1975	Regulation of financial institutions' disclosure of data related to home purchase, improvement, and refinancing
Community Reinvestment Act	1977	Banking regulations to reduce discriminatory credit practices in low-income neighborhoods, such as redlining
Housing and Community Development Act	1992	Title I-E on homeownership programs; Title II on home investment partnerships Title V on mortgage insurance and the secondary mortgage market
American Homeownership and Economic Opportunity Act	2000	Updated rules concerning continuation and termination of residential mortgages
American Dream Down Payment Initiative	2003	Helped first-time homebuyers with down payment and closing costs. Focus on low-income first-time homebuyers purchasing single-family homes. Assistance with down payment and closing costs.
Housing and Economic Recovery Act	2008	Reform of government-sponsored enterprises (GSE). Regulation and modernization of the Federal Housing Administration (FHA).
American Recovery and Reconstruction Act	2009	Extended first-time homebuyer's tax credit to December 1, 2009, and increased the maximum amount of the tax credit to $8,000 or $4,000 for married individuals filing separately
Dodd-Frank Wall Street Reform and Consumer Protection Act	2010	Established the Consumer Financial Protection Bureau to limit predatory lending practices and simplify home mortgage agreements.

Public, low-cost, and affordable housing. Most observers agree that public funds for assisted housing are inadequate to the size of the population who are eligible and who should be served. The number of available units has declined, and public willingness to provide needed funds is uncertain in the face of the current federal budget crisis brought on by fighting two wars and the rising cost of entitlements such as Social Security and Medicare.

Experts in the field have converged on the concept of "income integration"—a mix of low-income and moderate-income tenants as a way to strengthen neighborhoods and increase economic opportunity. Programs such as Move to Opportunity and HOPE VI that strive to disperse poor people into nonpoor neighborhoods are supposed to help those who move to become upwardly mobile. While these efforts have improved the image of public and affordable housing, they have several limitations. Subsidized housing units typically go to market rate after a limited period of time (such as 15 years, for example), so they do not solve the housing problem for poor people over the long term. Public housing is thus best paid for by public funds with no such time limits (Schwartz 2010). In addition, the use of HOPE VI, when limited to the inner city, fails to address regional patterns of employment and commuting that are crucial to work opportunity. Poor people, although newly housed, may not be able to find work or be able to get to it (Vankatesh 2008). In the face of the Bush Administration's 8 percent cuts in housing assistance between 2004 and 2006, and a cutback by Congress of 32 percent in capital funds, the Obama Administration's call for a 10.8 percent increase over the Bush budget is felt by many to be long overdue (Brassil 2010).

Ultimately, according to Vale (2000), the real battle is over types of tenants who should be able to live in public housing rather than types of structures to be built. Even though inner-city gentrification may have succeeded in raising the image of public housing within some cities, it is still necessary to think about the long-term need for public housing and especially how to protect poor children in large families and others who are excluded from existing accommodations and may be damaged by the hazards of poor housing in a poor neighborhood. Also at issue is the concentration of racial minorities in public housing. During the 1990s, Section 8 housing was largely given to white families, who found it easier to get into private apartments than blacks, who then ended up in public housing (Krzewinski 2001).

Homeownership. As prices cooled and foreclosures rose, the market fell out of subprime and other risky mortgages and triggered a collapse in the housing market (Schwartz 2010). In the wake of these events, major effort has gone into creating stricter financial regulations covering banks, mortgage funds, government-sponsored enterprises GSEs, and other related financial institutions. A key reform is the Dodd-Frank Wall Street Reform and Consumer Protection Act of 2010, which established a Bureau of Consumer Financial Protection to limit predatory lending practices and create mortgage instruments that are easier to understand. However, implementation of this legislation was strongly opposed by the banking and real estate lobbies (Nocera 2011). President Obama ended the impasse during the

Congressional recess of early 2012 by appointing the first director of the new Consumer Financial Protection Bureau.

Even more profound than strengthening the financial underpinnings of homeownership is the question of whether homeownership is the best form of housing for everybody, especially those with low and uncertain incomes (Schwartz 2010). Homeownership is not always sustainable or desirable. In many respects it has been oversold. Homeownership has important pitfalls because prices do not always rise. Mortgage-backed securities are only as valuable as the underlying mortgages. Moreover, such heavy reliance on homeownership as the major federal housing policy deprives public and subsidized housing of the resources needed. Use of tax-exempt bonds for construction of subsidized rental housing has proved risky when the bond market is not so stable as was expected. Yet most poor households will not be able to afford decent housing without some form of subsidy. Without such help, the alternative is overcrowding and substandard construction—which was the situation in the past.

Federal money is needed for an adequate supply of good supported housing, but it is harder to get than homeowner tax deductions. At the same time that funds for public housing were being cut, and despite the limitations of homeownership as the housing solution for everyone, Congress enacted a number of initiatives that gave further support to homeowners. The American Dream Down Payment Initiative in 2003 was intended to increase homeownership rates among low-income and minority households by supplementing the HOME Investment Partnership program (Brassil 2010). The Housing and Economic Recovery Act of 2008, through its neighborhood stabilization program, provided emergency assistance to state and local governments to acquire and redevelop foreclosed properties. The American Recovery and Reconstruction Act of 2009 extended tax credit to first-time homeowners and increased the minimum amount of the tax credit to $8,000. A summary of major legislation related to homeownership appears in Table 6.4.

Overarching the continuing question of relative investment in rental or home-owned housing is a third long-term issue, which is the continuing presence of racial discrimination in either market. Yes, there has certainly been progress in lessening discrimination since the passage of the Fair Housing Act in 1968 and its amendments in 1988, the Home Mortgage Disclosure Act of 1975, and the Community Reinvestment Act of 1977, as well as more recent legislation to curb abuses such as steering minority customers to minority neighborhoods and predatory lending. The reforms are aimed at protecting fairness in access to the market of available properties and mortgages at reasonable cost. All customers should be able to gain access to the type of property they desire and can afford (Schwartz 2010). Considerable progress was made in the 1990s when matched-pair audits showed a decrease in incidence of discrimination in the rental and home purchase markets. Blacks and Hispanics were able to originate relatively more home purchases than whites. But problems remain. There was an increase in geographic steering in the 1990s, although mortgage denials decreased sharply even though they were still higher for minorities than for whites. New forms of discrimination also appeared in the cost and terms of credit and predatory lending through high-cost subprime loans. Access to fair credit may have become more difficult. Schwartz (2010) describes three lingering problems: steering by real estate dealers to minority areas, more frequent denial of mortgages to minorities, and marketing of a dispropor-tionate share of high-cost subprime mortgages to minorities.

The persistence of racial discrimination and de facto segregation despite laws attempting to prohibit them is ample testimony that many minorities in American society do not have equal access to desirable housing and the kind of neighborhood that will promote their chances for upward mobility. A long tradition of sociological research on social class differences points to the connection between residential location and social status. New interdis-ciplinary research on education, neighborhoods, and social networks shows the strong connections between where a family lives and the life chances of its children.

Residence, Community, and Social Capital

Whereas sociologists may have spent relatively little effort on understanding housing policies, they have been the primary investigators of the connection between residential location and social class. From 1900 to 1950, community studies of Chicago; Muncie, Indiana; Newburyport, Massachusetts; and other towns and suburbs across the country became sociological classics. They depicted the connections between social class and the type of houses and parts of the community that separated lower-class people from the middle and upper classes. These were followed in the 1950s by studies of the new suburbs and the changes in community life that accompanied work in large organizations, with the necessity of long commutes between home and the job.

Then in the 1980s studies of community life suddenly became untethered from their physical location. Social networks and social capital became the focus of inquiry. The questions were not so much where a person lived and that person's status and role in the community. The new interest was instead directed to the nature of the social interaction itself and the power resulting from it. More social interaction generally produces more influence and social capital. Yet the relationship turns out to be circular. The people with the greatest social capital are the people with the most opportunity and the least exposure to toxic stress and chronic scarcity. Housing in good neighborhoods enables the families who live there to send their children to good schools and have their children play with wholesome companions. The counterparts to those who in the 1930s lived "across the tracks" are now the poor minorities who live in neighborhoods with poor schools and unsafe surroundings.

Thus over the course of a century, sociological study of social class, housing, and neighborhoods has shown that a family's residential location is a powerful variable that shapes economic opportunity and social interaction. Housing policy is indeed about far more than bricks and mortar, number of bedrooms, or the availability of a low-cost mortgage.

Housing and Social Class

Although Americans are famous for their belief in equality of all human beings, sociologists have always been intrigued by the manifestations of social inequality, especially in the ways that class and race are linked to a particular area of the city. Classic studies by Robert Park and his students at the University of Chicago in the early 1900s described the Gold Coast and the slum as well as the ethnic neighborhoods near the stockyards. Zones of transition evolved as the city grew larger, and upwardly mobile groups moved out, leaving behind deteriorating structures and decaying neighborhoods where poor people moved in (Park, Burgess, and McKenzie [1925] 1967; Zorbaugh 1976).

In small towns the old families and business owners lived in the big houses on the hill and the people who were struggling lived "across the tracks" or "in the flats." John Dollard (1937:2–3), a sociologist by training and famous for his work on stimulus-response theory, spent several months in a town in the South and described it in *Caste and Class in a Southern Town*, in which he traced the links between social position and residential location:

> It is a small town, just about large enough to qualify under the census as an urban area [not quite 2,500 people]. It is flat as a tennis court but with a bit of a tilt, the white people living on the upper half. Should floods come, the Negro quarter would be first under water. Southerntown is bisected by a railroad, and its tracks divide people according to color, the whites living on one side and the Negroes on the other. . . . On the white side of the town the

houses are, in general, commodious, well painted, shrubbed, and neat. Fans buzz in them during the summer months. They are screened and as cool as they can be in this climate. . . . The streets are paved in the white area and telephone wires run through the trees. . . . The other side of the tracks, sometimes called "nigger town," yields a different picture. Here the houses are small and cheap. . . . At night one sees kerosene lamps gleaming through the windows; in a few of the houses, electric bulbs. Only two paved streets traverse this area where 1,500 people live. . . . Behind the houses frequent privies testify to the fact that these people are not wholly included in our modern technology, as are those on the other side of the railroad tracks.

One hears similar themes in James West's description of Plainville in 1939–40, a town in the Southern Midwest of under 1,000 inhabitants. Although at the outset of his stay, town residents claimed that "We are all just one plain old class of American average working people here" (Withers 1945:viii), West found very clear class differences that were linked to whether a family lived on the good prairie land or in the hills. The prairie farms had more regular crops, more domestic animals, followed modern farming methods, and had greater wealth. The hill people were hunters and loggers, "patch farmers," and woodchoppers with only "scrub stock" and little wealth.

W. Lloyd Warner (1949:36) in researching Jonesville of the 1940s, a town of 6,000 people 50 miles from Chicago, quotes a local resident: "This town is divided into sections. Across the tracks is Ixnay; the northeast part of that section is called Frogtown. It is full of Polacks. The whole west side (south of the tracks), barring The Canal, is all right. But the outskirts on the far west side are kind of bad." In Newburyport, Massachusetts, the best part of town is Hill Street, which has predominantly large good houses in good repair whereas Riverbrook is avoided by the four highest classes and has more houses that are small and in bad repair. "In brief, as one descends in the class order the type of home becomes smaller and less preferable, and as we ascend the house tends to be larger and better. The upper classes get the better homes; the working classes, the ordinary houses; and the lower classes, the poorer ones" (Warner 1963:29).

To twenty-first century minds, many of these observations seem self-evident, yet at the time the studies were published they established an important sociological fact despite popular belief to the contrary. Social class *did* exist not just in people's minds but in the physical reality of residential location.

Suburbanization and the Organization Man

With the building of many vast suburbs in the 1950s, the central sociological questions about the connections between social class and community shifted to a more abstract and general plane. Instead of documenting social class distinctions within a stable self-contained community, sociologists became interested in how social class and community were changing not only internally but in relation to the big cities of which the suburbs were satellites. Books like *The Lonely Crowd* and *The Organization Man* described the new order of things.

One of the best-known sociological books of the 1950s and 1960s was *The Lonely Crowd: A Study of the Changing American Character*, by David Riesman (1950). What Riesman captured were the changes in social interaction that were occurring as a result of the rise of large corporations, which were replacing local and regional businesses. Living patterns were changing as the population shifted from rural areas and small towns to big metropolitan centers surrounded by suburbs. Gone were the traditional sources of authority and the forces of social control that had resided in the neighborhoods, schools, and churches where the organization men had grown up. The new generation no longer relied on their elders for the guidance that shaped earlier "tradition-directed" cohorts. Nor did they consult their internal moral gyroscopes for guidance on the right thing to do as did the previous "inner-directed" generation. Instead these new "other-directed" people looked to their peers for guidance. They cared about what others were doing and whether they themselves were accepted and well liked.

In *The Organization Man*, William H. Whyte (1957) took these themes even further. He used his observations of Park Forest, Illinois, an upscale suburb of Chicago, to argue that the rootlessness of the new corporation employees and their families was undermining former distinctions based on social class. At least half the population in the new suburbs was made up of corporation people being transferred from one post to another, and in their new situation the usual concept of social class no longer applied. The important common thread was instead that everyone had left home. Family background was no longer so relevant. Much more important now were "horizontal groupings" based on common organizational ties and neighborhood bonds with each other. Whyte (1957:201) observed that "in many American communities there has been a wholesale displacement from positions of power of the names that once 'meant' something." In Newburyport, as "the old upper-upper families of the beautiful houses on High Street" were giving way here and there, and the city saw "the slow disintegration of its eighteenth-century idol," it too joined the trend toward modernization by creating an industrial park to bring in new industry (Whyte 1957:301).

In the space of just two decades between the 1940s and the 1960s, the work of Riesman and Whyte marked the amazing shift from small-town, class-bound residential location and social interaction to the fluid and horizontal relationships that were linked to large-scale corporations and the new "rootless" suburbs. Social classes had not disappeared, however. They had merely become less evident as homogeneous residential districts expanded to make it less likely that inhabitants would encounter others of a different class during their daily rounds.

Social Networks and Social Capital

Just as Riesman and Whyte pointed to the changes in social interaction and communities that came with the rise of corporations and the suburbs, a later generation of sociologists would point to another major transformation in social interaction that could extend beyond local geographic boundaries. This is the phenomenon of "social networking," which was first illuminated by sociologists in the 1970s and has since become famous through such practical applications as Facebook and the 2010 movie *The Social Network*. Social networks, no matter how generalized and "virtual," usually begin with some kind of face-to-face interaction of people who are in physical proximity to each other. Thus they are typically embedded in residential location. These associations can be harmful (as in "cyber bullying") or empowering (as in job searches) because they are the means for creating and deploying the strength of group solidarity, which is known as *social capital*. Some communities by virtue of their affluence and educational levels and racial composition are rich in social capital while others are weak. It is important from a policy perspective to understand what makes social capital strong and how it can affect the life chances of families and children.

Several studies of job searches and equality in the schools have taught us why social capital is so important to individual and collective success. In 1974, Mark Granovetter (1974) wrote a brilliant thesis on how workers find jobs. He surveyed 100 men from Newton, Massachusetts, who had changed professional or managerial jobs within the previous five years and described how they had learned about the openings. He found, similar to what had been discovered for blue-collar workers, that roughly 70 percent had either applied directly to the job or had learned about it through a friend or acquaintance. Moreover, the men who had found work through informal connections were more satisfied and had higher pay than comparable applicants who had gone through an agency or a more impersonal process. Granovetter also discovered that tips coming through friends and associates made the search more efficient and less likely to end up in a blind alley. Since a friend was likely to know more about the job and its likely fit to the applicant, the relationship could smooth the new worker's entry and help him learn the ropes.

The importance of networks and social capital was further developed by James Coleman in his work on educational equality and achievement. In *The Adolescent Society: The Social Life of the Teenager and Its Impact on Education,* he pointed to the influence of peer networks and horizontal associations on grades and leadership in high school (Coleman 1961). In his nationwide study of racial equality in the schools he showed that the academic performance of minority students is better in those schools where most of the other students come from families with better educational backgrounds and greater income (Coleman 1966). Somewhat surprisingly, Catholic parochial schools did better than the public schools in encouraging achievement by both black and white students. The parochial students were almost a grade ahead of their peers in public schools; moreover, they placed a greater value on scholastic success. The racial difference was smaller and decreased from elementary to high school, whereas it increased in the public schools. The explanation appeared to lie in the stronger consensus on goals in the parochial than in the public schools (Coleman 1990a).

Coleman developed these insights into a theory about the connection between shared social norms and collective efficiency. In his theory of social capital he shows how mutual trust and cooperation can substitute for other resources. By helping each other, a group gets work done more efficiently and with less material investment. For example, farmers who take turns working on each other's farms during the hay-baling season can be more profitable and efficient by working together and saving money on labor and tools than if they each were to operate independently (Coleman 1990b).

A very new study by Latina social scientist Sylvia Domínguez (2011) uses insights about social networks in two public housing projects and their surrounding neighborhoods to explain several immigrant women's ability to climb out of poverty. Domínguez interviewed 19 poor Latina mothers on welfare in East Boston and South Boston to discover what factors enabled them to leave public housing and in some cases become homeowners in their countries of origin. The successful ones were not only self-starters (SPAs, "Self-Propelling Actors"); they also knew how to leverage their contacts to find assistance, jobs, help for their children, and other opportunities that enabled them to become upwardly mobile. Those in South Boston did somewhat better because of the "bridges" that they had to such persons as the nun, Sister Magdalena, who through her connection to the Catholic Church and the surrounding community was able to link the immigrant women to community authorities and social service workers. In addition, more of the immigrants in South Boston were SPAs who believed in the immigrant narrative of eventual upward mobility and were thereby emboldened to take advantage of existing resources.

If the social capital of a community (its norms, mutual trust, and reciprocity) helps members to achieve their goals, it is necessary to understand better the mechanisms and processes by which the social environment affects life outcomes. Life course theory identifies the key factors and dynamics by which residential location affects individual life outcomes.

Neighborhoods, Networks, and Life Chances

If influential social networks are critical to helping individuals achieve their goals, the mechanisms by which they operate must be spelled out more clearly. In his ecological theory of development, Urie Bronfenbrenner (1979) described the widening circles of influence on children that begin with the immediate family and extend to the neighborhood and the school. He had learned from his own experience of growing up on the 3,000-acre campus of a state institution for the "feeble-minded," where his father was the superintendent. When normal children were erroneously assigned by the courts to the institution, their scores on the Stanford-Binet IQ test declined after a time to the point that his father was unable to get them transferred. When, however, his mother was able to get certain children to work in the house and to benefit from her close attention and supervision, their scores rose and they were able to leave the institution.

In *Children of the Great Depression: Social Change in Life Experience*, Elder (1974) demonstrates how growing up in a deprived family during the 1930s produced different life outcomes in adulthood for the children of deprived and nondeprived families. When interviewed two decades later, in the 1950s, the deprived boys had more vocational stability and greater relative occupational achievement then the nondeprived boys. The girls from deprived families were especially devoted to domesticity and stopped work when they were married. Elder explained the outcomes for both groups as a reaction to the experiences of their childhood. Thus girls from the deprived families who had to help with the housework because their mothers were working learned to value the luxury of being able not to work outside the home whereas girls from the nondeprived families, whose mothers were at home, were more likely to view the opportunity to combine paid work and family life in a positive light.

There are four key causal variables in life course theory: (1) the historical and cultural context, (2) social networks, (3) human agency, and (4) the timing of events (the age at which major transitions occur) (Elder and Giele 2009; Giele and Elder 1998). Housing arrangements and neighborhoods provide the cultural matrix and social networks in which individual human agency is enabled and important life events (e.g., marriage, childbirth, getting a job) occur. Several recent studies indicate the importance of the way that family background, neighborhood composition, and sense of control are connected to individual achievement or failure.

Impact of Cultural Differences

Of the many kinds of possible cultural difference (such as based on race, religion, or nationality) the two most prominent are social class and race. Both features are highly associated with income and educational differences between communities that in turn affect the quality of the schools and the safety of the neighborhood.

Social class and parenting styles. In *Unequal Childhoods: Class, Race, and Family Life,* Annette Lareau (2003) describes how middle-class parents actively cultivate their children's skills and talents whereas poor and work-ing-class parents more or less take it for granted that their children will grow up naturally if they are properly cared for. These styles largely deter-mine whether children finish high school and get into college. Despite hav-ing reasonable SAT scores and high aspirations, the children whose parents have less education and income get less coaching in how to navigate the various requirements and deadlines. As a result, more of them fail to finish high school and fill out the applications for college (Lareau and Weininger 2008). These dynamics are behind the fierce efforts of middle-class parents to live in middle-class communities where the schools are good. They know that a good education is required to maintain middle-class status and to avoid downward mobility.

Race, nationality, and immigrant history. Being white carries a huge advan-tage because it is easier to live in a good neighborhood with a good school system even if you have rather low income and limited education. For example, Gary Orfield and Nancy McArdle (2006) found that in the Boston area over half of poor whites, despite low incomes, lived in suburbs in 1999 compared with only 10 percent of blacks and 15 percent of Latinos. Closely related to being a minority race is being a recent Latino immigrant. Domín-guez (2011) finds that being a first-generation immigrant is an advantage for upward mobility because recent immigrants are motivated with the promise of the American dream and a belief in their own capacity to control events.

Nor have they yet experienced the socialization as second-class citizens which overtakes the second generation.

Influence of Neighborhood Networks

The type of community experienced during childhood profoundly shapes life chances later on. Elder and Conger (2000), in their study of Iowa farm youth during the Iowa farm crisis of the 1980s, demonstrated the ways in which size and strength of a community shapes the lives of adolescents. During the crisis many family farmers lost their farms. The children from families in small towns where they were involved in 4-H, church activities, and school events had better grades, more involvement in school events, and a greater sense of confidence and competence than the children in the larger towns where the families had fewer social connections and were less involved in civic, church, and school affairs.

In his book *There Are No Children Here: The Story of Two Boys Growing Up in the Other America,* Kotlowitz (1991) documents life in an inner-city housing project in Chicago from the time it was built in the 1950s to its sad deterioration and loss of hope over a succeeding 30-year period. Families who started out in a shiny new building with great aspirations about the future gradually broke apart and saw their children threatened by violence and the temptations of petty crime. The residents ended up discouraged in the face of repeated failure at school and efforts to make a better life.

The big question is what leads such potentially healthy neighborhoods into decay, and on the other hand, what protects the safety, housing quality, and schools of those communities that continue to be desirable. In their review of major studies of neighborhood quality and its effect on adolescent behavior, Sampson, Morenoff, and Gannon-Rowley (2002) conclude that poor neighborhood quality predicts a host of social ills that include high infant mortality, low birth weight, child maltreatment, high rates of high school dropout, delinquency, teenage childbearing, and such adverse health events as homicide, suicide, and accidental injury. These authors then examine the characteristics of the neighborhoods that are particularly associated with negative behavioral and health indicators. Repeatedly they discover that adverse outcomes are linked to *concentrated disadvantage,* which is in turn highly correlated with low rates of homeownership, residential instability, and a high proportion of single-parent families. These characteristics are related to "place stratification" by social class, race, and family structure as well as geographic isolation of African Americans.

Still, these correlations do not explain the dynamic mechanisms by which such features operate to produce high crime, poor health, and low achievement in some areas but not others. Sampson and colleagues (2002) probed further and found four types of neighborhood mechanisms that make a difference: (1) strong social ties and interaction that (unlike gangs) are oriented to the public good and are a resource that can safeguard the neighborhood; (2) norms that promote collective efficiency and allow adults to intervene on behalf of children, which is only possible when there is mutual trust and shared expectations; (3) presence of numerous public institutions such as libraries, schools, childcare, and organized social and recreational opportunities that are actively used by residents and address the needs of children and youth; and 4) spatial arrangements and architecture in the area that are conducive to social interaction and pedestrian traffic and do not divide or isolate residential buildings by no man's lands of parking lots and large commercial buildings. Taken together, these neighborhood features add up to the degree of neighborhood control over deviant behavior. When ties are weak and norms unclear, the sanctions also are weak because the residents are unwilling to intervene and do not feel empowered by the group to administer the sanctions that stop unwanted behavior. The opposite picture is found in communities of concentrated affluence where residents feel empowered and entitled to call the police and demand punishment of action they do not like (Brooks-Gunn, Duncan, Klebanov, and Sealand 1993). But it takes economic resources, residential stability, and a sense of inner worth on the part of the residents to enforce the rules.

Besides allowing for control of antisocial behavior, neighborhood quality also appears to affect physical and mental health. In their review of neighborhood studies, Sampson and colleagues (2002) also asked what explains the connection between poor neighborhood quality and problematic mental health. They found that low neighborhood cohesion is linked to risk-taking behavior, high-risk sex, deviant peer affiliations, and greater mental distress such as seen in depression or suicide. It is well known that social support is a key resource for individual health and is associated in the general population with better health and lower mortality (National Institute on Aging 2011). Not surprisingly then, residents of poor neighborhoods, with their low social cohesion, are at greater risk for poor mental and physical health. These deficient settings also are implicated in stunted child development. One of the greatest threats is early and continued exposure to severe stress.

Developmental Consequences of Exposure to Toxic Stress

Where social capital may ultimately have the greatest impact is on individual development. Those neighborhoods where social ties are weak and trust is low also are typically places of concentrated disadvantage. People are anxious about their safety, about paying the rent, and about having enough food. Stress on parents can lead to harsh discipline and maltreatment of the children. Under these conditions stress is high, and infants and young children are especially vulnerable to harmful consequences for their physical, emotional, and cognitive development.

Researchers of the National Scientific Council on the Developing Child (2009) have assembled findings from a variety of psychological, economic, and animal studies to show that high levels of stress—such as brought on by deprivation, violence, and lack of social support—can damage the growing infant brain so that neuron density is visibly stunted by the age of 9 months and serious difficulty in learning is visible in delayed language acquisition and emotional development by age 2. The outlook for success in school is low even before the child has reached kindergarten. For adults also, the signs of chronic stress are visible in such health indicators as high blood pressure, diabetes, and elevated levels of stress response hormones such as adrenaline and cortisol. Evans, Brooks-Gunn, and Klebanov (2011) have spelled out the pathways that lead from living in a poor neighborhood to difficulties in school and adolescence as follows:

Poverty

Cumulative Risk Exposure

Chronic Stress

Low Achievement

The implication of these findings for the American economy and its future workforce are tremendous. An interdisciplinary team including Nobel economist James Heckman have put together findings from economics, developmental psychology, and neurobiology to conclude that the early environmental influences and negative effects of poverty are so important in early brain development and subsequent damage to learning capacity that the future workforce of the nation is at risk unless early intervention can protect disadvantaged children's capacity "for intellectual flexibility, problem solving skills, emotional resilience, and the capacity to work with others in a constantly changing and highly competitive economic environment" (Knudtson et al. 2006:10161). If as these authors say, "Prevention is more effective and less costly than remediation," the question is how this can be done. This chapter concludes with a brief review of the various efforts currently in progress to strengthen disadvantaged neighborhoods and promote the healthy development of children and families who are at special risk of school failure and long-term dependency. Consistent with the theoretical work of James Coleman (1988), these experimental neighborhood-based programs are building social capital in order to protect and increase the human capital (i.e., the education, skills, and problem-solving ability) of their residents.

Neighborhood Initiatives to Strengthen Families and Children

This chapter began with the American Dream and the central place that homeownership has in realizing that dream. But the dream cannot come true unless families have sufficient drive, education, and skills to gain the income that makes ownership possible. The stark reality is that many poor Americans are now caught in a vicious cycle where they are trapped in housing and in neighborhoods that destroy their initiative and sabotage their children's likelihood of ever being able to do well enough in school and gain good enough jobs to be able to escape a downward spiral. These are conditions where pure individual efforts and free market mechanisms are inadequate. Some sort of public or collective intervention is necessary to strengthen such beneficial factors as neighborhood cohesion, social capital, and educational resources.

The federal government has initiated several new programs that focus more on community mobilization than housing. The U.S. Department of Education in 2011 launched the Promise Neighborhood Initiative to energize school and community partnerships in 21 cities throughout the nation (U.S. Department of Education 2011). Also in 2011, the Department of Health and Human Services under the Affordable Care Act authorized $100 million for grants to create healthier communities by addressing chronic diseases, tobacco use, preventive measures, physical exercise, and environmental hazards (U.S. Department of Health and Human Services 2011a).

A variety of social programs address different aspects of strengthening families, and they range all across the age spectrum, from early child care programs to parent education, prenatal classes, neighborhood self-help associations, and youth development programs. Of particular interest in this chapter on housing and neighborhoods are the programs aimed at minority youth and children, and poor families.

YouthBuild USA. In 1978, a small group of teenagers in East Harlem decided to renovate a building in their neighborhood. Under the leadership of Dorothy Stoneman, what began with only volunteer help and small donations has gradually grown into a national organization that boasts 100,000 largely poor and minority youth who have come through its doors and in the process have learned construction and leadership skills, finished their GEDs, and secured well-paying jobs that have put them on the road to economic independence. There are currently over 4,000 young people, ages 16 to 24, in more than 400 sites around the country. As a sign of its success, YouthBuild USA recently received $75.8 million from HUD to construct or renovate single-family houses, low-cost and affordable housing, and apartment buildings (U.S. Department of Labor 2011). In some of the programs, over half the participants have had a prison record. Working in the program enabled them to finish school, gain important skills, make decisions, and take control of their lives. They now feel respected and appreciated by the community, and their contributions have affected whole neighborhoods. One participant recalled, "I've seen an entire block change thanks to the renovation of one house. All it takes is for a few people to start making improvements, and pretty soon community spirit starts to revive and the whole neighborhood is renewed. And seeing young men and women in the lead gives a community hope" (Piotrowski 1997:4).

Harlem Children's Zone. In 1990 Geoffrey Canada became the president of a nonprofit organization that at the time provided help to poor families and children in Harlem. Gradually the organization grew from a community center and charter school to offer a spectrum of programs for parents and infants and support for students through high school. Seeing that there was always a waiting list for the highly sought after charter school, Canada began to rethink the scope of the enterprise and decided to create a zone of almost 100 blocks in central Harlem that would include the community center, a "baby college," the existing charter school, and various other programs to compensate for the chronic disadvantage experienced by the African American population of the area (Tough 2008). The results have been dramatic. The black kids at entry into the middle school tested at the 39th percentile among New York City students in math. By eighth grade the typical student was in the 74th percentile; Promise Academy had succeeded in eliminating the difference in math performance between black students and the city average for white students. Commentator David Brooks (2009) attributes this dramatic success to a "no excuses" focus on standards of proper behavior, good manners, and a demand for academic excellence. The experiment confirms the importance of intense social support and consensus on the value of achievement. Moreover, in keeping with the ideal of prevention and of starting early, the Harlem Children's Zone encompasses not only a large physical area but concern for the child from infancy through high school (Harlem Children's Zone 2011).

The Family Independence Initiative. The newest example of promising efforts to help families and communities out of poverty began in Oakland, California, in 2001. Rather than use the social services model that helps people by meeting their needs and compensating for their deficits, Lim Miller, its founder, insists that families themselves provide help to each other rather than depend on the experts. "F.I.I. creates a space for families that encourages sense of control, desire for self-direction, and mutual support" (Bornstein 2011). By supporting the initiative of the member families and getting them to ask for help and give support to each other, the project has been remarkably successful. The organization gives out computers to keep track of any change in income, assets, debts, health, education, skills, social networks, and civic engagement. For every success reported it offers $30, up to a maximum of $200 a month. But families have to take the lead. The families typically want to avoid giving advice. Most people are shy and modest at first, then eventually learn to hold each other to account by such questions as, "Didn't you say you were going to get your G.E.D.? Where are you with that?" (p. 12). In a couple of years household incomes increased by one-quarter (not including the $30 payments) and by three years they had risen 40 percent. Again the principles of social capital formation combined with encouragement of individual initiative appear to have worked in the beneficial ways that Coleman (1988) predicted. Social capital is a critical factor in the formation of human capital.

Conclusion

Housing does indeed locate a family in a setting that can either promote or hinder general happiness, productivity, and child development. Sociologists have generally shown very little interest in housing policy, but they have been leaders in understanding how residential location is linked to social class, race, and general life chances.

This chapter began with a descriptive profile of housing in America and how it has changed over the last century. The biggest overall shift has been from a rural to urban economy, with the great majority of the population now living in metropolitan areas that span central cities and suburbs. Between 1939 and 1992 the proportion of the population living on farms dropped from 25 percent to less than 1 percent. The fraction of homeowners rose from under one-half of all households in 1940 to over two-thirds today. Household floor space increased by half, along with number of bedrooms and baths. While house values increased dramatically from 1972 to 2000, thereby endowing their owners with substantial appreciation on their assets, the situation of renters became more onerous. Not only were their incomes lower than that of homeowners, but also the proportion of their income spent on housing could total as much as 25 percent or 30 percent. Even though renters whose costs exceed 30 percent of income are eligible for assistance, only half of those eligible get any help. As to homeownership, the collapse of the housing bubble in 2007–2010 removed some of the luster from the American Dream. Many working-class and minority first-time homebuyers faced foreclosure, and the rate of homeownership declined from its peak of 70 percent.

Changes in housing policy paralleled the demographic shift from cities to suburbs. The greatest growth and biggest public investment went into construction of over 1 million homes per year throughout the 1950s, as homebuyers took advantage of low-interest home loans and tax write-offs for mortgage costs and local property taxes. Public support for rental housing and subsidized units was much less generous, producing only a tiny fraction of the number of units of single-family houses built during the same period. Accompanying the schemes for public housing was a belief in urban renewal that would first clear the slums and then replace dilapidated and crowded buildings with shiny new high-rise apartments. By the late 1970s, however, it was clear that these policies had been a failure because they scattered former residents to the suburbs and created isolated ghettos of poor people who were unable to create a robust new community.

Housing legislation, since the 1980s, has moved in the direction of creating individualized row houses while also subsidizing construction for mixed-income housing. Rather than concentrate poor people in one project, there is now an effort to disperse them into nonpoor areas through rental vouchers or access to subsidized mixed-income units. The lion's share of public tax expenditures still goes to homeowners, but progress in support for subsidized housing has made it much more varied. Rather than a single strategy of slum clearance and building big housing projects, government support now goes to rental housing in several forms: public housing, subsidized mixed-income housing, and Section 8 vouchers for subsidized rentals. Efforts to make the sale of mortgages more responsible and transparent also have succeeded in the establishment of the Consumer Financial Protection Bureau in 2011. Its purpose is to make lending and credit transactions much more understandable to the average layperson. These reforms also will presumably protect the public against other major financial disasters of the kind that led to the Great Recession of 2008–2010.

Where sociological insights have really led the way is in understanding the impact of environment on families as it is mediated through social class, social networks, and social capital. Dollard, Warner, and others documented the power of social class differences in small-town America. Riesman and Whyte followed in the 1950s to show how social class hierarchies had to some extent dissolved in the face of corporate transfers and suburban living. Relationship to peers and "horizontal associations" had gained ascendancy. The next insight of sociologists was to understand the importance of social networks and social capital to housing and the neighborhood. Granovetter, Coleman, and Sampson and colleagues illuminated the impact of social networks on many aspects of social life, especially the vitality of neighborhoods. Shared trust, norms of reciprocity, and an interest in collective purpose create *social capital* that can be deployed in ways that lead to civic engagement, community improvement, and good outcomes for families and children.

Finally, all these forces—the different types of housing, the character of the surrounding neighborhood, and the strength of community ties—bear on the inhabitants' chances for upward mobility. Poor communities that are characterized by *concentrated disadvantage* (i.e., sparse public institutions, inability to control deviant behavior, and scarcity of material resources) are places of high and chronic stress that interfere with the cognitive, emotional, and physical well-being of the residents. Affluent communities, on the other hand, are able to insist on high standards, intervene in deviant behavior, and promote school quality and institutional resources that enable their children to succeed.

To assure an intelligent and well-trained workforce for the future, it is in the interest of the whole nation to find ways that will prevent the stunting of child development in poor communities and lay the foundation for upward mobility and all-around competence in its adult citizens. Several experimental programs have had stunning success in showing how positive growth can be encouraged. *YouthBuild USA* is a construction program for poor and minority youth, which is now funded by HUD, that teaches construction skills, rehabilitates youths who have had a court record, and at the same time brings hope to disadvantaged districts by renovating the housing there. The *Harlem Children's Zone* has effected a transformation in a 100-block section of Central Harlem. Its programs embrace the African American children in the area, from infancy through high school, with social support and high expectations. The program has accomplished dramatic success in getting children to raise their test scores, finish high school, and prepare for college. The *Family Independence Initiative* that began in Oakland, California, in 2002 is still small but also has reported remarkable improvement in incomes of the poor families who are its members. Rather than getting help from experts, the participants themselves articulate goals, monitor their successes, and hold each other to account.

In sum, "Location, location, location," turns out to be a mantra not only for real estate agents but also for sociologists of family policy. The ecology of residential location is like a natural habitat in which all the plants and animals are interdependent. So it is in the housing field: Changing demography and social policies affect whoever lives in the neighborhood, and the resulting community affects the inhabitants for good or for ill. The challenge for future policy makers is to take these truths into account in any new efforts to improve the nation's housing.

7

Family Heritage, Identity, and Citizenship

P revious chapters in this book covered three defining functions of families—caregiving, economic support, and a place to live. This chapter treats a fourth key function—the transmission of a cultural heritage to children and their legitimation as citizens in the nation at large. Sociologists have always paid a great deal of attention to the family's importance in the socialization of children—the molding of their identity through language, distinctive customs, and patterns of life. But very little explicit attention has been given to the family as the most formative influence in whether a child attains full citizenship (as compared with "second-class citizenship") in the larger society.

There appear to be three main reasons for this lack of attention to the family's role in helping children to attain full citizenship. The primary reason is that the family's socializing role is thought of as a private matter rather than a public concern. Second, the problems of racial, ethnic, and religious inequality have been treated as primarily due to social forces outside the family such as segregation, prejudice, and discrimination. As a result, public policy to achieve equal rights has focused on expanding legal rights to voting, access to public accommodations, equal education, and employment opportunity, not on how to help families combat negative stereotypes and demeaning expectations. Finally, the reigning explanations of changes and variation in legal and social rights of citizenship have focused primarily on the actions of the state—whether the nation has a single language requirement, is tolerant of multicultural traditions, or insists on the primacy of its own distinctive national culture. Experts such as Bloemraad (with Korteweg and Yurdakul 2008) point out that another kind of explanation of second-class status is possible but has been given insufficient attention, namely, the "agency," or actions of minority groups themselves. It is in the matter of agency that the family is particularly important. Schools, religious congregations, the media, and friends and neighbors also transmit culture by rewarding compliance and punishing deviance. But the family is the crucible where all these influences come together.

More than any other single group, the family preserves and transmits the main elements of any culture and shapes the identity of the person. In the words of Carola and Marcelo Suárez-Orozco (2001:vii), "The main function of the family is the transfer of skills, values, and world views to the next generation." As cultural diversity increases in the United States, minority families are confronted with choices about maintaining their language, beliefs, and customs, and helping their children to internalize the dominant culture. Conversely, the families whose culture is the dominant one must learn to deal not only with those unlike themselves but also with the challenges of gaining the education and skills that will serve them in the face of globalization and new economic challenges.

These questions become especially important in defining the requirements of citizenship. If a person is black, or Jewish, or foreign born, is that individual entitled to the same rights and privileges as those of the native majority? At the societal level these questions are worked out in the Constitution, the laws, and public policy. For example, Martin Luther King turned to the provisions and ideals in the Constitution and Declaration of Independence as the basis for defending the rights of black citizens. He fought to close the gap between what was in the founding documents and what actually happened to blacks in voting, public accommodations, housing, and employment. The day-to-day enactment of the tensions between American ideals and race prejudice is played out in the ways that families interact with their community. The matter of family identity is included here as an essential but largely ignored aspect of family policy.

Questions of racial, religious, and ethnic equality are not just matters of public policy, but of *family* policy, because it is birth into a family of origin that determines a person's race, religion, and language group. These basic markers have affected the definition of citizenship in the U.S. Constitution. One must be born in the United States or of citizen parents to be a *natural* citizen.[1] This single requirement for natural citizenship is in stark contrast

---

[1]Place of birth and family of origin are therefore critical to qualification for citizenship. Recently immigration authorities have seen cases of affluent foreign-born mothers who arrive in the United States for a brief stay in order to have their babies born here and assure their American citizenship (Medina 2011a).

to the much more elaborate requirements of *naturalization* to become a citizen, which are five-year residence, English literacy, passing a civics test, and assurance of some basis for economic support. Whether one is *born* in the United States or *adopted* by parents who are citizens, *natural* citizenship is inevitably defined by relationship to a family of origin.

To identify the relevant aspects of family policy that apply to transmission of culture and legitimation of citizenship, this chapter uses a comparative strategy to highlight differences in family experiences between the majority and the most and least successful minority racial, ethnic, religious, and immigrant groups. From the nineteenth century on, modern societies have also been concerned with assuring *social* citizenship to all their members, which means, in addition to the right to vote and hold property, belonging as a full member to the society and being entitled to all its rights, protections, and privileges (Bloemraad et al. 2008; Marshall 1964). Thus a sign of denial of these privileges is to be treated like a "second-class citizen," which Myrdal and his coauthors (with Sterner and Rose 1944) found widespread in a massive study of the situation of American Negroes up to World War II. Such basic social rights as public education, access to public accommodations, and respectful treatment were not being accorded to them as to the white majority.

Family identity bears on these issues of social citizenship not just in terms of a person's birthplace inside or outside the United States, but also in terms of the cultural background of the family and the material and social resources at its command. A family's cultural tradition and living situation weigh heavily in determining the life chances of family members. This chapter treats these issues from a sociological perspective by describing and analyzing how families differ in the ways that they transmit their heritage to their children.

The chapter is divided into four parts. The first section describes the family's role in shaping identity by presenting examples of both downward and upward mobility and how the family's role differs in each. The second part provides a descriptive profile of the important minority religious, racial, ethnic, and immigrant communities that support families and that also contribute to identity formation and the transmission of a cultural heritage. A third section takes up current controversies surrounding immigration since 1965 and the important questions related to citizenship and the family that are raised by the presence of several million undocumented residents. The chapter closes with a theory of adaptation and inclusion that helps to account for the progress that has been made up to the present in the integration of minority religious, ethnic, and racial groups into American society. The process of inclusion offers guidance as ways to integrate illegal immigrant families and their children into American society. Family membership is so intimately connected with citizenship that any workable immigration policy must take family factors into account. The most promising initiatives are those that create a path to citizenship by providing access to higher education for children of undocumented immigrants. Immigration policy intersects with family policy when it strengthens the family's authority and capability of encouraging its children to complete their education and aim for jobs and careers that lead them into the American mainstream rather than to marginalization and downward mobility.

The Family's Influence on Identity Formation

Much of what we read today about prejudice and discrimination against blacks, Jews, Hispanics, or undocumented immigrants occurs in a public setting such as schools, public accommodations, or the workplace. The persistent questions concern whether these settings provide equal opportunity, whether they punish favoritism, or whether they offer extra support for those who are disadvantaged in the pecking order of society. Actions of public institutions, however, are only one factor in the equation that makes for individual success. Another factor is the family. Not only does family origin determine the markers that are the basis for discrimination. The family is also the crucible of identity formation and the adaptive behaviors that prepare its members either to accept humiliation and exclusion or to persist in the face of prejudice and discrimination.

The type of adaptive behavior that a family inculcates in its members is especially shaped by its own goals and values. But the family's action alone does not determine a member's ultimate fate. Of significant importance also are expectations and stereotypes from outside the family, the availability of social support from mentors and educators and employers, and the particular assets such as income, housing, and the resources to pay for "extras" such as music lessons or travel. These elements come together to affect the ways that families adapt to their situation and in turn instill a particular mode of adaptation in their children. Over the past century in America it appears that the negative influence of being from a minority family has somewhat diminished if the family has adequate economic resources. For African Americans in particular, who faced the greatest barriers to assimilate and to achieve full citizenship, the mood is much more hopeful. As Ellis Cose (2011) reports in *The End of Anger: A New Generation's Take on Race and*

Rage, the election of President Obama removed the glass ceiling in the minds of many blacks. This optimism, however, was not due to the election alone but was built on 30 years of progress in electing black officials to public office and promoting black men and women through elite educational institutions to top positions in business and the professions. Even though such positive results are limited to a relatively few members of the black middle class, the fact that such change occurred at all is testimony to a very different field of opportunity from what existed 50 years ago.

In Cose's account, the individuals with the most dramatic success stories come from families who deliberately positioned their children in situations that could lead to their success. Thus the story of moving from second- to first-class citizenship is the story of the *interaction* between the family and the surrounding society. Just as some black middle-class families have become more hopeful and deliberately chose the strategies that would give their children a better life, so also the society has become more welcoming than 50 years ago in offering opportunities to outstanding members of disadvantaged minority groups. The new outlook of the younger generation is the product of new ways of bringing up children that were made possible by the concrete gains of the post–Civil Rights generation. The greater economic and political success of that generation enabled them to insist on the importance of their children's getting a good education. This in turn resulted in a self-concept in this successful younger generation that is still relatively rare. They see themselves as intelligent, competent, and responsible—potential winners—a self-image that was both difficult to instill and to sustain in the Jim Crow era.

For an earlier generation, even during the Jim Crow era and de facto segregation, education was emphasized as the primary vehicle for gaining opportunity. Stable working-class blacks who found economic security through factory work and unionized jobs in the auto, steel, and mining industries had the resources to send their children to college. The majority went to traditional black colleges and a few (like W. E. B. DuBois) went to elite white institutions like Harvard. This is important because the creation of a black professional middle class *before* the civil rights revolution was made possible by working-class blacks with stable families. (Martin Luther King came from such a family.) Hence, the disappearance of factories and the loss of industries to other parts of the world adversely affected poor blacks and poor whites. They did not have a comparable route to security (Williams 2011).

Cose recognizes that his sample of black Harvard MBA graduates and alumnae of A Better Chance (for talented high school girls and boys of minority background) are not typical of their generation.[2] Nevertheless, he is documenting the leading edge of a new wave of black consciousness that turns old stereotypes on their head and gives insight into the life stories of those who are able to make such dramatic gains. I find in these stories four elements that are typical of pioneers who depart from traditional expectations. First, they have a distinct *identity* as being different or unusual in some way, often that they are the best students in the class. Second, they have mentors or supportive *personal or institutional networks* that help them to succeed. Third, they have a high level of *personal motivation* and desire to achieve. Finally, they use *innovative strategies* that are adaptive and flexible; they are ready to risk trying new approaches in order to prevail (Giele 2009). If one reviews various accounts of how different members of minority religious, racial, and ethnic groups have been able to "make it," it turns out that their families have had a role in helping them in each of these four respects. Conversely, those who have become discouraged and resigned to defeat have lacked one or more of these sources of support.

Two Contrasting Vignettes

The simplest way to convey the entire picture of family influence on identity formation is to contrast two extreme examples. The first is a subtle and detailed portrait by sociologist Lee Rainwater (1966) of a young woman from a lower-class Negro family living in a St. Louis housing project in the 1950s. The other is one of the examples given by Ellis Cose (2011) of a very successful young African American woman who grew up in a black neighborhood in Brooklyn but was able to leave there, graduate from Swarthmore, and become a top-level assistant to several big-city mayors. Both of these women faced what Pettigrew (1966) has termed the *stigma* of race. So how does one explain the striking success of the younger woman, and what role did each girl's family play in shaping her fate?

Rainwater's account of the poor family living in a Negro ghetto in the 1950s is not only peculiar to the pre–civil rights era; it is also a description of a destructive family dynamic that dooms Esther Johnson to early childbearing and long-term dependency. Cose's description of a successful young

---

[2]For example, Deval Patrick, who came from a single-parent family in Chicago, became the first African American governor of Massachusetts in 2007. When he was in the eighth grade, he was sponsored by A Better Chance to attend Milton Academy, an elite private school outside Boston, from which he went on to attend Harvard College and Harvard Law School.

African American in this decade describes a changed social climate in which there is more opportunity for education and economic success. Yet, here also, the family dynamic is crucial in positioning Desiree Peterkin Bell at the door to educational achievement and career success.

The single most obvious difference is the historical period in which both young women came of age. Rainwater (1966) describes a 16-year-old girl, Esther Johnson, living in a black public housing project in St. Louis in the 1950s. Before the civil rights revolution Negroes are still living under the weight of the Jim Crow caste system. It is standard practice to treat colored people as members of an inferior race—primitive, less intelligent, unbridled in sexual activity, and prone to violence—fit only for unskilled work as laborers or domestic servants (Dollard, 1937; Pettigrew 1966). This racial ideology not only served the interests of the superior white caste but was also internalized as a negative identity by the Negro family and its members. That identity ultimately served as an adaptation by helping them accept discriminatory and exploitive labor practices and humiliating social encounters. The social supports were absent that would give the person an alternative identity as competent, responsible, and worthy of respect and fair treatment. The poverty of Esther's family and its disorganization worked against any hope or motivation for achievement. Despite manifold efforts to hold off some boys' advances and reduce the frequency of sexual activity, both Esther and her sister became pregnant. But no one was particularly surprised. The care of the babies would be the responsibility of their overburdened mother while they and their siblings and half siblings continued a dissolute lifestyle of drinking, frequent sexual activity, and hanging out with the peer group. The overall picture of the family is one of the elder Mrs. Johnson's inability to control her household. In Rainwater's account the brothers and sisters call each other names and cast aspersions on their mother and her marital history as well as their own paternity, as in "These kids don't even know who their daddy is" (Rainwater 1966:189). The entire social structure contributes to a socialization process that keeps them in their place. As Rainwater (1966:193) observes,

[I]n Negro slum culture growing up involves an ever increasing appreciation of one's shortcomings, of the inability of finding a self-sufficient and gratifying way of living. . . . To those living in the heart of the ghetto, black comes to mean not just "stay back," but also membership in a community of persons who think poorly of each other, who attack and manipulate each other, who give each other small comfort in a desperate world. Black comes to stand for a sense of identity as no better than these destructive others. The individual feels that he must embrace an unattractive self in order to function at all.

Or, what is attractive gets redefined. For example, having a baby as an unwed teenager looks normative because many in the housing projects and the neighborhood have children and are also not married (Williams 1990).

What a hopeful contrast comes from the description of Desiree Peterkin Bell! When Ellis Cose interviewed her in 2010 she was communications director for Mayor Booker of Newark and previously had had a comparable position for Mayor Bloomberg of New York as well as the mayor of Indianapolis. Desiree had come of age more than two decades after the civil rights revolution. By then a significant number of black women and men had become mayors, governors, and members of Congress. African American racial identity was no longer inevitably stigmatized. Moreover, social and institutional supports were greatly improved. The Equal Pay Act of 1963 and the Civil Rights Act of 1964 outlawed discrimination by race. Head Start, the ABC (A Better Chance) program, special scholarship opportunities, and affirmative action by schools and colleges showed that great progress could be made toward racial equality with an expansion of educational opportunity. Desiree was identified as one of those talented young people for an ABC program in Pennsylvania, and her mother encouraged her to go. Although it meant leaving her family and neighborhood in Brooklyn, she turned down the acceptances that she had already received from top high schools in New York City such as Bronx Science. She reported that

> My mother, to her credit, really saw it as an opportunity for me to get a little further ahead than anyone else. And that meant stepping outside the world that I knew and creating a whole new network of relationships, of friends, of people of support (Cose 2011:18).

Her mother's encouragement reinforced her motivation to set high goals and take advantage of the opportunities that would not have been open to her if she had stayed at home. (In fact, one of her childhood friends—also very bright—became pregnant at the age of 14 and gave up going to college.) While this plan felt risky—to go to a good high school in an elite suburban community far from home, it was an innovative strategy that set her on the path to unusual success.

In sum, these two stories, although they represent two ends of a continuum from failure to success, show the differences in the process of forging a negative or positive identity. To gain a positive self-image in the face of stigma there must first of all be a cultural climate that punishes discrimination and promotes equality. A second requirement is supportive social and institutional surroundings. Then within this encompassing cultural and institutional matrix, the family must have enough authority and resources to promote a sense of purpose and desire for achievement in its children. Finally, the results are seen in the capacity of the younger generation who have experienced these benefits to move beyond the world of limited opportunity and truncated expectations that was experienced by their parents and grandparents. The Negro girl who grew up in the St. Louis ghetto of the 1950s would never leave it whereas the African American girl who left her familiar neighborhood in Brooklyn in the 1990s to attend a suburban mostly "white" high school out of state and then go to a good college had some hope of reaching the top of the American social and corporate structure.

The theory of identity formation can also be used to explain upward mobility and assimilation among new immigrants who are now being studied by demographers, psychologists, and various other social scientists. The 1965 Immigration Act opened the country once again to large-scale immigration that had been slowed to a trickle by quotas based on national origin that were established by the Immigration Act of 1924. The result has been a new kind of immigrant who does not "assimilate" or "melt" into American society along the straight-line trajectory that was followed by second and third generations of white Europeans. The situation is now much more complex because of the more diverse racial origins of the migrants and because of a service-oriented economy that offers less chance of upward mobility to laborers and blue-collar workers. Blocked mobility in turn causes families to adopt new strategies for socializing their children that result in a wider array of possible identities—"immigrant," "transnational," "ethnic," or (black or white) "American." A wealth of new research on recent immigrants gives a window on how these different adaptations emerge. Our central question is which of these identities is most likely to lead to upward mobility and eventual success in joining American society, and how are they formed.

Identity Formation in the Face of Stigma

The most striking difference between immigrants before and after 1965 is skin color. The 1965 Immigration Act stemmed from the civil rights movement, but no one expected that so many people would come from countries all over the world (Ludden 2006). Nor did Congress foresee the challenges that would be faced by people whose appearance did not blend in with the white majority. Over time, however, experience has shown that while the first generation may not feel the full impact of racial stigmatization because they continue to see themselves as "foreign," the second generation is no longer immune to racism and in many cases actually experiences downward mobility. This outcome is, of course, entirely counter to the American Dream. Against this backdrop, a central question is what factors enable some of the second generation to succeed while others fall into what may become a permanent underclass.

Carola and Marcelo Suárez-Orozco (2001) describe the primary issue as one of "social mirroring." The first generation may not even notice the racial slurs and slights, but the second generation does. Their better knowledge of English and greater interaction with schools and the peer group sensitize them to the negative image of themselves and they begin to internalize it. But some ethnic groups have social customs and networks that buffer these negative experiences and offer positive support as well. Immigrant Chinese families, for example, typically draw their community around them, insist on following their traditions, and keep up their language while at the same time expecting that the children will do well in school and bring honor to the family name (Zhou 2009).

In her book *Black Identities: West Indian Immigrant Dreams and American Realities,* Mary Waters (1999) describes the West Indian immigrants in New York City who come from places like Jamaica, Haiti, and other countries in the Caribbean. Some immigrants of West Indian parentage, like Colin Powell, have done extraordinarily well. Waters discovers from her interviews with 83 young people in the New York City area that West Indians are likely to distance themselves from American blacks and emphasize their Caribbean origins. Their reputation for hard work, for not being angry and difficult in interpersonal relationships, and their willingness to take menial jobs without feeling subservient stands them in good stead. Their higher labor force participation rates, educational attainment, and greater ability to advance to middle-class status are partly the result of resisting the negative image of their race. In addition, they bring with them the experience of having been in the majority where bankers, teachers, and other managers and professionals were black. This is a very different experience from that of African Americans who have a legacy of slavery and see mostly whites in positions of power.

This form of adaptation, maintaining a dual "transnational" identity as being from another country while also working and living in America, preserves a positive identity that enables the self-discipline and motivation that are necessary for upward mobility. The children who are not inoculated against the negative expectations of their race suffer a loss of self-esteem and are then vulnerable to an angry "oppositional" attitude that makes them sensitive to slights, less confident in the classroom, and less willing to take the low-level jobs that are available because they seem to affirm their low status by demanding an involuntary subservience (Ogbu 1990).

These processes of "symbolic violence" and "psychological disparagement" are typical where racial and ethnic inequalities are highly structured as with Algerians in France, Koreans in Japan, and Mexicans in California.

Not surprisingly, various nationalities differ in their reports of being thought of negatively in America. As Carola and Marcelo Suárez-Orozco (2001) discovered in their study of immigrants, fully four-fifths of the darkest nationalities—Dominican and Haitian—reported that most people thought of them in negative terms compared with two-thirds of Central Americans and less than half of the Chinese.

Supportive Networks and Institutions

A positive fabric of ethnic social networks can help protect the second-generation child from downward mobility. Social activities and language schools maintain the ethnic community and give an alternative positive basis for identity over against the gangs and antisocial peer groups that are associated with urban blacks. Waters (1999) notes that the West Indians in New York who were best protected from a negative identity were those involved in the church, the parochial schools, and after-school programs held at the church. The priest could act as go-between who represented respect for the ethnic traditions of the parents as well as the interests and feelings of the young people. Ethnic networks and cultural events helped to reinforce the authority of the parents while also preventing isolation among the young. The positive culture and achievement-oriented culture of these ethnic associations was in marked contrast to the Americanized peer group who ostracized good students for "acting white."

Supports and influences from outside the family also affect identity through established institutions such as schools and the workplace. Waters (1999) describes the crumbling violence-ridden inner-city high schools where she did her research in the early 1990s. She feared for her own safety because of the guns and knives that were smuggled into the school every day and were especially used against good students. In these "racially isolated" [all-black] schools many students never came to class but hung out in the schoolyard and were a menace to other students and to some of the teachers. The academic standards were low because many students were ill prepared when they came from the islands, and the most talented students were creamed off by the citywide competitive high schools. The result was that the greatest likelihood of success came to those who were selected for a scholarship or who went to a private or parochial school or one of the city high schools with entrance exams.

Family Resources and Parental Authority

The family is the ultimate crucible of identity, for it is parents' resources and authority that are either weak or strong enough to enforce the ambitious standards that the family holds for its children. Parents almost invariably immigrate with the purpose of finding a better life for themselves and their children. But some are more successful than others in seeing their dreams realized. Portes and Rumbaut (2001:77) find that some nationalities are stronger than others in family composition and human and cultural capital, and as a result, their children are more likely to do well in school and attain a higher social status. Laotians, Cambodians, and Filipinos are more likely to have intact families and the education and employment that have made them more successful, whereas Haitian and Mexican children were disadvantaged in these respects from the beginning.

Another aspect of family resources is family composition. The families with two parents and all the children living under one roof tend to be better able to envision a brighter future and actually reach it. Better-educated parents know how to reinforce what is learned in school. Those parents who are successful are clear on their goals. As Min Zhou (2009) reports, Chinese parents make clear their standards of success: Live in your own home. Be your own boss. Send your children to the Ivy League.

Family Socialization Practices

It is a subtle thing to get children to obey in the face of conflicting demands and rewards from inside and outside the home. The West Indian parents whom Waters (1999) observed were at a loss to know how to discipline their children because corporal punishment both at home and at school had been their standard method in their home country. But this is not allowed in the New York City public schools, and children learned that they could call the welfare office if they were disciplined by a spanking or beating. The result was a loss of parents' control at home and teachers' control at school. Children were disruptive in the classroom and disrespectful of their teachers. Physical punishment as a method of childrearing is in stark contrast to that of parents who use reminders of their sacrifice to motivate their children.

Zhou (2009) presents a contrasting portrait among Chinese and other Asian immigrants. Children don't necessarily want to work as hard as their parents expect. They want to go to the ballgame, have fun, and do what other kids do. They accuse their parents of being "feudal," "stubborn old heads," and the like. But even though these immigrant children may be embarrassed by their parents' poor English and old-fashioned ways, parents who have sacrificed so much by working two or three shifts and taking menial jobs usually keep the upper hand because their children come to understand that doing well in school helps to pay back their parents for all that they have done.

The difference in outcomes is clear. Portes and Rumbaut (2001:231) summarize the process when it is working well:

> . . . the processes of adaptation and success in outcomes build on each other, leading to predictable consequences. Hence, parental success in opening the doors to the American middle class translates into higher educational ambitions among children and greater confidence in reaching these goals. Higher parental status and unbroken families support fluent bilingualism and other manifestations of selective acculturation that, in turn, increase self-esteem, reinforce aspirations, and lower psychological distress. A favorable mode of incorporation and early academic achievement in school also set the grounds for an optimistic outlook on the future.

Waters (1999) notes that the "ethnic," or transnational, adaptation (which is similar to what Portes and Rumbaut term "selective acculturation") bridges the world of the old country and the new and is by far the most successful in propelling children into the middle class. Of the "ethnics" in her sample, 57 percent were middle class compared with only 36 percent of those who identified with American blacks and 7 percent of those who retained their immigrant identity. Put more starkly, Waters (1999:331) concludes,

> They [immigrants] come here to have a better standard of living for themselves and their children, and they are becoming American as the way to do it. Yet the economic payoff seems to go to those who are the least Americanized among the post-1965 immigrants. Why? For one thing, American culture seems to have a bad effect on the children of immigrants. The less Americanized they are the better they do in school, the more time they spend on homework, the less materialistic they are, and the less they challenge their parents' and teachers' discipline and authority. Discrimination is the other key to this puzzle. The more immigrant or ethnic the immigrants are, the more likely they are to have access to jobs and information from social networks, and the more likely employers are to prefer to hire them then native minorities.

A Descriptive Portrait of American Diversity

Over and over again, when one reviews the American kaleidoscope of religions, races, and nationalities, a central theme emerges. No matter how discriminated against or how much an outsider, the minority in most cases, although not all, is eventually absorbed into the majority. One big exception appears to be if the group is black, since African Americans are different from all other groups in having had to overcome a legacy of slavery. Another exception is the case of those from a despised ideological or religious minority such as the Jews in former times or Muslims today. In the case of Jews, many had European ancestry and shared the rabbinical tradition of learning that proved an asset for them in joining the melting pot. This process of gradual acceptance of outsiders by the majority and the acquisition by the newcomers of mainstream behaviors and values has been called *assimilation.* Some scholars question whether the process still operates as it did in the past because the new immigrants since 1965 are so unlike the white mostly European and Christian groups who came before them.

I will argue, however, that the relevant process is *inclusion,* which is still going on even though the new waves of immigrants differ widely from earlier waves in their religious, racial, and national origins. The process of inclusion has been described by Parsons (1966b) as a series of four changes that accompany modernization: (1) an increase in the demand for specialization and improved performance in order to meet new demands and challenges, (2) upgrading of their qualifications by participants in order to get positions that meet the new demands, (3) changes in the laws and norms to include formerly excluded groups whose contributions are needed, and (4) a generalization of values to find common ground and thereby incorporate the ideals of the formerly excluded groups.

The process of inclusion, however, is by no means automatic. History has shown that equal rights for women and civil rights for people whose ancestors had been slaves came only after decades of struggle. Social movements had to organize in order to keep up the pressure for change. The resistance from the dominant society was sometimes violent, and altogether the process of winning these rights took a very long time. Even then the victories were not 100 percent complete. The aggrieved have to keep a watchful eye and keep insisting on their rights. In addition, according to the Surgeon General's Report (2001),

> Ethnic and racial minorities in the United States face a social and economic environment of inequality that includes greater exposure to racism, discrimination, violence, and poverty. Living in poverty has the most measurable effect on the rates of mental illness. People in the lowest strata of income, education, and occupation (known as socioeconomic status) are about two to three times more likely than those in the highest strata to have a mental disorder.

In the face of such strong evidence that discrimination persists against stigmatized religious and racial groups, it is still important to explain how progress can occur. For example, how has it been possible that religious outsiders in America—from the Jews to modern-day Buddhists, Hindus, Muslims, and

Sikhs—have managed to achieve greater acceptance over time? How is it that American blacks no longer face legalized school segregation and egregious civil rights violations that were pervasive only decades ago? Parsons' theory of inclusion helps to explain the growing acceptance of minority religious, racial, and ethnic groups such as Africans, Arabs, Asians, and some groups of Native Americans. The following summary sketches the supporting evidence for this admittedly positive and hopeful interpretation of overall trends in religious, ethnic, and racial diversity. There is still plenty of evidence for continuing discrimination and exclusion, but the miracle is that over time these hateful behaviors have generally diminished rather than increased. The sociological challenge is to spell out the steps that lead to favorable outcomes at the family level. Legitimation of a family's religious, racial, and ethnic identity is an important asset that enables it to socialize its children more effectively and enable its members to participate more fully in the civil society. Family policy thus has a role in helping to legitimate family identity as well as give support to the other key family functions of caregiving, economic support, and residential location that were treated in previous chapters.

The Changing Landscape of Religion in America

For many, establishing an ethnic identity is importantly but indirectly connected to participation in a particular religious tradition. Yet in the United States, with its separation of church and state, the connection of religion to acculturation and citizenship is often unrecognized. Everyone knows that the Pilgrims and Puritans came to America in the seventeenth century seeking religious freedom. What is not so clear is how this initially Christian country was able to establish a Constitution that both protected the right of freedom of speech and religious freedom and at the same time refused to establish or privilege any single religious tradition or denomination as deserving precedence over any other. Eck (2001) illustrates how this tension has been resolved in recent times by the U.S. Department of Defense. The Armed Forces Chaplains Board handles requests for religious accommodations from many sources. Its purpose is to facilitate the free exercise of religion by all members of the military, which includes religious accommodations even for such small groups as the Wiccans. Although the Wiccans had been accommodated for over 20 years, the release of a news article reporting the practice unleashed a storm of protest. The response for the chaplains by Captain Gunter was very simple:

"The Department of Defense does not evaluate, judge, or officially sanction any religious faith. It is not up to us to judge religions or to make a list of denominations or religious groups that are officially acceptable. It is up to us to ask what the religious need of the member is. That's the important thing."

Captain Gunter recalled a typical phone call, this one from a Roman Catholic woman who asked, "Are you telling me that the Department of Defense recognizes Wicca?" He responded to her, "It may come as a shock to you, madam, that the Department of the Defense does not recognize the Roman Catholic Church" (Eck 2001:359).

Given this peculiarly American acceptance of a variety of religious beliefs, let us now survey the current landscape of religious diversity in the United States. In addition to giving a rough idea of the number and size of different religious groups, this summary will also touch on the way that religious and ethnic minorities have been treated, how they have adapted to American society, and how in the process the individuals and families identified with them have experienced gradual inclusion.

A profile of religious diversity. American society has been characterized as the "most diversely religious people on earth" (T. Smith 2002:577). Yet the dominant stream is still Protestant, although the size of that majority continues to decline. Protestants include all those Christian denominations formed since the Reformation in the sixteenth century, including Baptists, Lutherans, Methodists, Presbyterians, and even Mormons. In the 1972 General Social Survey, 62.5 percent of Americans identified themselves as Protestant, 27.4 percent as Catholics, 3 percent as Jews, 5.1 percent as None, and 1.9 percent as Other. By 2002, the figures for all the main religious groups had declined: Protestants to 52.4 percent, Catholics to 25.5 percent, and Jews to 1.5 percent. But the number stating their religion as None rose sharply to 13.8 percent and Other to 6.9 percent (T. Smith and Kim 2005).

Demographers explain these changes by several contributing factors. The exponential growth in non-Judeo-Christian beliefs is largely related to immigration from South Asia which increased the Hindu population, and from Korea, Japan, and Taiwan which increased the Buddhist population. But the rise in numbers professing no religious affiliation (None) turns out to have a rather surprising explanation. When asked further about their beliefs, most of these people turn out to have religious faith but what they mean is that they don't belong to a church or any specific religious group (Smith and Kim 2005). In addition, many of those who give no religious affiliation are political liberals who reject the socially conservative views of the religious right (Hout and Fischer 2002). In addition, within Protestantism there is a further decline among the mainstream denominations in relation to evangelical Christians. This change is due in large part to lower rates of childbearing among Methodists, Presbyterians, and similar established groups compared with conservative Protestants (Hout, Greeley, and Wilde 2001).

As to the nature of the growing segment of the American population who adhere to non-Judeo-Christian religious identities, estimates of the size of different groups vary widely. While the General Social Survey put the total in 2002 at 6.9 percent, the National Election Studies put the proportion at 2.7 percent and a 2007 Pew survey at 3.0 percent (Pew Forum on Religion & Public Life 2007). T. Smith (2002) estimated there were 2.3 million Buddhists, 1.1 million Hindus, and 1.9 million Muslims in the United States in 2000. All in all, three faiths—Buddhism, Hinduism, and Islam—account for about half of the people who designate their religion as Other. The remainder includes other Eastern religions such as Jainism, Sikhism, and Taoism as well as Native American religions, and pagan and Wiccan adherents.

Religious and ethnic discrimination and adaptation. From the beginning of the Republic to the present, every single minority religious or ethnic group other than the supposed WASP majority of white Anglo-Saxon Protestants can recount numerous examples of discrimination. Roger Williams, who believed in separation of church and state, and Anne Hutchinson, a dissenter who believed in freedom of conscience, were both banished to Rhode Island in 1637 to 1638 for failing to submit to the authority of the Puritan establishment of Massachusetts Bay. In 1834 the Ursuline convent in Charlestown, Massachusetts, was burned by an angry mob as a result of rumors about the blind obedience required of the sisters under the weight of Roman Catholic authority (Welter 1987). German-language newspapers and churches died out in Midwestern cities and towns as anti-German sentiment spread during World War I. Who has not heard of the desecration of Jewish synagogues and cemeteries even in recent times? With the post-1965 immigration from India and the Far East came Buddhists and Hindus and Muslims mobilizing to build temples and mosques and being faced with suspicion that threw obstacles in their way. In 1983 a group swinging clubs and hurling paint vandalized the new Hindu-Jain temple outside Pittsburgh; they destroyed the marble deities and tore into pieces the *Granthe,* the sacred book, and exited having scribbled "Leave" in black paint on the main altar (Eck 2001).

These examples of prejudice and discrimination against any group who are religiously, ethnically, or culturally different are a well-known feature of human behavior. What is more surprising are the remarkable tales of triumph by which the practice and celebration of these very differences become a means to acculturation of the group and at the same time to acceptance by the host society. Even though no one religion is recognized by the American government, it turns out that identification with a particular religious tradition creates a path to positive civic participation and to citizenship in its broadest sense. Oscar Handlin (1964:20), the venerable social historian of American immigration, stated the case as follows:

> The fact that the churches take for granted the common antecedents of their members permits them to serve an important function, in addition to that of divine worship; and conversely that further emphasizes their ethnic character. These bodies are the custodians of tradition and of the sacred objects, rituals, and forms of expression which men cherish. When faced with the significant incidents in human life—birth, marriage, and death—people wish to have the emotional assurance of a connection with the ancestral past. At such moments the church and the family converge in an association which cements ethnic loyalties. Religion too is the custodian of ethnic values. In a general sense, Americans share a common moral position derived from their Judeo-Christian heritage.

Handlin's insights are echoed by contemporary immigration scholars who understand the value of familiar religious and family rituals and a "common moral position" in aiding the process of acculturation. The same processes are at work among the new Eastern religions. Portes, Rumbaut, Fernandez-Kelly, and Haller (2006) document the vital role of the Haitian Cathedral in the lives of its communicants who congregate there not only for divine worship but also to participate in social activities and use a host of social services. Similarly, Eck (2001) describes the vibrant communities of Muslims who are involved in the humanitarian and educational work of their local mosques. Her luminous description of baby Buddha's birthday celebration at the Hsi Lai temple east of Los Angeles pictures the magnificent courtyard, grand staircase, gardens, and ornamented buildings as well as a touching account of a little girl and her mother proceeding through the rituals of the day. With a membership of over 20,000 largely Taiwanese immigrants and their families, this is the largest Buddhist temple in United States. In all these religious connections, as Handlin noted, family holidays and rites of passage are a part. In *Protestant, Catholic, Jew: An Essay in American Religious Sociology,* Will Herberg (1955) explained the resurgence of religious attendance in postwar America as a means of reaffirming one's ethnic roots. This is significant for family life because in the words of Carola Suárez-Orozco, a psychologist, and her husband Marcelo Suárez-Orozco, an anthropologist (2001:vii), "The main function of the family is the transfer of skills, values, and worldview to the next generation."

Putnam (with Campbell and Garrett 2010) discovers that the stronger an ethnic identity, the stronger a group's religious beliefs, which then correlates with likelihood of marrying a person of the same faith and continuing in that tradition as an adult. These religious and ethnic ties persist over time so that the geographic distribution of Lutherans by county, for example, corresponds to the geographic distribution of Germans and Scandinavians and is heaviest in the upper Midwest. By contrast, the groups who give their ethnicity as "American" are found in the old American South and correlate with the location of evangelical Protestants. These identities then sometimes become activated in a more political form of civic participation that varies from left to right. Across generations these religious and ethnic identities are likely to broaden with intermarriage and geographic and social mobility. Eck (2007) describes the many forms of religious blending now taking place with marriage: Muslim-Christian, Jewish-Buddhist, Christian-Hindu, as well as the more familiar combinations of Jewish-Christian, and Catholic-Protestant.

Religious and ethnic identity as a basis for citizenship. Robert Bellah (1992), a leading sociologist of religion, has noted that religious organizations are "schools for citizenship" because in their role as voluntary organizations they serve the function that de Tocqueville found so distinctively American and so basic to a democracy. By and large, religious adherence also appears to contribute to tolerance of other groups. Putnam and his colleagues (2010) find that over 90 percent of Americans believe that people not of their religious faith can go to heaven. Robert Bellah in his studies of American religious practice, *Habits of the Heart: Individualism and Commitment in American Life* and *The Good Society,* argued that discipleship in religious life when properly understood *entails* citizenship in a democratic society or in one that is trying to be democratic (Bellah 1985, 1991, 1992). Thus the Reverend Martin Luther King (1967) founded his appeal for justice and civil rights for the Negro and other oppressed groups on Biblical language and core beliefs of Christians and Jews:

> Let us be dissatisfied until from every city hall, justice will roll down like waters and righteousness like a mighty stream. Let us be dissatisfied until that day when the lion and the lamb shall lie down together, and every man will sit under his own vine and fig tree and none shall be afraid. Let us be dissatisfied. And men will recognize that out of one blood God made all men to dwell upon the face of the earth.

Evidence that the many different religious practices of the new immigrants are working in this positive way comes from Diana Eck's (2001) massive 10-year study of religious pluralism in America. There she describes the vibrant ethnic communities that celebrate their new life in America by building mosques and temples, interacting with the IRS and zoning boards, making architectural adaptations that fit better into the American landscape, and cooperating with civic organizations to win acceptance and legitimacy in the eyes of the community. This process was begun as early as the 1920s by Lebanese Muslim autoworkers in the Ford plant in Dearborn, Michigan, who by 1938 had organized to construct a mosque. The process of engaging with the larger society continues right up to the present and now includes Muslims from many nationalities including the Nation of Islam. New immigrant scientists and engineers from India by 1978 had constructed a large Hindu temple in Ashland, Massachusetts, and similar efforts have occurred all over the nation. Eck (2007:221) observes that religion helps immigrants become American through participation in a process that not only strengthens their ethnic identity but also engages them in a constructive and cooperative way with the larger society. By 2000, there were 1,400 mosques in the United States, over 2,000 Buddhist temples, and well over 500 Hindu temples.

Despite the hostility shown Arab-Americans and Muslims following the Oklahoma City bombing and the 9/11 attack on the World Trade Center, the outlook for integration of Muslims into American life is generally positive. One important factor is the high level of education and relatively high income of the Muslim community, with the average mosque goer in 2005 having a bachelor's degree or more and earning $75,000 a year. This is very different from the situation of the alienated and less educated Muslims in Britain and Europe. Portes et al. (2006, p. 339) conclude that:

> The best long-term course of action toward Islam is that which has thus far yielded so many instances of success in the incorporation of immigrants to America: respect for the rights of all in the marketplace of ideas and a hands-off policy from all *peaceful* religious institutions and groups, allowing them to seek and find the best course of adaptation for their members. There is no need to tell a young Muslim girl not to wear a headscarf. In due time, that scarf will come off or be replaced by one worn with a distinctive American flair.

The single most important departure from this positive pattern of religious involvement in acculturation is the limited interaction of the Roman Catholic Church with the large number of recent immigrants from Mexico. Portes and colleagues (2006) contrast this situation with the historic role of the Catholic hierarchy during the last century in integrating Irish, Italians, and Cubans into the larger society. The most important factor was the extensive system of parochial education that was centered in the eastern and midwestern United States and in which even now 25 percent of Catholic children are enrolled. In the West and Southwest, however, only 4 percent of

Mexican Americans are enrolled in parochial schools. The Catholic hierarchy has also been slow to incorporate Mexican priests. There are several reasons for this failure, one being the fact that Mexicans return to their home villages periodically where they practice a mixture of formal Catholic rituals along with indigenous folk customs that are at odds with official church doctrine. One other factor is the traditional domination by the Irish in the Catholic hierarchy of the northern and eastern United States compared with the dominance of the Spanish and Portuguese in Latin America. The demographers like Portes and others (2006) see the absence of engagement by the Church as a great loss to Mexican Americans of chances for a better education and upward mobility. One result is that an estimated 25 percent of Mexican Americans have left the Church to join evangelical sects.

Profile of the New Immigrants: Nationality and Race

The recent wave of immigrations between 1965 and 2000 is comparable in size to that from 1901 to 1925, about 17 million. But national origins and racial composition are very different. Oscar and Mary Handlin (1948) described four major waves of immigration between 1815 and 1924. The first came after the Napoleonic wars of the early nineteenth century and lasted up to the Civil War. Some 7.5 million Europeans from England, Scotland, Wales, Ireland, and southern Germany, who were facing the shock of modernization, left to escape poverty and find a better life. The second great wave lasting from the Civil War to the 1890s brought another 8 million people—many Norwegians, Swedes, and Finns. Sweden, for example lost 25 percent of its population during this period (my maternal grandparents among them) who left as a result of a double catastrophe—a potato famine and a crash in the herring catch. Between the 1890s and 1924 some 20 million more arrivals came from southern Europe—Czechs, Slovaks, Hungarians, Slovenians, Serbs, Poles, Russians, Italians, Romanians, Greeks, and Turks. Then in 1924 came the quota system and a drastic reduction of immigration. Between 1924 and World War II only 200,000 refugees were admitted. Between the end of the war and 1965 when the Immigration Reform Act was passed, only a trickle of refugees and skilled technicians were allowed in.

The 1924 quota system was replaced by new rules to allow 290,000 new immigrants per year (not counting spouses and minor children). Of that number, 170,000 were to come from the Eastern Hemisphere and 120,000 from the Western Hemisphere. The aim was both to unify families and fill labor needs (Zhou 2001). Although immigration reform was passed in 1965 because it extended principles of civil rights to other nations and races, Congress had little idea that so many people would come from so many different nations and cultures. In the nearly half century of immigration that has ensued, questions of nationality, race, and assimilation have been reformulated as a result of the great diversity in national origins, patterns of acculturation, and racial characteristics.

Variation in national origins. It is instructive to learn the relative magnitude of immigration from various countries of origin and to see how this distribution has changed over time. In 1850, 92 percent of immigrants came from Europe compared with only 15 percent in 2000. Whereas immigration from Latin America and Asia was negligible in the nineteenth century, by 2000 half of all migrants came from Latin America, one-quarter from Asia, 6 percent from other areas, and 2.5 percent from Canada (Ueda 2007:15). As shown in Table 7.1, of the top 12 migrant groups in 2000, almost one-third (29.4 percent) came from Mexico; 4.4 percent from the Philippines; just over 3 percent, respectively, from India, China, and Vietnam; and 2–3 percent each from Cuba, Korea, Canada, Germany, the Dominican Republic, and the former USSR (Portes and Rumbaut 2006:46).

Alternative paths to acculturation and upward mobility.   Given the much more heterogeneous population of current foreign-born residents, it is not

Table 7.1   National Origins of Immigrants to the United States, 1850–2000 (As a percentage of the foreign-born population)

Year	Europe	N. America	L. America	Asia	Other Regions
1850	92.2	6.7	---	---	---
1900	86.0	11.4	---	---	2.6
2000	15.3	2.5	51.4	25.5	5.7
Top 12 Immigrant Groups in 2000	Germany 2.3 USSR 2.0	Canada 2.6	Mexico 29.4 Cuba 2.8 El Salvador 2.6 Dom. Rep. 2.2	India 3.3 China 3.2 Vietnam 3.2 Korea 2.8	Philippines 4.4
2009	12.7	2.1	53.1	27.7	4.5
Top 11 Immigrant Groups in 2009		Canada 2.1	Mexico 29.8 El Salvador 3.0 Guatemala 2.1 Cuba 2.6 Dom. Rep. 2.1	China 5.2 India 4.3 Vietnam 3.0 Korea 2.6	Philippines 4.5

Sources: Ueda (2007:15); Portes and Rumbaut (2006:46); U.S. Census Bureau (2010a:2).

surprising that their paths toward assimilation and upward mobility have varied widely. Asian Americans have been characterized as the "model minority" because of their higher educational attainment and higher income. Those with the darkest skin, however, no matter what their nationality, have fared much less well. Two principal indicators of differential success are available in statistics on occupational status, median wages, and median net worth. Socioeconomic status varies widely by country of origin because of differences in human capital at the time of entry. For example, in 1990 almost half of Indian immigrants had a professional occupation, compared with 20–30 percent of Chinese, Filipinos, Koreans, and Jamaicans, and only 14 percent of Haitians and 17 percent of Vietnamese (Zhou 2001:208). Further differences in male wages, poverty level, and net worth are correlated with these general rankings, as shown in Table 7.2.

Table 7.2 Wages, Income Status, and Net Worth by Ethnicity

Median Male Wages as a Percentage of White Median Male Wages		
Ethnicity	1940	1990
Blacks	43.3	74.5
All Hispanics	64.2	67.3
Puerto Ricans (Lo)	82.9	74.5
Cubans (Hi)	—	86.6
Blacks as % of Hispanics	67.4	100.7

Income Status of Male Workers, 1997 (in percentage)			
Ethnicity	Poor	Middle Class	Affluent
White	12	54	34
Black	16	65	19
Hispanic	17	69	14

Net Worth at the Median, 2003 (in dollars)			
White	71,886		
Latin American	15,834	Lo: El Salvador 1,929	Hi: Cuba 37,517
Asian American	66,085	Lo: Vietnam 30,851	Hi: Hong Kong/Taiwan 161,254
Caribbean	6,183	Lo: Haiti 3,696	Hi: Jamaica 27,705

Sources: Hao (2007:94, 152, 193); J. Smith (2001:53, 67).

Besides differences in human capital that are reflected in educational attainment and occupational level, a further important distinction is immigration status. Undocumented immigrants are obviously at an enormous disadvantage with respect to protection from exploitation as workers and gaining access to social services and education. Portes and Rumbaut (2006, p. 21) distinguish three major occupational groups (unskilled and semi-skilled laborers, professionals, and entrepreneurs) and classify immigrant groups by four possible types of legal status—unauthorized, temporary legal residents, permanent legal residents, and refugees. Of greatest public concern have been the unauthorized migrant laborers who come from Mexico, El Salvador, Guatemala, and Haiti. But there are also skilled workers and professionals from China, Dominican Republic, and India who practice their professions without legal permits. There are also undocumented entrepreneurs who open small informal businesses in Chinese, Indian, or Korean enclaves.

The lack of proper legal status is obviously a huge impediment to the acculturation and upward mobility of undocumented immigrants and their families. They live in the shadows to avoid deportation and the even more frightening possibility that they can be sent back to their home country without their American-born children.

The outlook for differentiation by race. The Handlins (1948) document the hardening of a belief system about racial differences that began with slavery and then was expanded to include Asians, Jews, and even natives of southern and eastern Europe. Prior to the Civil War, southern whites used race inferiority as a means to fight the abolitionist doctrine of equality. Then after the Civil War the South was allowed to keep its social system by treating Negroes as a permanently inferior race with provision for "separate but equal" accommodations that were protected by the Supreme Court decision in *Plessey v. Ferguson* (1896), which at the same time nullified the intent of the 14th Amendment. The idea of innate racial differences had by then spread to Orientals and resulted in the halt of all Chinese immigration after 1882 as well as anti-Japanese sentiment in the early 1900s. The Spanish-American War of 1898 further eroded ideals of equality by introducing a colonialist orientation that denied full rights of citizenship to former Spanish colonies that came under American control such as Puerto Rico and the Philippines. From 1900 to the much more restrictive immigration legislation of 1924, there was a determined campaign to reverse the traditional American openness to immigration and restrict it to people similar to the Anglo-Saxon breed who were presumed to be responsible for American prosperity up to that point. The "old" immigrants had been mainly Teutonic and

Protestant. "New" immigrants included Slavs and Jews and somewhat darker-complexioned people from southern Europe and the Levant. The new racial ideology evolved from all these strands—the southern caste system, the importation of Chinese to build the railroads, the imperialist Spanish-American War, and the variegation of European nationalities. According to the Handlins (1948:21) many respected American academics (including sociologist E. A. Ross and economist John R. Commons) in the decade after 1910 concluded that certain ethnic groups including the Jews were inferior or inassimilable and that the native born were imperiled by "cross-breeding" with inferior stocks.

Today this history is not only outdated but shocking. Yet current observations that racial discrimination still retards acculturation are sobering. In 1942, Gunnar Myrdal and colleagues (1944) completed a massive study of the Negro situation in America and concluded that for most Americans, the situation of the Negro posed an embarrassing moral dilemma between the high American ideals of equality and democracy and the actual prejudice and discrimination against one race which contradicted those ideals. More recent observers like Gans (2007) and J. Hochschild (2007) picture two starkly different possible scenarios—one in which assimilation continues to be almost impossible for people who are brown or black; and the other in which income, education, and power have the capacity to "whiten" even those who are dark and thereby assimilate them into the majority. Omi (2001:245) explains the reason for this uncertainty: "The massive recent influx of new immigrant groups has destabilized specific concepts of race, led to a proliferation of identity positions, and challenged prevailing modes of political and cultural organization."

The new understanding of the relation between race and chances of acculturation is best expressed by Portes and Rumbaut (2001) in their concept of "segmented assimilation." Rather than the earlier image of assimilation as blending into the melting pot, these authors describe three main trajectories, one in which acculturation leads to downward mobility, a second that is mostly but not always successful, and a third that leads to upward mobility and a bicultural identity. The three main background factors that shape these outcomes are (1) the initial class position and human capital of the family when it arrives, (2) the strength of the family to resist negative racial associations, and (3) the strength of family in combination with the larger ethnic community. Those who have all three types of resources are best able to resist negative racial stereotypes, steer a path away from dead-end jobs, and avoid the downward pull of inner-city racial subcultures. Asians, to the extent that they have been able to marshal all three positive forces, have been more likely to succeed than the Latin

American and Caribbean groups who have come into the country with less education, fewer family resources, and a weaker ethnic community. As a result there has been much concern about the "immigrant paradox" in which the second generation in some ethnic groups have been found to be worse off in terms of health and economic status than their immigrant parents. Yet according to psychologist Huong H. Nguyen (2006:325–326), "Even the U.S.-born Latinos who remain 'ethnic' remain healthier. Hence, it could be that immigrant and ethnic youth have a protective quality related to their culture, but as they become 'Americanized' or 'minorities' in a racially stratified context, this protection is eroded. . . . The more we can discern the causes and pathways involved, the better we can inform policies aimed at decreasing these disparities."

Changes in Immigration Policy

Since the founding of the Republic, there have been many fascinating twists and turns in the regulations governing immigration and the requirements to become a citizen. For example, in the years between 1790 and 1798 the length of required residence was raised from two years to 14 years and then was dropped back to five years in 1802, where it stands to this day. Chinese immigrants and contract laborers were excluded between 1882 and 1952, and differences were removed from the regulations as they applied to women and men (Waters, Ueda, and Marrow 2007).

My summary begins with the legislation most relevant to our time, the restrictive quotas of 1924 that were the first to put a drastic limit on immigration to America. These restrictions lasted until the civil rights revolution in the 1960s. Since that time, it has become clear that the new immigrants are different from the old in their racial characteristics and countries of origin. In addition, the long-standing flow of laborers back and forth from Mexico has been changed by intensified border control with the unintended consequence of actually increasing the number of undocumented immigrants. This change, in addition to welfare reform in the 1990s and greater concern about terrorists since 2001, has resulted in a sea change in the political discussion surrounding immigration. Although national polls show that a majority of the U.S. population believes that paths should be created for the undocumented to achieve legalization, the opposition wishes to stop all illegal entry and punish anyone who assists or turns a blind eye on those who have overstayed their visas or slipped through the border.

Although immigrants from Mexico are by far the largest single nationality group among the foreign born, counting their number is tricky because of the changes in border control policy since 1986. Massey (2011) points out that for many years Mexican migrant workers had freely crossed back and forth over the border to perform seasonal migrant labor and then returned home. Efforts to seal the border, however, have made it more difficult for migrants to return to Mexico, with the undesirable result of increasing and dispersing the number of undocumented residents who lack legal and social protection. Restricting the movement of labor while at the same time encouraging North American free trade is a contradictory policy (Massey, Durand, and Malone 2002).

To explain how these major changes have come about and where they appear to be headed, this account first describes the major turning points in immigration law and describes the dynamics of immigration as understood by demographers who have studied the process.

Major Turning Points in Recent Immigration Law

Following the imposition of a national quota system in 1924 that sought to mirror the mainly European ethnic groups who had immigrated earlier, there was a 40-year period of relative stability in which those people who had come before 1924 had a chance to be absorbed into the larger society. During this period the biggest changes were of a humanitarian nature—laws executed in the 1940s to admit refugees and displaced persons as well as GIs and their fiancées and war brides. During this time, the most significant change was the Immigration Act of 1952, which removed all exclusions based on race and those discriminatory regulations that distinguished between men and women. (See Table 7.3.)

The Immigration Act of 1965 was a bold departure from this earlier state of affairs. Civil rights sentiment suddenly rent the placid curtain of preference for European immigrants and opened the door to 360,000 new immigrants per year, over half of whom were to come from the Eastern Hemisphere. Yet Congress did not expect to have more than a few thousand immigrants from each country per year, a prediction that turned out to be a gross underestimate (Ludden, 2006). Not only did hundreds of thousands take the opportunity to come, but they also brought their relatives under the family unification provisions of the Act in a well-known demographic phenomenon known as "chain migration."

Many skilled workers—engineers from India, medical professionals from the Philippines, service workers from the Caribbean, and agricultural workers from Mexico—filled important labor needs. But the movement of one group was particularly problematic. Ever since the 1920s, thousands of agricultural and service workers had moved to and fro across the border to

Table 7.3   Major Legislation Related to Immigration Since 1924

Legislation	Year	Provisions
Immigration Act of 1924	1924	Set up national-origin quota system. In conjunction with Immigration Act of 1917 set policy until 1952.
Added laws to govern admission of various new classes of immigrants	1943–1948	Importation of temporary farm labor. Alien registration. Admission of war brides, G.I. fiancées, displaced persons, and persons of Indian and Filipino descent.
Immigration Act of 1952	1952	Codification of previous laws. All races now eligible (e.g., Chinese). No discrimination by sex. National quotas revised with preference for skilled workers.
Immigration Act: Amendments of 1965	1965	Abolished national origin quota system, eliminating national origin, race, or ancestry as basis. Limit of 170,000 from W. Hemisphere and 190,000 from E. Hemisphere. Preference system for family reunification and skilled workers.
Immigration Reform and Control Act of 1986 (IRCA)	1986	Stricter border control. Legalization (amnesty) for 1.7 million aliens who had entered unlawfully or had expired visas and had been residents since 1982. Created category of Seasonal Agricultural Workers (SAWs) with amnesty for 1.3 million resident workers and reporting requirement for employers.
Immigration Act of 1990	1990	Major overhaul of immigration law. Increased total immigration cap to 700,000 for 1992–1994 and 675,000 thereafter, of which 480,000 family-sponsored, 140,000 work-sponsored, and 55,000 "diversity immigrants."
North American Free-Trade Agreement Act (NAFTA)	1993	Facilitated temporary entry on a reciprocal basis between the United States and Canada and Mexico
Personal Responsibility and Work Opportunity Reconciliation Act of 1996 (PRWORA)	1996	Restrictions on eligibility of legal immigrants for means-tested public assistance. Restriction on public benefits for illegal aliens and nonimmigrants.

Legislation	Year	Provisions
Illegal Immigration Reform and Immigrant Responsibility Act of 1996 (IIRIRA)	1996	Set up measures to control U.S. borders, protect legal workers through worksite enforcement, and remove deportable aliens. Further restrictions on benefits for aliens.
Nicaraguan Adjustment and Central American Relief Act of 1997 (NACARA)	1997	Permanent legal status for 150,000 Nicaraguans and 5,000 Cubans without their having to show hardship. Hardship relief available for 200,000 Salvadorans and 50,000 Guatemalans as well as immigrants from former USSR.
Uniting and Strengthening America by Providing Appropriate Tools Required to Intercept and Obstruct Terrorism Act of 2001 (PATRIOT Act)	2001	Tripled number of Border Patrol, Customs Service, and INS personnel at points of entry. Elaboration of electronic surveillance, cooperation with FBI, and detention of aliens suspected of terrorist intent or activity. Legal limitations on judicial review of habeas corpus proceedings.
Homeland Security Act of 2002	2002	Transferred INS functions to the Department of Homeland Security, where immigration enforcement was assigned to Border and Transportation Security and immigration services to Citizenship and Immigration Services.
Assorted state laws in Alabama, Arizona, Georgia, Indiana, and Utah to criminalize illegal immigrants	2010–2011	State initiatives such as authorizing police to check documentation of suspected illegal immigrants, charge them with an offense, and punish anyone who has helped them. These measures are being contested in federal courts by the federal government.

Source: Waters, Ueda, and Marrow (2007).

Mexico. During World War II a special *bracero* program was begun in 1942 that lasted until 1964 and met labor needs by importing workers from Mexico. From 1950 on, however, there was increased concern about the size of the flow. High fertility in Mexico that more than doubled its total population between 1950 and 1980 (from 26.3 million to 69.7 million) together with a 7-to-1 ratio of U.S. to Mexican wages for manual labor, resulted in almost one-third of all immigrants coming from Mexico alone (Portes and Rumbaut 2006:352; Zolberg 2007). The presence of so many Hispanics excited fears about their continued use of Spanish instead of English, their ethnic enclaves that made them seem slow to assimilate, and the possibility that they might be taking jobs away from native residents while also using social services paid for by U.S. taxpayers.

The Immigration Reform and Control Act of 1986 (IRCA) tightened the border while also giving amnesty to approximately 1,700,000 immigrants who had arrived before 1982 and to 1,300,000 seasonal agricultural workers (SAWs) who had come to harvest crops and had stayed in the United States rather than return to Mexico. Despite these measures, however, the number of undocumented Mexican immigrants continued to rise dramatically, eventually leading to harsh initiatives in several states such as Alabama, Arizona, California, and Georgia to identify and punish immigrants who lacked the proper legal papers.

Two other new concerns grew up in addition to worries about Mexican migration. The first was access by undocumented aliens to welfare benefits, schools, medical care, and social services. In California, Proposition 187 was passed in 1994 to deny such public benefits to illegal immigrants but was declared unconstitutional in 1997 because regulation of immigration is the sole province of the federal government, and access to welfare services is covered at the federal level by the welfare reform of 1996 (PRWORA) and the Illegal Immigration Reform and Immigrant Responsibility Act of 1996 (IIRIRA).

The second new issue for immigration policy was national security, which was raised by the threat of terrorism as it was experienced in the World Trade Center bombing of 1993, the Oklahoma City bombing of 1995, and the Al Qaeda attacks of September 11, 2001. These events led to further tightening of the borders, electronic surveillance, and stricter screening for suspected terrorists through the PATRIOT Act of 2001 and the Homeland Security Act of 2002. In the process the Immigration and Naturalization Service (INS) was closed, and its functions were handed over to the Department of Homeland Security and Citizenship and Immigration Services, as shown in Table 7.3.

Following 40 years of restricted immigration from 1924 to 1965, the succeeding expansion of immigration brought roughly 30 million new foreign-born residents (of whom 10 million were unauthorized) and greatly increased the demographic diversity of the nation (Hoefer, Rytina, and Baker 2011). But the current mood seems to be shifting once again from openness to a concern for tightening the borders and turning away those eager to find a better life in America. For example, major criticisms of the 1965 legislation include the loss of Anglo-European cultural dominance, claims that immigrants take lower wages, and that immigrants are more likely to be on public assistance (Johnson 2002).

Understanding the Dynamics of Immigration Flows

Population experts provide a larger understanding of the dynamics behind immigration. It is not just that poor people want to escape poverty by getting into a rich country, or that rich countries want to protect their wealth by keeping out poor people or by exploiting their labor—although there is a grain of truth in both these perspectives. Nor is it true that putting up higher barriers will necessarily stop the flow. Instead, the migration of populations is related to supply and demand for labor in an integrated global economy. Advanced industrial countries whose birth rates have fallen and whose populations have more education and higher incomes have fewer people available to take service jobs and manual labor positions that require less education and yield lower pay. These countries need workers who will fill those positions. Conversely, the people in poor countries who want a better life and more opportunities for their children are drawn to the positions available in more affluent nations and are willing to take less well-paid jobs and endure lower status for the promise of greater opportunities for their children. Especially in a global economy where transportation and communication jumps across national boundaries, these ebbs and flows of migration are so powerful that even with borders that are supposedly closed, people manage to get across because there are employers who need and want their services, smugglers who enable their crossing, and family and friends who will facilitate their settlement once they have entered the country.

One further observation is noteworthy: These population flows do not last forever but appear to be self-limiting to periods of no more than 80 to 90 years duration (Massey et al. 2002). For example, Sweden in the nineteenth century saw one-quarter of its population leave to escape poverty and famine (about 20,000 people per year came to the United States between 1868 and 1873). Since 1970, however, Swedish immigrants have averaged only about 1,000 per year (Immigration-online.org 2011). Like liquid or gas that flows from high to low pressure areas, and finally reaches its level, so also population flows run out of steam once the costs and benefits on either side of a border become more nearly equal. Understandably, of course, such a dynamic raises the specter that affluent countries may lower their standard of living in the process. Zolberg (2007) in fact notes that most affluent countries want to keep their borders as closed as possible. However, few would argue that past immigration caused any decline in the United States. Instead, the waves of nineteenth and early twentieth century immigrants helped to settle the frontier, dig the canals, build railroads, mine coal, and manufacture everything from textiles and shoes to steel, cars, and labor-saving appliances.

Portes and Rumbaut (2006) analyze the current malaise over immigration in the United States in terms of a "disconnect" between protectionist ideologies and the actual dynamics of migration. Negative public opinion about immigration tends to divide into two camps, one of "intransigent nativism" that tries to keep the new people out and the other of "forced acculturation" that asks for immediate assimilation and exclusive use of English. The economic and social realities of immigration are ignored by both the nativists and the advocates of forced acculturation. The economic reality is that the "hourglass" labor market needs foreign labor both at the top in the professions and at the bottom in the manual and service occupations. The social reality is that networks between family members and between employers and workers enable newcomers to cross national boundaries even if they lack proper documentation. These networks are conduits of information and provide help in finding points of entry, links to jobs, and access to host communities.

The disconnect between ideology and realities of the immigration process can be seen in the startling statistics recently provided by Jiménez and López-Sanders (2011) on the results of current enforcement policy along the Mexican border. Although the number in the border patrol has more than tripled from 5,878 to 18,319, and the amount of money spent on enforcement has more than quadrupled from $568 million to $2.7 billion, the population of unauthorized immigrants continued to increase, from 3.5 million in the United States in 1990 (18 percent of the foreign-born population) to 12 million in 2007, (30 percent of all foreign born).

Jiménez and López-Sanders see the current mood in public opinion to be not only one of reducing illegal immigration but of creating a new "illegal class" of those already here. They identify four unintended and perverse consequences of such a policy: (1) an actual increase in unauthorized immigration, (2) a dispersion of the immigrant population beyond traditional ethnic communities, (3) creation of barriers to successful acculturation of the immigrants into host communities, and (4) disruption of intergenerational dependence between children (who may be born in the United States) and their alien parents. Like many other observers of the immigration process, these authors recommend creation of paths to legal citizenship for those who are as yet unauthorized. The big question is whether such a reform can be accomplished in the current political climate.

Alternative Scenarios for the Future

Massey and Sánchez (2010), basing their projections on a long-term study of Mexican immigration, have posed two stark scenarios for immigration policy of the future. One is that the United States will turn away from its historical openness to new citizens and create a permanent underclass of those who manage to enter but are never able to gain legal status. The other alternative is to legislate policies that create paths to citizenship by using the contributions and labor power of the newcomers as a positive basis for giving them full civil and social rights of membership in American society.

The emerging story of diversity in America has been one of exclusion, prejudice, and discrimination against outgroups, which in the end have gradually faded and been replaced first by grudging acknowledgment and later by unselfconscious acceptance. The question now is whether that story will have a major exception in the case of unauthorized immigrants. The answer can perhaps be found by reviewing earlier cases where formerly excluded groups became accepted and by projecting how a similar process might work in the current case of unauthorized residents who are foreign-born.

From Exclusion to Inclusion

In *The Negro in America*, a landmark review of the civil rights situation of the 1960s, Talcott Parsons (1966a), a leading sociological theorist and one of the book's editors, reflected on the long history of prejudice against Catholics and Jews. He then suggested that analogous processes of differentiation from a stereotyped image might be repeated even with respect to a racial minority.

A principal objection to the Catholics was the threat of their listening to priests and papal authority instead of consulting their own conscience and individual rights as citizens. The fact that many were former peasants who might be subservient to outside authority added weight to this concern. But several factors eventually eased these worries and ultimately made acceptance of Catholics a nonissue. One positive feature was the pluralism within the Catholic Church that ranged from the Irish and Germans to Poles and Italians. Another was the fact that the Irish spoke English and therefore seemed less foreign, as well as were dominant in the American Catholic hierarchy. Catholics furthermore succeeded in higher education and the professions, and they moved out of urban enclaves into settings that bespoke their upward mobility. The crowning achievement was the election of John F. Kennedy, the first Catholic president, which finally put to rest worries about political influence by the Catholic Church. In addition, the communist scare and the activity of Senator Joe McCarthy displaced anxiety about foreign control by the Church to another target.

In the case of anti-Semitism, the nature of the "foreign" threat was different. Instead of being subservient to an outside authority, Jews were thought of as the peddlers and middlemen who made profits from buying and selling but did not actually produce the commodities or manufacturers from which they profited. Moreover, they were seen to be "clannish," meaning that they appeared to be more loyal to their own group than to the native population with whom they did business. These prejudices gradually faded, however, as the occupations of Jews became more diverse, and they moved into a wider range of professions and trades. Their intellectual leadership and their philanthropy to a broad array of colleges and universities, museums, hospitals, and other charities also demonstrated their commitment to groups outside their own. Gradually Jews, like Catholics, have been accepted into the mainstream, and their presence in Congress and the U.S. Supreme Court is testimony to a turning of the tide.

Although Parsons pointed to the possibility that a similar kind of acceptance might be extended to the American Negro, progress in 1966 was not yet far enough along to make a convincing case to that effect. Now, 45 years later, there are more signs that his hope was justified. Perhaps chief among these is the election of president Obama, who as an African American has attained the highest office of the land—a parallel to JFK's leap over the barrier of being a Catholic. Also, similar to the growing representation of Jews and Catholics in positions of societal leadership, we see the increasing presence of African American leaders of foundations, corporations, and universities, and as members of state legislatures and the U.S. Congress. This change is evident despite the continuing presence of poverty and unemployment among many urban blacks that has been so well described by William Julius Wilson (1987) in *The Truly Disadvantaged*.

From these examples it is possible to distill several principles about the conditions that help to dispel prejudice and discrimination and promote inclusion. Gordon Allport (1954), in *The Nature of Prejudice,* identified four necessary conditions for overcoming prejudice between majority and minority racial or religious groups: (1) contact between persons of equal status, (2) absence of competition, (3) a need for cooperation, and (4) a common goal. In fact, the 1948 desegregation of the United States Armed Forces was consistent with these principles and with research late in the war on the effect of inserting Negro platoons into white combat units. The white soldiers in integrated fighting units liked the experiment and showed less prejudice toward Negro soldiers than those who had not shared such a common experience (Merton, Stouffer, and Lazarsfeld 1950).

A review of the dynamics of inclusion as they work in the case of Catholics, Jews, and African Americans shows that progress is made when these four conditions were present. *Contact between people of equal status* was accomplished when Catholics were no longer only peasants, when Jews were no longer only peddlers or middlemen, and when Negroes were no longer confined to the status of servants but reached higher ranks of industry and government. Working with people of equal status in a similar line of work or on the battlefield resulted both in an *absence of competition* and a *need to cooperate.* Finally, over time and as a result of working together, the majority eventually saw that the minority were in many ways people just like themselves with *common goals.* The opportunity to work together, unfortunately, has remained mostly in the workplace. Living space (neighborhoods and housing) and public schools still reflect separation of the races. Consequently, *social* integration has moved much more slowly.

Given these lessons, an important current question related to immigration is how to reduce prejudice against the foreign born as well as how to incorporate undocumented immigrants into the societal mainstream. What is needed is not only a socio-psychological theory such as Allport's on how to reduce individual prejudice but also a theory of the conditions necessary for a social system to facilitate inclusion. In the political climate, leading up to the 2012 presidential election, in which there is a standoff between the Tea Party Republicans and Republican and Democrat centrists, Americans appear divided into two main factions—one that believes in less government, local control, and lower taxes, and the other that believes that government can best respond to protecting the general welfare by providing or assuring basic services like health care and Social Security. These different views have always been present but have became more stark and vocal with rising economic inequality and the Occupy Wall Street demonstrations of 2011. These confrontations may go on for some time, but it is unlikely that they will continue very long at the same intensity. For the purpose of perceiving a long-term pattern in the resolution of such conflicts, Parsons' (1966b) theory of adaptive upgrading is a useful guide.

Systems Theory and Immigration Policy

A central conceptual framework among all the social sciences is the idea of society as a system of interdependent parts. Political scientists focus on governments, economists on the economy, and sociologists on the system as a whole—population, family, government, the economy, the media, and the way that they all relate to each other as well as to the larger global system. Thus to economists and sociologists in particular, it is unrealistic to believe that any sovereign nation can simply close its borders without taking into account the labor needs of the future and the family ties that pull foreign-born persons into the internal system.

In his book *Immigrants and Boomers: Forging a New Social Contract for the Future of America,* demographer Dowell Myers (2007) uses this understanding of the interconnected national society to argue that the aging population in America really *needs* the new young people raised by immigrant families to be capable and well trained so that they can take the jobs of the future and pay the taxes that will support the older generation. Along with other experts, Myers views the effort to deny the newcomers and their children access to public services and public education as a shortsighted folly that fails to recognize the long-term benefit of making these outsiders fully productive citizens. Instead, Americans should realize that the immigrants and the nation have a shared destiny that requires a new social contract in which present investment in the young will pay off later in their support of older adults and retirees. Myers (2007:253) spells out what he means by a new social contract:

> The grown children who have been educated with taxpayer assistance will not simply be workers. They will also enter the ranks of taxpayers, and if they are well enough trained, they will command well-paying jobs that support healthy tax contributions. Those will be dearly needed if we are to support so many elderly at such a high level of retirement benefits.

Myers goes on to spell out a similar exchange in the homebuyer market. Older people will want to sell, and the younger generation will need to be sufficiently educated so that they have the income to buy the houses available. "Thus the buyer and seller relationship will link the fortunes of different generations and that linkage will echo a different relationship found earlier when the older generation supported investment in the education of these future homebuyers" (Myers 2007:253). This social contract is particularly important for California, which in the past received many residents from outside, especially Mexico. But since 1970 the fertility rate in Mexico has fallen from 6.8 to 2.4 children per women, which is likely to reduce the immigration rate, and thus it will be ever more important to have "home grown" young people who will take the jobs and pay the taxes of the future.

The theory of adaptive upgrading. Myers' vision of a new social contract that incorporates new elements of society to achieve greater productivity and a higher standard of living is consistent with a long sociological tradition begun by Emile Durkheim ([1893] 1964) in *The Division of Labor in Society* and refined by Talcott Parsons for modern times. Durkheim demonstrated that as the rules and institutions within society become more complex and specialized, the members become more interdependent. Among the higher animals that have a specialized heart, brain, and other organs, cutting out one organ is fatal whereas a lower animal with less specialized organs such as a flatworm can survive if it is cut into pieces. Analogously, the constituent parts of simpler societies based on family units or tribal groups can survive if they are separated or suffer injury. But in complex societies, change to one major institutional component such as the economy affects everything else. Durkheim called the integration of the simpler segmented societies *mechanical solidarity* and that of the complex societies *organic solidarity*. One way to think of a solution to the immigrant problem is to strengthen borders and create a class of illegal residents, which would be consistent with mechanical solidarity and would attempt to maintain the status quo. Another way is to create a path to citizenship which would increase organic solidarity and in the process improve efficiency and productivity.

In his theory of adaptive upgrading, Parsons (1966b) took Durkheim's framework further by incorporating twentieth century experience with labor unions, women's rights, racial integration, and other social movements to spell out four conditions that promote inclusion and organic solidarity. First, the processes that trigger inclusion begin with new demands on the system that force change in the old social structure and reward new more specialized roles *(structural differentiation)*. Second, previous tasks and skills are improved in order to meet the new demands *(upgrading)*. Third, there is recognition that some current outsiders have skills and talents that need to be brought in to strengthen the overall enterprise *(inclusion)*. Finally, there is recognition that the former outsiders share many of the same values and goals as the insiders *(generalization of values)*. As will be shown below, current legislative initiatives to create a path to citizenship for undocumented immigrants are consistent with this process of adaptive upgrading.

Current policy initiatives to control immigration and citizenship. Some recent efforts by the states to control immigration within their borders have been quite draconian. Perhaps best known is the law passed by Arizona in 2010 to empower police to identify, prosecute, and detain undocumented residents in the course of their normal duties (Archibold 2010). In 2011, Alabama passed an even harsher law to criminalize not only the undocumented resident but any citizen or group who transports or houses that person. Employers can have their licenses revoked. The law has been protested by church leaders as an affront to practice of their moral obligation to help others. Even conservative Fox News has labeled the law a disaster for farmers who, following enactment of a similar law in Georgia, hired criminals to do the harvest while banning undocumented migrants. The result was such a labor shortage that tomatoes and cucumbers lay rotting in the fields (Nowrasteh 2011).

The major alternative to these retributive approaches is to make the border more conducive to temporary visits and to create paths to citizenship for undocumented residents. Durand and Massey (2004) document the perverse consequences of tightening the border with Mexico. There has been an *increase* in undocumented migrants who started out as seasonal workers but never returned to Mexico because they would have become ensnared in the border control. In the meantime, undocumented workers are exploited with low wages and poor working conditions. Rather than close or open the borders entirely, Durand and Massey (2004) advocate a philosophy of *managing migration more effectively.*

An effective management of international migration requires a clear ethical stance. Massey and colleagues (2002) enumerate five principles formalized in the U.N. Declaration of Human Rights and the Helsinki Accords: (1) people should be free to leave their country of birth or citizenship without state interference; (2) migrants in a receiving nation should receive full legal rights and access to the judiciary system; (3) steps should be taken to minimize the number of undocumented workers and residents through regularization programs, temporary work visas, and moderate border enforcement; (4) sending nations should guarantee reciprocal rights of entry and legal protection to citizens of receiving societies; and (5) immigration policy should not be imposed unilaterally but with multilateral agreements such as govern trade.

A second requirement of effective immigration control and management is that it be based on an accurate understanding of the reasons for immigration. Three misconceptions are particularly common: one, that the sending nation will inundate the receiving nation with desperately poor people; second, that the flow is entirely unidirectional such that remittances home are overlooked as well as their positive effect on the economic development of the sending nation; and third, that migration flows last forever. In fact, it is not the poorest people who migrate, nor the poorest nations who send the migrants. Instead, people are more likely to migrate from developing countries and for a variety of reasons in addition to higher wages such as opportunities to gain credit, to make investments, and the like. The income they send back to their home communities translates into capital that furthers economic development of their home country. As a result, these exchanges don't last forever; a particular migration flow may be as brief as three to four decades, as in the case of South Koreans coming to the United States between 1965 and 2005, or as long as eight or nine decades in the case of European migration during the nineteenth century. These time-limited flows are referred to as "migration humps," and effective management will attempt to limit the height and duration of the hump.

No system to implement these ethical principles or manage immigration can be effective without multilateral collaboration. Massey and his coauthors (2002:156–157) point out that international migration does not occur evenly across potential receiving countries but follows well-established routes that are laid down by war, colonialism, investment, trade, or family ties. Thus the present U.S. limitation of 20,000 immigrants per year from any one country is a poor fit to the reality of the huge number coming from Mexico and far fewer from other nations. A better standard would be ethnically neutral criteria based on trade relations, treaties, or historical ties. Rather than repressive border enforcement, a better strategy would be to "cultivate the natural inclination of migrants to remain abroad temporarily by facilitating return migration and the repatriation of funds. Receiving societies would work with sending countries to create binational institutions capable of maximizing the positive effects of migradollars [sic] and fully harnessing their developmental potential" (Massey, Durand and Malone 2002:157).

The one prominent example of recent legislative efforts to regularize the status of undocumented residents is the DREAM Act (Development, Relief, and Education for Alien Minors), which was passed by the U.S. House of Representatives but voted down by the Senate in December 2010. The Act was widely supported by educators and authorities on immigration, but it failed because it was seen as an entering wedge for providing amnesty to undocumented immigrants and as a costly investment in education that might not pay off if many dropped out of school before completing the two-year requirement. Proponents argued instead that young people with a better education would hold better jobs and pay higher taxes that would more than pay for the investment. The law would have given young people under 30 who had been brought to this country illegally before they were 16, and who had lived in the United States continuously for at least five years, the right to pursue citizenship if they had a high school diploma and had completed at least two years of college or served in the military (Knickerbocker 2010).

Despite the setback of the federal DREAM Act, a similar idea has received a positive reception in California. The California DREAM Act cannot offer citizenship (authorization of which is reserved to the federal government). It does, however, allow *undocumented immigrant college students to receive publicly funded financial aid* if they came to this country before the age of 16, completed at least three years of high school, and graduated. Like the demographers who point to the long-term benefits of incorporating undocumented residents into the mainstream, Assemblyman Cedillo, the lead author of the bill, has persistently argued that the state will soon have to replace 1 million older workers and that students who have demonstrated tremendous talent and resilience should be educated for the future benefit of the state (Medina 2011b).

Clearly the idea of flexible multilateral treaties to manage immigration as well as DREAM legislation to regularize productive but undocumented young people are measures that depend on understanding that the nation and the global order are interdependent systems that benefit from normal population flows. Better management of immigration and new paths to citizenship are ways to achieve greater organic solidarity in which families continue to have a critical role. In order to carry out their socialization function successfully, families need assurance that they and their children are eligible to become citizens or legal residents. Thus successful integration of minority and immigrant groups depends on actions by *both* governments and families. Only then can native minorities, foreign-born residents, and unauthorized immigrants eventually be included as full citizens of American society.

Conclusion

Discussion of identity and citizenship has not been a traditional part of what is considered family policy. This is a serious omission because the family of origin determines an individual's birthplace, ethnicity, life chances, and civil rights. This chapter has traced a wide arc that runs from socialization and acculturation of the individual in the family environment to larger religious, racial, and ethnic communities that are shaped by the international dynamics of migration.

A key theme throughout is the fact that progress has been made in the inclusion of minority groups into full citizenship in American society. At the level of individual socialization and family dynamics it is clear that those who are most successful in being acculturated and achieving upward mobility come from families with greater human capital (the parents have more education and hold more secure jobs). These families are also more strongly connected to their religious and ethnic communities and are able to resist the downward pull of negative racial stereotypes and lower-class affiliation. Those in the second generation who are bicultural (with a secure foot in both American society and their ethnic heritage) are most likely to succeed.

But families do not operate in a vacuum. The changing demographic landscape that has brought in more non-Christians, nonwhites, and non-Europeans to American shores has both created problems of prejudice against the new outgroups and at the same time provided more robust community support for the minority religious and ethnic communities that have grown up in the wake of the immigration reform of 1965. Hindus, Buddhists, and Muslims have built their temples and mosques and in the process initiated their members not only into their religious communities but have enabled their participation in the larger civil society. These religious and ethnic communities mark important family events such as birth, marriage, and death. They also serve as schools for citizenship.

Immigration policy and the laws of citizenship constitute the institutional umbrella that influences the actions of both families and ethnic communities. The record shows five dramatic turning points in immigration policy since the early 1900s. The first important change was establishment of a national quota system in 1924. The second was the immigration reform of 1965 that abolished the national quotas and significantly raised the annual immigration limit to 360,000 people, more of whom were to come from Asia and the Eastern Hemisphere than from the Western Hemisphere. A third shift was the Immigration Reform and Control Act of 1986 that tightened the border with Mexico and at the same time offered amnesty to 3 million temporary and unauthorized residents. The welfare reform laws of 1996 constituted a fourth major development, which limited access by immigrants to public assistance and welfare benefits. The fifth and most recent change came about with heightened concern for protection of national security, which was implemented through the provisions of the PATRIOT Act of 2001 and the Homeland Security Act of 2002.

The nation now stands at a crossroads with respect to its future immigration policy. One school of thought is that enforcement against illegal aliens should be much stricter. This view has resulted in a number of state laws in Arizona and Alabama, and local jurisdictions to criminalize undocumented residents and sanction employers who hire them. Proponents of these laws are bitterly opposed to any kind of amnesty and instead advocate exclusion of unauthorized immigrants from access to public services or other kinds of assistance from private persons or charitable organizations. A more positive view, which is advocated by experts on immigration, is that movement of populations across national borders is a natural and time-limited process that benefits both sending and receiving countries. Rather than trying to shut off immigration, the public goal should be to manage it effectively. Immigration policy should be consistent with the U.N. Declaration of Human Rights and should work with national immigration flows to encourage temporary residence rather than to harden border controls that have been shown to increase the undocumented population. The national quotas need not be equal for every country but should follow already established paths of migration and be devised by multilateral treaties.

Those who regard immigration as a positive force when it is well managed also advocate ways of regularizing the status of the currently undocumented by creating paths to citizenship. The federal DREAM Act is one such example which, although it failed to pass Congress in 2010, remains a goal. In 2011 California passed the California Dream Act, which provides state funding to young undocumented aliens to finish two years of college. The argument for this legislation is that eventual contributions from future taxpayers will more than repay the cost to the public.

Past experience has shown that long excluded groups—whether Catholics, Jews, middle-class African Americans, or Muslims—have eventually achieved inclusion and acceptance as full citizens of American society. Several steps are necessary for inclusion to occur. Higher demands require adaptation and upgrading of everyone's qualifications. In the process there is more contact between equals from majority and minority groups, with the result that competition is submerged and cooperation enhanced. Insiders and outsiders are led to an appreciation of their common humanity and the values that they share. The current controversy over the proper treatment of undocumented residents defines a new line of difference between majority and minority groups. It seems likely that in the long run the new minority will also achieve inclusion into the mainstream. But at this moment, it is unclear whether that will be a matter of years or of decades.

8

Family, Government, and the Safety Net

U nlike economic, environmental, or defense policy, the term *family policy* is unfamiliar to most people. Even among family sociologists, family policy is usually linked to specific domains such as child poverty, work–family balance, or the Family and Medical Leave Act of 1993. Family policy tends to be lumped under the general topic of social policy, but so doing blurs what is distinctive about it. Most people are unaware of the extent to which government programs support many different kinds of families. For that reason a significant portion of the American public believes government should be smaller yet at the same time they demand that their benefits from Social Security and Medicare continue without change.

Scholars of family policy have a responsibility to educate both students and voters by showing them just how many areas of family life are at least partly dependent on government programs and policies. American citizens also need a coherent picture of why various family policies came into being—why they were thought to be necessary, and who worked to see them established. The descriptive challenge is to document the range of family-related policies that already exist but which most people take for granted. The previous chapters of this book have listed the vast array of programs and policies that apply to caregiving, economic security, housing and living space, and transmission of cultural, racial, and national identity. The analytic challenge is to show why the main elements of American family policy are also found in other modern societies, even though there is significant variation in their coverage and implementation.

A central thesis of this book is that family policy is not a random collection of specific programs. It is instead an adaptive societal response to the family's need for support in carrying out its four key functions—caregiving, economic provision, finding a place to live, and transmission of cultural identity and citizenship. Family policy came about because of economic modernization and changes in family structure that resulted in the decline of agriculture, smaller families, greater longevity, and more women in the labor force. Caregiving could no longer be confined to the home or be done by women alone. Economic security could no longer be based on working the land. Residential location was no longer determined by living on a farm or working at a nearby mill. Transmission of cultural heritage and eligibility for citizenship became less certain with racial desegregation and a diverse influx of immigrants. In the face of these challenges family policy became the nation's adaptive strategy for supporting key family functions when the family alone was unable to do so. Under normal circumstances the family is the place most people turn to for help. It is their ultimate safety net, what Christopher Lasch (1977) termed "a haven in a heartless world." But if a family member suffers a catastrophic illness, can't find a job, or risks being homeless or living in an unsafe place, the larger community and the nation are increasingly agreed that an institutionalized safety net should be available to support and supplement the basic work of the family. This ideal is still far from being realized in practice, but the principle is widely shared.

This sociological explanation of the growth of family policy as an adaptation to modernization is different from a primarily historical explanation that emphasizes the impact of specific historical events such as war, depression, or the outcome of a particular election. The sociological explanation also differs from a political or institutional analysis that attributes policy development primarily to the actions of interest groups and political leaders or the structure of American government. Rather, the focus of this book is on the broad similarities between American family policy and that of other advanced economies. The similarities are the result of the shared experience of modernization and the way modern nation states have responded to widespread change in family structure. The question to be explained is why the main elements in government programs to support the family are not unique to America. The answer is that modernizing governments have to meet similar challenges, as do families. Not surprisingly, the policy solutions in each country also share broad similarities.

This concluding chapter steps out of the descriptive picture of the many elements of American family policy that were presented in previous chapters and places them within the larger context of the nation as a whole.

The central theoretical argument of the chapter is that family policy is an evolutionary adaptation to the challenges presented by modernization of the economy and of the family. The adaptation occurs at several levels of society that are described here in top-down order: first, at the *national level* in the emergence of the modern American welfare state; second, at the *institutional level* in the creation of laws, programs, and agencies providing specialized support such as health care or housing; third, in the *community of family policy makers* that includes academics, program officials, the helping professions, and advocates; and finally, at the *action level,* the search for ways to meet specific new challenges of the future.

At the national level, the most important and dramatic evolutionary changes that laid the groundwork for family policy occurred during the 1930s. Like other modern nation states, America faced the challenge of modernization and the loss of traditional community and family supports to individuals. Social welfare policies in the United States, as in other countries, created pension and insurance systems, social services for needy families, and help with nutrition, health care, and housing, which were delivered through bureaucratic agencies that managed the new social programs.

At the institutional level, family policy in America did not become a conscious goal until the 1960s and 1970s when the women's movement and rise of single-parent and dual-earner families challenged established expectations of what families should be and should do. Over time, as a result of action by advocates for children, women, and poor people, a consensus gradually evolved that accepted diversity of family structure and agreed on the importance of supporting key family functions, especially caregiving and economic security.

At the collectivity level, a community of family policy makers began to take shape that ranges from data gatherers to members of Congress. Longitudinal studies make it possible to understand the factors leading to individual and family hardship or well-being. Agencies and workers implement the policies and programs that have been legislated at the state and federal level. Interest groups and lawmakers develop policy proposals and pass legislation that extend benefits to ever larger segments of the American population.

Now, at the level of future action, the current question before the nation is which human needs are most pressing for the country as a whole and must be addressed for the greater good of the nation. Should the priorities be on health care, education, support of the aging population, or cutting the deficit? How should human needs be measured against the importance of national defense, modernizing the infrastructure, or supporting research and technological innovation? In the family policy field, at least, the answer is clear that investment in children and the future labor force of the nation trump all other concerns. The emerging narrative of family policy in America is that the future strength of the nation will be built on the strength of families.

Family Policy in the Modern American Welfare State

Since the welfare crisis of the mid-1990s when President Clinton pledged "to end welfare as we know it," and a Republican Congress under the leadership of Newt Gingrich instituted welfare reform, the term *welfare* has taken on a distorted meeting in many circles to indicate an undeserved handout. But the idea behind social welfare as most people understand it in the Preamble to the Constitution of the United States is that it should be universally available.

> We the people of the United States, in order to form a more perfect union, establish justice, insure domestic tranquility, provide for the common defense, promote the general welfare, and secure the blessings of liberty to ourselves and our posterity, do ordain and establish this Constitution for the United States of America.

A modern term which approximates the broader concept of welfare is *well-being,* and as such includes all the freedoms mentioned in the Preamble: justice, peace, liberty, safety, and the blessings of liberty and domestic tranquility. In a famous set of lectures on *Class, Citizenship, and Social Development,* T. H. Marshall (1964) outlined the expansion of citizens' rights. With the abolition of serfdom in Europe that preceded the French Revolution, governments in the eighteenth century granted basic *civil rights* to their citizens—freedom of speech, of movement, and contract (to marry and to take work as they wished). Nineteenth century governments expanded *political rights* for the common people—the right to organize into labor unions, to be a member of the body politic and to vote without owning land. In the twentieth century, governments granted *social rights* to citizens by providing access to basic necessities such as food and shelter as well as health care and education. After World War II, the old Poor Laws of England that once took away civil rights of paupers in return for aid were repudiated by the Labor government. Social reforms by "the welfare state" broadened access to education, established the National Health Service, and built low-income housing. Government now paid not only for traditional state functions, such as defense, road-building, and regulation of commerce, but also for programs to support the well-being of the general population, especially those in greatest need.

Not only in Great Britain, but also in the United States and other countries such as Canada, France, and the nations of Scandinavia and the communist bloc, similar changes were occurring to broaden government responsibility for a variety of social services and economic supports to the general population. In the United States, as elsewhere, there was debate over whether such programs were "socialistic" and thus a danger to free enterprise. Critics argued that if people were "on the dole" they would lose incentive to work. Advocates contended that poor people were generally not poor because they were lazy but because of circumstances beyond their control. They had poor health, less education, and low-paying jobs; and yet they contributed to society, and the society in turn owed them a fair share of its wealth and resources.

At the same time that the popular debate was raging over the threats and virtues of socialism and capitalism, economists and sociologists were observing that similar changes were taking place in modern governments around the world, regardless of political regime. Economists Clark Kerr and John T. Dunlop (with Harbison and Myers 1960) counted five major types of political regime that had evolved not only to regulate their particular industrial economies but also to provide social goods to their people. Esping-Andersen (1990:1) writes, "What once were night-watchman states, law-and-order states, militarist states, or even repressive organs of totalitarian rule, are now institutions predominately occupied with the production and distribution of social well being."

Marshall's history and Kerr and colleagues' generalizations are among a series of observations on the nature and structure of the welfare state that help us to understand how modern government became a seedbed for the emergence of family policy in the United States. The story has several parts. First, modern governments must deal with the challenges posed by industrialism and modernization in general. Second, the policies and programs to meet these challenges have two principal goals—regulating the new capitalist economy and promoting the general welfare. Third, to accomplish these tasks requires a new kind of bureaucratic state run by managers who focus on specialized areas of reform but at the same time depend on a general consensus to support their actions. Fourth, three principal values—liberty, equal rights, and social justice—serve as touchstones for setting priorities and resolving conflicts.

The Challenge of Modernization

The new industrial economy requires a new relation of the workplace to the family. Factories need labor and, according to Kerr and his coauthors

(1960), the people are eager to work, and family and religion make the adaptation by ceding control to employers. But at the same time, there is no longer a need for so many children and large families to work the land. The modernizing nations of Europe began to see their birth rates decline and wondered how to replenish the population. Folbre (2009) attributes much of the British social reform ideas at the turn of the nineteenth century to a general concern that women's rights, women's rising employment, and access to birth control were causing a decline in fertility that had to be stemmed by active government measures to support children and family life. Similarly, in France and Sweden during the interwar period, family allowances and subsidies for large families came into being (Myrdal [1934] 1968).

Another demographic challenge was aging of the population. As industrial systems recruited younger workers and sent older workers into retirement, and longevity increased due to health advances, it became necessary to provide for the economic security of the older population. Wilensky and Lebeaux (1958) thus link the timing of the earliest welfare state initiatives to an awareness of the demographic revolution in aging and longevity.

In the economy, modernization also requires a new relationship between industry and the state. For the sake of efficiency, more specialized activity necessitates coordination and some standardization of rules in order to foster cooperation and the smooth operation of markets. Thus the modern state must take an active role in regulation that promotes integration and coordination of the many specialized sectors of the economy—business, labor, agriculture, and distribution. Kerr and his co-authors (1960:289) conclude that, ". . . industrialism cannot function well according to either atomistic or monistic models. . . . The discipline of the labor gang no longer suffices." There has to be some degree of decentralization, but a large measure of central control by the state is also required. This is achieved through consent and cooperation of labor, management, professionals and clients, and numerous nongovernmental organizations.

A third challenge to the modern state is the looming potential for the alienation and social unrest that results from the displacement of old loyalties to family and community by vast new opportunities for gaining wealth or the risk of becoming unemployed and impoverished. Social reform organizations, women's groups, and labor unions become experts at pointing out corruption, exploitation, and unfair advantages of owners over workers and of men over women (Quadagno 1987; Rueschemeyer and Skocpol 1996). No government wants to preside over a revolt by its citizens. Governments respond to these protests by instituting programs and policies to foster compliance and consensus. The result is a series of measures that give help to the "respectable poor" and "to the stranger who by reason not of personal bond commands it without asking" (Wilensky and Lebeaux 1958:141). The new social welfare is effective in offering assistance even though it assumes a certain amount of social distance between the helper and those who are helped.

Programs and Policies of Welfare-State Regimes

Given the desire of political leaders and the government to forestall social unrest, why is it that its hallmark social policies, like the Social Security Act of 1935, turn out to be pension and social insurance systems, social services for needy families, and help with nutrition, health care, and housing? But this is only the "non-economic" aspect of the modern welfare state. On the economic side there are also a series of innovations like the public employment schemes of the Depression era that together with social programs form a larger system in which the nation's economic and social welfare systems are intertwined and affect each other.

Kerr and other economists in the late 1950s surveyed the various types of modern states that had emerged around the world and found that they dealt with the new industrialism in similar ways. Social protests were much less common than had been expected (and than Marx had predicted). Instead governments were taking a central role in negotiating cooperative agreements between different power groups (such as corporations and labor unions), and the operation of nongovernmental organizations. Rather than class war and blood running in the streets, Kerr and his fellow economists (1960) predicted that a flood of paperwork would be much more likely.

Economist John Kenneth Galbraith (1958), in *The Affluent Society,* pointed to the "externalities," or unintended costs, produced by modern economic growth. Like Schumpeter (1958) before him, who saw in the new industrialism an inevitable connection between creativeness and destructiveness, Galbraith noted that greater filth accompanies greater wealth. Producers of goods also produce waste, polluted water and air, and do not pay the costs which typically fall on the poor who live in the shadow of factories or near noisy highways. Who then should pay these costs? Titmuss (1975:74) voiced a new ethic in the modern welfare state— that the costs of economic development should not be allowed "to lie where they fall" [on the poor] but should be shouldered by the nation at large. The modern state thus must deal with the economy as well as attend to the lives of the people at large.

While earlier observers recognized the mutual effect of economic and social policy on each other, it was not until the groundbreaking work of Gøsta Esping-Andersen (1990) that it became clear how social welfare and the economy affect each other as component parts of a single welfare-state regime. Unlike countries of continental Europe or Scandinavia, neo-liberal capitalist regimes such as the United States give relatively more weight to individual initiative and competition within the private sector and favor action by the private sector whenever possible rather than by the public sector.

Although all types of regime contain the basic institutions of the welfare state such as retirement insurance, subsidies for poor families and children, and assistance for those who need help with food or housing, the size and nature of these programs differ. Market-oriented regimes like the United States rely heavily on employers and the private sector to provide benefits alongside the basic supports that come from government. Despite America's less generous family policy than that of Germany and Sweden, employment opportunities for women were better in the United States. A larger proportion of women were found in managerial positions and professional occupations than in the corporatist or socialist state regimes.

Many critics have deplored the late arrival and limited reach of American social policy. Yet Esping-Andersen's work is a reminder that there are trade-offs between the breadth and generosity of the social welfare system and the nature and pace of the economy. Growth in the economies of Germany and Sweden during the 1980s was more limited than in the United States. Thus there may be a grain of truth in conservative neo-liberal claims that universal income benefits that come from the state rather than from employers are a potential damper on free-market incentives.

Institutional Innovations: Bureaucracy and Management

Not only does the modern welfare state have similar economic and social functions in modern nations, but it also has a similar structure. Observers of modern state formation repeatedly mention bureaucracy and management by administrators as distinctive features (Kerr et al. 1960; Quadagno 1987; Rueschemeyer and Skocpol 1996). Since bureaucracy is so familiar to most of us—in universities, corporations, and social services—it seems at first strange that its presence in government should be worthy of any particular mention. The prevalence of bureaucracy in government is significant, however, for three reasons. First, bureaucracy is a modern social invention with specialized offices that operate according to a well-understood set of rules that represent a rational approach to authority. This is a modern advance beyond traditional lineage-based or class-based authority which can be arbitrary and irrational (Weber 1947). Second, bureaucracy is a fairer and more efficient way of steering the economy and delivering social assistance than by authoritarian leaders or a corrupt political machine. Third, government by numerous specialized bureaucratic units can be more responsive to a variety of popular demands. This differentiated structure can both prevent social protest and better respond to the demands that come from many different quarters.

The advent of bureaucracy in government is so widely accepted because it is a successful adaptation to the many varieties of economic and social interests. Kerr and colleagues (1960:292) see the main theme of modern industrial society as pluralism: "Class warfare will be forgotten, and in its place will be the bureaucratic control of interest group against interest group. The battles will be in the corridors instead of the streets, and memos will flow instead of blood."

Flora and Heidenheimer (1981) suggest that the modern state is a new system of control that manages competing demands of distributing elites, service bureaucracies, and social clienteles. The state encompasses all of these elements and referees their struggles for power. Kerr and coauthors (1960:8) observe that, "Everywhere [in the industrialization process] there develops a complex web of rules binding the worker into the industrial process, to his job, to his community, to patterns of behavior. Who makes the rules? What is the nature of those rules? Not the handling of protest but the structuring of the labor force is *the* labor problem in economic development," and it is the state that deals with this problem.

Given the complexity and the importance of rules, conformity may be rigid in the workplace, leading to William H. Whyte's (1957) characterization of the "organization man." But Kerr and colleagues (1960:295) see the possibility that this very conformity may generate a predisposition for greater freedom and diversity in private life. "The new slavery to technology may bring a new dedication to diversity and individuality." In hindsight, it seems possible to interpret the increasing diversity in contemporary family structure as the manifestation of the quest for freedom in private life that Kerr and his colleagues speculated might accompany industrialization and the modern state.

What is the larger meaning of this theme that notes the coincidence of bureaucratic development with the emergence of the modern state? It is a sociological instance of form following function. Modernization creates a more complex and differentiated labor force. As industrialization spawns a more varied array of manufacturers, producers, distributors, business and accounting firms, a larger umbrella of shared understanding that is embodied in rules, offices, and "bureaus" with defined duties is needed to hold everything together and accomplish coordination across many domains of activity. Bureaucracy is the social form that can meet these demands—hence its ubiquitous presence in all types of welfare-state regimes.

Of course, there is a common stereotype of the bureaucrat, described by Merton (1968), as a rigid and narrow rule-bound official who is more faithful to the letter than the spirit of the law. But this stereotype should not blind us to the advances made possible by the growth of bureaucracy in the modern state. The positive significance of bureaucracies can be appreciated through the insights of Durkheim's great classic, *The Division of Labor in Society* (1893/1964), which outlines the transformations by which modernization proceeds. Increasing specialization and differentiation of roles in any social group threatens its coherence and unity. Fortunately, however, the interdependence that results from specialization also engenders organic solidarity and consensus. Thus in a bureaucracy, the rules—and consensus on how to operate under the rules—can hold together the increasingly complex operations of modern industrialism.

The division of labor and the emergence of organic solidarity are visible in the modern economy in the complex interplay between banks, brokers, corporations, stockholders, consumers, and workers. Laws and financial policy ("rules" that are created by the state) govern the money supply, mortgage rates, interest on loans, the minimum wage, and such matters as the extension of unemployment insurance. On the social welfare side, other laws and social policies (also "rules") govern eligibility for health care coverage, assistance to needy families, Social Security benefits, student loans, housing standards, and many other "nonmarket" goods and services. The social workers, doctors, therapists, and office workers in this sector are the "bureaucrats" who administer the rules and operate within them. By all accounts of the emergence of the modern state, the creation of bureaucratic structures for managing the economy and general social welfare was a great advance beyond the patronage, favoritism, and callousness toward the powerless that prevailed in earlier times.

Freedom, Equality, and Social Justice as Touchstone Values

Against the major narrative of welfare-state development around the world, the American case, despite its limited and largely implicit family policy, still stands out as similar to other regimes in having developed major social programs to support elders, children, and needy families. But the United States follows the "liberal"[1] type of welfare-state regime in emphasizing liberty and

---

[1]The term "liberal," as used by Esping-Andersen and political theorists, refers to reliance on capitalist or free-market mechanisms and freedom of individual choice. When used by Americans in everyday discourse, the term "liberal" usually means just the opposite—"left-wing" or even socialistic.

freedom of the individual whereby it delivers many social benefits through a combination of public and private means, always emphasizing the need to keep economic incentive alive by avoiding assistance that will make would-be workers into complacent dependents. Along with this emphasis on freedom Americans also value equality and social justice, which are central principles in other modern states as well.

The American emphasis on liberty turns the meaning of equality in economic affairs into "equality of opportunity" rather than "equality of results." Equality of opportunity is a value compatible with the liberal economic idea of Adam Smith's concept of the "invisible hand" in which the market is thought to reward the best price, the most efficient method of production, and the highest-quality product. Freedom and liberty also become associated with the economic virtue of acting primarily on the basis of self-interest rather than the interests of others. The principle of letting the market decide is used to justify decisions made on the basis of cost and price rather than loyalty, fairness, or such other noneconomic virtues. However, Nancy Folbre (2009), Julie Nelson (2006), and other feminist economists have noted that a theory of economics focused on profit and economic growth simply assumes the presence of the unpaid domestic labor of women in the home and the community without which it would be impossible to keep the labor force healthy and available for work and the children ready for school. Once the unpaid labor of women, retired persons, and volunteers is added to the factors that lead to economic success, it becomes clear that self-interest in the market and the altruism at home are in need of each other. Thus modern capitalism is locked in a firm embrace with welfare programs to promote well-being of the national household.

On the social welfare side of the modern state (as distinct from the economic side), social justice is the key guiding principle. The concept of social justice is less well understood than liberty or equality. It is perhaps best understood as the ideal of "fair play" in which no one is given an unfair advantage and allowance is made for those who start from behind or are otherwise handicapped in ways beyond their control. This understanding of social justice is famously illustrated by the philosopher John Rawls (1971) in *A Theory of Justice*. He proposes that if one were behind a "veil of ignorance" about one's own "original position" as being either favorably or unfavorably situated, one would devise a "just" social order where a disadvantaged person would receive help and a well-endowed person would be required to give help.

Britons during and after World War II grasped clearly the idea of social justice and the obligation to distribute "fair shares" of national resources because everyone had lived through a period of dire austerity and could empathize with anyone in need. T. H. Marshall (1964:321–322) summed up the mood of the times:

> Solidarity grew without a break through the war and into the first years of peace. The Beveridge Report was a bestseller because it offered, while the war was still in progress, a blueprint of what the nation was fighting for. British war drives were expressed in terms of social justice. The Welfare State could enjoy a ready-made consensus. But the crucial point is, I believe, that the Welfare State was born into a world of austerity—of rationing, price control, coupons, rent restriction, and houses requisitioned for the use of the homeless. It was not that these restrictions on the free market were regarded as good in themselves and desirable elements in the new social order: . . . But they provided as a background to the welfare legislation a society committed to "fair shares" and to a distribution of real income which could be rationally justified and was not the unpredictable result of the supposedly blind forces of a competitive market, in which everybody was entitled to take as much as he could get.

The challenge for the modern welfare state is to reconcile these two values of liberty and social justice by implementing measures that will enhance equality of opportunity and guarantee fair shares of the income distribution. Over the last half century, economists and social reformers have battled over the relative merits of an emphasis on keeping markets as unfettered as possible to promote capitalism and economic growth or to encourage investment in "nonmarket" goods such as the social services, education, and health care. Conservative economists led by Milton and Rose Friedman (2002) argue that big government and much of state regulation stifle growth and progress, encourage inefficiency and overspending, and interfere with individual freedom. The Friedman principle of keeping government to the needed minimum would privatize Social Security, national parks, and the postal system. Economists in the Keynesian mold argue instead that government regulation and government spending are necessary for building and improving infrastructure, education, and health care and will in the long run lead to economic growth. Expressed in the starkest terms, the arguments are between a conservative approach to economic improvement through the operation of private property and self-interest in the market and a progressive approach to increase general well-being through public investment based on altruistic principles that express solidarity and stimulate mutual aid within the community.

In *The Gift Relationship: From Human Blood to Social Policy*, Richard Titmuss (1971), the famous British social welfare theorist, strikingly illustrates the failure of a market approach to provide help to "strangers" (i.e., nonfamily members, people other than friends). By a careful comparison of the origins, cost, and quality of donated blood in Great Britain and the United States, he demonstrates that the cost per pint of blood in England and Wales in 1968 was the equivalent of $4.80 whereas in the United States it could range from $15 to $100 per pint depending on blood type (such as Rh negative) or the nature of the medical procedure in which it was to be used.

How could this be? Titmuss recounts the dramatic story of a lawsuit in Kansas City in 1964 that charged Kansas City hospitals and doctors with monopolistic practices because they had avoided using blood collected from prisoners and skid row derelicts who had been paid for their donations by two local blood banks with questionable reputations. The Federal Trade Commission accused the hospital association of restraining trade by creating a monopoly and prevailed in the court judgment, leading to a cost of $500,000 in fines and court charges to the professionals who were forced to shut down their safer blood bank and use commercial services instead. The whole episode had the effect of raising costs dramatically in other parts of the United States. Laboratories had to check more carefully blood supplied by prisoners and others who had been paid for their blood, and this added to the cost. Doctors ordered twice as much blood as needed to ensure an adequate supply, resulting in waste after the expiration date had passed, again adding to the cost. By contrast, blood in England and Wales was regulated by the National Health Service. The donors were healthier, much more likely to be volunteers than paid donors, and with less need for complicated testing for hepatitis and other impurities or for advance orders of more supplies than needed. Titmuss concludes that by any economic standard such as economic efficiency, administrative efficiency, cost per unit, or quality, the commercial approach was a failure. The voluntary, government-regulated supply was much more efficiently produced, cost less, and was of much higher quality.

Just as the feminist economists argue that the profit-oriented economy cannot operate effectively without the contributions of the altruistic work of families, friends, and neighbors, the moral of the gift relationship is that there is likely to be a better outcome when nonmarket considerations and altruistic virtues are included in the explanation of success or failure.

At the same time, social welfare advocates have to be realists about the costs of social programs and the adequacy of revenue to fund them. The so-called "fiscal crisis of the welfare state" has been a serious concern around the world for several decades. The crisis stems from global integration where tax breaks are given to multinational corporations, the ascendance of a service economy that yields lower taxes, and rising costs that come from an aging population and other social expenditures. Expense outruns revenue and large deficits threaten national solvency (Avi-Yonah 2000; Korpi 2003;

Quadagno 1987). In 2011–2012 Greece, Italy, Portugal, and Spain were on the brink of financial default because their social programs (pensions, unemployment insurance, educational subsidies, etc.) were costing more than the amount of money in their coffers. In the United States also, a similar concern surrounds Medicare and Social Security, which are in danger of running out of money as all the baby boomers reach retirement and incur increased medical costs. Social welfare advocates thus have to attend to basic economic principles by revising social programs (extending the retirement age, raising premiums on high earners, cutting medical costs, etc.) in order to ensure the long-term viability of the safety net.

In the final analysis, the values of liberty, equality, and social justice *(fraternité)* are realized in two ways of understanding equality—as both liberty of the individual to pursue opportunity, and as provision of a level playing field. Also embedded in this intertwined credo is the principle of the social body of which each individual is a part and outside of which no individual can survive.

The Nature and Purpose of Family Policy in America

Although a number of European countries established explicit national family programs and policies in the 1930s to reverse the decline in births, the concern with establishing a family policy in the United States did not emerge until the 1960s. Until that time family policy was largely seen as synonymous with child welfare and maternal and child health. Implicit policy was to support the husband-wife (breadwinner-homemaker) family with children by assuring men a "family wage" and by giving assistance to widows with children (as in Aid to Dependent Children). The emergence of family policy as a topic for discussion was precipitated by several new developments, among them the release of the Moynihan report in 1964, *The Negro Family: a Case for Natural National Action* (Rainwater and Yancey 1967) and the rise of the new feminist movement. Once family policy was on the public agenda, the question arose as to how it should be developed. Over time, social movements and interest groups contributed their ideas on what American family policy should cover. A contentious debate emerged in the 1970s and 1980s over whether family policy should try to influence family structure and form or should be neutral on questions of divorce, single-parent families, and dual-earner couples (Berger and Berger 1983; Steiner 1981). The debate is still unresolved, but there is clear acceptance of greater diversity as seen, for example, in several states' authorization of same-sex marriage. What the record seems to show is that a stronger consensus has developed around the need for public support of healthy family functioning.

Awakening to Family Policy in America

Up until the 1960s, American family policy was unquestioned because it was unstated. Mothers without husbands to support their families, many of them widows, were eligible for ADC benefits. Two-parent families with breadwinner-fathers and homemaker-mothers were the norm. The baby boom obviated any worry about population replacement. It was a period of political consensus with full employment and a rising standard of living. Men with no more than a high school education could earn a salary equivalent to some professionals.

Beginning in the 1960s, however, and continuing to the present, these demographic conditions changed dramatically, as did the general political and cultural climate. *The Other America: Poverty in the United States* (Harrington 1962) revealed that one-fifth of the nation was living in poverty. The fuel crisis of the 1970s and a gradual loss of manufacturing jobs resulted in an economic downturn in the 1970s. The Moynihan Report noted that 21 percent of African American families in 1965 were headed by a woman, making them eligible for welfare aid, compared with 9 percent of white families and that the ratio of nonmarital births among blacks was eight times the white ratio. These figures were signs of an upward trend in what Moynihan interpreted as a crisis in the Negro family. Thus began a long-term discussion of how to support poor families without in some way worsening their condition by making them split apart in order to receive welfare assistance. Moreover, as more mothers throughout the country joined the labor force, a new question arose concerning the justice of welfare assistance to single mothers to stay at home with their children when the majority of married women with children were then in the paid labor force.

These changes in economic and demographic conditions called into question the implicit family policy of the AFDC program that was based on the traditional idea of helping poor children rather than providing a universal benefit to all families. Scholars, policy makers, and the general public began to think about *family* policy as distinct from children's policy or aging policy. In addition, the re-energized women's movement that became visible in the 1970s was asking for day care and maternity leaves for working mothers.

In the face of such challenges, existing child-oriented and antipoverty policies came under critical scrutiny. Social scientists, government officials, and social service workers all took a hand at defining what American family policy was or should become.

Defining the Goals of American Family Policy

Different groups brought different perspectives to the question. Social scientists like Reuben Hill developed a typology of five different approaches to family life that are used in family studies—interactional, structural-functional, situational, institutional, and developmental—and said that the most useful of these for policy purposes was the structural-functional or system approach to families (Hill and Hansen 1960; Hill 1971). Social workers like Alvin Schorr (1969), Robert Moroney (1976; 1986), and a special committee of the National Conference on Social Welfare (1978) all put forward conceptual frameworks to describe the scope and content of family policy. Zill and Rogers (1988) reviewed social indicators of child well-being (health, educational achievement, poverty) and suggested the kinds of programs needed to remedy any deficits.

Various research institutes and foundations also took a role in surveying the needs and the resources available for developing a national family policy. In 1974, the National Science Foundation provided a small grant to survey current family policy development in the United States (Giele and Lambert 1975). The National Research Council (1976) and the Carnegie Corporation Council on Children (Keniston and Carnegie Council on Children 1977) developed reports on the topic, although with some difficulty in reaching consensus on their recommendations (Steiner 1981:22–23). In 1977 the National Institutes of Mental Health funded three multiyear academic training programs in family policy at the University of Minnesota, headed by Reuben Hill; Duke University, headed by Carol Stack; and at the Heller School of Brandeis University, headed by Roland Warren and Robert Perlman.

Various policy makers approached the project of developing a national family policy as something analogous to other government initiatives to protect the environment or provide safeguards to workers. Senator Walter Mondale in 1973 held Senate hearings on the changing state of the American family, and this became one of the themes of the 1976 presidential campaign of Carter and Mondale. Out of these efforts came the Family Impact Seminar (Family Impact Seminar 1976–1998) based in Washington, which reviewed over a thousand federal programs for their potential effect on family life. The Seminar reported that 269 programs administered by 17 different federal agencies had potential effects on at least one of three dimensions of family life—membership, material support, or health and caregiving (Bane 1980).

The wider public also became involved. President Carter called for a White House Conference on Families in 1979 that signaled the new broader approach to family policy. Since the first White House Conference on Children in 1909 and the founding of the Children's Bureau in 1912 there had been periodic White House conferences that resulted in significant recommendations for improved services to children and families. Those earlier events generated consensus and program innovations, but the White House Conference on Families was different in making clear a major cultural divide related to family structure. Conservatives wanted to endorse the traditional two-parent family and see government policy as a means to strengthen it while discouraging other forms. Feminists and progressives, on the other hand, wanted to support families in general by providing universal childcare, flexible schedules for working parents, and better remuneration for part-time work.

Despite many perspectives on what should be the goals of American family policy, an implicit consensus appears to have emerged among policy makers and academics that the chief purpose of American family policy is to support the healthy *functioning* of families regardless of whether their form and composition are traditional or not. As Bane and Jargowsky (1988:253) concluded from their review of American family policy, ". . . no government policies that are feasible within the American political context could appreciably change American family structure. In particular, no government policy will reverse the increase in the proportion of children in female-headed families." Even earlier, Bane (1980:171) had emphasized that the main focus of family policy should be to help families to be "healthy and functional." She argued that, "Policy is judged by the extent to which it provides these needed supports, which tend to include income security, jobs, housing, healthcare, and social services."

The late Reuben Hill (1971), one of the leading American sociologists of the family, in his 1970 presidential address to the International Sociological Association, showed the usefulness of combining a systems approach with his own developmental focus on how families change in age and composition over time. The advantage of the systems approach or "structural-functional" model is that it includes the concept of adaptation and thus can comprehend change in functioning as well as change in structure over time.

My review of contemporary family policy in America is likewise based on a conception of the family as a social system within the larger society (along with other institutions such as the economy, education, defense, etc.). Both Hill and Parsons see the family system as having four main functions. They have been articulated by Parsons (1966b) in his theory of action as adaptation (A), goal attainment (G), integration (I), and legitimation (L). Hill lists four properties of systems that parallel those of Parsons: (1) the tasks they perform to meet the needs and demands of their members and those of their environment (similar to G), (2) the interrelatedness of positions or the interdependence of component parts that form their structures (similar to I), (3) boundary maintenance tendencies that serve to differentiate systems from other social systems in their environment (similar to L), and (4) equilibrium and adaptive propensities that tend to ensure their viability as social systems (similar to A) (Hill 1971; Zimmerman 1988:74–75). In my framework, *adaptation* by the family is accomplished primarily through income provision that pays for material and other necessities. The main task or *goal* of the family in modern times is caregiving. *Integration* of the family into the larger society is linked to residence in a given place that connects the family to neighborhood, schools, and voting district. The *legitimation* function defines the family's identity through its legal standing and its cultural, racial, and ethnic heritage as well as transmission of this heritage. The earliest version of this formulation appears in Giele (1979).

Table 8.1 summarizes the dimensions of family life that reviewers of family policy have identified as relevant. One of the most inclusive listings of issues under the rubric of family policy appears in Zimmerman (1988:21):

> Family policy not only represents a perspective, but also a field of activity. As a field, it includes such programs as family planning, food stamp programs, income maintenance programs such as Aid to Families with Dependent Children (AFDC), unemployment compensation, supplemental security income, and so forth; foster care, adoptive services, homemaker service, day care, home based parent aid, and family therapy. In more recent years it also has included employment services, and manpower and training programs, housing, health services of various kinds, nutrition programs, child development programs, a range of personal social services, special programs for women, and services for elderly members and their adult children. It also includes a whole body of family law having to do with family relationships and obligations, such as marital rape laws, child support laws, child custody, cohabitation, marriage and divorce, and so forth. The criterion of family well-being, however, extends its domain even further, into such areas of activity as taxation, land use, energy, defense, transportation, the environment, highway safety, and hazardous waste. In other words, as earlier definitions suggest, family policy connotes all activities promoted or sanctioned by government that affect families, directly or indirectly.

It is striking, as shown in Table 8.1, that all the major books and articles on American family policy between the 1960s and the 1990s mention caregiving as central. The majority also mention adequate income and economic assistance for those who are poor. A few mention housing and public education, but many fewer include transmission of cultural heritage or citizenship. Both the heavy clustering in caregiving and the lesser attention given to housing and transmission of family identity indicate the lack of a clear theoretical framework for identifying the central functions of family life.

Using a theory of family functions based on a system model has three advantages. The first advantage is parsimony: The list of functions is limited and avoids redundancy. The second is generalization: A clear conceptual scheme organizes data that are relevant to many types of family. The third gain is in generation of hypotheses that are a guide to evidence that others may have overlooked or seen as outside the family policy field (such as housing or immigration policy). The four-part theoretical scheme is thus a powerful tool for organizing the vast field of data and government programs related to family policy such as presented in the central chapters of this book on caregiving, economic provision, housing, and citizenship.

In relation to the four major functions by which the conceptual models are classified in Table 8.1, there are two other dimensions that writers frequently identified which relate to what Kamerman and Kahn (1978) refer to as "target groups." Target groups are the structural units—individuals and families—on whom policy has an impact. Included in target groups are population categories such as children, aged, handicapped, and poor people, as well as types of family such as cohabiting, married, single-parent, or same-sex unions. Family policy is here classified primarily in terms of function with the understanding that all the main target groups will be covered. Such a classification is consistent with the dominant theme among scholars of family policy, which is that its primary purpose is to support healthy family functioning rather than to serve any one population group or family type.

The Role of Social Movements and Interest Groups

The social scientists, social workers, and policy makers who were trying to figure out what family policy was or should be were willy-nilly responding to prevailing ideas and social institutions that were already firmly established by the women's groups and social reformers of an earlier era. The dominant theme of these pioneers was child protection and maternal health and well-being. The Children's Bureau established in 1912 and the Women's Bureau established in 1920 were the main instruments for policy implementation. The causes they had espoused were the ending of child labor, the protection of women workers from dangerous working conditions, and universal health care for mothers and children that was provided by the Sheppard-Towner Act during the 1920s.

The enactment of the Social Security law of 1935 extended these early efforts to help poor mothers and children through establishment of Aid to Dependent Children (ADC). But the advent of Old Age Assistance and Social Security for retirees was a new approach in that it focused on adults

Table 8.1 Descriptions of American Family Policy, 1967–1994

Year	Author	Caregiving (G)	Economics (A)	Residence (I)	Citizens (L)
1967	Sussman (1967) *Journal of Marriage and the Family* (entire issue)	Health & Mental Health	Economic Programs	Housing & Education	"Social Authority" of Family
1968	Schorr (1969) *Explorations in Social Policy*	Childcare Social Services	Public Assistance Job Training	Housing	Immigration, Racial Equality
1976	National Research Council (1976), *Toward a National Policy for Children & Families*	Health, Childcare, Social Services	Economic Resources		
1977	Rice (1977) *American Family Policy: Context and Content*	Health, Service Integration	Industry Income		
1978	National Conference on Social Welfare, and National Commission on Families and Public Policy (1978) *Families and Public Policies in the United States: Final Report of the Commission*	Care for Sick, Young, & Elderly	Income & Jobs	Education	
1978	Kamerman and Kahn (1978) *Family Policy: Government and Families in Fourteen Countries* (chapter on United States)	Health & Social Services, Daycare, etc.	Income Transfer Programs	Housing & Education	
1980	Aldous and Dumon, *The Politics and Programs of Family Policy* (chapter by Bane, 1980)	Health Care, Social Services	Income Security, Jobs	Housing	Indian Affairs

(Continued)

Table 8.1 (Continued)

Year	Author	Caregiving (G)	Economics (A)	Residence (I)	Citizens (L)
1986	Moroney (1986), *Shared Responsibility: Family and Social Policy*	Care for Dependents, Health	Income Supports & Insurance	Housing & Education	
1988	Zimmerman (1988) *Understanding Family Policy: Theoretical Approaches*	Health & Social Services Foster care	Food, SSI Unemployment Insurance Job Training	Housing	
1988	Cherlin, *The Changing American Family and Public Policy* (chapter by Bane and Jargowsky 1988)	Childcare, Adolescents' Health	Parental leave, etc.		
1994	Jacobs and Davies (1994), *More Than Kissing Babies?: Current Child and Family Policy in the United States*	Childcare, Adolescents AIDS Education Care of Disabled	Family Leave Family-Friendly Workplace	Help for the Homeless	Race and Class Equality Issues

rather than children and on giving aid to individual recipients rather than family units. Thus during the 1930s and 1940s, there was no ready-made constituency or reform agenda for constructing a policy for families in general rather than for a variety of needy individuals.

By the late 1950s and early 1960s, however, new voices were being heard and questions were being raised about the efficiency of ADC (Schorr 1969), the hidden social controls that kept women out of the labor force (Friedan 1963), and changes in sexual mores and family stability (Thornton et al. 2007). Policies aimed at individual target groups no longer seemed adequate to the task of protecting and promoting family health and well-being.

The new women's liberation movement that surfaced in the late 1960s and was at its apogee in the early 1970s was a major contributor to the ideas of what might be done. The women faculty members who banded together to set up childcare centers in universities in the 1970s (Campbell 1973) or the innovations to provide childcare at a factory like the Stride Rite Shoe Corporation in Massachusetts were typical of family-related innovations at workplaces around the country. Also prominent among ideas for reform were more flexible schedules for mothers and fathers of young children. For the first time, in the 1970s, one might see a parent who was a graduate student or even a teacher bringing a child to the classroom to play or read quietly in the corner.

Ferment was all around, and family sociologists were taking an active role in defining the issues. Scholars from sociology, economics, psychology, and political science were also engaged in broad reviews of changes in work and family structure. One of the most influential was Rosabeth Moss Kanter (1977). In her report, *Work and Family in the United States: A Critical Review and Agenda for Research and Policy,* to the Russell Sage Foundation, she described the close interdependence of work life and family life and noted how generally work–family connections had been ignored.

Social workers were also active in defining the new situation of families in the economy and the nation. Rather than women's equality, the most important theme in their work was poverty alleviation and care for dependents who could not look after themselves, a group that included children, the elderly, the physically and mentally handicapped, and others trapped in poverty. Alvin Schorr (1969), a social worker who had program responsibilities in the U.S. Department of Health Human Services and the Office of Economic Opportunity in the 1960s, made observations on the ADC program that helped to expand the program to *families* with dependent children (AFDC) by covering unemployed fathers as well as mothers and children. Social workers like Sheila Kamerman, a faculty member at the Columbia University School of Social Work, also had a role in shaping family policy through her testimony at Congressional hearings related to the Pregnancy Disability Act, the Family Support Act of 1988, and the Family and Medical Leave Act of 1993. In addition, Kamerman and Kahn (1978) in their book *Family Policy: Government and Families in Fourteen Countries* gathered descriptions of policies and programs in Europe and North America.

Besides feminists and social workers, a third major group with an interest in creating family policy includes the various public representatives who met in the 1979 White House Conference on the Families held in Baltimore, Minneapolis, and Los Angeles to define the types of help that families need—home care for elders, help for the handicapped, childcare, flexible hours, tax reform, and the like. Some delegates wanted a clear prohibition of abortion but were not successful in their appeal. However, a definition of family as two or more people related by blood, marriage, or adoption was accepted (White House Conference on Families 1980).

It was the immense range of topics proposed as policy goals that provoked Gilbert Steiner's (1981) title, *The Futility of Family Policy*. Rather than become lost in the swamp of ideological conflict over defining the right kind of family, or a policy broad enough to cover many different situations, Steiner argued that it would be more productive simply to focus on those in greatest need. This sidestepped the question of policy to support the family as a necessary social institution and focused instead on help to the neediest individuals.

Diversity of Family Forms, Consensus on Family Functions

The upshot of disagreement on goals among advocates of family policy was the eventual eclipse of efforts to define family narrowly or to favor one form over another. Murray's (1984) suggestion that black female-headed families had become more common so that they could qualify for welfare benefits was questioned by William Julius Wilson (1987) in *The Truly Disadvantaged: The Inner City, the Underclass, and Public Policy*. Wilson argued that the causal arrow went the other way, from the poverty and unemployment of black males to black women's reluctance to marry them. Thus, from the standpoint of family policy advocates, it was reasonable to be skeptical about the possibility of making any difference in family structure, given so much uncertainty about the causes of teenage pregnancy, divorce, and single parenting. A more modest aim that had a better chance of being realized was to support healthy family functioning and in the process to strengthen family structure.

Some conservative gains may have contributed to a retreat from focusing on family structure as an object of family policy. During the Reagan Administration, the passage of the JOBS program and Family Support Act made important changes in welfare programs that instituted work requirements. This trend was consolidated in the welfare reform legislation of 1995. In addition, the Defense of Marriage Act of 1996 defined marriage as a contract between a man and a woman and thereby postponed a more inclusive definition of marriage to include same-sex unions. So also, the famous article by Barbara Dafoe Whitehead (1993), "Dan Quayle Was Right" (endorsing Quayle's position that out-of-wedlock births were not acceptable), generated a huge positive response. The article also stimulated a broad discussion of changing attitudes about sex, divorce, and childbearing as well as recognition that the causes and remedies for these trends were not easy to identify. What now seems to be an implicit consensus is that family policy should apply to a diverse range of family types and provide help when needed.

Creation and Implementation of Family Policy in America

The picture of American family policy quickly becomes very complex when one considers how it is formulated and carried out. Developing family policy is only part of the process of social change; the rest is implementation. When policy is created, the system is adapting to specific needs by creating programs that will address a problem on a more general scale ("scaling up"), and program officials and legislators codify rules about how to proceed. When policy is applied, the personnel in government agencies and service organizations implement these principles and specify how they should be put into practice "on the ground." Adaptation moves up the hierarchy of social control from specific instances to general principles. Implementation moves down the hierarchy from general regulations to specific applications. The cycle is similar in various types of social change and social reform as seen, for example, in the way that gender role change comes about as adaptation to changes in the economy and women's lives that affect the laws and norms of society. The new laws and norms are then implemented in ways that reinforce the new patterns of behavior (Giele 1988:296).

The story of the creation and implementation of family policy in America can be told either way—as a process of adaptation or of implementation. The path of adaptation is easier to follow. It begins with changes in individual and family behavior and leads to practical attempts to solve social problems by creating broader policies. There are several major groups involved. One group monitors and interprets changes in individual and family behavior. This is the community of social scientists who collect data and populate the think tanks and academic centers. A second group are the employees of social service and government agencies such as agency personnel and social service workers who not only help to shape policies in their field of expertise but also carry them out. A third group are the advocates, interest groups, and law-makers who propose new laws and see that they are passed. Finally, in the court of general public opinion, some policies are approved and others rejected. The following review is a sketch of these various members of the family policy community and their roles in the policy-making process.

Scientific Studies of Families and Children over Time

In the whole process of devising policies that will help families, someone has to take responsibility for defining the situation—saying what the problems are and what needs to be done. Social scientists have performed that responsibility in the family policy field. There is a division of labor among the scholars, statisticians, and data entrepreneurs in acquiring and analyzing the facts and evaluating the results. Named here are just a few of the most outstanding examples of major databanks, and academic, foundation, and government centers concerned with social policy for children and families.

Longitudinal surveys and databanks. A major breakthrough in social science information gathering was developed during and after World War II in the form of panel studies and longitudinal surveys. Rather than collecting information from respondents at a single point in time (as in the decennial census), these surveys follow individuals over a period of years by repeating the questions to the same group of respondents at regular intervals. The method was pioneered by Lazarsfeld, Berelson, and Stouffer in such studies as *The American Soldier* and *The People's Choice: How the Voter Makes Up His Mind in a Presidential Campaign,* which followed changes in attitudes over time (Lazarsfeld, Berelson, and Gaudet 1965; Merton et al. 1950).

The longitudinal technique was then adapted to the study of family events and changes in individual lives over time. Five longitudinal surveys are frequently cited in published works on family-related policy as well as the Inter-University Consortium for Political and Social Research, which archives data and documentation from these and other studies:

- The Wisconsin Longitudinal Study (WLS) surveyed the Wisconsin high school class of 1957 and their parents, and later their siblings and spouses in 1957, 1964, 1975, 1992, 2004, and 2006 (Hauser 2009; Wisconsin Longitudinal Study 2011).
- The National Longitudinal Surveys (NLS) sponsored by the Labor Department were begun in 1966 to study labor market activities and other significant life events of young men and older men, and young and mature women; they have since been augmented by surveys of youths and young women and their children in 1979 and 1997 (U.S. Department of Labor 2011).
- The Panel Study of Income Dynamics (PSID), launched in 1968, began as the "Five Thousand Family Study" with major funding from the National Science Foundation. It is the longest-running longitudinal survey in the world and has provided data for over 3,000 publications (Institute for Social Research 2011).
- The Survey of Income and Program Participation (SIPP) is conducted by the U.S. Census and began in 1983 as a longitudinal survey to gather information on poverty, income, employment, and health insurance coverage (U.S. Census Bureau 1983–).
- The National Study of Households and Families (NSFH) launched Wave I in 1987–1988, Wave II in 1992–1994, and Wave III in 2001–2003 and covered

cohabitation, dating and marriage, childbearing, household task allocation, and consequences of divorce (National Survey of Families and Households 1987–1988). The study ended in 2006.

- The Inter-University Consortium for Political and Social Science (ICPSR), located at the Institute of Social Research of the University of Michigan, contains downloadable data from the preceding five surveys as well as many more (Inter-University Consortium for Political and Social Research 1961).

Centers for study of family and children's policy. As new data sources have been developed, various academic centers and nonprofit organizations have also charted emerging trends and their causes. During the 1970s, a number of organizations monitored changes in families, women's roles, rights of minorities, and the situation of children. The Russell Sage Foundation produced *Indicators of Change in the American Family* (Ferriss 1970). The United States Commission on Civil Rights (1979) published *Social Indicators of Equality for Minorities and Women*. Louis Harris, together with the Roper Organization (1974), conducted *The Virginia Slims American Women's Opinion Poll*. General Mills, Inc., and Yankelovich Skelly and White, issued several reports on family income (1975), child well-being (1977), and health (1979). The U.S. Census Bureau compiled *Issues in Federal Statistical Needs Relating to Women* (Reagan 1979). The Urban Institute published *Women in the Labor Force in 1990* (R. Smith 1979). These are just a few of the reports produced during the early discussion of women's changing roles and the feasibility of developing a national family policy.

Alongside these early efforts at stocktaking, there emerged a number of specialized academic centers. Some like that at the Columbia University School of Social Work led by Sheila Kamerman and Alfred Kahn or the Center on Economics and Politics of Aging at the Heller School of Brandeis University were most prominent in the 1970s and 1980s. Others like the Andrus Center on Gerontology at the University of Southern California, the Poverty Center at the University of Wisconsin, or the Harvard/MIT Joint Center on Housing Studies continue among the leading centers in their fields.

New centers for research and training in family and children's policy have also emerged over the last two decades. The Sloan Foundation (2011) Work and Family Research Network under the leadership of Kathleen Christensen established a series of centers on work and family that have "played a pivotal role in developing this new field of work–family scholarship by providing the only source of sustained funding for researchers in sociology, psychology, anthropology, political science, labor economics and industrial relations to conduct interdisciplinary research on issues faced by working families." Seven centers focusing on different aspects of the problem were located at University of Chicago, Cornell

University, University of California at Berkeley and Los Angeles, Emory University, University of Michigan, and MIT. The Network is now centered at the University of Pennsylvania, with partners at Boston College, Georgetown Law Center, and the Families and Work Institute. A host of other centers too numerous to count have sprung up in universities and the government to examine current issues related to the lives of children, youth, and families, a sure indication of growing concern with family-related questions (Work and Family Researchers Network 2012).

Agencies and Workers: The Implementers of Family Policy

In his influential book *Street-Level Bureaucracy: Dilemmas of the Individual in Public Services,* Michael Lipsky (1980) demonstrates that a policy is only as good as the actions of the people who administer it. The street-level bureaucrat is always solving dilemmas that come from reconciling the goal and intent of a general policy with the particular needs and demands of the people being served. The way the official solves these questions becomes the policy as it is applied. Sometimes ancillary considerations—personal ambition, racial bias, or political favor—distort the mission.

A recent example of a miscarriage of policy was aired by National Public Radio in a profile of South Dakota's treatment of Native American children by its Department of Social Services (DSS). A disproportionate number of Indian children are being taken away from their families under the rationale that they are being "neglected" (which usually means that they are poor). The NPR reporters discovered that a federal law meant to protect Native Americans in fact provides more money for placing Indian children than white children with foster families. If an Indian child who has been placed is later adopted, the state receives even more money ($4,000 per child), so there is an incentive for the DSS to take these children, place them in foster care, and put them up for adoption (Sullivan and Walters 2011). When department officials and caseworkers were asked by the reporters about the propriety of these actions, they justified them in terms of what they saw as their duty to prevent neglect and to take children out of situations that they considered unsafe but which were regarded as normal by the Indians. The white caseworkers were apparently without any awareness of the injustice and cruelty of their actions. Native American caseworkers and foster families reported that they were hardly ever called upon, even though official policy directs that they be consulted first.

In contrast with such a misguided example of implementation, a new form of offering assistance is being adopted by caseworkers and program directors. Referred to as *participant direction* or the *capabilities approach,* any interaction with clients emphasizes human dignity and the development of a person's capacities whatever they may be. The capabilities approach means that a person with Down syndrome is not treated as totally incompetent but is accorded the dignity and freedom to make decisions wherever possible (Nussbaum 2011). Professionals in caregiving who encourage self-direction and management (agency) on the part of their clients are implicitly using a capabilities approach in what is termed "participant direction" (PD). This orientation is now being implemented in service systems for caregiving to persons with limited cognitive abilities or frail elders by consulting and complying with clients' wishes wherever possible and in some cases even giving them charge of budget management and choice of caregivers (Sciegaj and Capitman 2004; Warfield and Leutz 2011).

The methods of the Family Impact Seminars (2011–) and their focus on taking a family perspective are consistent with the capabilities and PD approaches in encouraging as much autonomy of families as possible in the work of professional caregivers. Although Karen Bogenschneider (2006), the current head of the Family Impact Seminars, does not describe her work either as participant direction or a capabilities approach, she has in fact used similar methods in a successful youth project in rural Wisconsin. The purpose of the program in 22 communities was to create a more supportive environment for youth. The basic principles were for the professional university extension agents to work with community participants to identify their strengths and wishes and help them organize in a way that would bring about several desired goals—giving youths a place to gather, limiting alcohol use, and increasing youth engagement in community life. The elements of this success story in policy implementation actually correspond with the theory of action—identification of goals (G), adaptive mobilization of skills and resources to attain the goals (A), integration of efforts by all the players (I), and legitimation (L) from outside community members and experts.

A third example of dynamic implementation of family-friendly initiatives can be found in the private sector. Rapaport and Bailyn (1996), under the auspices of the Ford Foundation, explored ways that employers and fellow workers can take family needs and women's and men's different work and family obligations into account in ways that benefit workers as well as corporations. Following months of observation and discussion with employees and managers at Xerox Corporation, Tandem Computers, and Corning, Inc., the authors showed that a dual lens on demands of work and family both changes the culture and also promotes cooperation across different departments within the company. More flexible work routines and a culture that takes family needs into account can actually energize workers and help the enterprise become *more* efficient than with a rigid separation of work and family life.

Policy Makers: Interest Groups and Lawmakers

In his review of the social science literature on policy making, Paul Burstein (1991) names three main steps in the process of achieving an established policy: (1) agenda setting, (2) development of policy proposals, and (3) the struggle for adoption of one proposal or another. By far the most is known about agenda setting, perhaps because making a list of many desirable policy goals is easier than narrowing the list to just a few rules or laws that are specific and popular enough to gain acceptance. The nineteenth century women's rights movement, for example, did not succeed until its broad demands for social equality of women were narrowed to the very specific proposal of woman suffrage (Giele 1995). It is the same with family policy. Compared with innumerable requests for preschool childcare, flexible hours, and paid maternity leave, the Family and Medical Leave Act of 1993 is quite limited in coverage; it is unpaid and does not apply to firms with fewer than 50 employees. Nevertheless, it represents a considerable step beyond what existed before.

Agenda setting and policy proposals. One large group of family policy proposals is oriented to strengthening family *functions* by providing help with caregiving or flexible work schedules. Many, however, have never reached the stage of policy proposals that could be enacted into law. The Conference Board outlined potential employee benefit programs in 1989. Private employers would offer a combination of benefits ranging from fitness programs and on-site childcare to pensions, health insurance, and counseling for different stages of the life cycle—time of hiring, marriage, childbearing, divorce, and retirement (D. Friedman and Gray 1989).

One of the most comprehensive outlines for an American policy agenda to integrate work and family appears in *Families that Work: Policies for Reconciling Parenthood and Employment* by Gornick and Myers (2003). The authors compare several key policies such as family leave, vacations, regulation of working time, preschool childcare, and public schooling in the United States and 11 other nations. In 2000, nine European countries and Canada gave at least 12 weeks of paid maternity leave whereas the United States gave none. Other countries typically guarantee three weeks paid vacation compared with none in the United States. Publicly funded childcare and good pay for early childcare workers are similarly present in the other countries but almost nonexistent in America. Given these comparisons and the high level of American mothers' employment, Gornick and Myers present an implicit agenda for work–family integration in the United States. Similar cross-national comparisons and wish-list agendas are to be found in other aspects of family functioning such as health care, poverty alleviation, public education, and immigration.

A second type of family policy agenda has to do with family *structure*—measures that can strengthen and promote marriage, reduce nonmarital births, or lower the high rate of divorce. The original Family Impact Seminar (Family Impact Seminar 1976–1998) was established in 1976 "to promote a family perspective in public policies and programs and to build capacity for family-centered policymaking." Over a 30-year period it conducted nearly 50 field studies and analyses of the impact of federal legislation on families, and presented them to federal policy makers, on topics ranging from child abuse and foster care to poverty reduction and homelessness. As the Seminar closed after more than 30 years of operation, Theodora Ooms (1998:4), one of the founding directors, summarized one of its central themes:

> Society has a large stake in strengthening marriages. Children should be our central concern and, in general, they fare better when raised by two parents. Marriage also typically improves the health and economic well-being of adults, stabilizes community life, and benefits civic society.

Another group focused on family structure, the Institute for American Values since its founding in 1987, has published authoritative position papers on such topics as trends in marriage, divorce, parenting, and changing patterns of reproduction and sexual behavior. The thrust of these publications is to question the viability of new practices such as conception by donor sperm, shared parenting in intentional families, and the potential harm from a tension between adult rights and children's needs. A current goal is "To increase the proportion of children growing up with their two married parents" (Institute for American Values 2011).

One very conservative organization focused on family structure, but without the scholarly authority of the previous examples, is the Family Policy Network. This group aggressively promotes adoption instead of abortion and a fundamentalist Christian and traditional form of family life. The Network explicitly opposes abortion, civil unions, same-sex marriage, and homosexuality (Family Policy Network 2011).

There appears to be no single formula about how to develop proposals or find the advocates who will initiate them. The one factor that distinguishes agenda setting from the proposal stage is specificity and narrowing of the objective as well as translation into a form that can ultimately gain wide support. Whereas putting an issue on the public agenda is primarily a matter of prioritizing a wish list, creating a proposal requires spelling out the precise steps to accomplish the goal. This can be done in several ways. As in the case of the women's suffrage movement or pressure to establish the Children's Bureau, interest group members learned by a process of trial and error what measures could gain traction and how to mobilize broad popular support (Giele 1995; Skocpol 1992).

Policy proposals concerning the family are now more likely to originate with legal and academic experts and family-oriented think tanks than with social movements or pressure groups. Sherry Wexler (1997), in her study of the adoption of the Family Support Act of 1988 and the Family and Medical Leave Act of 1993, has shown how testimony before Congress by experts was aligned with their own personal experience and professional outlook. The Family Support Act, which extended assistance to welfare mothers, also instituted work requirements and was influenced mainly by social workers and legislators who had a helping orientation toward poor clients of the program. Their approach was thus less empathic and more oriented to providing assistance to less fortunate people than to help people like themselves. By contrast, the women lawyers who worked to pass the Family and Medical Leave Act gained experience by securing passage of the Pregnancy Discrimination Act of 1978. They thought of the people they were helping as women employees and professionals like themselves, and their main effort was to get approval for time off without particular effort to assure that the leave would be paid.

The main initiators of family policy proposals today are academic centers devoted to the study of families and children such as those founded and supported by the Sloan Foundation. Outside of this group, the single most active center with the greatest outreach is the Policy Institute for Family Impact Seminars allied with the venerable Institute for Research on Poverty at the University of Wisconsin. It is the mission of the Seminars "to strengthen family policy by connecting state policymakers with research knowledge and researchers with policy knowledge. The Institute provides nonpartisan, solution-oriented research and a family impact perspective on issues being debated in state legislatures" (Family Impact Seminars 2011–). The principal mode of operation is to work through policy makers at the state level by helping them to identify existing problems of families and children. This approach is advantageous and efficient because it builds on the expertise of scholars, specialized agencies, and lawmakers to put particular issues on the agenda and to develop concrete proposals. Once these steps are accomplished, it is much easier to work toward adoption of the policies being proposed.

Policy adoption. With the focus of the Family Impact Seminars over the last decade on state family policies, it is not surprising that the best available descriptions of policy adoption are at the state level. Wisensale (1989) documented the way in which a family policy agenda in Connecticut was narrowed from 16 proposals to 12 that were adopted by the Legislature in 1987 along with a budget of $34 million for implementation. Wisensale explained this remarkable success as the result of several fortuitous factors. The Democrats were in power both in the governorship and the legislature. The focus was on improving the lives of children rather than on any single "benchmark" type of family, and the family leave measure was limited to state employees rather than extended to all workers.

A second example of success in adoption of family policy comes from Hutchins' (1998) comparative study of Connecticut, Kentucky, Ohio, and Washington. State policy making in these cases accomplished better integration of services for children and families. Hutchins attributed success to cabinet-level coordination that identified potential areas of duplication or gaps in home service programs. Cooperation among agencies in the executive branch of government produced a more integrated approach and was accomplished by coordination from the top through the governor's cabinet.

At the national level similar studies are needed of the ways in which family policy proposals gain traction and are eventually adopted. Attention is due the role of legendary legislative leaders like Representative George Miller (D–CA), the founding chairman of the House Select Committee on Children, Youth and Families, which from 1983 through 1991 initiated and influenced congressional efforts to help poor children and their families. Another powerful friend of children and families was Senator Ted Kennedy (D–MA), who successfully sponsored a variety of legislation touching on immigration, health insurance, disability discrimination, mental health benefits, and children's health insurance. Outside the Congress are important advocates like the Children's Defense Fund (2011), led by Marian Wright Edelman (1987; 2008), that are also due credit for their persistent concern for poor children and families.

In describing the process of policy adoption, the actions of the courts and the judicial branch of government should not be overlooked. Much of marriage and divorce law has been built through the accretion of case law. Lawyers have developed proposals and promoted their acceptance. With their help, no-fault divorce laws swept the nation in the 1970s and 1980s. In the past decade the courts have also held a key role in affirming or rejecting the constitutionality of same-sex marriage laws. In 2004 Massachusetts became the first state to authorize same-sex marriage through a decision of the Massachusetts Supreme Court.

Family Values and Family Policy

In addition to changes in family structure and behavior, big cultural shifts also push solutions in one direction or another, thereby coloring all three layers of family policy formation—the social scientists' work on social indicators, street-level implementation of policies, and the passage of new policies. Mary Ann Glendon (2006:xiii–xiv) sums up what has been termed the "The Great Disruption" and its effect on family law.

> . . . Rising affluence, accelerating geographical mobility, increasing labor force participation of women (including mothers of young children), more control over pro-creation and greater longevity.

> . . . provided a favorable climate for law revision . . . . Family law systems were completely overhauled, often very hastily in the 1970s and 1980s.

> . . . When the entire complex of changes is viewed together, it is apparent that the story the law tells about family life has been substantially rewritten. The legal narrative now places much more emphasis on the rights of individual family members than on familial responsibilities. Marriage is treated less as a necessary social institution designed to provide the optimal environment for child rearing than as an intimate relationship between adults.

> . . . It thus seems evident that among the most pressing issues for family law and policy in the future will be those arising from the impaired ability of families to socialize the next generation of citizens, and the diminished capacity of society's support institutions (family, government, mediating structures of civil society) to furnish care for the very young and other dependent persons.

Increased attention to women's independence and adults' needs has lessened attention to children's needs, a trend that has provoked heated discussion of "family values." Liberals and progressives typically argue for greater freedom of choice and conservatives defend certain constraints on freedom that are associated with the traditional family. Norval Glenn (1997) in a detailed evaluation of 20 family textbooks criticized the majority for a lopsided portrayal of family life in which the benefits of marriage to adults and the costs of marital breakup to children received far too little attention. He also found that the majority of the textbooks failed to cite the extensive psychological literature on sex differences and their place in family life, as though men's and women's roles and motivations are completely interchangeable and any differences are purely the result of socialization or social construction.

A middle ground is beginning to take shape between an emphasis on individual liberation and the reproductive and social benefits of family life.

There is increasing awareness that self-realization and family obligations are in fact both necessary. Martha Nussbaum (2011) makes clear that individuals' basic capabilities cannot be realized without the work of facilitating institutions like the family, schools, and the state. Derek Bok (2010:17), in his investigation of *The Politics of Happiness: What Government Can Learn From the New Research on Well-Being,* finds that marriage is one of the six factors that account for most of the variation in well-being (along with social relationships, employment, perceived health, religion, and quality of government).

In her dissertation, Meg Lovejoy (2012) investigates the new social sexual practice of hooking up and discovers that along with the benefits of immediate gratification and a sense of agency, women who engage in this practice also experience depression and disappointment. In such fleeting encounters there is little connection between intimacy and commitment to protect against being sexually abused and exploited. The concept of "family values" is relevant in this context, although sometimes interpreted as exclusively pro-family, and therefore opposed to the kind of autonomy implied in hooking up. Economist Nancy Folbre, however, sees family values as a contrast to market values. To her the term conveys "ideas of love, obligation, and reciprocity," which are associated with the "invisible heart" and the caregiving that is at the core of family life. The invisible heart of the family is Folbre's complement to Adam Smith's "invisible hand" of the market. She writes, "[T]he invisible hand of markets depends upon the invisible heart of care" (Folbre 2001:xviii). Thus both functionally oriented family policy to improve and protect family well-being and structurally oriented family policy to protect marriage and children's interests are necessary to the healthy functioning of the nation as a whole.

The Future of American Family Policy

This chapter has traced the history and changing definition of family policy in America since the 1930s in three ways: by showing the similarities and differences between the United States and other welfare capitalist regimes, by telling how family policy emerged out of general social policy, and by describing the process through which family policy is formed and implemented.

This final section takes up the current political and financial concerns surrounding American social welfare policies. How will legislation limit a huge government deficit that is partly fueled by social welfare spending for Social Security and Medicare? How can the country meet these challenges and at the same time protect families and children and vulnerable populations? In recent years the predominant solution has been a market-based focus on economic growth, which is thought by many to be the primary ingredient for a higher standard of living. But there is an alternative view gaining ground among leading economists and public intellectuals, which is that economic growth without investment in human capital and infrastructure is not an automatic guarantee for greater happiness or improved health and well-being of the general population. The following account spells out the alternative "capabilities approach" at four levels of American society: (1) *values*—the contrasting assumptions and ideals underlying the market-based and capabilities theories, (2) *institutions*—the structural changes required for society to improve the general health and well-being of the nation, (3) *families and communities*—the specific programs designed to strengthen adults' and children's prospects, and (4) *individuals*—nurturance of the basic capabilities that especially depend on family care and that must receive extra investment by the larger society when family resources are inadequate.

Values: Economic Growth and the Pursuit of Happiness

Virtually everybody agrees that economic growth is a desirable thing. Health and nutrition improve; there are fewer poor people; illiteracy becomes a thing of the past. The theoretical and policy question is how economic growth and improvements in life are related to each other. Is economic growth the fundamental driver of health and happiness, or is it the other way around—that you need to have a healthy, well-educated, and well-cared-for population in order to achieve economic growth? The conventional wisdom until recently has been that prosperity and a rising GDP were the first requirement and that health and well-being would follow. Perhaps this is true for the early steps of modernization. This theory goes back to Adam Smith and the metaphor of the market as an "invisible hand" in which individuals by pursuing their self-interest will in the end find economic solutions that serve the best interests of all.

The formulation that sees economic growth as the first requirement is now being seriously questioned, perhaps because economic development has now matured and the challenges have changed accordingly. Psychologists Wilkinson and Pickett (2010) in a comparison of physical and psychological health find that countries like the United States with its impressive economic growth also have a highly unequal distribution of income and a host of ills, even though their aggregate standard of living is high. They are worse off in education, mental and physical health, violence, imprisonment, obesity, drug abuse, and teenage births (Matthaei and Wollman 2011).

Such disappointing indicators have prompted leading economists from John Galbraith (1958) to Amartya Sen (1999), James Heckman (Heckman, Krueger, and Friedman 2003), and Nancy Folbre (2001) to advocate an alternate theory, which is that governments have to invest as much or more in the health and education of their populations, their human capital, as in technology and equipment. Martha Nussbaum (2011), a philosopher who has worked with Sen, spells out this alternative theory in *Creating Capabilities: The Human Development Approach*. The end in view is not economic growth but social justice and the maximum realization of every individual's human potential. This includes good health, education, personal and political freedom, and opportunities for leisure and for being a parent—a list of 10 "basic capabilities" in all.

Basic capacities cannot be realized without a surrounding social structure that makes them possible. Nussbaum gives as evidence her observations on differences among Indian states such as Kerala and Gujarat. Kerala, with more social investment, has a population with better health, much higher literacy, and greater political participation. The capabilities approach thus posits the need for social institutions that make possible the realization of human potential. In the United States, the economists who have criticized the invisible hand of the market as insufficient for improving health and well-being point to the social institutions that are needed to make possible the realization of human potential. This is where social policy and family policy come into the picture.

Institutions: Government Initiatives and Regulatory Reform

Esping-Andersen (2007) compares U.S. social mobility, postsecondary levels of education, and health with that of several European countries where the income distribution is less unequal and the percent of national income (GDP) spent on social benefits is higher. Given the American pride in equality of opportunity and the idea that anyone can attain the American Dream, the results of these comparisons are shocking. In contrast with Norway, Sweden, and Denmark, young people in the United States showed no greater mobility since World War II than earlier generations, whereas in the Scandinavian social democracies the rates are higher for younger groups than the older groups.

Ironically, however, the politics of many industrial economies have turned to the right. Ever since Reagan and Thatcher, the neoliberal market-based ideology of economic growth and reduced social welfare expenditures has gained ground all across Europe as well as in the United States. There has been a slow erosion of the safety nets and social welfare provisions of those democratic countries where trade unions and center-left parties were once in power. Kuttner (2011) recounts his interviews with a number of European leaders and documents evidence from Sweden, Netherlands, Germany, France, and the United Kingdom, where conservative political majorities have dismantled or weakened the universal systems of education and social protection that were once in place. In Sweden, for example, where virtually all workers were once members of trade unions, and thus in a powerful position vis-à-vis employers, union membership has since eroded. Where all schools were once supported by government funds, now 40 percent of children attend alternative schools, some of which are run by multinational corporations that pay no taxes because they are located in offshore tax havens. Nor does this dynamic seem likely to change. The last time the Social Democrats were in power in Sweden was 2006, and they are not likely to return to power soon. Kuttner concludes that once the conservatives gained control they used their power to make it difficult for the Social Democrats to return. Similar consolidation of power by conservatives has occurred in the United States.

The budget and deficit crisis of 2011 in the United States has exposed basic contradictions between what people want—continuation of Medicare and Social Security—and their demands for smaller government and low taxes. The impasse is part of what inspired the Occupy Wall Street movement in the fall of 2011 to call attention to inequality in the income distribution and risky investments and banking practices that brought wealth to brokers and financiers but financial ruin to many ordinary people. Leaders of the Occupy movement, however, have failed to construct concrete policy proposals. By mid-November 2011 a number of camps in Oakland, New York City, Philadelphia, and Portland, Oregon, were dismantled by city officials and police. Although the journalist Nicholas Kristof (2011a) tried to help the organizers by suggesting specific measures such as a tax on financial transactions, closing tax loopholes on carried interest and founders' stocks, and protecting big banks against themselves, the demands of the movement did not become clearer. Yet the movement, in the rapidity of its growth, signified widespread malaise with the economic and political direction of the nation, especially a growing frustration with income inequality and political gridlock in the face of high unemployment and a budget crisis.

In the midst of this turmoil, T. Friedman and Mandelbaum (2011) have put forward a list of five concrete proposals to address what they see as the decline of American competitiveness and equal opportunity. In their book *That Used to Be Us: How America Fell Behind in the World It Invented and How We Can Come Back,* the authors observe that the United States is falling behind other developed countries on a number of indicators: proportion of the population in poverty, educational attainment, and health. They propose that to restore United States to its leading position as a land of opportunity and leader in economic growth and innovation, the nation must return to some of the institutional initiatives and safeguards that fueled earlier prosperity but have since been eroded. A first requirement is investments in public education and support for students to get to the postsecondary level. Second is an open immigration policy of the kind that brought in energetic workers and contributed to economic growth during the past century. A third need is to restore regulation of the financial markets and prevent the kind of meltdown that occurred in 2008–2009. Fourth is the need to update and improve the national transportation and communications infrastructure—railroads and airports that are as good as those in Singapore and Hong Kong. Finally, the government needs to put funding into research as it did following World War II but which has declined steadily since the 1970s.

The Friedman and Mandelbaum proposals call for investment both in the nation's physical infrastructure and its investment in socially shared resources. No individual or group of individuals is likely to make such efforts. For example, government investment in research may not be immediately profitable, but it lays the foundation for future innovation. A good example is the Internet, which was first developed as the ARPANET in the late 1960s by the U.S. Department of Defense.

These proposals imply a larger rather than smaller role for government. Why should that be, especially given the conservative critique of big government as contrary to the Constitution and the Founders' intent to protect individual freedom and liberty? The reason that it is government that must create the policies and take the action needed is the paradox that Garrett Hardin (1968) in a famous article in *Science* termed "The Tragedy of the Commons." Where the common pasture is open to every cow, it is in the interest of the herder to graze as many of his cattle there as possible because his gain is +1 for every cow, and such is true for all the other herders. But the degradation of the pasture that ensues from overgrazing is far less than –1 for each herder because that cost is distributed among all the other owners. It is not in the herder's self-interest to limit his grazing to prevent spoiling of the commons. Thus the invisible hand does not work in situations where limits on self-interested action must be imposed for the greater good. This is what Galbraith (1958:283–284) meant when he wrote about the unloveliness, congestion, and long-term degradation of the environment that accompanies an affluent society. Government action, regulation, and investment are needed in those situations where individual self-interest operating alone will never be adequate to construct the programs and institutions that will serve the common good.

But where does the family come into this broad set of government institutions that range from educational investment to financial regulation? Families are affected by these measures (for example, by shortening commuting time with better transportation). Families also implement and carry the benefits of these reforms to their members—children, adults, and elders. This is the point where the capabilities approach is implemented on the ground, where social policies and family policies are enacted in families' and children's lives so that basic capabilities of individuals can be realized.

Families and Communities as Enablers of Human Potential

In his review of the scientific literature on what constitutes happiness, Derek Bok (2010) found that all the evidence points to marriage and having children as more important to happiness than income. Other than possible self-selection of happy people into marriage, it is not exactly clear by what mechanisms marriage and family promote happiness. Protection against loneliness and depression are prominent as well as better mental and physical health. A healthy family relationship and integration into a community together constitute an environment that nurtures the adults, youth, and children who inhabit them.

Nussbaum (2011:18) tells us that the full expression of human capability will only happen when a person has freedom and opportunities available in the political, social, and economic environment. Societies should thus provide for their people "a set of opportunities, or substantial freedom, which people may or may not exercise in action. The choice is theirs." This protects a person's powers of self-definition without imposing any one set of values. The great task of government and public policy is therefore "to improve the quality of life for all people, as defined by their capabilities." Theda Skocpol (2000) spells out the elements needed to construct a family-friendly environment: child allowances, health care, work–family accommodation (availability of part-time schedules and childcare), and Social Security, including Medicare and Medicaid.

A key means to improve diverse capabilities and increase upward mobility is to provide a good education to all children. But as the noted Nobel economist James Heckman and his coauthors (2003) have emphasized, "learning begets learning," which means that unless the child has already developed some basic skills before going to school, that child will face difficulties and may never finish high school, let alone attain a postsecondary qualification, which is becoming increasingly necessary in a technologically advanced society. Developing such a capacity to learn, especially among poor and underprivileged families, requires additional societal investment both in helping mothers to get further education (so that they can take employment, which increases family income as well as their own autonomy in the household) and to provide access to early childcare.

In *From Neurons to Neighborhoods: The Science of Early Childhood Development,* Jack Shonkoff and Deborah Phillips (2000), under the auspices of the National Research Council, have shown that the child's brain during the first three years of life is almost infinitely malleable either for developing curiosity and a capacity for learning or for becoming limited and rigid in response. The latter may be the result of poor nutrition, neglect or abuse, or an impoverished environment that fails to stimulate and reward curiosity and learning. Shonkoff's and Heckman's work suggests how critical the early family and childcare environment is in laying the foundation for a healthy educated adolescent and adult life and for the nation's future workforce (see also the Center on the Developing Child 2011). Esping-Andersen (2007) likewise argues that bringing children to their full potential requires a societal investment in their health, education, and early socialization that cannot be accomplished without investment in the families of children.

The preponderance of the scientific evidence thus argues for more rather than less investment in the social welfare of families and children. The countries with the greatest social mobility, best health, and highest educational attainment have more generous and universal policies that support the key family functions of caregiving, economic provision, decent housing, and equal treatment of all citizens, which affirms their dignity and their capabilities. There is a growing belief that America will have to do likewise if it is to live up to the ideals of equal opportunity and freedom of which it is so proud.

Conclusion

This concluding chapter has placed the many specific kinds of family policy in a larger context. It further shows that the United States is similar to other advanced industrial societies in having an extensive system of social protection as part of what the Danish economist Esping-Andersen has termed a welfare capitalist regime. Across the industrial world, economic modernization, greater longevity, and urbanization exposed individuals and families to new risks of poverty and dependency that required governments to intervene with supportive measures that provided public support to health care, housing, public education, and retirement pensions. The process was accelerated in Britain by the austerity of the war years. In the United States, the war on poverty and the women's movements of the 1960s raised consciousness about the need for a more comprehensive family policy that would address the needs of single-parent families and dual-earner households. What should be included in family policy was debated by scholars and advocates from the late 1960s to the early 1990s. But there was controversy about whether *family* policy was really needed, and if so, how it would be implemented.

Nevertheless, an implicit consensus has emerged that family policy should focus on supporting family functions more than on trying to influence family structure. It turns out that there is considerable agreement on the primary functions of the family. Caregiving is first and foremost the distinctive work of the family, but economic provision, housing and schooling, and transmission of racial and cultural heritage are also recognized and are consistent with a more general system theory that posits four key functions of goal attainment, adaptation, integration, and legitimation.

Although family policy is still an unfamiliar term to many, it turns out that there is a large and differentiated community of people concerned with issues and policies that fall under the family policy rubric. These groups are related to each other in an ascending hierarchy of generality from data gathering, delivery of services, and making new policies, to more general values and public attitudes that focus attention on one problem rather than another. Social scientists and data analysts work at the most specific level and have developed impressive databanks on changes in individual and family behavior over time. Workers in social agencies deliver services and at the same time implement policy at the ground level. Further up the hierarchy are the advocates, policy centers, and legislators who recommend and adopt given measures. Finally, at the highest level of generality are the public opinion leaders and the general public who define what is wrong and what it is important to improve in the lives of families, children, and the society as a whole.

All these matters related to social protection and family well-being are highly relevant to the current fiscal crisis faced by the United States as well as other advanced welfare capitalist societies around the globe. Against this backdrop, the most pressing current question is how American family policy can be extended to cover more people and still be paid for. This question raises the issue of national priorities and America's devotion to individualism and free enterprise, which currently appears to threaten needed investment in human capital and the well-being of society as a whole. Forward-thinking critics urge institutional reforms that will better enable families to develop the human potential and basic capabilities of children, parents, and lone individuals. What is required is a better balance of liberty with equality of opportunity. Only then can America treat all men and women as created equal and live up to the Founders' vision of promoting the general welfare and ensuring the pursuit of happiness.

References

Abbott, Grace. 1938. *The Child and the State*. Chicago: University of Chicago Press.

Abbott, Grace. 1941. *From Relief to Social Security: The Development of the New Public Welfare Services and Their Administration*. Chicago: University of Chicago Press.

Adams, Kathryn Betts. 2009. "Older Adult Services." Pp. 240–262 in *Delivering Home-Based Services: A Social Work Perspective*, edited by S. F. Allen and E. M. Tracy. New York: Columbia University Press.

Addison, Gillian. 2007. *Grandmothers Raising Grandchildren in Massachusetts: Challenges and Triumphs*. PhD dissertation, Heller School for Social Policy and Management, Brandeis University. Ann Arbor, MI: University Microfilms.

Administration for Children and Families. 2011a. "Child Care and Development Fund (CCDF) Performance Measures." Office of Child Care. U.S. Department of Health and Human Services. Retrieved March 10, 2011 (http://www.acf.hhs.gov/programs/occ/ccdf/gpra/measures.htm).

Administration for Children and Families. 2011b. "Low Income Home Energy Assistance Program." U.S. Department of Health and Human Services. Retrieved March 10, 2011 (http://www.acf.hhs.gov/programs/ocs/liheap/).

Afterschool Investments. 2007. *School-Age Children in Regulated Family Child Care Settings*. U.S. Department of Health and Human Services, Administration for Children and Families Child Care Bureau.

Alan Guttmacher Institute. 1994. "President Speaks out on Pop Aid as Congress Moves toward Increased Funding." *Washington Memo*, July 7, 10(2), 4. Retrieved August 1, 2009 (http://www.ncbi.nlm.nih.gov/pubmed/12318808).

Allen, Jodie T. 2007. "Negative Income Tax." *The Concise Encyclopedia of Economics*. Retrieved December 17, 2011 (http://www.econlib.org/library/Enc1/NegativeIncomeTax.html).

Allen, Susan F. 2009. "Early Childhood Programs." Pp. 81–110 in *Delivering Home-Based Services: A Social Work Perspective*, edited by S. F. Allen and E. M. Tracy. New York: Columbia University Press.

Allport, Gordon W. 1954. *The Nature of Prejudice*. Cambridge, MA: Addison-Wesley.

Amato, Paul R. 2004. "The Consequences of Divorce for Adults and Children." *Journal of Marriage and the Family* 62(4):1269–1287.

Amato, Paul R. 2005. "The Impact of Family Formation Change on the Cognitive, Social, and Emotional Well-Being of the Next Generation." *The Future of Children* 15(2):75–96.

Angel, Jacqueline L. and Ronald J. Angel. 2006. "Minority Group Status and Healthful Aging: Social Structure Still Matters." *American Journal of Public Health* 96(7):1152–1159.

Angel, Ronald J., and Jacqueline L. Angel. 2006. "Diversity and Aging in the United States." Pp. 94–110 in *Handbook of Aging and the Social Sciences,* edited by R. H. Binstock and L. K. George. New York: Academic Press.

Applebaum, Teddy. 2011. "Wellesley Family Attempts Living on Food-Stamp Budget." *Wellesley Townsman,* February 3. Retrieved March 10, 2011 (http://www.wicked local.com/wellesley/features/x1916608983/Wellesley-family-experiments-with-food-stamp-diet#axzz1gzcQcUbJ).

Archibold, Randal C. 2010. "Arizona Enacts Stringent Law on Immigration." *New York Times,* April 24, A1.

Ariès, Philippe. 1962. *Centuries of Childhood: A Social History of Family Life.* New York: Vintage Books.

Avi-Yonah, Reuven S. 2000. "Globalization, Tax Competition, and the Fiscal Crisis of the Welfare State." *Harvard Law Review* 113(7):1573–1676.

Axinn, June, and Herman Levin. 1975. *Social Welfare: A History of the American Response to Need.* New York: Dodd, Mead.

Bailyn, Lotte. 1993. *Breaking the Mold: Women, Men, and Time in the New Corporate World.* New York: Free Press.

Bailyn, Lotte, Ann Bookman, Mona Harrington, and Thomas A. Kochan. 2006. "Work-Family Interventions and Experiments: Workplaces, Communities, and Society." Pp. 651–664 in *The Work and Family Handbook: Multi-Disciplinary Perspectives, Methods, and Approaches,* edited by M. Pitt-Catsouphes, E. E. Kossek, and S. A. Sweet. Mahwah, NJ: Lawrence Erlbaum.

Baker, Elizabeth H., Laura A. Sanchez, Steven L. Nock, and James D. Wright. 2009. "Covenant Marriage and the Sanctification of Gendered Marital Roles." *Journal of Family Issues* 30(2, February):147–178.

Baltes, Paul B., and Margret M. Baltes. 1990. *Successful Aging: Perspectives from the Behavioral Sciences.* New York: Cambridge University Press.

Bane, Mary Jo. 1980. "Toward a Description and Evaluation of United States Family Policy." Pp. 155–190 in *The Politics and Programs of Family Policy,* edited by J. Aldous and W. Dumon. Notre Dame, IN: University of Notre Dame Press.

Bane, Mary Jo, and Paul A. Jargowsky. 1988. "The Links between Government Policy and Family Structure: What Matters and What Doesn't." Pp. 219–261 in *The Changing American Family and Public Policy,* edited by A. J. Cherlin. Washington, DC: Urban Institute Press.

Barnett, Rosalind C. 1999. "A New Work-Family Model for the 21st Century." *Annals of the American Academy of Political and Social Science* 562 (March):143–155.

Barnett, Rosalind C., and Caryl Rivers. 1996. *She Works/He Works: How Two-Income Families Are Happier, Healthier, and Better-Off.* San Francisco, CA: Harper.

Barrett, Nancy Smith. 1978. "Data Needs for Evaluating the Labor Market Status of Women." In *Issues in Federal Statistical Needs Relating to Women.* Washington, DC: U.S. Bureau of the Census.

Beacon Hill Village. 2010. "City Living Just Got Easier." Retrieved May 12, 2010 (http://www.BeaconHillVillage.org).

Beauvoir, Simone De. [1949] 1953. *The Second Sex.* New York: Knopf.

Becker, Gary S. 1981. *A Treatise on the Family.* Cambridge, MA: Harvard University Press.

Beecher, Catharine E., and Harriet Beecher Stowe. 1869. *The American Woman's Home: Or, Principles of Domestic Science; Being a Guide to the Formation and Maintenance of Economical, Healthful, Beautiful, and Christian Homes.* New York: J. B. Ford.

Belenky, Mary Field. 1986. *Women's Ways of Knowing: The Development of Self, Voice, and Mind.* New York: Basic Books.

Belkin, Lisa. 2003. "The Opt-out Revolution." *The New York Times Magazine,* October 26:42. Retrieved September 22, 2011 (http://www.nytimes .com/2003/10/26/magazine/26WOMEN.html).

Bell, Carolyn Shaw. 1972. "A Full Employment Policy for a Public Service Economy." *Social Policy* 3 (September/October):12–19.

Bellah, Robert Neely. 1985. *Habits of the Heart: Individualism and Commitment in American Life.* Berkeley: University of California Press.

Bellah, Robert Neely. 1991. *The Good Society.* New York: Knopf.

Bellah, Robert Neely. 1992. *The Broken Covenant: American Civil Religion in Time of Trial.* Chicago: University of Chicago Press.

Berger, Brigitte, and Peter L. Berger. 1983. *The War over the Family: Capturing the Middle Ground.* Garden City, NY: Anchor.

Bergmann, Barbara R. 1995. "Becker's Theory of the Family: Preposterous Conclusions." *Feminist Economics* 1(1, Spring):141–150.

Bergmann, Barbara R. 1996. *Saving Our Children from Poverty: What the United States Can Learn from France.* New York: Russell Sage Foundation.

Bernard, Jessie Shirley. 1973. *The Future of Marriage.* New York: Souvenir.

Bianchi, Suzanne M., and Marybeth J. Mattingly. 2004. "Time, Work and Family in the United States." Pp. 95–118 in *Changing Life Patterns in Western Industrial Societies,* edited by J. Z. Giele and E. Holst. London, England: Elsevier.

Bianchi, Suzanne M., and Sara B. Raley. 2005. "Time Allocation in Families." Pp. 21–42 in *Work, Family, Health, and Well-Being,* edited by S. M. Bianchi, L. M. Casper, and R. B. King. Mahwah, NJ: Lawrence Erlbaum.

Blair-Loy, Mary. 2003. *Competing Devotions: Career and Family among Women Executives.* Cambridge, MA: Harvard University Press.

Blake, Judith (Ed.). 1982. *Demographic Revolution and Family Evolution: Some Implications for American Women.* Bethesda, MD: U.S. Department of Health and Human Services, Public Health Service, National Institutes of Health.

Blank, Rebecca M. 2009. "Economic Change and the Structure of Opportunity for Less-Skilled Workers." Pp. 63–91 in *Changing Poverty, Changing Policies,* edited by M. Cancian and S. Danziger. New York: Russell Sage Foundation.

Blankenhorn, David. 1995. *Fatherless America: Confronting Our Most Urgent Social Problem.* New York: Basic Books.

Blau, Francine D., Marianne A. Ferber, and Anne E. Winkler. 2010. *The Economics of Women, Men and Work.* Boston: Prentice Hall.

Blehar, Mary. 1979. "Runaways Revisited." Pp. 523–539 in *Families Today: A Research Sampler on Families and Children,* edited by E. L. Corfman. Washington, DC: U.S. Government Printing Office.

Bloemraad, Irene, Anna Korteweg, and Gödkçe Yurdakul. 2008. "Citizenship and Immigration: Multiculturalism, Assimilation, and Challenges to the Nation-State." *Annual Review of Sociology* 34:153–179.

Blossfeld, Hans-Peter. 2009. "Comparative Life Course Research: A Cross-National and Longitudinal Perspective." Pp. 280–306 in *The Craft of Life Course Research,* edited by G. H. Elder and J. Z. Gielçe. New York: Guilford Press.

Bogenschneider, Karen. 2000. "Has Family Policy Come of Age? A Decade Review of the State of U.S. Family Policy in the 1990s." *Journal of Marriage and the Family* 62(4, November):1136–1159.

Bogenschneider, Karen. 2006. "How Can Professionals Team up with Communities to Influence Local Policymaking? Guidelines from Wisconsin Youth Futures." Pp. 277–290 in *Family Policy Matters: How Policymaking Affects Families and What Professionals Can Do,* edited by K. Bogenschneider. Mahwah, NJ: Erlbaum.

Bok, Derek Curtis. 2010. *The Politics of Happiness: What Government Can Learn from the New Research on Well-Being.* Princeton, NJ: Princeton University Press.

Bookman, Ann. 2008. "Innovative Models of Aging in Place: Transforming Our Communities for an Aging Population." *Community, Work & Family* 11(4):419–438.

Bookman, Ann, and Mona Harrington. 2007. "Family Caregivers: A Shadow Workforce in the Geriatric Health Care System?" *Journal of Health Politics Policy and Law* 32(6):1005–1041.

Boonstra, Heather. 2002. "Teen Pregnancy: Trends and Lessons Learned." *The Guttmacher Report on Public Policy* 5(1):7–10.

Bornstein, David. 2011. "Out of Poverty, Family-style." *New York Times,* (The Sunday Review, 12): Retrieved July 14, 2011 (http://opinionator.blogs.nytimes.com/2011/07/14/out-of-poverty-family-style/#more-99433).

Boyer, Peter J. 2008. "Ohio Postcard Eviction: The Day They Came for Addie Polk's House." *The New Yorker,* November 24, 2008. Retrieved December 21, 2011 (http://www.newyorker.com/reporting/2008/11/24/081124fa_fact_boyer#ixzz1hD77D300).

Brandeis University. 2010. "Life Span Initiative on Healthy Aging." Retrieved May 11, 2010 (http://www.brandeis.edu/lifespaninitiative/).

Brassil, Margaret M. 2010. *The Creation of a Federal Partnership: The Role of the States in Affordable Housing.* Albany: State University of New York Press.

Bronfenbrenner, Urie. 1979. *The Ecology of Human Development: Experiments by Nature and Design.* Cambridge, MA: Harvard University Press.

Bronzaft, Arline L. 1991. "Career, Marriage, and Family Aspirations of Young Black College Women." *The Journal of Negro Education* 60(Winter):110–118.

Brooks, David. 2008. "The Conservative Revival." *The New York Times,* May 9. Retrieved September 19, 2011 (http://www.nytimes.com/2008/05/09/opinion/09brooks.html).

Brooks, David. 2009. "The Harlem Miracle." *New York Times,* May 8, A31.

Brooks-Gunn, Jeanne, Greg J. Duncan, Pamela Kato Klebanov, and Naomi Sealand. 1993. "Do Neighborhoods Influence Child and Adolescent Development?" *American Journal of Sociology* 99(2):353–395.

Bumpass, Larry L. 1998. "The Changing Significance of Marriage in the United States." Pp. 63–79 in *The Changing Family in Comparative Perspective: Asia and the United States,* edited by K. O. Mason, N. O. Tsuya, M. K. Choe, and N. Daigaku. Honolulu: University of Hawaii Press.

Bureau of Labor Statistics. 2009a. "Civilian Labor Force Participation Rates by Age, Sex, Race, and Ethnicity." *Employment Projections:* Retrieved December 12, 2011 (http://www.bls.gov/emp/ep_table_303.htm).

Bureau of Labor Statistics. 2009b. "Employment Characteristics of Families in 2008." Washington, DC: Retrieved May 3, 2010 (http://www.bls.gov/news.release/famee.nr0.htm).

Burstein, Paul. 1991. "Policy Domains: Organization, Culture, and Policy Outcomes." *Annual Review of Sociology* 17:327–350.

Burt, Martha R. 2010. "Life after Transitional Housing for Homeless Families." U.S. Department of Housing and Urban Development. Retrieved July 24, 2011 (http://www.urban.org/publications/1001375.html).

Cain, Glen George. 1966. *Married Women in the Labor Force: An Economic Analysis.* Chicago: University of Chicago Press.

Cain, Louis P. 2006. "Transportation." Pp. 4–761 to 4–778 in *Historical Statistics of the United States,* edited by S. B. Carter, et al. New York: Cambridge University Press.

Campbell, Jean. 1973. "Women Drop Back In: Educational Innovation in the Sixties." Pp. 93–124 in *Academic Women on the Move,* edited by A. S. Rossi and A. Calderwood. New York: Russell Sage Foundation.

Cancian, Maria and Sheldon Danziger. 2009. *Changing Poverty, Changing Policies.* New York: Russell Sage Foundation.

Carbone, June R. 1994. "A Feminist Perspective on Divorce." *The Future of Children* 4(1):183–209.

Carden, Maren Lockwood. 1974. *The New Feminist Movement.* New York: Russell Sage Foundation.

Carey, Benedict. 2007. "Friends with Benefits, and Stress Too." *The New York Times,* October 2. Retrieved September 19, 2011 (http://www.nytimes.com/2007/10/02/health/02sex.html).

Carson, Judith Hall. 2009. *Mothers as Partners in Early Childhood Education: Comparison of an Even Start and a Family Resource Center Program.* PhD dissertation,

Heller School for Social Policy and Management, Brandeis University. Waltham, MA.

Carter, Susan B. 2006. *Historical Statistics of the United States*. New York: Cambridge University Press.

Case, Karl E. 2010. "A Dream House after All." *New York Times*, September 2, A35.

Center on the Developing Child, Harvard University. 2011. "Science of Early Childhood." Retrieved November 20, 2011 (http://developingchild.harvard.edu//topics/science_of_early_childhood/).

Cere, Dan. 2000. *The Experts' Story of Courtship: A Report to the Nation*. New York: Institute for American Values.

Chafetz, Janet Saltzman. 1991. "The Gender Division of Labor and the Reproduction of Female Disadvantage Toward an Integrated Theory." Pp. 74–94 in *Gender, Family, and Economy: The Triple Overlap*, edited by R. L. Blumberg. Newbury Park, CA: Sage.

Cherlin, Andrew J. 2009. *Public & Private Families: An Introduction*. Boston: McGraw-Hill.

Children's Defense Fund (U.S.). 2011. Retrieved November 22, 2011 (http://www.childrensdefense.org/).

Christensen, Kathleen E. 2005. "Lessons to Be Learned." Pp. 449–457 in *Being Together, Working Apart: Dual-Career Families and the Work-Life Balance*, edited by B. L. Schneider and L. J. Waite. New York: Cambridge University Press.

Clayton, Obie, Ronald B. Mincy, and David Blankenhorn. 2003. *Black Fathers in Contemporary American Society: Strengths, Weaknesses, and Strategies for Change*. New York: Russell Sage Foundation.

Cohen, Nathan E., and Maurice F. Connery. 1967. "Government Policy and the Family." *Journal of Marriage and the Family* 29(1):6–17.

Coleman, James Samuel. 1961. *The Adolescent Society: The Social Life of the Teenager and Its Impact on Education*. New York: Free Press of Glencoe.

Coleman, James Samuel. 1966. *Equality of Educational Opportunity*. Washington, DC: U.S. Department of Health Education and Welfare Office of Education.

Coleman, James Samuel. 1988. "Social Capital in the Creation of Human Capital." *American Journal of Sociology* 94:S95–120.

Coleman, James Samuel. 1990a. *Equality and Achievement in Education*. Boulder, CO: Westview Press.

Coleman, James Samuel. 1990b. *Foundations of Social Theory*. Cambridge, MA: Harvard University Press.

Coltrane, Scott. 1996. *Family Man: Fatherhood, Housework, and Gender Equity*. New York: Oxford University Press.

Coltrane, Scott and Michele Adams. 2001. "Men's Family Work: Child-Centered Fathering and the Sharing of Domestic Labor." Pp. 72–99 in *Working Families: The Transformation of the American Home*, edited by R. Hertz and N. L. Marshall. Berkeley: University of California Press.

Connell, R. W. 1995. *Masculinities*. Berkeley: University of California Press.

Coontz, Stephanie and Donna Franklin. 1997. "When the Marriage Penalty Is Marriage." *The New York Times,* October 28, A23.

Cose, Ellis. 2011. *The End of Anger: A New Generation's Take on Race and Rage.* New York: Ecco.

Coser, Lewis A., and Rose Laub Coser. 1974. "The Housewife and Her Greedy Family." Pp. 89–102 in *Greedy Institutions: Patterns of Undivided Commitment,* edited by L. A. Coser. New York: Free Press.

Council on Contemporary Families. 2009. "Unconventional Wisdom, Volume 2." Retrieved November 23, 2009 (http://www.contemporaryfamilies.org/sub template.php?t=pressReleases&ext=uwisdom).

Cowgill, Donald O. and Lowell Don Holmes. 1972. *Aging and Modernization.* New York: Appleton-Century-Crofts.

Craig, Lee A. 2006. "Household Production." Pp. 2–59 to 2–62 in *Historical Statistics of the United States,* edited by S. B. Carter et al. New York: Cambridge University Press.

Crown, William. 2001. "Economic Status of the Elderly." Pp. 352–368 in *Handbook of Aging and the Social Sciences,* edited by R. H. Binstock and L. K. George. San Diego, CA: Academic Press.

Csikai, Ellen. 2009. "Hospice and End-of-Life Care." Pp. 263–284 in *Delivering Home-Based Services: A Social Work Perspective,* edited by S. F. Allen and E. M. Tracy. New York: Columbia University Press.

Dash, Eric. 2011. "Banks Amass Glut of Homes, Chilling Sales." *New York Times,* May 23, A1.

Davis, Karen, Cathy Schoen, Michelle Doty, and Katie Tenney. 2002. "Medicare versus Private Insurance: Rhetoric and Reality." *Health Affairs* 30(10, October, 9). Retrieved October 13, 2011 (http://content.healthaffairs.org/content/suppl/2003/12/03/hlthaff.w2.311v1.DC1).

Dembowitz, Marti. 2007. "The Individuals with Disabilities Education Act (IDEA): Evolving Philosophies, Goals, and Implications for Students with Disabilities." Unpublished paper, Heller School for Social Policy and Management, Brandeis University, Waltham, MA.

Denavas-Walt, Carmen, Bernadette D. Proctor, and Jessica C. Smith. 2010. "Income, Poverty, and Health Insurance Coverage in the United States: 2009." *Current Population Reports, P60–238.* U.S. Census Bureau. Washington, DC: U.S. Government Printing Office. Retrieved March 10, 2011 (http://www.census.gov/prod/2010pubs/p60-238.pdf).

Deparle, Jason and Robert Gebeloff. 2010. "Once Stigmatized, Food Stamps Find Acceptance." *New York Times,* February 11, A 22.

Dewitt, Larry. 2009. "Historical Background and Development of Social Security." *Social Security Online* (updated): December 6, 2011. Retrieved January 1, 2012 (http://www.socialsecurity.gov/history/briefhistory3.html).

Dill, Bonnie Thornton, Maxine Baca Zinn, and Sandra Patton. 1993. "Feminism, Race, and the Politics of Family Values." *Philosophy & Public Policy* 13:13–18.

Dobelstein, Andrew W. 2009. *Understanding the Social Security Act: The Foundation of Social Welfare for America in the Twenty-First Century.* New York: Oxford University Press.

Dollard, John. 1937. *Caste and Class in a Southern Town.* New Haven, CT: Yale University Press.

Domínguez, Silvia. 2011. *Getting Ahead: Social Mobility, Public Housing, and Immigrant Networks.* New York: New York University Press.

Doty, Michelle M., Mary Jane Koren, and Elizabeth L. Sturla. 2008. "Culture Change in Nursing Homes: How Far Have We Come? Findings from The Commonwealth Fund 2007 National Survey of Nursing Homes." New York: The Commonwealth Fund.

Douthat, Ross and Reihan Salam. 2008. *Grand New Party: How Republicans Can Win the Working Class and Save the American Dream.* New York: Doubleday.

Downs, Anthony. 1977. "The Impact of Housing Policies on Family Life in the United States since World War II." *Daedalus* 106(2):163–80.

Duffy, Mignon. 2005. *One Hundred Years of Buying Care: Gender, Race, Immigration, and Market Care Work in the Twentieth Century.* PhD dissertation, Heller School for Social Policy and Management, Brandeis University. Ann Arbor, MI: University Microfilms.

Durand, Jorge, and Douglas S. Massey. 2004. *Crossing the Border: Research from the Mexican Migration Project.* New York: Russell Sage Foundation.

Durkheim, Emile. 1947. *The Elementary Forms of the Religious Life, a Study in Religious Sociology.* Glencoe, IL: Free Press.

Durkheim, Emile. [1893] 1964. *The Division of Labor in Society.* New York: Free Press.

Dybwad, Rosemary Ferguson. 1990. *Perspectives on a Parent Movement: The Revolt of Parents of Children with Intellectual Limitations.* Cambridge, MA: Brookline Books.

Eck, Diana L. 2001. *A New Religious America: How a "Christian Country" Has Now Become the World's Most Religiously Diverse Nation.* San Francisco, CA: HarperSanFrancisco.

Eck, Diana L. 2007. "Religion." Pp. 214–227 in *The New Americans: A Guide to Immigration since 1965*, edited by M. C. Waters, R. Ueda, and H. B. Marrow. Cambridge, MA: Harvard University Press.

Edelman, Marian Wright. 1987. *Families in Peril: An Agenda for Social Change.* Cambridge, MA: Harvard University Press.

Edelman, Marian Wright. 2008. *The Sea Is So Wide and My Boat Is So Small: Charting a Course for the Next Generation.* New York: Hyperion.

Edin, Kathryn, and Laura Lein. 1997. *Making Ends Meet: How Single Mothers Survive Welfare and Low-Wage Work.* New York: Russell Sage Foundation.

Eichler, Margrit. 1997. *Family Shifts: Families, Policies, and Gender Equality.* Toronto, Canada: Oxford University Press.

Elder, Glen H. 1974. *Children of the Great Depression: Social Change in Life Experience.* Chicago: University of Chicago Press.

Elder, Glen H. and Rand Conger. 2000. *Children of the Land: Adversity and Success in Rural America*. Chicago: University of Chicago Press.

Elder, Glen H. and Janet Z. Giele. 2009. *The Craft of Life Course Research*. New York: Guilford Press.

Elderweb. 2011. "1915–1934: State Old Age Assistance Programs." Retrieved February 2, 2011 (http://www.elderweb.com/book/export/html/2896).

Ellender, Stacey. M. 2005. *Assisted Reproduction: Defining and Evaluating the Multiple Outcomes of Technologically Advanced Interventions*. PhD dissertation, Heller School for Social Policy and Management, Brandeis University. Waltham, MA.

Elliott, Diana B. 2009. "America's Family and Living Arrangements: 2007." *Current Population Reports* P20–561 September.

Elshtain, Jean Bethke. 1995. *Democracy on Trial*. New York: Basic Books.

Employee Benefit Research Institute. 2010a. "Participation in Employee Benefit Programs." *EBRI Databook on Employee Benefits:* Retrieved March 10, 2011 (http://www.ebri.org/pdf/publications/books/databook/DB.Chapter%2004.pdf).

Employee Benefit Research Institute. 2010b. "Trends in Retiree Health Benefits Offered by Employers." *Fast Facts,* February 24 (#156): Retrieved April 24, 2012 (http://www.ebri.org/pdf/FFE156.24Feb10.Final.pdf).

Employment and Training Administration. 2011. "Monthly Program and Financial Data." Retrieved April 11, 2011 (http://workforcesecurity.doleta.gov/unemploy/5159report.asp).

England, Paula. 1992. *Comparable Worth: Theories and Evidence*. New York: Aldine de Gruyter.

England, Paula, Michelle Budig, and Nancy Folbre. 2002. "Wages of Virtue: The Relative Pay of Care Work." *Social Problems* 49(4, November):455–473.

Erickson, David James. 2009. *The Housing Policy Revolution: Networks and Neighborhoods*. Washington, DC: Urban Institute Press.

Esping-Andersen, Gøsta. 1990. *The Three Worlds of Welfare Capitalism*. Princeton, NJ: Princeton University Press.

Esping-Andersen, Gøsta. 2007. "Equal Opportunities and the Welfare State." *Contexts* 6(3):23–27.

Esping-Andersen, Gøsta. 2009. *The Incomplete Revolution: Adapting to Women's New Roles*. Malden, MA: Polity.

Evan B. Donaldson Adoption Institute. 2011. "Research: Adoption Facts." Retrieved December 8, 2011 (http://www.adoptioninstitute.org/research/international adoption.php).

Evans, Gary W., Jeanne Brooks-Gunn, and Pamela Kato Klebanov. 2011. "Stressing Out the Poor: Chronic Physiological Stress and the Income-Achievement Gap." *Pathways* (Winter):16–21.

Facing Up to the Nation's Finances. 2011. "Facts and Figures." Retrieved April 5, 2011 (http://www.facingup.org/why-it-matters/facts-figures).

Faludi, Susan. 1991. *Backlash: The Undeclared War against American Women*. New York: Crown.

Family and Home Network. 2011. "Family and Home Network: Helping Families Spend Generous Amounts of Time Together." Retrieved September 20, 2011 (http://www.familyandhome.org).

Family Impact Seminar. 1976–1998. "Federal Family Impact Seminar Reports." Retrieved November 19, 2011 (http://familyimpactseminars.org/index.asp?p=1&page=pub_federal).

Family Impact Seminars. 2011–. "Connecting Policymakers and Professionals to Build Research-Based Family Policy." Retrieved November 18, 2011 (http://familyimpactseminars.org/index.asp?p=1&page=home).

Family Policy Network. 2011. "Family Policy Network: Informing Christians, Confronting the Culture." Retrieved November 18, 2011 (http://familypolicy.net/).

Family Research Council. 2011. "An Instant Read on America's Social Health." Retrieved December 6, 2011 (http://www.frc.org/).

Familyfarmer.Org. 2011. "Voices of the Family Farm." Retrieved December 21, 2011 (http://www.familyfarmer.org/sections/guest.html).

Farley, Reynolds. 1996. *The New American Reality: Who We Are, How We Got Here, Where We Are Going.* New York: Russell Sage Foundation.

Ferree, Myra Marx and Beth B. Hess. 1994. *Controversy and Coalition: The New Feminist Movement across Three Decades of Change.* New York: Twayne Publishers.

Ferriss, Abbott Lamoyne. 1970. *Indicators of Change in the American Family.* New York: Russell Sage Foundation.

Fleischer, Doris Zames and Frieda Zames. 2001. *The Disability Rights Movement: From Charity to Confrontation.* Philadelphia: Temple University Press.

Flora, Peter and Arnold J. Heidenheimer. 1981. *The Development of Welfare States in Europe and America.* New Brunswick, NJ: Transaction Books.

Folbre, Nancy. 2001. *The Invisible Heart: Economics and Family Values.* New York: New Press.

Folbre, Nancy. 2009. *Greed, Lust & Gender: A History of Economic Ideas.* Oxford, England: Oxford University Press.

Foner, Nancy. 1994. *The Caregiving Dilemma: Work in an American Nursing Home.* Berkeley: University of California Press.

Food and Nutrition Service. 2011. "Supplemental Nutrition Assistance Program." United States Department of Agriculture. Retrieved March 8, 2011 (http://www.fns.usda.gov/snap/rules/Legislation/about.htm).

Francis, Judith. 1992. *At Home During the Day: A Study of Experienced Family Day Care Providers.* Ph.D. dissertation, Heller School for Social Policy and Management, Brandeis University. Ann Arbor, MI: University Microfilms, 1993.

Friedan, Betty. 1963. *The Feminine Mystique.* New York: Norton.

Friedberg, Leora. 2007. "The Recent Trend Towards Later Retirement." *Work Opportunities for Older Americans,* March. 9. Retrieved April 24, 2012 (http://globalag.igc.org/pension/us/2007/laterretirement.pdf).

Friedman, Dana and Wendy B. Gray. 1989. "A Life Cycle Approach to Family Benefits and Policies." *Perspectives No. 19.* New York: The Conference Board.

Friedman, Milton and Rose D. Friedman. 2002. *Capitalism and Freedom*. Chicago: University of Chicago Press.

Friedman, Thomas. 2008. "Anxious in America." *The New York Times,* June 29, 10. Retrieved September 19, 2011 (http://www.nytimes.com/2008/06/29/opinion/29friedman.html).

Friedman, Thomas L. and Michael Mandelbaum. 2011. *That Used to Be Us: How America Fell Behind in the World It Invented and How We Can Come Back*. New York: Farrar Straus and Giroux.

Furstenberg, Frank F., Jeanne Brooks-Gunn, and S. Philip Morgan. 1987. *Adolescent Mothers in Later Life*. New York: Cambridge University Press.

Furstenberg, Frank F., Richard Lincoln, and Jane A. Menken. 1981. *Teenage Sexuality, Pregnancy, and Childbearing*. Philadelphia: University of Pennsylvania Press.

Galbraith, John Kenneth. 1958. *The Affluent Society*. Boston: Houghton Mifflin.

Galbraith, John Kenneth. 2000. "Keynes's Impact on America: FDR and the New Deal." Interview, September 28. Retrieved October 15, 2011 (http://www.pbs.org/wgbh/commandingheights/shared/minitext/int_johnkennethgalbraith.html#2).

Gallagher, James J. 1996. "Policy Development and Implementation for Children with Disabilities." Pp. 171–187 in *Children, Families, and Government: Preparing for the Twenty-First Century,* edited by E. Zigler, S. L. Kagan, and N. W. Hall. New York: Cambridge University Press.

Gallagher, Maggie. 1996. *The Abolition of Marriage: How We Destroy Lasting Love*. Washington, DC: Regnery.

Gans, Herbert J. 2007. "Ethnic and Racial Identity." Pp. 98–109 in *The New Americans: A Guide to Immigration since 1965,* edited by M. C. Waters, R. Ueda, and H. B. Marrow. Cambridge, MA: Harvard University Press.

Garfinkel, Irwin and Sara McLanahan. 1986. *Single Mothers and Their Children: A New American Dilemma*. Washington, DC: Urban Institute Press.

Garfinkel, Irwin, Sara McLanahan, and Philip K. Robins. 1994. *Child Support and Child Well-Being*. Washington, DC: Urban Institute Press.

Gardiner, Karen N., Michael E. Fishman, Plamen Nikolov, Asaph Glosser, and Stephanie Laud. 2002. "State Policies to Promote Marriage: Final Report." Washington, DC: U.S. Department of Health and Human Services. Retrieved September 20, 2011 (http://aspe.hhs.gov/hsp/marriage02f/).

Garfinkel, Irwin, Lee Rainwater, and Timothy M. Smeeding. 2010. *Wealth and Welfare States: Is America a Laggard or Leader?* New York: Oxford University Press.

Garreau, Joel. 1991. *Edge City: Life on the New Frontier*. New York: Doubleday.

Gavanas, Anna. 2004. *Fatherhood Politics in the United States: Masculinity, Sexuality, Race and Marriage*. Urbana: University of Illinois Press.

Gelfand, Donald E. 2006. *The Aging Network Program and Services*. New York: Springer.

General Mills, Inc., and Yankelovich Skelly and White. 1975. *A Study of the American Family and Money*. Minneapolis, MN: General Mills.

General Mills, Inc., and Yankelovich Skelly and White Inc. 1977. *Raising Children in a Changing Society*. Minneapolis, MN: General Mills.

General Mills, Inc., and Yankelovich Skelly and White Inc. 1979. *Family Health in an Era of Stress*. Minneapolis, MN: General Mills.

George, Linda K. 2006. "Perceived Quality of Life." Pp. 320–336 in *Handbook of Aging and the Social Sciences*, edited by R. H. Binstock and L. K. George. Boston: Academic Press.

Gerson, Kathleen. 1993. *No Man's Land: Men's Changing Commitments to Family and Work*. New York: BasicBooks.

Gerson, Kathleen. 2010. *The Unfinished Revolution: How a New Generation Is Reshaping Family, Work, and Gender in America*. New York: Oxford University Press.

Giele, Janet Zollinger. 1978. *Women and the Future: Changing Sex Roles in Modern America*. New York: Free Press.

Giele, Janet Zollinger. 1979. "Social Policy and the Family." *Annual Review of Sociology* 5:275–302.

Giele, Janet Zollinger. 1980. "Adulthood as Transcendence of Age and Sex." Pp. 151–173 in *Themes of Work and Love in Adulthood*, edited by N. J. Smelser and E. H. Erikson. Cambridge, MA: Harvard University Press.

Giele, Janet Zollinger. 1982a. "Cohort Variation in Life Patterns of Educated Women, 1910–1960." *Western Sociological Review* 13(1):1–24.

Giele, Janet Zollinger. 1982b. "Family and Social Networks." Pp. 41–74 in *International Perspectives on Aging: Patterns, Policies, and Challenges*, edited by R. H. Binstock, N. Chow, and J. H. Schulz. New York: United Nations Fund for Population Activities.

Giele, Janet Zollinger. 1988. "Gender and Sex Roles." Pp. 291–323 in *Handbook of Sociology*, edited by N. J. Smelser. Newbury Park, CA: Sage.

Giele, Janet Zollinger. 1993. "Woman's Role Change and Adaptation, 1920–1990." Pp. 32–60 in *Women's Lives through Time: Educated American Women of the Twentieth Century*, edited by K. Hulbert and D. Schuster. San Francisco: Jossey-Bass.

Giele, Janet Zollinger. 1995. *Two Paths to Women's Equality: Temperance, Suffrage, and the Origins of Modern Feminism*. New York: Twayne Publishers.

Giele, Janet Zollinger. 1996. "Decline of the Family: Conservative, Liberal, and Feminist Views." Pp. 89–115 in *Marriage in America*, edited by D. Popenoe, J. B. Elshtain, and D. Blankenhorn. Totowa, NJ: Rowman and Littlefield.

Giele, Janet Zollinger. 1998. "Innovation in the Typical Life Course." Pp. 231–263 in *Methods of Life Course Research: Qualitative and Quantitative Approaches*, edited by J. Z. Giele and G. H. Elder. Thousand Oaks, CA: Sage.

Giele, Janet Zollinger. 2006. "The Changing Gender Contract as the Engine of Work-and-Family Policies." *Journal of Comparative Policy Analysis* 8(2):115–128.

Giele, Janet Zollinger. 2008. "Homemaker or Career Women: Life Course Factors and Racial Influences among Middle Class Americans." *Journal of Comparative Family Studies* 39(3):392–411.

Giele, Janet Zollinger. 2009. "Life Stories to Understand Diversity by Class, Race, and Gender." Pp. 236–257 in *The Craft of Life Course Research*, edited by G. H. Elder, Jr. and J. Z. Giele. New York: Guilford Press.

Giele, Janet Zollinger and Glen H. Elder. 1998. *Methods of Life Course Research: Qualitative and Quantitative Approaches.* Thousand Oaks, CA: Sage.

Giele, Janet Zollinger and Mary Gilfus. 1990. "Race and College Differences in Life Patterns of Educated Women, 1934–1982." Pp. 179–198 in *Changing Education: Women as Radicals and Conservators,* edited by J. Antler and S. K. Biklen. Albany, NY: State University of New York Press.

Giele, Janet Zollinger and Joan Dahr Lambert. 1975. "Current Family Policy Development in the United States; Preliminary Report to the National Science Foundation." Cambridge, MA: Radcliffe College.

Giele, Janet Zollinger and Leslie F. Stebbins. 2003. *Women and Equality in the Workplace: A Reference Handbook.* Santa Barbara, CA: Abc-Clio.

Gil, David G. 1970. *Violence against Children: Physical Child Abuse in the United States.* Cambridge, MA: Harvard University Press.

Gilligan, Carol. 1982. *In a Different Voice: Psychological Theory and Women's Development.* Cambridge, MA: Harvard University Press.

Gillis, John R. 1996. *A World of Their Own Making: Myth, Ritual, and the Quest for Family Values.* New York: Basic Books.

Gittell, Jody Hoffer. 2009. *High Performance Healthcare: Using the Power of Relationships to Achieve Quality, Efficiency and Resilience.* New York: McGraw-Hill.

Glendon, Mary Ann. 1977. *State, Law, and Family: Family Law in Transition in the United States and Western Europe.* New York: North-Holland.

Glendon, Mary Ann. 1979. "The Shell Foundation Lectures, 1978–1979: The New Family and the New Property." *Tulane Law Review* 53:697.

Glendon, Mary Ann. 1987. *Abortion and Divorce in Western Law.* Cambridge, MA: Harvard University Press.

Glendon, Mary Ann. 2006. "Foreword." Pp. xiii–xv in *Reconceiving the Family: Critique on the American Law Institute's Principles of the Law of Family Dissolution,* edited by R. F. Wilson. New York: Cambridge University Press.

Glenn, Evelyn Nakano. 1992. "From Servitude to Service Work: Historical Continuities in the Racial Division of Paid Reproductive Labor." *Signs: Journal of Women in Culture & Society* 18(1):1–43.

Glenn, Evelyn Nakano. 2001. "Creating a Caring Society." *Contemporary Sociology* 29(1):84–94.

Glenn, Norval D. 1997. "A Critique of Twenty Family and Marriage and the Family Textbooks." *Family Relations* 46(3, July):197–208.

Glenn, Norval D. and Elizabeth Marquardt. 2001. *Hooking up, Hanging out, and Hoping for Mr. Right: College Women on Dating and Mating Today.* New York: Institute for American Values.

Goldin, Claudia Dale. 1997. "Career and Family: College Women Look to the Past." Pp. 20–58 in *Gender and Family Issues in the Workplace,* edited by F. D. Blau and R. G. Ehrenberg. New York: Russell Sage Foundation.

Goldin, Claudia Dale. 2004. "The Long Road to the Fast Track: Career and Family." *Annals of the American Academy of Political and Social Science* 596(November):20–35.

Goldin, Claudia and Lawrence F. Katz. 2008. *The Race between Education and Technology*. Cambridge, MA: Harvard University Press.

Goldscheider, Frances K. and Linda J. Waite. 1991. *New Families, No Families?: The Transformation of the American Home*. Berkeley: University of California Press.

Gordon, Linda. 1994. *Pitied but Not Entitled: Single Mothers and the History of Welfare, 1890–1935*. New York: Free Press.

Gornick, Janet C. and Alexandra Heron. 2006. "The Regulation of Working Time as Work-Family Reconciliation Policy: Comparing Europe, Japan, and the United States." *Journal of Comparative Policy Analysis* 8(2):149–166.

Gornick, Janet C. and Marcia Meyers. 2003. *Families That Work: Policies for Reconciling Parenthood and Employment*. New York: Russell Sage Foundation.

Granovetter, Mark S. 1974. *Getting a Job: A Study of Contacts and Careers*. Cambridge, MA: Harvard University Press.

Green House Project. 2011. "The Green House Project." Retrieved December 28, 2011 (http://thegreenhouseproject.org/).

Gutman, David. 1977. "The Cross-Cultural Perspective: Notes toward a Comparative Psychology of Aging." Pp. 202–253 in *Handbook of the Psychology of Aging*, edited by J. E. Birren and K. W. Schaie. New York: Van Nostrand Reinhold.

Guyton, Gregory P. 1999. "A Brief History of Workers' Compensation." *The Iowa Orthopaedic Journal* 19:106–110.

Handlin, Oscar. 1964. *Out of Many: A Study Guide to Cultural Pluralism in the United States*. New York: Anti-Defamation League of B'nai B'rith.

Handlin, Oscar and Mary Flug Handlin. 1948. *Danger in Discord: Origins of Anti-Semitism in the United States*. New York: Anti-Defamation League of B'nai B'rith.

Hanssen, Gail M. 1997. *Extending Families: How Adoptive Parents Transition to Openness*. Ph.D. dissertation, Heller School for Social Policy and Management, Brandeis University. Waltham, MA.

Hao, Lingxin. 2007. *Color Lines, Country Lines: Race, Immigration, and Wealth Stratification in America*. New York: Russell Sage Foundation.

Harbin, Gloria L., R. A. Mcwilliam, and James J. Gallagher. 2000. "Services for Young Children with Disabilities and Their Families." Pp. 387–415 in *Handbook of Early Childhood Intervention*, edited by J. P. Shonkoff and S. J. Meisels. New York: Cambridge University Press.

Hardin, Garrett. 1968. "The Tragedy of the Commons." *Science* 162 (13 December) : 1243–1248.

Harlem Children's Zone. 2011. "History." Retrieved July 24, 2011 (http://www.hcz.org/about-us/history).

Harrington, Michael. 1962. *The Other America: Poverty in the United States*. New York: Macmillan.

Harvard Living Wage Campaign. 2003. "Labor Abuses Continue at Harvard." Retrieved January 11, 2011 (http://www.hcs.Harvard.edu/~pslm/livingwage/portal.html).

Hauser, Robert M. 2009. "The Wisconsin Longitudinal Study: Designing a Study of the Life Course." Pp. 29–50 in *The Craft of Life Course Research*, edited by G. H. Elder and J. Z. Giele. New York: Guilford Press.

Haveman, Robert. L. 2009. "What Does It Mean to Be Poor in a Rich Society?" Pp. 387–408 in *Changing Poverty, Changing Policies*, edited by M. Cancian and S. Danziger. New York: Russell Sage Foundation.

Hayes, Cheryl D., John L. Palmer, and Martha J. Zaslow. 1990. *Who Cares for America's Children?: Child Care Policy for the 1990s*. Washington, DC: National Academy Press.

Heckman, James J. 2006. "Catch 'Em Young." *Wall Street Journal*, January 10, A14.

Heckman, James J., Alan B. Krueger, and Benjamin M. Friedman. 2003. *Inequality in America: What Role for Human Capital Policies?* Cambridge, MA: MIT Press.

Hehir, Thomas. 2002. "Eliminating Ableism in Education." *Harvard Educational Review* 72(1):1–32.

Helson, Ravenna and James Picano. 1990. "Is the Traditional Role Bad for Women?" *Journal of Personality & Social Psychology* 59(1):311–320.

Hendricks, Jon and Laurie Russell Hatch. 2006. "Lifestyle and Aging." Pp. 301–319 in *Handbook of Aging and the Social Sciences*, edited by R. H. Binstock and L. K. George. Boston: Academic Press.

Herberg, Will. 1955. *Protestant, Catholic, Jew: An Essay in American Religious Sociology*. Garden City, NY: Doubleday.

Hernandez, Donald J. 1993. *America's Children: Resources from Family, Government, and the Economy*. New York: Russell Sage Foundation.

Hetherington, E. Mavis and John Kelly. 2002. *For Better or for Worse: Divorce Reconsidered*. New York: W. W. Norton.

Hill, Reuben. 1971. "Modern Systems Theory and the Family: A Confrontation." *Social Science Information* 10(5):7–26.

Hill, Reuben and Donald A. Hansen. 1960. "The Identification of Conceptual Frameworks Utilized in Family Study." *Marriage and Family Living* 22(4):299–311.

Hochschild, Arlie Russell. 1975. "Inside the Clockwork of Male Careers." Pp. 47–80 in *Women and the Power to Change*, edited by F. Howe and Carnegie Commission on Higher Education. New York: McGraw-Hill.

Hochschild, Arlie. 1989. *The Second Shift: Working Parents and the Revolution at Home*. New York: Viking.

Hochschild, Arlie Russell. 2001. "The Nanny Chain." *The American Prospect*: December 19. Retrieved December 13, 2011 (http://prospect.org/article/nanny-chain).

Hochschild, Jennifer L. 2007. "Pluralism and Group Relations." Pp. 164–175 in *The New Americans: A Guide to Immigration since 1965*, edited by M. C. Waters, R. Ueda, and H. B. Marrow. Cambridge, MA: Harvard University Press.

Hoefer, Michael, Nancy Rytina, and Bryan C. Baker. 2011. "Estimates of the Unauthorized Immigrant Population Residing in the United States: January 2010." Office of Immigration Statistics, Policy Directorate, U.S. Department of Homeland Security. Retrieved September 3, 2011 (http://www.dhs.gov/xlibrary/assets/statistics/publications/ois_ill_pe_2010.pdf).

Hofstadter, Richard. 1955. *The Age of Reform: From Bryan to F.D.R.* New York: Knopf.

Holden, Karen and Charles Hatcher. 2006. "Economic Status of the Aged." Pp. 219–237 in *Handbook of Aging and the Social Sciences,* edited by R. H. Binstock and L. K. George. New York: Academic Press.

Holmstrom, Lynda Lytle. 1972. *The Two-Career Family.* Cambridge, MA: Schenkman.

Holzer, Harry J. 2009. "Workforce Development as an Antipoverty Strategy: What Do We Know? What Should We Do?" Pp. 301–329 in *Changing Poverty, Changing Policies,* edited by M. Cancian and S. Danziger. New York: Russell Sage Foundation.

Horn, Wade F., David Blankenhorn, and Mitchell B. Pearlstein. 1999. *The Fatherhood Movement: A Call to Action.* Lanham, MD: Lexington Books.

Hout, Michael and Claude S. Fischer. 2002. "Why More Americans Have No Religious Preference: Politics and Generations." *American Sociological Review* 67 (2, April):165–190.

Hout, Michael, Andrew Greeley, and Melissa J. Wilde. 2001. "The Demographic Imperative in Religious Change in the United States." *American Journal of Sociology* 107(2, September):468–500.

Hutchins, John. 1998. "Coming Together for Children and Families: How Cabinet-Level Collaboration Is Changing State Policymaking." Washington, DC: Family Impact Seminar.

Immigration-Online.Org. 2011. "Swedish Immigration." *Encyclopedia of Immigration.* Retrieved September 5, 2011 (http://immigration-online.org/285-swedish-immigration.html).

Institute for American Values. 2011. "Center for Marriage and Families." Retrieved November 18, 2011 (http://www.americanvalues.org/).

Institute for Child, Youth, and Family Policy. 2011. Retrieved November 28, 2011 (http://icyfp.brandeis.edu/).

Institute for Research on Poverty. 2011. "What Are Poverty Thresholds and Poverty Guidelines?" Retrieved February 11, 2011 (http://www.irp.wisc.edu/faqs/faq1.htm#hhs).

Institute for Social Research. 2011. "Panel Study of Income Dynamics." Retrieved November 17, 2011 (http://psidonline.isr.umich.edu/).

Inter-University Consortium for Political and Social Research. 2011. "Inter-University Consortium for Political and Social Research." Retrieved November 17, 2011 (http://www.icpsr.umich.edu/icpsrweb/ICPSR/).

Isaacs, Katelin P. and Julie M. Whittaker. 2011. "Temporary Extension of Unemployment Benefits: Emergency Unemployment Compensation (Euco8)." *Congressional Research Service:* Retrieved April 11, 2011 (http://economic-legislation.blogspot.com/2011/03/temporary-extension-of-unemployment_25.html).

Jacobs, Francine Helene and Margery W. Davies. 1994. *More Than Kissing Babies?: Current Child and Family Policy in the United States.* Westport, CT: Auburn House.

Jacobs, Jerry A. and Kathleen Gerson. 2004. *The Time Divide: Work, Family, and Gender Inequality.* Cambridge, MA: Harvard University Press.

Jacobs, Jerry A., Kathleen Gerson, and Janet C. Gornick. 2004. "American Workers in Cross-National Perspective." Pp. 119–147 in *The Time Divide: Work, Family, and Gender Inequality*, edited by J. A. Jacobs and K. Gerson. Cambridge, MA: Harvard University Press.

Jiménez, Tomás R. and Laura López-Sanders. 2011. "Unanticipated, Unintended, and Unadvised: The Effects of Public Policy on Unauthorized Immigration." *Pathways* (Winter):3–7.

Johnson, Ben. 2002. "The 1965 Immigration Act: Anatomy of a Disaster." *FrontPageMagazine.com*. Retrieved September 3, 2011 (http://archive.frontpagemag.com/readArticle.aspx?ARTID=20777).

Johnson, Richard W., Desmond Toohey, and Joshua M. Wiener. 2007. "Meeting the Long-Term Care Needs of the Baby Boomers: How Changing Families Will Affect Paid Helpers and Institutions." Washington, DC: The Urban Institute.

Johnston, William Robert. 2011. "Historical Abortion Statistics, United States." *Abortion statistics and other data—Johnston's Archive:* January 17. Retrieved December 7, 2011 (http://www.johnstonsarchive.net/policy/abortion/ab-unitedstates.html).

Kahne, Hilda. 1985. *Reconceiving Part-Time Work: New Perspectives for Older Workers and Women*. Totowa, NJ: Rowman & Allanheld.

Kahne, Hilda and Zachary Mabel. 2010. "Single Mothers and Other Low Earners: Policy Routes to Adequate Wages." *Poverty & Public Policy* 2(3):113–149. Retrieved April 20, 2011 (http://www.psocommons.org/ppp/vol2/iss3/art7).

Kamerman, Sheila B. 1995. "Families: Theoretical and Policy Issues." *Encyclopedia of Social Work*:927–935.

Kamerman, Sheila B. and Alfred J. Kahn. 1976. *Social Services in the United States: Policies and Programs*. Philadelphia: Temple University Press.

Kamerman, Sheila B. and Alfred J. Kahn. 1978. *Family Policy: Government and Families in Fourteen Countries*. New York: Columbia University Press.

Kanter, Rosabeth Moss. 1972. *Commitment and Community; Communes and Utopias in Sociological Perspective*. Cambridge, MA: Harvard University Press.

Kanter, Rosabeth Moss. 1977. *Work and Family in the United States: A Critical Review and Agenda for Research and Policy*. New York: Russell Sage Foundation.

Keniston, Kenneth and Carnegie Council on Children. 1977. *All Our Children: The American Family under Pressure*. New York: Harcourt Brace Jovanovich.

Kerr, Clark, John T. Dunlop, Frederick H. Harbison, and Charles A. Myers. 1960. *Industrialism and Industrial Man: The Problems of Labor and Management in Economic Growth*. Cambridge, MA: Harvard University Press.

King, Martin Luther. 1967. "Where Do We Go from Here?" *Address to the Southern Christian Leadership Conference:* August 16. Retrieved August 20, 2011 (http://en.wikiquote.org/wiki/Martin_Luther_King,_Jr.#Where_Do_We_Go_From_Here.3F_.281967.29).

Kinsella, Kevin G. 1992. "Changes in Life Expectancy 1900–1990." *American Journal of Clinical Nutrition* 55(June, 6 Suppl):1196S–1202S.

Klerman, Lorraine V. 1996. "Child Health: What Public Policies Can Improve It?" Pp. 188–206 in *Children, Families, and Government: Preparing for the Twenty-First Century*, edited by E. Zigler, S. L. Kagan, and N. W. Hall. New York: Cambridge University Press.

Knickerbocker, Brad. 2010. "DREAM Act for Minors in the US Illegally Stopped in the Senate." *Christian Science Monitor*, December 18, 2010. Retrieved July 24, 2011 (http://www.csmonitor.com/USA/Politics/2010/1218/DREAM-Act-for-minors-in-the-US-illegally-stopped-in-the-Senate).

Knitzer, Jane. 1996. "Children's Mental Health: Changing Paradigms and Policies." Pp. 207–232 in *Children, Families, and Government: Preparing for the Twenty-First Century*, edited by E. Zigler, S. L. Kagan, and N. W. Hall. New York: Cambridge University Press.

Knudtson, Eric I., James J. Heckman, Judy L. Cameron, and Jack P. Shonkoff. 2006. "Economic, Neurobiological, and Behavioral Perspectives on Building America's Future Workforce." *Proceedings of the National Academy of Sciences* 103(27):10155–10162.

Kobrin, Frances E. 1976. "The Primary Individual and the Family: Changes in Living Arrangements in the United States since 1940." *Journal of Marriage and the Family* 38(2):233–239.

Kohn, Melvin. 1995. "Social Structure and Personality through Time and Space." Pp. 141–68 in *Examining Lives in Context: Perspectives on the Ecology of Human Development*, edited by P. Moen, G. H. Elder, K. Lüscher, and U. Bronfenbrenner. Washington, DC: American Psychological Association.

Korpi, Walter. 2003. "Welfare-State Regress in Western Europe: Politics, Institutions, Globalization, and Europeanization." *Annual Review of Sociology* 29:589–609.

Kotlowitz, Alex. 1991. *There Are No Children Here: The Story of Two Boys Growing up in the Other America*. New York: Doubleday.

Kotok, Alan. 2008. "Student-Veterans Come Marching Home: A New GI Bill for Scientists." *Science Career Magazine*, June 6. Retrieved September 19, 2011 (http://sciencecareers.sciencemag.org/career_development/previous_issues/articles/2008_06_06/caredit_a0800083).

Koven, Seth and Sonya Michel. 1993. *Mothers of a New World: Maternalist Politics and the Origins of Welfare States*. New York: Routledge.

Kozol, Jonathan. 1991. *Savage Inequalities: Children in America's Schools*. New York: Crown.

Kreider, Rose M. and Renee Ellis. 2011. "Number, Timing, and Duration of Marriages and Divorces: 2009." *Current Population Reports*: P70–125. Retrieved December 6, 2011 (http://www.census.gov/prod/2011pubs/p70-125.pdf).

Kristof, Nicholas D. 2010. "Our Banana Republic." *New York Times*, November 7, WK10.

Kristof, Nicholas. 2011a. "The Bankers and the Revolutionaries." *New York Times*, October 2, SR11.

Kristof, Nicholas D. 2011b. "Equality, a True Soul Food." *New York Times*, January 2, WK10.

Krzewinski, Lisa M. 2001. "Section 8's Failure to Integrate: The Interaction of Class-Based and Racial Discrimination." *Boston College Third World Law Journal*, 21: Issue 2/4. Retrieved December 22, 2011 (http://lawdigitalcommons.bc.edu/twlj/vol21/iss2/4/).

Kuttner, Robert. 2011. "Histories Missed Moment." *The American Prospect* 22 (8 October):18–25.

Ladd-Taylor, Molly. 1993. "'My Work Came Out of Agony and Grief': Mothers and the Making of the Sheppard-Towner Act." Pp. 321–342 in *Mothers of a New World: Maternalist Politics and the Origins of Welfare States*, edited by S. Koven and S. Michel. New York: Routledge.

Landry, Bart. 2000. *Black Working Wives: Pioneers of the American Family Revolution.* Berkeley: University of California Press.

Lareau, Annette. 2003. *Unequal Childhoods: Class, Race, and Family Life.* Berkeley: University of California Press.

Lareau, Annette and Elliot B. Weininger. 2008. "Class and the Transition to Adulthood." Pp. 118–151 in *Social Class: How Does It Work?*, edited by A. Lareau and D. Conley. New York: Russell Sage Foundation.

Lasch, Christopher. 1977. *Haven in a Heartless World: The Family Besieged.* New York: Basic Books.

Laumann, Edward O. and Robert T. Michael. 2000. *Sex, Love, and Health in America: Private Choices and Public Policies.* Chicago: University of Chicago Press.

Lazar, Kay. 2008. "439,000 More Get Health Coverage; State Shows Big Gains in Landmark Program." *The Boston Globe,* August 20. Retrieved December 13, 2011 (http://www.healthlawadvocates.org/news?id=0011).

Lazarsfeld, Paul Felix, Bernard Berelson, and Hazel Gaudet. 1965. *The People's Choice: How the Voter Makes Up His Mind in a Presidential Campaign.* New York: Columbia University Press.

Leiby, James. 1978. *A History of Social Welfare and Social Work in the United States, 1815–1972.* New York: Columbia University Press.

Leland, John. 2010. "New Program for Buyers, with No Money Down." *New York Times,* September 5, A 19.

Letablier, Marie-Thérèse. 2004. "Work and Family Balance: A New Challenge for Policies in France." Pp. 189–209 in *Changing Life Patterns in Western Industrial Societies*, edited by J. Z. Giele and E. Holst. Amsterdam, Netherlands: Elsevier.

Levin, Diane E. and Jean Kilbourne. 2008. *So Sexy So Soon: The New Sexualized Childhood, and What Parents Can Do to Protect Their Kids.* New York: Ballantine Books.

Levine, James A. 1976. *Who Will Raise the Children?: New Options for Fathers (and Mothers).* Philadelphia: Lippincott.

Levinson, Daniel J. 1979. *The Seasons of a Man's Life.* New York: Ballantine Books.

Levy, Frank. 1998. *The New Dollars and Dreams: American Incomes and Economic Change.* New York: Russell Sage Foundation.

Lewandowski, Cathleen A. and Katharine Briar-Lawson. 2009a. "Child Welfare." Pp. 134–159 in *Delivering Home-Based Services: A Social Work Perspective*, edited by S. F. Allen and E. M. Tracy. New York: Columbia University Press.

Lewandowski, Cathleen A. and Katharine Briar-Lawson. 2009b. "Social Policy Context." Pp. 55–77 in *Delivering Home-Based Services: A Social Work Perspective*, edited by S. F. Allen and E. M. Tracy. New York: Columbia University Press.

Lipset, Seymour Martin. 1996. *American Exceptionalism: A Double-Edged Sword*. New York: W. W. Norton.

Lipsky, Michael. 1980. *Street-Level Bureaucracy: Dilemmas of the Individual in Public Services*. New York: Russell Sage Foundation.

Lorber, Judith. 1994. *Paradoxes of Gender*. New Haven, CT: Yale University Press.

Louis Harris and Associates, and Roper Organization. 1974. *The Virginia Slims American Women's Opinion Poll*. S.l.: Louis Harris and Associates.

Lovejoy, Meg. 2012. *Is Hooking up Empowering for College Women? A Feminist Gramscian Perspective*. Ph.D. dissertation, Department of Sociology, Brandeis University. Waltham, MA.

Lowrey, Annie. 2012. "Tax-Cut Bill Includes Updates to Jobless Benefits System." *New York Times*, February 22, A16.

Ludden, Jennifer. 2006. "1965 Immigration Law Changed Face of America." *National Public Radio:* May 9. Retrieved August 9, 2011 (http://www.npr.org/templates/story/story.php?storyId=5391395).

Luker, Kristin. 1984. *Abortion and the Politics of Motherhood*. Berkeley: University of California Press.

Madland, David and Karla Walter. 2009. "Unions Are Good for the American Economy." *Center for American Progress:* Retrieved April 19, 2011 (http://www.americanprogressaction.org/issues/2009/02/efca_factsheets.html).

Magnuson, Katherine and Elizabeth Votruba-Drzal. 2009. "Enduring Influences of Childhood Poverty." Pp. 153–179 in *Changing Poverty, Changing Policies*, edited by M. Cancian and S. Danziger. New York: Russell Sage Foundation.

Marquardt, Elizabeth. 2006. *The Revolution in Parenthood: The Emerging Global Clash between Adult Rights and Children's Needs*. New York: Institute for American Values.

Marshall, T. H. 1964. *Class, Citizenship, and Social Development: Essays*. Garden City, NY: Doubleday.

Martin, Joyce A., Brady E. Hamilton, and Stephanie J. Ventura. 2011. "Births: Final Data for 2009." *National Vital Statistics Reports*, 60(1, November):1–72. Retrieved April 24, 2012 (http://www.cdc.gov/nchs/data/nvsr/nvsr60/nvsr60_01.pdf).

Mason, Karen Oppenheim and Larry L. Bumpass. 1975. "U.S. Women's Sex-Role Ideology, 1970." *American Journal of Sociology* 80(5):1212–1219.

Mason, Karen Oppenheim, Noriko O. Tsuya, and Minja Kim Choe. 1998. *The Changing Family in Comparative Perspective: Asia and the United States*. Honolulu: University of Hawaii Press.

Mass. Law Reform Institute. 2002. "Teen Parents and Welfare Reform." Retrieved April 25, 2012 (http://www.masslegalhelp.org/income-benefits/teen-parents-welfare-reform.pdf).

Massachusetts Workforce Development System. 2011. "Executive Summary FY 2011." *Career Center Performance Reports:* Retrieved April 25, 2011 (http://www.massworkforce.org/_uploads/iss/1116B.pdf).

Massey, Douglas S. 2011. "Isolated, Vulnerable and Broke." *New York Times,* August 5, A23.

Massey, Douglas S., Jorge Durand, and Nolan J. Malone. 2002. *Beyond Smoke and Mirrors: Mexican Immigration in an Era of Economic Integration.* New York: Russell Sage Foundation.

Massey, Douglas S. and Magaly Sánchez. 2010. *Brokered Boundaries: Creating Immigrant Identity in Anti-Immigrant Times.* New York: Russell Sage Foundation.

Matthaei, Julie and Neil Wollman. 2011. "Why the Occupy Movement Is Good for Our Health." Retrieved November 19, 2011 (http://www.commondreams.org/view/2011/11/08-2).

May, Elaine Tyler. 2008. *Homeward Bound: American Families in the Cold War Era.* New York: Basic Books.

McCarty, Maggie, Libby Perl, Bruce E. Fotte, Katie Jones, and Meredith Peterson. 2008. "Overview of Federal Housing Assistance Programs and Policy." *Congressional Research Service,* (RL34591):1–36. Retrieved April 24, 2012 (http://congressionalresearch.com/RL34591/document.php?study=Overview+of+Federal+Housing+Assistance+Programs+and+Policy).

McKenna, Christine. 2010. "Child Care Subsidies in the United States: Government Funding to Families (2010)." *Work and Family Researchers Network,* Retrieved April 25, 2012 (https://workfamily.sas.upenn.edu/wfrn-repo/object/ad3j1t5wq2hm2h26).

McLanahan, Sara and Christine Percheski. 2008. "Family Structure and the Reproduction of Inequalities." *Annual Review of Sociology* 34(1):257–76.

McLanahan, Sara and Gary D. Sandefur. 1994. *Growing up with a Single Parent: What Hurts, What Helps.* Cambridge, MA: Harvard University Press.

Mead, Lawrence M. 1996. "Welfare Reform and Children." Pp. 51–76 in *Children, Families, and Government: Preparing for the Twenty-First Century,* edited by E. Zigler, S. L. Kagan, and N. W. Hall. New York: Cambridge University Press.

Medicaid.Gov. 2011. "Children." *Medicaid & CHIP Program Information:* Retrieved December 17, 2011 (http://www.medicaid.gov/Medicaid-CHIP-Program-Information/By-Population/Children/Children.html).

Medina, Jennifer. 2011a. "Arriving as Pregnant Tourists, Leaving with American Babies." *New York Times,* March 28, A1.

Medina, Jennifer. 2011b. "Legislature in California Set to Pass a Dream Act." *New York Times,* September 1, A16.

Merle, Renae. 2010. "Minorities Hit Harder by Foreclosure Crisis." *Washington Post,* June 19. Retrieved September 19, 2011 (http://www.washingtonpost.com/wp-dyn/content/article/2010/06/18/AR2010061802885.html).

Merton, Robert King. 1968. "Bureaucratic Structure and Personality." Pp. 195–206 in *Social Theory and Social Structure.* New York: Free Press.

Merton, Robert King, Samuel Andrew Stouffer, and Paul Felix Lazarsfeld. 1950. *Studies in the Scope and Method of "The American Soldier."* Glencoe, IL: Free Press.

Michel, Sonya. 1993. "The Limits of Maternalism: Policies toward American Wage-Earning Mothers During the Progressive Era." Pp. 277–320 in *Mothers of a New World: Maternalist Politics and the Origins of Welfare States,* edited by S. Koven and S. Michel. New York: Routledge.

Michel, Sonya. 1999. *Children's Interests/Mothers' Rights: The Shaping of America's Child Care Policy.* New Haven, CT: Yale University Press.

Mincer, Jacob. 1962. "Labor Force Participation of Married Women." Pp. 63–105 in *Aspects of Labor Economics: A Conference of the Universities—National Bureau Committee for Economic Research,* edited by National Bureau of Economic Research. Princeton, NJ: Princeton University Press.

Mincy, Ronald B. and Hillard Pouncy. 2007. "Baby Fathers and American Family Formation: Low Income Never-Married Parents in Louisiana before Katrina." *An Essay in the Future of the Black Family Series.* New York: Institute of American Values. Retrieved September 20, 2011 (http://familyscholars.org/2007/01/01/baby-fathers-and-american-family-formation/).

Mishel, Lawrence R., Jared Bernstein, and Heidi Shierholz. 2009. *The State of Working America 2008/2009.* Ithaca, NY: Institute for Labor Relations.

Mitchell, J. Paul. 1985. *Federal Housing Policy and Programs: Past and Present.* New Brunswick, NJ: Center for Urban Policy Research Rutgers University.

Modell, John. 1989. *Into One's Own: From Youth to Adulthood in the United States, 1920–1975.* Berkeley: University of California Press.

Moen, Phyllis. 1992. *Women's Two Roles: A Contemporary Dilemma.* New York: Auburn House.

Moon, Marilyn. 2006. "Organization and Financing of Health Care." Pp. 380–396 in *Handbook of Aging and the Social Sciences,* edited by R. H. Binstock and L. K. George. Boston: Academic Press.

Moren-Cross, Jennifer L., and Nan Lin. 2006. "Social Networks and Health." Pp. 111–126 in *Handbook of Aging and the Social Sciences,* edited by R. H. Binstock, L. K. George, S. J. Cutler, J. Hendricks, and J. H. Schulz. Boston: Academic Press.

Moroney, Robert. 1976. *The Family and the State: Considerations for Social Policy.* New York: Longman.

Moroney, Robert. 1986. *Shared Responsibility: Family and Social Policy.* New York: Aldine.

Mothers of Color at Home. 2011. "Mocha Moms, Inc." Retrieved December 6, 2011 (http://www.mochamoms.org/).

Murray, Charles A. 1984. *Losing Ground: American Social Policy, 1950–1980.* New York: Basic Books.

Myers, Dowell. 2007. *Immigrants and Boomers: Forging a New Social Contract for the Future of America.* New York: Russell Sage Foundation.

Myrdal, Alva Reimer. [1934]1968. *Nation and Family: The Swedish Experiment in Democratic Family and Population Policy.* Cambridge, MA: MIT Press.

Myrdal, Alva and Viola Klein. 1956. *Women's Two Roles, Home and Work.* London, England: Routledge & Paul.

Myrdal, Gunnar, Richard Mauritz Edvard Sterner, and Arnold Rose. 1944. *An American Dilemma: The Negro Problem and Modern Democracy.* New York: Harper & Brothers.

National Alliance to End Homelessness. 2011. "Issues." Retrieved May 21, 2011 (http://www.endhomelessness.org/section/issues).

National Association of Realtors. 2012. "Metropolitan Area Median Prices and Affordability." Retrieved April 25, 2012 (http://www.realtor.org/topics/metro politan-area-median-prices-and-affordability).

National Conference on Social Welfare, and National Commission on Families and Public Policies. 1978. *Families and Public Policies in the United States: Final Report of the Commission.* Columbus, OH: National Conference on Social Welfare.

National Council on Disability. 2005. "The State of 21st Century Long-Term Services and Supports." Retrieved May 15, 2010 (http://www.ncd.gov/publications/2005/ 12152005).

National Housing Law Project. 2011. "Choice Neighborhoods Initiative: A Work in Progress." Retrieved December 21, 2011 (http://nhlp.org/node/1474).

National Institute on Aging. 2011. "Mourning the Death of a Spouse." Age page. Retrieved March 30, 2011 (http://www.nia.nih.gov/health/publication/mourning-death-spouse).

National Research Council and Advisory Committee on Child Development. 1976. *Toward a National Policy for Children and Families.* Washington, DC: National Academy of Sciences.

National Scientific Council on the Developing Child. 2009. "Excessive Stress Disrupts the Architecture of the Developing Brain." *Working paper #3:* Retrieved July 25, 2011 (http://developingchild.harvard.edu/).

National Survey of Families and Households. 1987–88. "National Survey of Families and Households." Retrieved November 17, 2011 (http://www.ssc.wisc.edu/nsfh/bib.htm).

Nelson, Julie A. 2006. *Economics for Humans.* Chicago: University of Chicago Press.

New Jersey Department of Labor and Workforce Development. 2011. "Workers' Compensation." Retrieved April 7, 2011 (http://lwd.dol.state.nj.us/labor/wc/ content/stats.html).

Newport, Frank and Lydia Saad. 2011. "Americans Oppose Cuts in Education, Social Security, Defense." *Gallup Politics.* Retrieved February 23, 2012 (http:// www.gallup.com/poll/145790/americans-oppose-cuts-education-social-security-defense.aspx).

Nguyen, Huong H. 2006. "Acculturation in the United States." Pp. 311–329 in *The Cambridge Handbook of Acculturation Psychology,* edited by D. L. Sam and J. W. Berry. Cambridge, UK: Cambridge University Press.

Nichols, Carol Ann. 2002. *Providing Foster Care: A Study of the Challenges for Regular and Kinship Foster Parents and the Child Welfare Community.* PhD dissertation, Heller School for Social Policy and Management, Brandeis University. Ann Arbor, MI: University Microfilms.

Nocera, Joe. 2011. "An Advocate Who Scares Republicans." *New York Times,* March 19, B1.

Nowrasteh, Alex. 2011. "Alabama's Immigration Law Is a Train Wreck." *Foxnews. com,* September 2.Retrieved September 6, 2011 (http://www.foxnews.com/opinion/2011/09/02/alabamas-immigration-law-is-train-wreck/).

Nussbaum, Martha Craven. 2011. *Creating Capabilities: The Human Development Approach.* Cambridge, MA: Harvard University Press.

Oakley, Ann. 1975. *Woman's Work: The Housewife, Past and Present.* New York: Pantheon Books.

O'Brien, Ruth. 2004. *Voices from the Edge: Narratives about the Americans with Disabilities Act.* New York: Oxford University Press.

Ogbu, John U. 1990. "Minority Status and Literacy in Comparative Perspective." *Daedalus* 119(2):141–168.

Oliveira, Victor, Elizabeth Racine, Jennifer Olmsted, and Linda M. Ghelfi. 2002. "The WIC Program: Background, Trends, and Issues." *Food Assistance and Nutrition Research,* Report No. FANRR27. Retrieved May 15, 2010 (http://www.ers.usda.gov/publications/fanrr27/).

Oliver, Melvin L. and Thomas M. Shapiro. 2006. *Black Wealth, White Wealth: A New Perspective on Racial Inequality.* New York: Routledge.

Omi, Michael A. 2001. "The Changing Meaning of Race." Pp. 243–263, Vol. 1 in *America Becoming: Racial Trends and Their Consequences,* edited by N. J. Smelser, W. J. Wilson, and F. Mitchell. Washington, DC: National Academy Press.

Ooms, Theodora. 1998. *Toward More Perfect Unions: Putting Marriage on the Public Agenda.* Washington, DC: Family Impact Seminar.

Oppenheimer, Valerie Kincade. 1970. *The Female Labor Force in the United States: Demographic and Economic Factors Governing Its Growth and Changing Composition.* Berkeley: University of California, Institute of International Studies.

Oppenheimer, Valerie Kincade. 1982. *Work and the Family: A Study in Social Demography.* New York: Academic Press.

Oppenheimer, Valerie Kincade. 1994. "Women's Rising Employment and the Future of the Family in Industrial Societies." *Population and Development Review* 20(2):293–342.

Orfield, Gary and Nancy McArdle. 2006. "The Vicious Cycle: Segregated Housing, Schools and Intergenerational Inequality." Harvard University, Joint Center for Housing Studies. Retrieved July 24, 2011 (http://www.jchs.harvard.edu/sites/jchs.harvard.edu/files/w06-4_orfield.pdf).

Overturf Johnson, Julia. 2005. "Who's Minding the Kids? Child Care Arrangements: Winter 2002." *Current Population Reports:* 70–101. Retrieved May 15, 2010 (http://www.census.gov/prod/2005pubs/p70-101.pdf).

Park, Robert Ezra, Ernest Watson Burgess, and Roderick Duncan McKenzie. [1925] 1967. *The City*. Chicago: University of Chicago Press.

Parke, Ross. D. 2004. "Development in the Family." *Annual Review of Psychology* 55:365–399.

Parsons, Talcott. 1966a. "Full Citizenship for the Negro American? A Sociological Problem." Pp. 709–754 in *The Negro American,* edited by T. Parsons and K. B. Clark. Boston: Houghton Mifflin.

Parsons, Talcott. 1966b. *Societies: Evolutionary and Comparative Perspectives.* Englewood Cliffs, NJ: Prentice-Hall.

Perun, Pamela J. and Janet Zollinger Giele. 1982. "Life after College: Historical Links between Women's Education and Women's Work." Pp. 375–398 in *The Undergraduate Woman: Issues in Educational Equity,* edited by P. J. Perun. Lexington, MA: Lexington Books.

Peterson, Richard R. 1996. "A Re-Evaluation of the Economic Consequences of Divorce." *American Sociological Review* 61(June):528–536.

Pettigrew, Thomas F. 1966. "Complexity and Change in American Racial Patterns: A Social Psychological View." Pp. 325–359 in *The Negro American,* edited by T. Parsons and K. B. Clark. Boston: Houghton Mifflin.

Pew Forum on Religion & Public Life. 2007. "U.S. Religous Landscape Survey." Retrieved August 20, 2011 (http://religions.pewforum.org/reports#).

Pew Research Center. 2007. "As Marriage and Parenthood Drift Apart, Public Is Concerned about Social Impact." *Pew Research Center Publications:* Retrieved December 7, 2011 (http://pewresearch.org/pubs/526/marriage-parenthood).

Piotrowski, Leslie Johnson. 1997. "These Heroes Wear Hard Hats." *Ford Foundation Report* (Summer-Fall):1–4.

Piven, Frances Fox and Richard A. Cloward. 1971. *Regulating the Poor: The Functions of Public Welfare.* New York: Pantheon Books.

Polanyi, Karl. 1944. *The Great Transformation.* New York: Octagon Books.

Popenoe, David. 1996. *Life without Father: Compelling New Evidence That Fatherhood and Marriage Are Indispensable for the Good of Children and Society.* New York: Martin Kessler Books.

Popenoe, David, Jean Bethke Elshtain, and David Blankenhorn. 1996. *Promises to Keep: Decline and Renewal of Marriage in America.* Lanham, MD: Rowman & Littlefield Publishers.

Portes, Alejandro and Rubén G. Rumbaut. 2001. *Legacies: The Story of the Immigrant Second Generation.* Berkeley: University of California Press.

Portes, Alejandro and Rubén G. Rumbaut. 2006. *Immigrant America: A Portrait.* Berkeley: University of California Press.

Portes, Alejandro, Rubén G. Rumbaut, Patricia Fernandez-Kelly, and William Haller. 2006. "Religion: The Enduring Presence." Pp. 299–342 in *Immigrant America: A Portrait,* edited by A. Portes and R. G. Rumbaut. Berkeley: University of California Press.

Putnam, Robert D., David E. Campbell, and Shaylyn Romney Garrett. 2010. *American Grace: How Religion Divides and Unites Us.* New York: Simon & Schuster.

Quadagno, Jill. 1987. "Theories of the Welfare State." *Annual Review of Sociology* 13:109–128.

Rainwater, Lee. 1966. "Crucible of Identity: The Negro Lower-Class Family." Pp. 160–204 in *The Negro American,* edited by T. Parsons and K. B. Clark. Boston: Houghton Mifflin.

Rainwater, Lee, Martin Rein, and Joseph E. Schwartz. 1986. *Income Packaging in the Welfare State: A Comparative Study of Family Income.* New York: Oxford University Press.

Rainwater, Lee and William L. Yancey. 1967. *The Moynihan Report and the Politics of Controversy.* Cambridge, MA: MIT. Press.

Rapoport, Rhona and Lotte Bailyn. 1996. *Rethinking Life and Work: Toward a Better Future. A Report to the Ford Foundation Based on a Collaborative Research Project with Three Corporations.* New York: Ford Foundation.

Rapoport, Rhona and Robert N. Rapoport. 1976. *Dual-Career Families Re-Examined: New Integrations of Work & Family.* London, England: M. Robertson.

Rawls, John. 1971. *A Theory of Justice.* Cambridge, MA: Harvard University Press.

Reagan, Barbara Benton. 1979. *Issues in Federal Statistical Needs Relating to Women.* Washington, DC: U.S. Department of Commerce, Bureau of the Census.

Reinharz, Shulamit. 2009. *On Becoming a Social Scientist: From Survey Research and Participant Observation to Experiential Analysis.* New Brunswick, NJ: Transaction Books..

Reynolds, Morgan. 2009. "A History of Labor Unions from Colonial Times to 2009." *Mises Daily Index:* Retrieved April 22, 2011 (http://mises.org/daily/3553).

Rice, Robert M. 1977. *American Family Policy: Context and Content.* New York: Family Service Association of America.

Rich, Motoko. 2010. "Factory Jobs Return, but Employers Find Skills Shortage." *New York Times,* July 1, A1.

Rich, Motoko. 2011. "Many Jobs Seen as Failing to Meet the Basics." *New York Times,* April 1, B1.

Riesman, David. 1950. *The Lonely Crowd: A Study of the Changing American Character.* New Haven, CT: Yale University Press.

Robert Wood Johnson Foundation. 2010. "The Green House Model: Pinnacle for Culture Change Movement." *Vulnerable Populations.* Retrieved December 28, 2011 (http://www.rwjf.org/pr/product.jsp?id=63828).

Roberts, Sam. 2010. "U.S. Plans New Measure for Poverty." *New York Times,* March 2. Retrieved April 27, 2010 (http://www.nytimes.com/2010/03/03/us/03poverty.html).

Roos, Patricia A. 1985. *Gender and Work: A Comparative Analysis of Industrial Societies.* Albany: State University of New York.

Rossi, Alice S. 1964. "Equality between the Sexes: An Immodest Proposal." *Daedalus* 93(2):607–652.

Rossi, Alice S. 1984. "Gender and Parenthood." *American Sociological Review* 49(1):1–19.

Rothman, David J. 1971. *The Discovery of the Asylum: Social Order and Disorder in the New Republic.* Boston: Little, Brown.

Rothman, Sheila M. 1978. *Woman's Proper Place: A History of Changing Ideals and Practices, 1870 to the Present.* New York: Basic Books.

Rowe, John W. and Robert Louis Kahn. 1998. *Successful Aging.* New York: Pantheon Books.

Rubin, Roger Harvey. 1976. *Matricentric Family Structure and the Self-Attitudes of Negro Children.* San Francisco: R and E Research Associates.

Rueschemeyer, Dietrich and Theda Skocpol. 1996. *States, Social Knowledge, and the Origins of Modern Social Policies.* Princeton, NJ: Princeton University Press.

Ruggles, Steven. 1997. "The Rise of Divorce and Separation in the United States, 1880–1990." *Demography* 34(4):455–466.

Ruggles, Steven. 2006. "Family and Household Composition." Pp. 655–659 in *Historical Statistics of the United States Millennial Edition Online,* edited by S. B. Carter, S. S. Gartner, M. R. Haines, A. L. Olmstead, R. Sutch, G. Wright, and S. Ruggles. New York: Cambridge University Press.

Ruhm, Christopher J. 2005. "How Well Do Government and Employer Policies Support Working Parents?" Pp. 313–325 in *Work, Family, Health, and Well-Being,* edited by S. M. Bianchi, L. M. Casper, and R. B. King. Mahwah, NJ: Lawrence Erlbaum.

Russo, Francine. 1997. "Can the Government Prevent Divorce?" *Atlantic Monthly,* 280(4):28–42.

Ryder, Norman B. 1965. "The Cohort as a Concept in the Study of Social Change." *American Sociological Review* 30(6):843–861.

Sampson, Robert J., Jeffrey D. Morenoff, and Thomas Gannon-Rowley. 2002. "Assessing Neighborhood Effects: Social Processes and New Directions in Research." *Annual Review of Sociology* 28:443–478.

Sandler, Bernice. 2011. "All about Bernice Sandler." Retrieved January 2, 2012 (http://www.bernicesandler.com/id2.htm).

Schaie, K. Warner. 1977. "Quasi-Experimental Research Designs in the Psychology of Aging." Pp. 39–58 in *Handbook of the Psychology of Aging,* edited by J. E. Birren and K. W. Schaie. New York: Van Nostrand Reinhold.

Schneider, Barbara L. and Linda J. Waite. 2005. *Being Together, Working Apart: Dual-Career Families and the Work-Life Balance.* New York: Cambridge University Press.

Scholz, John Karl, Robert Moffitt, and Benjamin Cowan. 2009. "Changing Poverty and Changing Antipoverty Policies." Pp. 203–241 in *Changing Poverty, Changing Policies,* edited by M. Cancian and S. Danziger. New York: Russell Sage Foundation.

Schor, Juliet. 1991. *The Overworked American: The Unexpected Decline of Leisure.* New York: Basic Books.

Schorr, Alvin L. 1961. *Filial Responsibility in the Modern American Family.* Washington, DC: Social Security Administration.

Schorr, Alvin Louis. 1969. *Explorations in Social Policy.* New York: Basic Books.

Schottland, Charles I. 1967. "Government Economic Programs and Family Life." *Journal of Marriage and the Family* 29(1, February):71–123.

Schram, Sanford F. and Joe Soss. 2001. "Success Stories: Welfare Reform, Policy Discourse, and the Politics of Research." *The Annals of the American Academy of Political and Social Science* 577(1):49–65.

Schulz, James H. and Robert H. Binstock. 2008. *Aging Nation: The Economics and Politics of Growing Older in America*. Baltimore, MD: Johns Hopkins University Press.

Schumpeter, Joseph Alois. 1958. *Capitalism, Socialism and Democracy*. S.l.: Peter Smith.

Schwartz, Alex F. 2010. *Housing Policy in the United States*. New York: Routledge.

Sciegaj, Mark and John A. Capitman. 2004. "Consumer-Directed Community Care: Race/Ethnicity and Individual Differences in Preferences for Control." *Gerontologist* 44(4):489–99.

Seccombe, Karen. 2011. *"So You Think I Drive a Cadillac?": Welfare Recipients' Perspectives on the System and Its Reform*. Boston: Allyn & Bacon.

Seeley, John R. 1956. *Crestwood Heights: A Study of the Culture of Suburban Life*. New York: Basic Books.

Sen, Amartya Kumar. 1999. *Commodities and Capabilities*. New York: Oxford University Press.

Seniorlink, Inc. 2009. "Seniorlink, Inc. Named Better Government Award Winner in Pioneer Institute Competition." *Business Wire*. Retrieved April 25, 2012 (http://www.thefreelibrary.com/Seniorlink,+Inc.+Named+Better+Government+Award+Winner+in+Pioneer...-a0203226959).

Shanas, Ethel. 1973. "Family-Kin Networks and Aging in Cross-Cultural Perspective." *Journal of Marriage and Family* 35(3):505–511.

Shapiro, Joseph P. 1993. *No Pity: People with Disabilities Forging a New Civil Rights Movement*. New York: Times Books.

Sheehy, Gail. 1976. *Passages: Predictable Crises of Adult Life*. New York: Dutton.

Shirk, Cynthia. 2008. "Medicaid and Mental Health Services." *National Health Policy Forum*, October 23. Background Paper – No. 66. Retrieved March 12, 2012 (http://www.nhpf.org/library/details.cfm/2680).

Shonkoff, Jack P. and Deborah Phillips. 2000. *From Neurons to Neighborhoods: The Science of Early Childhood Development*. Washington, DC: National Academy Press.

Shonkoff, Jack P., Deborah Phillips, and National Research Council (U.S.). Committee on Integrating the Science of Early Childhood Development. 2000. *From Neurons to Neighborhoods: The Science of Early Childhood Development*. Washington, DC: National Academy Press.

Shoreline Community College. 2011. "WorkFirst Program." Retrieved April 25, 2011 (http://www.shoreline.edu/workfirst/).

Short, Kathleen S. 2011. "Who Is Poor? A New Look with the Supplemental Poverty Measure." Retrieved April 5, 2011 (http://www.census.gov/hhes/povmeas/methodology/supplemental/research.html).

Shorto, Russell. 2008. "No Babies?" *New York Times Magazine*, June 29. Retrieved September 19, 2011 (http://www.nytimes.com/2008/06/29/magazine/29Birth-t.html).

Silberner, Joanne. 2008. "MS Patient Falls into American Insurance Gap." *National Public Radio,* July 24. (Morning Edition): Retrieved April 25, 2012 (http://www.wbur.org/npr/92067101/ms-patient-falls-into-american-insurance-gap).

Simmel, Georg. 1955. *Conflict and the Web of Group Affiliations.* Glencoe, IL: Free Press.

Sklar, Kathryn Kish. 1993. "The Historical Foundations of Women's Power in the Creation of the American Welfare State, 1830–1930." Pp. 43–93 in *Mothers of a New World: Maternalist Politics and the Origins of Welfare States,* edited by S. Koven and S. Michel. New York: Routledge.

Skocpol, Theda. 1992. *Protecting Soldiers and Mothers: The Political Origins of Social Policy in the United States.* Cambridge, MA: Harvard University Press.

Skocpol, Theda. 1995. *Social Policy in the United States: Future Possibilities in Historical Perspective.* Princeton, NJ: Princeton University Press.

Skocpol, Theda. 2000. *The Missing Middle: Working Families and the Future of American Social Policy.* New York: W. W. Norton.

Sloan Foundation. 2011. "Workplace, Work Force and Working Families." Retrieved November 17, 2011 (http://www.sloan.org/program/32/page/84).

Smelser, Neil J. 1959. *Social Change in the Industrial Revolution; An Application of Theory to the Lancashire Cotton Industry, 1770–1840.* London, England: Routledge & Paul.

Smith, James P. 2001. "Race and Ethnicity in the Labor Market: Trends over the Short and Long Term." Pp. 52–97, Vol. 2 in *America Becoming: Racial Trends and Their Consequences,* edited by N. J. Smelser, W. J. Wilson, and F. Mitchell. Washington, DC: National Academy Press.

Smith, Ralph Ely. 1979. *Women in the Labor Force in 1990.* Washington, DC: Urban Institute.

Smith, Tom W. 2002. "Religious Diversity in America: The Emergence of Muslims, Buddhists, Hindus, and Others." *Journal for the Scientific Study of Religion* 41(3, September):577–585.

Smith, Tom W., and Seokho Kim. 2005. "The Vanishing Protestant Majority." *Journal for the Scientific Study of Religion* 44(2, June):211–223.

Sobek, Matthew. 2006. "Occupations." Pp. 2–35 to 2–40 in *Historical Statistics of the United States,* edited by S. B. Carter, et al. New York: Cambridge University Press.

Social Security Online. 2011a. "Social Security Beneficiary Statistics." *Actuarial Publications:* January 19, 2011. Retrieved April 8, 2011 (http://www.socialsecurity.gov/OACT/STATS/OASDIbenies.html).

Social Security Online. 2011b. "SSI Federal Payment Amounts for 2012." *Automatic Determinations:* October 19, 2011. Retrieved December 31, 2011 (http://www.socialsecurity.gov/OACT/COLA/SSI.html).

Stacey, Judith. 1996. *In the Name of the Family: Rethinking Family Values in the Postmodern Age.* Boston: Beacon Press.

Stebbins, Leslie F. 2001. *Work and Family in America: A Reference Handbook.* Santa Barbara, CA: Abc-Clio.

Steiner, Gilbert Yale. 1981. *The Futility of Family Policy.* Washington, DC: Brookings Institution.

Steiner, Gilbert Yale and Pauline H. Milius. 1976. *The Children's Cause*. Washington, DC: Brookings Institution.

Still, Mary C. and Joan C. Williams. 2006. "A Legal Perspective on Family Issues at Work." Pp. 309–326 in *The Work and Family Handbook: Multi-Disciplinary Perspectives, Methods, and Approaches*, edited by M. Pitt-Catsouphes, E. E. Kossek, and S. A. Sweet. Mahwah, NJ: Lawrence Erlbaum.

Stone, Deborah. 2000. "Caring by the Book." Pp. 89–111 in *Care Work: Gender, Labor, and Welfare States*, edited by M. Harrington Meyer. New York: Routledge.

Stone, Pamela. 2007. *Opting Out?: Why Women Really Quit Careers and Head Home*. Berkeley: University of California Press.

Stone, Robyn I. 2006. "Emerging Issues in Long-Term Care." Pp. 397–418 in *Handbook of Aging and the Social Sciences*, edited by R. H. Binstock and L. K. George. Boston: Academic Press.

Streitfeld, David. 2011. "House Prices Are Set to Hit Another Low." *New York Times*, May 31, A1.

Suárez-Orozco, Carola, and Marcelo M. Suárez-Orozco. 2001. *Children of Immigration*. Cambridge, MA: Harvard University Press.

Sullivan, Laura and Amy Walters. 2011. "Native Foster Care: Lost Children, Shattered Families." Retrieved October 25, 2011 (http://www.npr.org/2011/10/25/141672992/native-foster-care-lost-children-shattered-families).

Surgeon General of the United States. 1999. "Organizing and Financing Mental Health Services." *Mental Health: A Report of the Surgeon General*, Chapter 6:405–433. Retrieved May 15, 2010 (http://www.surgeongeneral.gov/library/mentalhealth/pdfs/c6.pdf).

Surgeon General of the United States. 2001. "Culture Counts." *Mental Health: Culture, Race, and Ethnicity*, Chapter 2. Retrieved December 26, 2011 (http://www.surgeongeneral.gov/library/mentalhealth/cre/execsummary-6.html).

Sussman, Dalia. 2009. "Tracking Public Opinion on Abortion: It's Tricky." *The Caucus: The Politics and Government Blog of the Times*, May 21. Retrieved August 5, 2009 (http://thecaucus.blogs.nytimes.com/2009/05/21/tracking-public-opinion-on-abortion-its-tricky/).

Sussman, Marvin B. 1967. "Editor's Comments." *Journal of Marriage and the Family* 29(1, February):5.

Swartz, Katherine. 2009. "Health Care for the Poor: For Whom, What Care, and Whose Responsibility?" *Focus* 26(2):69–74.

Tavernise, Sabrina. 2011. "Married Couples Are No Longer a Majority, Census Finds." *New York Times*, May 26, A22.

Thornton, Arland, William G. Axinn, and Yu Xie. 2007. *Marriage and Cohabitation*. Chicago: University of Chicago Press.

Titmuss, Richard Morris. 1971. *The Gift Relationship: From Human Blood to Social Policy*. New York: Pantheon Books.

Titmuss, Richard Morris. 1975. *Social Policy: An Introduction*. New York: Pantheon Books.

Tough, Paul. 2008. *Whatever It Takes: Geoffrey Canada's Quest to Change Harlem and America*. Boston: Houghton Mifflin.

Turk, Jema K. 2009. "The Division of Household Labor among Dual-Earner Couples." PhD dissertation, The Heller School for Social Policy and Management, Brandeis University. Waltham, MA.

Turnbull, Ann P., Vicki Turbiville, and H. R. Turnbull. 2000. "Evolution of Family-Professional Partnersips: Collective Empowerment as the Model for the Early Twenty-First Century." Pp. 630–650 in *Handbook of Early Childhood Intervention*, edited by J. P. Shonkoff and S. J. Meisels. New York: Cambridge University Press.

Ueda, Reed. 2007. "Immigration in Global Historical Perspective." Pp. 14–28 in *The New Americans: A Guide to Immigration since 1965*, edited by M. C. Waters, R. Ueda, and H. B. Marrow. Cambridge, MA: Harvard University Press.

Uhlenberg, Peter. 1969. "A Study of Cohort Life Cycles: Cohorts of Native-Born Massachusetts Women, 1830–1920." *Population Studies* 23(3):407–420.

Ungerson, Clare. 2000. "Cash in Care." Pp. 68–88 in *Care Work: Gender, Labor, and Welfare States*, edited by M. Harrington Meyer. New York: Routledge.

United States Commission on Civil Rights. 1979. *Social Indicators of Equality for Minorities and Women: A Report of the United States Commission on Civil Rights.* Washington, DC: The Commission.

U.S. Census Bureau. 1975. "Historical Statistics of the United States: Colonial Times to 1970." *Bicentennial Edition: Part 1.* Washington DC: U.S. Department of Commerce. Retrieved September 22, 2011 (http://www2.census.gov/prod2/statcomp/documents/CT1970p1-01.pdf).

U.S. Census Bureau. 1985. *Statistical Abstract of the United States, 1985.* Washington DC: U.S. Bureau of the Census.

U.S. Census Bureau. 2004. "Homeownership." *Historical Census of Housing Tables.* Retrieved May 23, 2011 (http://www.census.gov/hhes/www/housing/census/historic/owner.html).

U.S. Census Bureau. 2009a. "Americans with Disabilities Act: Population Distribution." *Facts for Features.* Retrieved April 25, 2012 (http://www.census.gov/newsroom/releases/archives/facts_for_features_special_editions/cb09-ff13.html).

U.S. Census Bureau. 2009b. "Births, Deaths, Marriage, and Divorce." *Statistical Abstract of the United States.* Section 2. Retrieved April 25, 2012 (http://www.census.gov/prod/2008pubs/09statab/vitstat.pdf).

U.S. Census Bureau. 2009c. "Selected Social Characteristics in the United States: 2007–2009." *American Community Survey:* Table DP3YR-2. Retrieved April 25, 2012 (http://factfinder2.census.gov/faces/tableservices/jsf/pages/productview.xhtml?pid=ACS_09_3YR_DP3YR2&prodType=table).

U.S. Census Bureau. 2010a. "Place of Birth of the Foreign-Born Population: 2009." *American Community Survey Briefs,* October:1–5. Retrieved August 27, 2011 (http://www.census.gov/prod/2010pubs/acsbr09-15.pdf).

U.S. Census Bureau. 2010b. "Table 694. Poverty Thresholds by Size of Unit: 1980 to 2007." The 2010 Statistical Abstract, Retrieved April 25, 2012 (http://www.census.gov/prod/2009pubs/10statab/income.pdf).

U.S. Census Bureau. 2010c. "U.S. Census Bureau Reports Men and Women Wait Longer to Marry." Retrieved December 6, 2011 (http://www.census.gov/news room/releases/archives/families_households/cb10-174.html).

U.S. Census Bureau. 2011. "The 2012 Statistical Abstract." Retrieved February 12, 2012 (http://www.census.gov/compendia/statab/).

U.S. Department of Agriculture. 2011. "Official USDA Food Plans: Cost of Food at Home at Four Levels, U.S. Average, February 2011." *Center for Nutrition Policy and Promotion:* Retrieved December 17, 2011 (http://www.cnpp.usda.gov/ Publications/FoodPlans/2011/CostofFoodFeb2011.pdf).

U.S. Department of Education. 2011. "U.S. Department of Education Awards Promise Neighborhoods Planning Grants." Retrieved December 21, 2011 (http:// www.ed.gov/news/press-releases/us-department-education-awards-promise-neighborhoods-planning-grants).

U.S. Department of Health and Human Services. 2007. "School-Age Children in Regulated Family Child Care Settings." Washington DC: Retrieved March 12, 2012 (http://www.childcareresearch.org/childcare/resources/13725/pdf).

U.S. Department of Health and Human Services. 2008. "Transforming Mental Health Care in America: The Federal Action Agenda: A Living Agenda." Retrieved May 10, 2010 (http://www.samhsa.gov/Federalactionagenda/NFC_TOC.aspx).

U.S. Department of Health and Human Services. 2011a. "$100 Million in Affordable Care Act Grants to Help Create Healthier U.S. Communities." Retrieved December 21, 2011 (http://www.hhs.gov/news/press/2011pres/05/20110513b .html).

U.S. Department of Health and Human Services. 2011b. "Connecting Kids to Coverage: Steady Growth, New Innovation." *2011 CHIPRA Annual Report*, Retrieved March 12, 2012 (http://www.insurekidsnow.gov/chipraannualreport.pdf).

U.S. Department of Housing and Urban Development. 2008. "Characteristics of HUD-Assisted Renters and Their Units in 2003." Retrieved May 18, 2011 (http://www.huduser.org/portal/publications/pubasst/hud_asst_rent.html).

U.S. Department of Labor. 2011a. "National Longitudinal Surveys." Retrieved November 17, 2011 (http://www.bls.gov/nls/).

U.S. Department of Labor. 2011b. "US Labor Department Awards $75.8 Million for 76 YouthBuild Programs Nationwide." May 17. Retrieved March 10, 2012 (http://www.dol.gov/opa/media/press/eta/ETA20110737.htm).

U.S. Government Accountability Office. 2009. "Foster Care: State Practices for Assessing Health Needs, Facilitating Service Delivery, and Monitoring Children's Care—Highlights." Retrieved May 10, 2010 (http://www.gao.gov/products/ GAO-09-26).

U.S. Social Security Administration. 2011. "2012 Social Security Changes." *Fact Sheet:* November 29, 2011. Retrieved December 31, 2011 (http://www.ssa.gov/ pressoffice/colafacts.htm).

Vale, Lawrence J. 2000. *From the Puritans to the Projects: Public Housing and Public Neighbors.* Cambridge, MA: Harvard University Press.

Vankatesh, Sudhir. 2008. "To Fight Poverty, Tear Down HUD." *New York Times,* July 25, A19.

Villa, Richard A. and Jacqueline S. Thousand. 2005. *Creating an Inclusive School.* Alexandria, VA: Association for Supervision and Curriculum Development.

Village to Village Network. 2010. "Welcome to the Village to Village Network." Retrieved May 15, 2010 (http://vtvnetwork.clubexpress.com/).

Waite, Linda J. 2001. "Family as Institution." Pp. 5311–5314 in *International Encyclopedia of the Social & Behavioral Sciences,* edited by N. J. Smelser and P. B. Baltes. New York: Elsevier.

Waldfogel, Jane. 2009. "The Role of Family Policies in Antipoverty Policy." Pp. 242–265 in *Changing Poverty, Changing Policies,* edited by M. Cancian and S. Danziger. New York: Russell Sage Foundation.

Wallerstein, Judith S. 2003. "Children of Divorce: A Society in Search of Policy." Pp. 66–95 in *All Our Families: New Policies for a New Century: A Report of the Berkeley Family Forum,* edited by M. A. Mason, A. S. Skolnick, and S. D. Sugarman. New York: Oxford University Press.

Wallerstein, Judith S. and Sandra Blakeslee. 1989. *Second Chances: Men, Women, and Children a Decade after Divorce.* New York: Ticknor & Fields.

Wallerstein, Judith S. and Sandra Blakeslee. 2004. *Second Chances: Men, Women, and Children a Decade after Divorce* (15th-anniversary ed). Boston: Houghton Mifflin.

Warfield, Margi Erickson and Walter I. Leutz. 2011. "Assessing a Participant Directed Service System for Low Income Children with Autism." Paper presented at Conference on *Combating Autism Act Initiatives.* Washington, DC.

Warner, Judith. 2005. *Perfect Madness: Motherhood in the Age of Anxiety.* New York: Riverhead.

Warner, W. Lloyd. 1949. *Democracy in Jonesville: A Study of Quality and Inequality.* New York: Harper.

Warner, W. Lloyd. 1963. *Yankee City.* New Haven, CT: Yale University Press.

Waters, Mary C. 1999. *Black Identities: West Indian Immigrant Dreams and American Realities.* Cambridge, MA: Harvard University Press.

Waters, Mary C., Reed Ueda, and Helen B. Marrow. 2007. "Appendix: Immigration and Naturalization Legislation." Pp. 687–699 in *The New Americans: A Guide to Immigration since 1965,* edited by M. C. Waters, R. Ueda, and H. B. Marrow. Cambridge, MA: Harvard University Press.

Weber, Max. 1947. "Legal Authority with a Bureaucratic Administrative Staff." Pp. 329–341 in *The Theory of Social and Economic Organization,* edited by M. Weber, A. M. Henderson, and T. Parsons. New York: Oxford University Press.

Weber, Max. 1963. *The Sociology of Religion.* Boston: Beacon Press.

Weber, Max. 1968. *Economy and Society: An Outline of Interpretive Sociology.* New York: Bedminster Press.

Weitzman, Lenore J. 1985. *The Divorce Revolution: The Unexpected Social and Economic Consequences for Women and Children in America.* New York: Free Press.

Welter, Barbara. 1987. "From Maria Monk to Paul Blanshard: A Century of Protestant Anti-Catholicism." Pp. 43–71 in *Uncivil Religion: Interreligious Hostility in America,* edited by R. N. Bellah and F. E. Greenspahn. New York: Crossroad Publishing Company.

Wertheimer, Richard, Susan Jekielek, Kristin A. Moore, and Zakia Redd. 2005. "Government Policies as External Influences on Work-Family Trade-Offs." Pp. 157–165 in *Work, Family, Health, and Well-Being*, edited by S. M. Bianchi, L. M. Casper, and R. B. King. Mahwah, NJ: Lawrence Erlbaum.

Wexler, Sherry. 1997. *To Work and to Mother: The Politics of Family Support and Family Leave*. PhD dissertation, Heller School for Social Policy and Management, Brandeis University, Waltham, MA. Ann Arbor, MI: University Microfilms.

White House Conference on Families. 1980. "White House Conference on Families. Listening to America's Families: Action for the 80's." Washington, DC: White House Conference on Families.

Whitehead, Barbara Dafoe. 1993. "Dan Quayle Was Right." *Atlantic Monthly* 271(4):47–58. Retrieved September 20, 2011 (http://www.theatlantic.com/magazine/archive/1993/04/dan-quayle-was-right/7015/).

Whyte, William Hollingsworth. 1957. *The Organization Man*. Garden City, NY: Doubleday.

Widerquist, Karl, Michael Anthony Lewis, and Steven Pressman. 2005. *The Ethics and Economics of the Basic Income Guarantee*. Aldershot, United Kingdom: Ashgate.

Wilcox, W. Bradford, and Stephen L. Nock. 2006. "What's Love Got to Do with It? Equality, Equity, Commitment and Women's Marital Quality." *Social Forces* 84(3):1321–45.

Wilcox, W. Bradford. 2009. "The Evolution of Divorce." *National Affairs* 1: Fall. Retrieved December 9, 2011 (http://www.nationalaffairs.com/publications/detail/the-evolution-of-divorce).

Wilensky, Harold L. and Charles Nathan Lebeaux. 1958. *Industrial Society and Social Welfare; the Impact of Industrialization on the Supply and Organization of Social Welfare Services in the United States*. New York: Russell Sage Foundation.

Wilkinson, Richard G. and Kate Pickett. 2010. *The Spirit Level: Why Greater Equality Makes Societies Stronger*. New York: Bloomsbury Press.

Williams, Constance W. 2011. "Personal Recollections." Personal communication to J. Z. Giele. October 16, 2011.

Williams, Constance Willard. 1990. *Black Teenage Mothers: Pregnancy and Child Rearing from Their Perspective*. Lexington, MA: Lexington Books.

Wilson, William J. 1987. *The Truly Disadvantaged: The Inner City, the Underclass, and Public Policy*. Chicago: University of Chicago Press.

Wisconsin Longitudinal Study. 2011. "Wisconsin Longitudinal Study." Retrieved November 17, 2011 (http://www.ssc.wisc.edu/wlsresearch/).

Wisensale, Steven K. 1989. "Family Policy in the State Legislature: The Connecticut Agenda." *Review of Policy Research* 8(3, March):622–637.

Withers, Carl [James West, Pseud.]. 1945. *Plainville, U.S.A.* New York: Columbia University Press.

Wolff, Edward N. 2009. *Poverty and Income Distribution*. Malden, MA: Wiley-Blackwell.

Work and Family Research Network. 2012. Retrieved April 25, 2012 (https://workfamily.sas.upenn.edu/).

Young, Michael Dunlop and Peter Willmott. 1974. *The Symmetrical Family.* New York: Pantheon Books.

YouthBuild USA. 2011. "Rebuilding Our Communities and Our Lives." Retrieved December 7, 2011 (https://youthbuild.org/).

Zelizer, Viviana A. 1985. *Pricing the Priceless Child: The Changing Social Value of Children.* New York: Basic Books.

Zhou, Min. 2001. "Contemporary Immigration and the Dynamics of Race and Ethnicity." Pp. 200–242, Vol. 1 in *America Becoming: Racial Trends and Their Consequences,* edited by N. J. Smelser, W. J. Wilson, and F. Mitchell. Washington, DC: National Academy Press.

Zhou, Min. 2009. "Conflict, Coping, and Reconciliation." Pp. 21–46 in *Across Generations: Immigrant Families in America,* edited by N. Foner. New York: New York University Press.

Zigler, Edward and Elizabeth Gilman. 1996. "Not Just Any Care: Shaping a Coherent Child Care Policy." Pp. 94–116 in *Children, Families, and Government: Preparing for the Twenty-First Century,* edited by E. Zigler, S. L. Kagan, and N. W. Hall. New York: Cambridge University Press.

Zigler, Edward, Katherine Marsland, and Heather Lord. 2009. *The Tragedy of Child Care in America.* New Haven, CT: Yale University Press.

Zill, Nicholas and Carolyn C. Rogers. 1988. "Recent Trends in the Well-Being of Children in the United States and Their Implications for Public Policy." Pp. 31–115 in *The Changing American Family and Public Policy,* edited by A. J. Cherlin. Washington, DC: Urban Institute Press.

Zimmerman, Shirley. 1988. *Understanding Family Policy: Theoretical Approaches.* Newbury Park, CA: Sage.

Zolberg, Aristide R. 2007. "Immigration Control Policy: Law and Implementation." Pp. 29–42 in *The New Americans: A Guide to Immigration since 1965,* edited by M. C. Waters, R. Ueda, and H. B. Marrow. Cambridge, MA: Harvard University Press.

Zorbaugh, Harvey Warren. 1976. *The Gold Coast and the Slum: A Sociological Study of Chicago's near North Side.* Chicago: University of Chicago Press.

List of Tables

Index

Note: In page references, f indicates figures and t indicates tables.

About the Author

Janet Zollinger Giele (AB Earlham College, PhD Harvard University) is Professor Emerita of Sociology, Social Policy, and Women's Studies at the Heller School for Social Policy and Management of Brandeis University. From 1990 to 1996, she served as the founding director of the Family and Children's Policy Center, which was the forerunner of the present Institute on Children, Youth, and Families at the Heller School. Professor Giele's research and writing has focused on three interlocking interests—women's changing roles, aging and the life course, and family policy.

⑤SAGE research**methods**

The essential online tool for researchers from the world's leading methods publisher

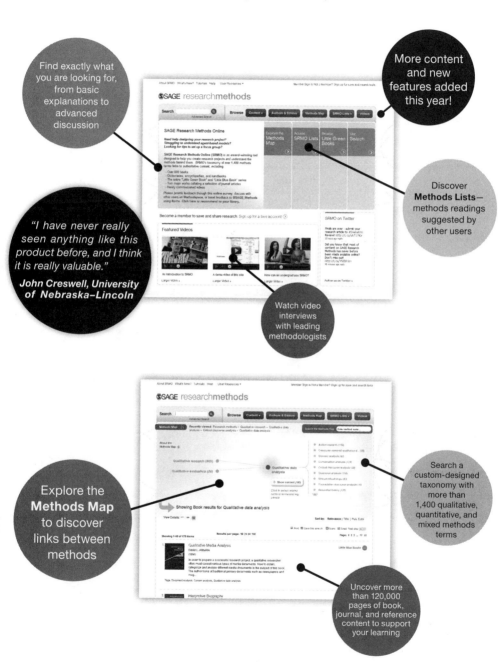

Find exactly what you are looking for, from basic explanations to advanced discussion

More content and new features added this year!

"I have never really seen anything like this product before, and I think it is really valuable."

John Creswell, University of Nebraska–Lincoln

Discover **Methods Lists**— methods readings suggested by other users

Watch video interviews with leading methodologists

Explore the **Methods Map** to discover links between methods

Search a custom-designed taxonomy with more than 1,400 qualitative, quantitative, and mixed methods terms

Uncover more than 120,000 pages of book, journal, and reference content to support your learning

Find out more at
www.sageresearchmethods.com